Corporate Power in Civil Society

Corporate Power in Civil Society

An Application of Societal Constitutionalism

David Sciulli

NEW YORK UNIVERSITY PRESS

New York and London

NEW YORK UNIVERSITY PRESS
New York and London

Library of Congress Cataloging-in-Publication Data
Sciulli, David.
Corporate power in civil society : an application osf societal
constitutionalism / David Sciulli.
p.   cm.
Includes bibliographical references and index.
ISBN 0-8147-9786-5 (cloth : alk. paper) —
ISBN 0-8147-9787-3 (pbk. : alk paper)
1. Corporation law—Social aspects—United States. 2. Judicial
power—Social aspects—United States. 3. Corporate governance—
United States. 4. Social responsibility of business—United States.
5. Social contract—United States. 6. Civil society—United States.
I. Title.
KF1416 .S396 2001
346.73'066—dc21   00-011744

Contents

Acknowledgments

Early drafts of this volume contained lengthy discussions of the history of corporate law in the United States along with this volume's discussion of contemporary debates over corporate law and judicial practice. Early readers, therefore, commented on what turned out to be two books—the first, historical part was published as *Corporations vs. the Court: Private Power, Public Interests*. I would like to thank James Burk, Isabelle Corbisier, and Catherine Riegle in particular for their careful reading and comments. I also noted in the earlier book scholarly meetings at which I presented my approach to corporations and law. Since then I had the opportunity to relate this approach to Talcott Parsons' more general social theory at a May 1999 conference in honor of Parsons' work, which was organized and hosted by Helmut Staubmann and Harald Wenzel at University of Innsbruck. I benefitted greatly from their comments as well as from those of Harold Bershady, Victor Lidz, Nicos Mouzelis, Hans Joas, and Jeremy Tanner.

As always, I am instructed by general discussions with Bill D'Antonio, Amitai Etzioni, Erwin Scheuch, and Masamichi Sasaki. And finally, I would like to thank Stephen Magro for seeing this project through, and also two anonymous reviewers for NYU Press who gave me detailed comments and suggestions for improvement.

Introduction

In monitoring how management governs publicly traded corporations, the American corporate judiciary bears two major responsibilities. One is to identify who acts on the corporation's behalf. Who has the authority and power to get things done in the corporation's name and, as a result, can be held legally responsible for the corporation's behavior? This is a question about the nature of corporate agency. The other major responsibility of the American corporate judiciary is to define (and limit) how corporations may conduct themselves in civil society. What standards of behavior does the corporate judiciary expect corporate officers to meet? Is the sole legitimate purpose of corporations to maximize profits or growth? Or do the courts expect corporate officers to conform to social norms, to meet extra-economic standards of behavior? These are questions about the nature of corporate purpose in civil society.

Since the founding of America, state courts (particularly today those of Delaware, California, New York, and New Jersey) have borne these two responsibilities. However, the ability of the corporate judiciary to meet either of them was in graver doubt in the late 1980s and early 1990s than at any time since the rise of giant corporations at the turn of the twentieth century. Some reasons for this are well known.

Beginning in the 1920s, business corporations increasingly decentralized their internal structures of authority. In the language of organization theory, corporations evolved from a unidivisional form, where both planning and daily operations were centralized at headquarters, to a multidivisional form. Today, middle managers at divisions are responsible for daily operations while top managers at headquarters dedicate themselves to planning and financing strategies. Yet some corporate divisions today are considerably larger than many centralized corporations were two and three generations ago. Moreover, the basic division of labor struck between middle managers and top managers has been followed by numerous other divisions, and then subdivisions, of power and authority. All of

1

this complicates judicial efforts to identify *the* corporate agent. If we bring into the picture the increasing tendency of corporations to operate across national markets (often using subsidiaries), and also the increasing economic competition they face in global markets, the courts' difficulties become even more understandable. Who (or what position) is to be held legally responsible for what a corporation does at a particular time, in a particular place?

In addition, the very idea that American state courts ought to identify normative, extra-economic "responsibilities" that corporate officers bear to the larger society, beyond their unavoidable burden to compete effectively in markets, has come under formidable challenge since the mid-1970s. An increasing number of influential judges and law professors—known as legal contractarians—question whether the corporate judiciary as an institution can or should impose *social norms* of behavior on directors, management, and controlling shareholders, and whether this institution is capable of doing so. Contractarians believe the entire matter of trying to define corporate purpose in legal terms is hopelessly anachronistic. How corporate officers conduct themselves within private companies, how they "govern" these companies, is a matter best left to competition in self-regulating product markets and capital markets. In their view, markets impose the only limitations on corporate activity that (a) make sense economically and (b) can be "enforced" with any consistency regardless.

We will see that this position has considerable merit in principle. We will also see, however, that it represents a dramatic departure from long-standing American judicial (and legislative) practice. Economic limitations on corporate purpose are narrowly instrumental and strictly pecuniary in their sanctions. They do not speak to broader issues: Whether and when do corporations either increase or decrease social wealth (what Adam Smith called the wealth of nations)? And whether and when do corporations broadly support or increasingly enervate and then challenge the basic institutional design of a democratic society? These broader issues, and particularly the "societal constitutional" issue of institutional design, continue to inform the behavior of the corporate judiciary, albeit often implicitly. We will call this broader view of corporate purpose, and the general political economic position of which it is a part, *republican vigilance.*

If we keep the issue of institutional design in mind, then contractarians' faith in markets seems disingenuous, and yet it remains a credible point of departure in analyzing the relationship between corporations and law. Their faith is that as long as corporate officers do not violate the same basic criminal and civil laws that apply to all other citizens, then self-regulating markets will otherwise restrain how they manage large corporate entities sufficiently in any society, and particularly in a democratic society. Contractarians are convinced, as are a great many members of the corporate judiciary and bar today, that however corporate officers decide to govern their firms internally, this cannot possibly pose a threat to a democratic society. We call this article of faith *liberal complacency*, and we will find that it is today's orthodoxy in the corporate judiciary and bar.

We can trace the origin of today's orthodoxy to the 1830s. This is when the corporate judiciary *began* abandoning the quite different general political economic position of the Founders, that of republican vigilance. American state courts began believing as an article of faith that when corporations increase their owners' private wealth, this simultaneously (a) increases social wealth and (b) automatically supports, rather than possibly challenges or enervates, the institutional design of a democratic society. Thus, in the first decades of the nineteenth century, the American corporate judiciary began abandoning concepts (and doctrinal options) that could help state courts to resist contractarians' faith in markets today.

There is a popular way of visualizing how otherwise lawful and profitable exercises of corporate power can harm the larger society. When corporations successfully increase their owners' wealth, they may nonetheless disrupt an existing balance between economic institutions (such as product, capital, and labor markets) and noneconomic institutions (such as families, communities, and voluntary associations).[1] The problem with this popular view, however, is that it does not establish that the existing balance just noted is truly basic to maintaining a democratic society as such. So this way of visualizing what is at stake in judicial monitoring of corporate governance is not one we will pursue here. Rather, we offer social scientists (and judges) a way of identifying (a) those institutional arrangements that are truly basic to a democratic society and (b) when changes in corporate governance unambiguously challenge or enervate these institutional arrangements.

For now, we simply repeat that contractarians have been remarkably successful in establishing liberal complacency as today's orthodoxy. They have convinced a large and growing number of judges and legal scholars that, in principle, otherwise lawful exercises of corporate power do not (and can not) harm the larger society, either purposefully or inadvertently. At best, some judges and legal scholars resist orthodoxy by pointing out that even lawful and profitable corporate behavior can potentially harm particular, readily identifiable, individuals or groups—say, by laying people off or by moving operations to another location. Yet even these seeming agnostics nonetheless typically assume that such harms can usually be priced so that, in principle at least, "victims" can be fully recompensed. With this, they operate within today's orthodoxy. They follow contractarians in narrowing the issue of corporate purpose to economic factors alone. In turn, they also accept the way contractarians portray the normative, extra-economic duties that the corporate judiciary imposes on corporate officers. Today's orthodoxy holds that these duties are anachronistic displays of "state paternalism." Thus, many judges and legal scholars no longer believe these normative limitations rest on truly settled principles of corporate law doctrine, despite the fact that American state courts have been imposing some of these limitations on corporate officers since the Founding.

Given its two crises of responsibility, the American corporate judiciary remains in the throes of its most thoroughgoing debate over basic principles of corporate law and corporate governance since the first stages of American industrialization and urbanization in the 1870s and 1880s. This was the period when, first, American pragmatism challenged corporate power in principle and then the Progressive movement did so in practice. Today's debate, too, moves well beyond academic concern with legal principles. Changes in legal doctrine covering corporate agency and corporate purpose directly influence the rulings of sitting judges. New judicial rulings on these matters, in turn, either open or close avenues for future corporate behavior. They also (arguably) open or close the same avenues for all other intermediary associations, from hospitals and universities to professional associations. Thus, new rulings on corporate agency and corporate purpose either reflect or anticipate larger shifts in the direction of social change in the United States.

One remarkable fact about today's debate over corporations and law is how little social theorists and other sociologists have participated in it. This is remarkable not only because corporations are the single most significant set of intermediary associations in American society. It is also remarkable because intermediary associations have long been a central concern of political theorists and then social theorists (from James Madison and Alexis de Tocqueville to the pragmatists and the Chicago School). In addition, classical European political philosophers and social theorists (from Georg Wilhelm Hegel to Emile Durkheim and Max Weber) also often drew attention to intermediary associations.

Sociologists' absence from today's debate over corporations and law is noteworthy because the two major responsibilities of the corporate judiciary—identifying the corporate agent and defining corporate purpose—are more sociological and institutional than economic or narrowly legal. Indeed, as a social theorist, I do not share legal scholars' fascination with the details of the corporate governance disputes that come before state courts. But I am very interested in whether (and then how) the corporate judiciary as an institution monitors corporate power. I am equally interested in how judges and legal scholars conceptualize what courts are doing, the principles of corporate law doctrine they believe best explain past and present judicial behavior and best predict future judicial behavior. Indeed, I will introduce sociological concepts that, I believe, provide a better account of what the corporate judiciary is doing and why. These same concepts will also allow us to predict what will happen if the corporate judiciary ever takes a "contractarian turn" and monitors corporate power in only narrowly economic ways.

The central contribution of this volume is to explain an empirical state of affairs in the world: How, when, and why does the corporate judiciary impose social norms of behavior on corporate officers in publicly traded companies? Any explanation for such norm-based judicial behavior, in turn, simultaneously provides an answer to three other questions: Why does the corporate judiciary not simply monitor the behavior of corporate officers in strictly market-mimicking ways? Why does it not simply facilitate the workings of product markets, capital markets, and especially a new market for control over corporations? Why does it not state explicitly, as a matter of corporate law doctrine, that the only legitimate purpose of corporations in American civil society is either to maximize profits (for shareholders) or else to maximize growth (for the corporate entity)?

As I introduce sociological concepts that account for the corporate judiciary's norm-based behavior, I simultaneously introduce major issues in today's debate over corporations and law. I also identify major legal scholars (including judges) engaged in this debate. This is a second contribution of this book. Social scientists are largely unaware that in the late 1980s and early 1990s the corporate judiciary suffered from what one prominent judge called "institutional angst." The hostile takeovers and leveraged buyouts of the 1980s cast the corporate judiciary adrift from its traditional moorings in corporate law doctrine. Social scientists are also largely unaware that judges remain "available" today to consider manifestly sociological approaches to the issues of corporate agency and corporate purpose. They seek new doctrinal rationales for normatively mediating corporate power in today's global economy. Judges have said as much, both implicitly in judicial rulings and more explicitly in speeches and journal articles.

In sharp contrast to the absence of most other social scientists in today's debate over corporations and law, economists are quite involved and quite aware of the controversies preoccupying the corporate judiciary and bar. They have greatly influenced this debate, particularly by lending support to contractarians' calls for courts to take a narrowly economic approach to the issue of corporate purpose. They have thereby helped to steer judges away from the idea that corporate power may carry *institutional* consequences for the larger society. Yet other judges are now convinced that economists and contractarians have gone too far. This is why they are now "available" to consider sociological alternatives, and especially those consistent with the corporate judiciary's more traditional reading of its two responsibilities.

A third contribution of this book is to bring the issue of corporate purpose more fully into view. Here I build on my first book, *Theory of Societal Constitutionalism*. In that volume I proposed that collegial organizations—in contrast to bureaucratic organizations, patron-client organizations, and even formally democratic organizations—uniquely institutionalize fidelity to procedural norms first identified by Harvard legal theorist Lon Fuller. I proposed that this ongoing procedural normative mediation of private power in civil society is what ultimately distinguishes the institutional design of democratic societies from that of formal democracies and imposed social orders. Now, in this volume, I explore whether and when the corporate judiciary protects collegial organizations in corporate governance structures, and endeavors to increase the number of these organizations across corporate America.

A fourth and related contribution of this book is to track the corporate judiciary's drift as an institution beginning in the mid-1970s. We will see that American state courts have been incrementally, unevenly, replacing traditional, substantive normative limitations on corporate power with procedural normative mediations. But we will also see that these courts falter at times in the midst of this still ongoing transition. In turn, legal scholars (to say nothing of economists) fail to isolate the source of this problem. Thus, judges' otherwise promising "procedural turn" is at times overtaken by the corporate judiciary's ongoing drift as an institution. Should it now rely increasingly on economic concepts, as contractarians prefer, or should it otherwise fail to update its own more traditional concepts, continued drift is likely. In today's flux of domestic and global economic change, this could well push the corporate judiciary beyond its institutional angst of the 1980s.

Further drift could result in a state of outright institutional crisis, leading ultimately to federalizing corporate law in whole or in part. Delaware courts in particular have a clear interest in seeing that this does not happen. What is certain, however, is that these courts, and the corporate judiciary as a whole, will not somehow arrive at a new equilibrium state, as if guided by a benevolent hidden hand, in the absence of new concepts that reconnect contemporary judicial practice to this institution's rich, decidedly extra-economic, traditions.

A final contribution of this book is to address larger sociological concerns. As I noted earlier, I am not interested in the details of the American corporate judiciary's activities as an institution. I leave this to legal scholars. I am also not interested in whether and how American (or other) corporations may increase their competitiveness in today's global economy. I leave this to economists. As a social theorist, I am interested in describing and explaining a shift in the direction of institutional change that began in the United States in the mid-1970s, that accelerated in the 1980s, and that concerns many judges and legal scholars today. I am interested in exploring what, if anything, is being done about this shift today by two major American institutions: the corporate judiciary and corporate governance structures. This is an eminently sociological issue.

1

Corporations and Civil Society
Institutional Externalities of Corporate Power

Hostile corporate takeovers and leveraged buyouts of publicly traded corporations in the United States disrupted the lives of millions of Americans in the 1980s. Although the typical business in the United States is not organized as a corporation, but rather as a proprietorship or partnership, corporations account for 90 percent of all business sales and receipts.[1] This is why reverberations stemming from the turbulence of the 1980s continue to be felt today on Wall Street, Main Street, and in boardrooms. Management, now more attuned to shareholder acquisitiveness, continues to restructure companies.[2] Business headlines routinely announce workforce cutbacks and at times medical benefit reductions and pension withholdings. From 1993 to 1995, 8 percent of all working Americans lost their jobs involuntarily.[3] Workers between the ages of 35 and 54 were 55 percent more likely to be laid off or otherwise experience a job loss than during the 1970s.[4]

A case can also be made, however, that turbulence in the 1980s prepared the way for inflation-free economic growth in the 1990s and today.[5] Beginning in mid-1997, the unemployment rate fell below 5 percent and has since inched down. Labor Department reports for October, released in November 1999, put unemployment at 4.1 percent, the lowest since January 1970. The rate for adult women—at 3.5 percent—is the lowest since 1953.[6] In such a tight labor market, even workers at lower wage levels—those being paid $6 to $11 an hour—are able to push for pay increases and more flexible hours.[7]

The economic turbulence of the 1980s had a second broad impact on American society, however, one more significant and certainly more enduring than today's job displacements and low unemployment. The hostile activity of the 1980s cast adrift from their traditional moorings three major institutions that structure—and control—corporate power in American society: corporate governance structures, the corporate judiciary, and corporate law doctrine. Our major concern in this book is to explore this second outcome of the 1980s. We wish to identify the larger, institutional consequences of today's changes in corporate governance, judicial practice, and legal doctrine. Put more succinctly, our focus in this book is to identify what we call *institutional externalities* of corporate power. Which changes in corporate governance, judicial practice, and legal doctrine support the institutional design of American society, the most basic institutional arrangements spanning the state and civil society? And which changes if any enervate and ultimately challenge this design, these arrangements?

The institutional externalities of corporate power are elusive. In the absence of concepts that specifically bring them into view, they elude ready observation and, therefore, empirical study.[8] We will see, however, that Delaware courts intervene into the internal governance of corporations at times on this ground. They operate on a traditional assumption unique to courts in equity, including Delaware's Chancery Court, that there is *some* relationship between corporate governance and institutional design. Economists and "legal contractarians" cannot explain this behavior by Delaware courts. They fail here precisely because their concepts obscure the institutional externalities of corporate power rather than bring them into view. "Legal traditionalists," legal scholars who continue to operate with more traditional legal concepts—including those employed by courts in equity—share Delaware courts' concern about corporate power. However, they approach the issue of institutional externalities in exceedingly general ways, as part of an inquiry into "corporate purpose." When contractarians ask them explicitly to point directly to some possible harms that corporate power might cause the larger society, traditionalists falter.

Both sets of legal scholars, therefore, share a difficulty. They have difficulty accounting fully for how Delaware courts analyze and resolve major corporate governance disputes. They have difficulty explaining the judicial behavior before them even as they describe this behavior, and the facts in dispute, in identical ways.

In this chapter we begin to present a framework of sociological concepts that we believe reveals (a) how to identify specifically the broader consequences of corporate power and (b) how to explain more fully the behavior of the corporate judiciary. On the one hand, it identifies the institutional externalities of corporate power today. On the other, it accounts for judicial behavior that contractarians and traditionalists acknowledge they cannot explain.[9] More generally, we propose that the success of any theory of corporate power in civil society—economic, legal, or social—stands or falls on its ability to describe, explain, and then possibly predict the empirical behavior of the corporate judiciary and the empirical consequences of corporate power.

We can begin to suggest the importance of such a theory by taking four steps. First, we define corporate governance and begin to consider its general, social importance. Second, we elaborate by distinguishing the institutional design of democratic societies from that of formal democracies and imposed social orders. Third, we draw two related distinctions that begin to reveal at least in a preliminary way the possible institutional externalities of corporate power, those that challenge or enervate institutional design. Finally, we review American courts' traditional role in monitoring corporate power.

I. Corporate Governance

"Corporate governance" refers to how decisions are made and, more importantly, how disputes are settled within publicly traded corporations.[10] The term draws our attention to a basic fact of any complex team activity: Team members are not simply individuals but also players of positions. As individuals, team members may harm a team by acting in their own self-interests. This is well known and does not concern us here. Less well known, and of concern, is another threat to team success, namely when members promote a position one-sidedly. Team members may act one-sidedly in their own "positional interest," thereby endeavoring to increase their "positional power" relative to that of other members in an honest belief that what is good for *anyone in their position* is good for the team. Thus, legal traditionalist Melvin Eisenberg (1989) distinguishes "positional conflicts" from traditional conflicts of interest (that is, self-dealing or lining one's own pockets at the team's expense) and shirking (that is, goldbricking).

Team success rests on whether *and how* conflicting positional interests are reconciled, that is, governed. This implies that effective governance also hinges on whether team leaders act relatively disinterestedly, by endeavoring to identify and then advance the collective interests of the whole, as opposed to acting one-sidedly in *their* positional interests. A central issue in any team activity, then, is how do members recruit and retain disinterested leaders?[11]

The corporation is a complex team activity.[12] Its governance is a multi-player game—involving directors, managers, shareholders, and "stakeholders"—that takes place within an identifiable *structure* of authority.[13] The term stakeholder is important but is also a catchall.[14] It refers to all corporate constituents whose primary contribution to the enterprise is neither ownership (shareholding) nor overall control (top management). Thus, the term includes bondholders, long-term suppliers, and middle managers as well as line employees, retirees, and even residents of the local communities in which corporations operate or are headquartered. All of these constituents have a "stake" in the enterprise but neither own it nor control it.

With our team analogy in mind, we can now see that corporate governance refers to two distinct processes. The first is whether and how corporate officers (directors, top managers, controlling shareholders) reconcile the competing positional interests of shareholders and stakeholders. The second distinct process of corporate governance is whether and how a *structure* of authority encourages corporate officers to act disinterestedly, in the corporate entity's collective interests, and discourages them from acting more one-sidedly, in their own positional interests.

Corporate governance therefore has little to do with how corporate officers settle personal squabbles and antagonisms at headquarters.[15] It also has little to do with how they deal more generally with constituents' self-interested behavior as individuals. Corporate governance has everything to do with the identifiable *structure* of authority within which corporate officers resolve disputes and make decisions over time. Does this structure institutionalize disinterested behavior by corporate officers, or does it permit directors, top managers, or controlling shareholders to act in their own positional interests?

Corporate governance is our central concern, but we cannot study it to the exclusion of everything else a corporation does. One major responsibility of top management, after all, is to see to it that the firm's governance function facilitates, rather than needlessly obstructs, the firm's production function, its competitiveness in securing resources and generating sales in domestic and global markets.[16] Top management falls short here when the governance function needlessly consumes resources, hampers decision making, or distorts corporate officers' scanning of markets for business opportunities. To prevent this from happening, top management endeavors to keep the ongoing, healthy competition for positional power within corporations from degenerating into trench warfare. Legal scholars call such warfare "positional conflicts." When a corporation's governance structure fails to resolve positional conflicts internally, when these conflicts reach state courts (in the form of a derivative suit, as we will see later), they become what legal scholars call "corporate governance disputes."

It is instructive to consider some examples of positional conflicts that often escalate into governance disputes in state court, without yet considering the issues involved:

- Must management maximize share price during a change in corporate control, to shareholders' immediate benefit? Or may management plan for the longer term, taking into account the stakes of other constituents, even as this also increases its positional power rather than maximizing shareholder wealth?
- When must a top management team facilitate the sale of its company to the highest bidder? When (and how) may management maintain or erect defenses against a particular bidder or against bidders in general?
- When (and how) does a board of directors adequately review a major corporate decision proposed by management—a sale of control, a defensive tactic—and when does a board fail to bear this responsibility?
- Is it permissible for individual directors or top managers to derive personal pecuniary benefits from a merger or any other corporate transaction?
- When, if ever, do the conflicts of interest of individual directors compromise the independence of the board? Is a board to be treated as a collection of individuals, whose possible conflicts are to be analyzed case by case? Or is a board to be treated as a collective entity, whose integrity can be violated by the actions of a few members?
- May management issue more shares of stock in order to dilute the voting power of controlling shareholders or a hostile bidder? May it otherwise substantially alter shareholder interests in the corporation? Is it acceptable to harm shareholder minorities while benefitting shareholder majorities or controlling shareholders?
- May top managers purchase control over the company they are managing from public shareholders—that is, may they "take it private" in an MBO, a management buyout? May they do so with outside financing secured by the company's assets? May they do so without offering the company for sale, to see if its market value for shareholders is greater than the share price management is offering?

The details of the cases above are not important for our purposes now, nor are the details of how the corporate judiciary decides them. What is important is that state courts intervene into the internal governance of corporations in order to resolve disputes like these, and they do so at times on decidedly normative grounds with an eye ultimately, we propose, to institutional design. They do not restrict themselves to calculating what is the most profitable outcome for shareholders or even necessarily for the corporate entity. Nor do they restrict themselves to compromises, to balancing the positional interests of corporate officers, shareholders, and stakeholders. This will become clear when we review major Delaware court cases of the 1980s and 1990s in Chapter 5.

We can see already that the internal governance of publicly traded corporations is embedded within a larger economic, political, social, and cultural environment.[17] This environment is comprised not only of economic pressures institutionalized in markets and political pressures institutionalized in state legislatures. It is also comprised of legal pressures institutionalized by courts and normative pressures institutionalized by elites' general (often implicit) understandings of what is acceptable and unacceptable conduct in their society and, more importantly, by their society's institutional design.[18]

The economic pressures on corporations are familiar, namely local, national, and global markets—product markets, capital markets, labor markets, and the new market for corporate control (that emerged in 1983). The pressures that state politics (and to a lesser extent national politics) exerts on corporations are somewhat less familiar but nonetheless well documented.[19] We touch on these pressures at times in this volume. But the central focus is on two other sets of pressures, those stemming from courts and corporate law tradition and those stemming from the relationship between corporate governance and institutional design, which courts can either monitor or neglect. Our goal is to identify when and why the corporate judiciary imposes social norms of behavior on corporate officers, and when this reflects an implicit or explicit effort on its part to support institutional design. At these moments the corporate judiciary is enforcing corporate law, to be sure. But corporate law tradition itself is instructing them to bring social norms to corporate governance disputes, not legal standards that are more strictly economizing, what legal scholars call market mimicking. The empirical behavior we wish to describe, explain, and predict, therefore, is when and why the corporate judiciary intervenes into corporate governance disputes on extra-economic grounds, on normative grounds.

The most important statutory laws broadly framing or mediating the internal governance of corporations are those contained in the General Corporation law of the state in which companies are incorporated. However, state courts do more than interpret and enforce these statutes. They also enforce certain mandatory rules of corporate governance independently of state statutes (and independently of common law contracts).[20] *Both General Corporation law and the courts' own mandatory rules, we propose, are windows to social norms and to the institutional design of the larger society. Changes in state statutes and mandatory rules therefore typically reflect, at times anticipate, changes in social norms and changes in institutional design.*[21]

II. Institutional Design

The institutional design of a democratic *society* goes further than normatively mediating governmental power short of abuse or arbitrariness. This is where the institutional design of a formal democracy stops and where the institutional design of an imposed social order already falls short.[22] The institutional design of a democratic society extends normative mediations of power from government to major intermediary associations in civil society. Putting this point formally, a democratic society prohibits those who hold positions of trust in at least some *structured situations* in civil society from exercising power one-sidedly, in their own positional interests. This general principle is the most fundamental tenet of the fiduciary law tradition that originated in fourteenth-century England, and on this basis the American corporate judiciary today prohibits corporate officers from exercising their positional power one-sidedly in corporate governance *structures*.[23] Today's judicial limits on corporate power are designed to prevent directors, management, and controlling shareholders from so altering a corporation's structure of governance that only its positional interests prevail in this structured situation.[24] In this way these limits at least indirectly encourage disinterested behavior by anyone who occupies a position of trust in a structured situation in American civil society.

There is no federal law in the United States that extends to the internal governance of corporations.[25] Beginning before the American founding, first colonial congresses, then state legislatures, and now state courts—not the Supreme Court, not Congress, and not any regulatory agency—

have monitored how corporations govern themselves and otherwise exercise private power in civil society. Today, the state courts of Delaware, California, New York, and New Jersey largely comprise what legal scholars call the corporate judiciary. This means that it is the responsibility of decentralized state courts, and ultimately of Delaware courts, to interrelate corporate governance, state corporate law, and the corporate judiciary's mandatory rules with social norms and the institutional design of the larger society. We will see in time that this qualifies the corporate judiciary in general, and Delaware courts in particular, as an environmental agent. The corporate judiciary and Delaware courts are corporate America's window to the larger society and, in turn, the larger society's window to corporate America.

By monitoring corporate governance with an eye to institutional design, Delaware courts perform what American social theorist Talcott Parsons called a pattern-maintenance function for the entire society.[26] This is our first way of wording our proposed account of Delaware courts' normative behavior. Indeed, it is not an exaggeration to say that Delaware's Chancery Court and Supreme Court together function as the constitutional court of the United States for all intermediary associations, for all powerful private bodies in American civil society.

The fact that corporations perform a governance function within an institutionalized environment that includes laws and social norms (as well as economic and political pressures) draws our attention to two legal issues and then to three decidedly sociological issues.[27] The legal issues are: How is the content of corporate law determined, including the content of state statutes and mandatory rules that place a "normative capsule" around corporate governance in particular?[28] How do state courts enforce these statutes and rules across cases, across particular governance disputes?

These issues are not our central concern, but we explore them at times as we raise and address the following three sociological issues: When and how do Delaware courts interrelate the internal governance of corporations, their state's General Corporation law, and their own mandatory rules to broader social norms and institutional design? How, if at all, do officers of particular corporations recognize and understand the broader social norms to which Delaware courts might hold them? When, and to what extent, do judicial interventions into the internal governance of corporations either reflect or anticipate changes in social norms and changes in institutional design?

III. Two Distinctions

In addressing these sociological issues, and particularly the third, we need to draw two conceptual distinctions. First, we distinguish intermediary associations from a larger, more amorphous category—organizations.

1. Intermediary Associations and Organizations

Intermediary associations are so called because, unlike other organizations, they simultaneously mediate the state's power and broaden individuals' loyalties beyond their families and primary groups.[29] Restaurants, retail stores, and small businesses typically do not have either effect, and so rarely qualify as intermediary associations. By contrast, corporations often have both effects. The same is true of organizational sites of professional practice such as hospitals, universities, museums, research and consulting facilities, and some governmental agencies.

We may appreciate the intermediary position corporations occupy in civil society by approaching it from both sides—that of the state and that of the individual. From the perspective of the state, the very presence of privately owned and controlled collective entities in civil society means that the state's power stops short of absolutism. The very presence of intermediary associations means that the state does not monopolize collective power in civil society, as is the case in more imposed social orders. However, this also means that corporations are just as capable as the state of exercising collective power in ways that are abusive or arbitrary, in ways that can challenge the institutional design of a democratic society. Just as we do not assume that public officials automatically discipline themselves short of arbitrariness as they carry out their duties, we have no greater reason to assume that corporate officers will be any more self-disciplining. We have no reason to assume that directors, top managers, and controlling shareholders will automatically discipline themselves short of acting one-sidedly as they advance their own positional interests in competition with others. Rather, we have every reason to assume that if courts fail to mediate *either* state power or corporate power short of one-sidedness, public and private arbitrariness will increase in frequency and broaden in scope across civil society.

Here is where the institutional design of a democratic society is put at risk. Whether we label arbitrary or one-sided power "public" or "private" is considerably less important than whether courts (a) recognize such exercises of power with consistency, (b) endeavor to mediate them, and thereby

(c) maintain institutional arrangements that distinguish a democratic society from formal democracies and, certainly, more imposed social orders.

Seen from the perspective of the individual, corporations and other intermediary associations do more than mediate state power. They can also elevate individuals' loyalties beyond their families and primary groups (including loyalties based on ethnicity, gender, religion, and class). In this way, too, intermediary associations contribute to the basic institutional design of a democratic society. But here again, this also means that when corporate power is exercised in arbitrary ways in civil society, individuals and primary groups may hunker down to protect themselves. They may then exhibit the familism and tribalism that mark unstable democracies and imposed social orders rather than fully institutionalized democracies.[30]

We can identify three ways, therefore, in which corporations and other intermediary associations differ from organizations. First, they contain structured situations in which officers exercise positional power over other constituents. When corporate officers advance their positional interests against bondholders, long-term suppliers, middle managers, line employees, and local communities, they exercise collective power over them in a structured situation. They are not operating within a more fluid site of self-interested contracting, a market. Whereas any market affords participants the option of exiting at any time at little cost, many corporate constituents lack this option. Rather, as power plays become patterned—become institutionalized—a corporation develops an identifiable structure of authority, a governance structure, from which participants cannot exit either readily or at little cost. Thus, and second, corporations and other intermediary associations differ from other organizations in that they contain such governance structures. These structures mediate how corporate and association officers may legitimately advance their own positional interests. Third, corporations and intermediary associations are not only aggregates of individuals (or of positions) but also entities in their own right. They have collective interests that are not always reducible to the positional interests of their leaders, their owners, or their stakeholders. These entities also compete with others in markets and, as they compete, exercise collective power in society.[31]

A. FROM ASSOCIATIONS TO DESIGN

Our first distinction, between intermediary associations and organizations, is important because it begins to reveal the relationship between corporate governance and institutional design. It also brings into view another way of wording our proposed explanation for the normative behavior of Delaware courts.

All organizations, intermediary associations included, perform a production function. They all compete for resources and customers (or clients). As they adjust their outputs to match their inputs, markets (or state budgets) discipline them. Assuming that organization leaders are not violating criminal or civil laws as they perform this function, courts are not needed to monitor this process. Courts certainly are not needed to intervene into the decisions organization leaders make regarding how best to perform their production function. Here is where markets best courts.

But we just showed that corporations and other intermediary associations are more than profit-driven commercial enterprises. They are also private governments in civil society. They not only perform a production function, with all other organizations, but also perform a governance function unique to intermediary associations.

Where any organization lawfully performing its production function attunes itself rather exclusively to economic pressures (from markets or state budgets), a corporation attunes itself to different pressures when *lawfully* performing its governance function. Corporate officers remain aware of economic pressures even here, to be sure, but they also attune themselves at least somewhat to the corporate judiciary, and thus to corporate law as well as norms institutionalized in the larger society. Where a lawfully performed production function is evaluated by economic standards, a lawfully performed governance function is evaluated simultaneously by these standards and more qualitative standards, those of legitimacy and equity or basic fairness.[32] How corporate officers lawfully perform a governance function invariably speaks in one way or another to institutional design; how they lawfully perform a production function typically does not. Delaware courts bear ultimate responsibility for seeing to it that intermediary associations perform a governance function in ways that broadly support, not possibly enervate, the institutional design of the larger society. This is our second way of wording our proposed explanation for Delaware courts' normative behavior.

B. DELAWARE COURTS UNDER PRESSURE

The problem today is that Delaware courts suffer from uncertainty when they impose norms of behavior on corporate officers as *mandatory rules*, what legal scholars call fiduciary duties. They are not sure why they should continue to require directors, top managers, or controlling shareholders to maintain the "integrity" of the governance function, as Delaware courts define it. The alternative is that state courts might substitute negotiated contracts for mandatory rules, substitute laissez faire in corporate governance for state paternalism. They might free corporate officers from fiduciary duties and thereby permit them to compete more one-sidedly for positional power, including the power to change the rules (the contracts) that will bind them (and corporate constituents) when governance disputes come before state courts.

Delaware courts are being pressured by accelerating competition in domestic and global markets and also by impressive arguments from economists and legal contractarians to focus more exclusively on facilitating corporations' production function.[33] They are being pressured to facilitate corporate officers' efforts to economize, to rationalize production, by relaxing all mandatory rules of governance. Thus, they are being pressured to restrict themselves to enforcing contracts that management negotiates with constituents from corporation to corporation and particularly contracts that receive shareholder approval. They are being pressured to stop enforcing mandatory rules of corporate governance because these rules by definition place normative limits on these negotiations, on tailoring governance *to* production.

If Delaware courts were to yield to these pressures, then their behavior would become market mimicking. The monitoring of corporate governance would no longer remain normatively mediating. Such judicial behavior, in turn, would redefine the corporation in the eyes of the law. The corporation would be defined legally as a power-neutral site of self-interested contracting, as an inculpable nexus or market cluster. It would no longer be defined legally as an entity, an intermediary association within which positional power can be exercised in ways that might (somehow) harm the larger society.[34]

2. Immediate and Institutional Externalities

Delaware courts are endeavoring today to justify to other state judges and to legal scholars more generally why they continue to impose norms of behavior on corporate officers rather than enforce contracts alone. They do so in written opinions in major corporate governance disputes. Our responsibility as sociologists is not to comb these opinions nor in other ways directly to enter into today's debate over corporations and law. Our responsibility is to account for Delaware courts' norm-based behavior, and particularly in light of all of the pressures being exerted on them to act otherwise, in market-mimicking ways. This project of empirical explanation nonetheless drives us, however reluctantly, to explore central issues in today's legal debate. As we endeavor to explain Delaware court behavior, we cannot avoid describing the norms—the fiduciary duties—these courts in fact impose on corporate officers. We also cannot avoid describing the criticisms contractarians direct at fiduciary duties and mandatory rules more generally.

And here is where we draw a second conceptual distinction. We distinguish immediate externalities of corporate decision making and corporate governance from institutional externalities. This distinction brings more sharply into view the relationship between corporate governance and institutional design. The concept of immediate externalities refers to substantive decisions made by corporate officers that harm discrete, readily identifiable constituents or third parties. These are effects of corporate power that economists and legal scholars identify and study—from pollution and layoffs to reductions in local or state tax contributions.[35] These externalities, however, do not account for why Delaware courts continue to impose norms of behavior on corporate officers in governance disputes. Nor do they account for why the corporate judiciary has acted in this way since the American founding. They account only for why courts impose criminal and civil penalties *in any context* and then otherwise leave everyone alone to conduct their lives as they see fit, including, in this case, leaving corporate officers alone to run their businesses, to exercise their business judgment.

By contrast, our concept of institutional externalities does account for the *corporate* judiciary's normative behavior in particular. It brings into fuller view the judicial behavior which economists and legal contractarians fail to explain (and often fail to see). It refers to a qualitatively different set of consequences of corporate decision making: Certain changes in corporate governance broaden the scope and increase the frequency of one-sidedness in structured situations, of one-sided exercises of *positional* power in civil society. These changes challenge or enervate certain social norms and, more importantly, potentially challenge or enervate the institutional design of a democratic society in particular. We propose that Delaware courts continue to impose norms of behavior on corporate officers as mandatory rules because Delaware judges remain concerned, however implicitly at times, about the possible institutional externalities of corporate power in American civil society. This is our third way of wording our proposed explanation for the norm-based behavior of Delaware courts. More than the rest of the corporate judiciary, Delaware courts remain concerned that certain changes in corporate governance can jeopardize a democratic society and, with this, undermine their own legitimacy as this country's constitutional court for intermediary associations.

A. FIDUCIARY DUTIES AND MANDATORY RULES

The norms of behavior that Delaware courts enforce as mandatory rules originated three centuries before the American founding, during the rise of English fiduciary law in the fourteenth century. The King's Chancellors began creating this tradition of law by imposing on barons norms of "equitable conduct" or "fair behavior" in their own manors. These norms went far beyond barons' legal obligations under common law and later under legislative statute. The Chancellors held that barons' private behavior on their own manors could have public consequences. In our terminology, they held that barons' seemingly private behavior could carry externalities—harmful consequences—for the institutional design of the kingdom. Thus, English chancellors intervened into barons' private affairs on what lawyers today call a "public law ground."

Being directly descended from this fourteenth-century principle applied to barons, American corporate law similarly directs judges' attention to the possible harms that powerful private persons can cause to institutional design. When judges impose fiduciary duties on corporate officers, they endeavor to maintain the integrity of private structures of governance. They endeavor to re-establish disinterested behavior in the relationship between (1) corporate officers who occupy positions of trust and (2) corporate constituents who occupy positions of dependence in structured situations. They thereby treat corporations as intermediary associations, not as market clusters or fluid sites of self-interested contracting. They also treat corporate officers as powerful "persons" whose conduct in private domains, like that of barons, can harm the larger social order—not just particular individuals or groups.

We find this legacy of England's fiduciary law tradition today in two "regimes" at the center of corporate law doctrine—corporate officers' duties of care and loyalty first to the corporate entity, then to shareholders (and, in certain circumstances, to selected stakeholders).[36] The duty of care essentially requires corporate officers to remain informed as they make decisions, including actively to seek the information they need as opposed simply to going along with their superiors' proposals. The duty of loyalty essentially requires corporate officers to avoid other business dealings that conflict with the corporation's collective interests. Taken together, both duties require corporate officers to exhibit some degree of independence and disinterestedness in their positions, to act with some degree of "fairness" and "equity." Thus, both duties normatively mediate one-sided behavior by those who occupy positions of trust in structured situations in American civil society. Neither fiduciary duty is relevant in the eyes of the law, therefore, when adults act one-sidedly at more fluid sites of contracting—whether as sellers or shoppers in a retail store or as contractors or suppliers in a spot market.

The duties of care and loyalty do not stem from common law (which covers property ownership and contracts) or from legislative statutes (which identify criminal and civil offenses). As in the fourteenth century, *the corporate judiciary today imposes fiduciary duties on corporate officers independently of contract law and statutory law.* Thus, the corporate judiciary literally places a value-added normative capsule around all of the transactions in which corporate officers otherwise engage lawfully by statute or contract. Our fourth way of wording our proposed explanation for Delaware court behavior is that this institution is uniquely responsible for mediating corporate officers' exercises of positional power at least short of one-sidedness or arbitrariness. Delaware courts may not be able to induce or compel corporate officers to act in disinterested ways in these important structured situations. But they can (a) identify when corporate officers advance their positional interests in one-sided ways and (b) rescind the transactions in which they act in these ways or else compensate those who suffer financial losses in these transactions.

We will see (in Chapters 5 and 10) that none of our four ways of characterizing Delaware court behavior are the explanations that Delaware judges typically provide for their decisions and opinions in major corporate governance disputes. We will see in fact that Delaware judges have difficulty articulating the general principle underlying their own norm-based behavior. This means that the corporate judiciary's continuing normative mediation of corporate officers' positional power is a contingent "social fact" at best. This ongoing norm-based behavior by state courts is not guaranteed by institutions of formal democracy (regularly held elections, competing political parties, and general First Amendment freedoms). Its continuation is not institutionalized either explicitly or implicitly by the Constitution of the United States. Its continuation is also not guaranteed by systemic or cross-national trends of social change, which Talcott Parsons called evolutionary universals (industrialization, formal democracy, a secure middle class, and widening access to postsecondary education).[37]

This means that should Delaware courts act in increasingly market-mimicking ways in coming decades, should they enforce contracts and statutes alone, corporate officers are hardly likely voluntarily to stop themselves short of exercising their power one-sidedly in their own positional interests, as if guided by an invisible hand. We can hardly assume that directors, top managers, or controlling shareholders will institutionalize restraints on their own positional power within corporate governance structures by contract in the absence of judicial monitoring informed by the fiduciary law tradition. Whether they ever act in such ways voluntarily is itself an empirical issue. But the empirical issue that concerns us now is more imminent, and more socially significant: Will the corporate judiciary continue to monitor the internal governance of corporations and other intermediary associations with an eye to its possible institutional externalities? Or will it follow economists and legal contractarians in seeing, at most, only the immediate externalities of corporate power?

B. FROM PERSONAL EXPERIENCE TO SOCIAL SIGNIFICANCE

Our distinction between the immediate and institutional externalities of corporate governance allows us to identify the larger social significance of corporate governance at three levels of analysis. Economists and legal scholars typically operate at the first two levels. At the first level, changes in a corporation's internal governance can increase the uncertainties that corporate officers, shareholders, and stakeholders experience in their everyday lives. Thus, the hostile takeovers and leveraged buyouts that swept across corporate America from 1983 to 1989 heightened rather suddenly the expectations that shareholders, investment bankers, and other investors had regarding acceptable levels of return on their investments (see Chapter 2). In search of higher returns in shorter periods of time, some investors opted to buy controlling shares in corporations with the express purpose of changing their management teams and business strategies. With this, investors literally created a new market for corporate control. Their increasingly self-interested behavior in this market soon altered the everyday lives of all corporate constituents, first and foremost the lives of management teams—directors, top managers, and middle managers. Then, in short order the new market reverberated across society to alter the lives of bondholders and long-term suppliers, then the lives of line employees and retirees, and finally the lives of residents of affected local communities.[38] Taking these changes together, they all qualify as immediate externalities of corporate governance and changes in corporate control.

Looking only a little more broadly, the new market for corporate control also altered the lives of elite and upper-middle class families in the United States that were not necessarily directly affiliated with any of the particular corporations being bought and sold (see Chapter 6). It goes without saying that families at more modest rungs of the economic ladder were also affected, in their own worlds. As one example of what happened to elites, consider the following headline from a page one story in the Sunday *New York Times* in 1992: "Rockefellers Trying to Keep a Fortune From Dissipating." With an estimated family fortune of between $5 billion and $10 billion, the Rockefellers are hardly living hand-to-mouth. But this family's fortune pales in comparison to that of Bill Gates or, for that matter, Ross Perot. Thus, much like other prominent American families, this family's expectations were heightened during the 1980s. By the early 1990s, the Rockefellers were prepared to live with greater risk:

> The Rockefellers are not alone in contending with low rates of return on many investment vehicles of the 1980s. Many people with big money are on the prowl for places to put some of it. "In the 1980s with investments in the stock market, the bond market, initial public offerings and real estate you almost couldn't go wrong," said David Hern, a senior vice president of the Northern Trust Company, which provides administrative and consulting services to wealthy families. "In the 1990s you're seeing the collapse of some of these investments and so you're seeing families at this level trying to fight the ravages of taxes and inflation by reaching into riskier direct investments."[39]

By looking more broadly still, we begin to bring into view the social significance of changes in corporate governance and changes in corporate control. Some changes in governance and control can be so unusual or innovative that judges may worry that they call into question first principles of corporate law doctrine, the courts' own fiduciary law tradition. No matter how Delaware judges respond to such questioning in practice—whether by upholding or adjusting these principles—they instruct other state judges more generally about how to understand the place and purpose of corporations in American society. Depending on how they respond, they may maintain, broaden, or narrow the range of ways in which corporate officers legitimately exercise their positional power. It is in this sense that corporate law is constitutional law for intermediary associations, for all structured situations in civil society.

> Corporate law, like most law, is primarily about the rule-oriented structuring of social power, and it is specifically about the rules that structure the orga-

nization of economic power. . . . [T]he powers and restrictions of corporate law are formulated with a view (at least in theory) toward achieving a set of rules for incorporated businesses that conduce to the public advantage. In the words of Professor Melvin Eisenberg, "corporate law is constitutional law" in this fundamental sense.[40]

IV. Traditional Judicial Monitoring of Corporate Power

1. Republican Vigilance, Liberal Complacency

From the American founding to the mid-1970s, the corporate judiciary's monitoring of corporate governance evolved from strict republican vigilance to increasing liberal complacency. Judicial oversight is marked by republican vigilance when state courts endeavor to identify and then normatively mediate institutional externalities of corporate power. Judges hold corporate officers accountable not only for the immediate harms they cause to particular constituents, which often stem from breaches of contract. Judges also hold corporate officers accountable for more subtle yet grander harms, which these judges believe they cause to fundamental institutional arrangements spanning the state and civil society. We can think of these harms as breaches of social order.

When judges remedy immediate externalities (breaches of contract), they intervene into a corporation's internal governance on what judges and legal scholars call a "private law ground." When they remedy institutional externalities (breaches of social order), judges intervene into a corporation's internal governance on what judges and legal scholars call a "public law ground." The situation today is not cut-and-dry, as we will see, but the American corporate judiciary has backed off considerably from its earlier republican vigilance in monitoring corporate governance. At the same time, Delaware courts in particular remain reluctant even today to embrace liberal complacency outright, to focus exclusively on the immediate externalities of corporate governance, on breaches of contract. Why?

Economists and contractarians have offered three explanations for why corporations exist (a question posed most influentially by Ronald Coase in 1937), and none account for the norm-based behavior of Delaware courts.[41] The first explanation is that corporations exist to produce goods and services efficiently, and problems arise when owners hire agents to manage corporations for them. This is a principal-agent approach, the central problem for which is how to reduce agency costs. A second explanation is that corporations exist to coordinate long-term productive activities; it is ineffi-cient to bring different investments together serially by contract. One way of filling gaps in long-term contracts—members' "understandings" of what is expected of them—is to assign control, along with property rights as an incentive to rule effectively, to one party. This is a property rights approach, the central problem for which is how best to allocate ownership in order to ensure effective control. A third explanation is that corporations are pro-duction teams in which an internal hierarchy is necessary to police shirking and opportunism by team members, irrespective of how one otherwise hires agents or assigns property rights. This is a hierarchy approach, the cen-tral problem for which is how the internal hierarchy can best benefit the principal, the owner.

However, the history of corporate law in the United States reveals yet a fourth, institutional explanation for why corporations exist, one that better accounts for the norm-based behavior of Delaware courts in monitoring corporate governance, the internal hierarchy. Corporations disperse collec-tive power from government to civil society. They thereby help to keep gov-ernment limited (while also helping to elevate individuals' loyalties beyond their families and primary groups). Thus, beyond all three economic ap-proaches to the corporation, we propose that American corporate law would encourage the presence of corporations *even if corporations turned out to be rather inefficient producers of goods and services.* American corpo-rate law would encourage this because dispersing collective power is a pub-lic good regardless. In turn, American corporate law would monitor how corporations exercise their collective power in civil society *even if corpora-tions turned out to be extraordinarily efficient.* Preventing private power from being exercised one-sidedly in structured situations in civil society is also a public good regardless.

This accounts, we propose, for the norm-based behavior of Delaware courts today. They endeavor to encourage commercial activity (which dis-perses collective power in civil society) but they also endeavor to prevent one-sided exercises of private power in structured situations in civil society. We conclude this way of thinking about corporations and courts with a brief review of the corporate judiciary's evolution as an institution.[42]

2. Corporate Law Doctrine Past and Present

Since the Founding, American state legislatures and state courts have op-erated with three distinct doctrinal approaches to the corporation, and contractarians today are successfully challenging the third. With the first doctrinal approach, from the colonial period to the 1820s and 1830s, state legislatures and state courts treated corporations as artificial "persons," as entities whose place and purpose in American society is dictated strictly by state statute.[43] When a state legislature granted a corporate charter to a private commercial enterprise, it conferred a limited set of rights on this new "legal person" in civil society, a legal person it had literally created. It essentially converted a business that lacked any independent claims on the state into a "person" that could make such claims on its "own" behalf, independently of its owners' and constituents' claims as individuals.

This first doctrinal approach, the "artificial entity" theory, is also called Hobbesian because it mirrors the way British philosopher Thomas Hobbes thought in the mid-seventeenth century about the relationship between *individuals* and the state. American state legislatures denied that *corporations* have inalienable rights, rights independent of the legal duties state legislatures imposed explicitly on them. After all, any team activity as complex as a corporation is clearly not self-sustaining "in nature" in the absence of state protection. Thus, corporations are indeed more like the way Hobbes thought of individuals in a "state of nature," as leading such a brutish life in the absence of state protection that they desperately relinquish any claims on the state. Corporations are not comparable to the way John Locke characterized individuals in nature, as living freely and affiliating themselves voluntarily with the state through a contract that limits its power. Thus, American state legislatures viewed corporations as state-created, "artificial persons" that, as such, may legitimately be required by law to serve a public interest in every activity. They did not view corporations as "natural persons" who legitimately advance their own private interests in most activities.

Given this Hobbesian view, American state legislatures compelled early corporations to perform all sorts of public services. They often mandated that corporations contribute to the general welfare by performing community services and by protecting not only owners and creditors but also employees. In addition, they prohibited corporations from otherwise maximizing their owners' private wealth directly or one-sidedly. They placed strict substantive limitations on what corporations could do and how they could do it, including the following:

- Until 1867, state legislatures did not apply bankruptcy law to corporations.[44]

- Until 1875, no state legislature granted corporations a legal right to accumulate wealth without restriction.[45]
- Until New Jersey developed the first General Corporation law, in 1888, every act of incorporation in the United States was more like an elaborate naturalization ceremony than like the formality of recognizing the birth of a citizen's child.[46]
- Until a 1910 Supreme Court decision, commercial activity in the United States was formally intrastate, not interstate. All General Corporation laws formally prohibited corporations from entering into interstate contracts even with unanimous shareholder approval.[47]
- As late as 1927, only 20 state legislatures permitted shareholder majorities to approve a merger; all others still required unanimous shareholder approval.[48]

If any incorporated business failed to meet its obligations to the public, or disregarded these substantive limitations, it activated "self-destruction" clauses in its certificate of incorporation, thereby ending its legal rights. In these ways, American state legislatures—not self-regulating markets—defined the legitimate place and purpose of corporations in American civil society.

With the second doctrinal approach, from the 1830s through the early stages of American industrialization and urbanization to the 1920s, the corporate judiciary increasingly treated corporations as "natural persons" with rights of their own. It *began* treating corporations as private commercial enterprises that legitimately advance their owners' interests.[49] This second doctrinal approach, the "natural entity" theory, is also called Lockean because it mirrors John Locke's more benign way of characterizing *individuals* in a state of nature. American state legislatures began conceding that incorporated businesses, like individuals, also have rights, including a right to accumulate private wealth without limit.

As the United States industrialized and urbanized, state courts adopted yet a third approach to the corporation. Beginning in the 1920s, this approach continued to orient the corporate judiciary to the mid-1970s. Since then it has come under increasing challenge, both in theory and in practice. Contractarians challenge this doctrinal tradition in theory, and the hostile activity of the 1980s exposed limitations in this doctrinal tradition in practice.

The third doctrinal approach emerged in the early 1920s as state courts began deferring to management's discretion in interpreting and then acting on the corporate natural person's collective interests. Citing what judges and legal scholars call the "business judgment rule," state courts largely insulated management's business decisions from judicial second-guessing. The courts adopted this third doctrinal approach outright when judges finally acknowledged two relatively new facts of corporate governance. First, they acknowledged that corporate agents are more likely to be elected boards of directors and appointed management teams than owning partners or controlling shareholders.[50] Second, they also acknowledged that this new management corporation is largely self-governing as a private commercial enterprise. It is capable of advancing legitimate private interests in American society independently of detailed statutory authorization or detailed judicial monitoring.[51] With this, state courts became less inclined to monitor management's business decisions on principle, on the basis of trying to meet some substantive ideal of the good society codified in corporate law doctrine.

As constitutional law for powerful private persons, corporate law identifies "rights" corporate officers legitimately exercise within structured situations in American civil society, including the contracts into which they may lawfully enter. Thus, corporate law identifies rights corporate officers may claim against the state. Corporate law also identifies duties corporate officers must bear when advancing either the corporate entity's collective interests or their own positional interests. *In both respects, these rights and duties reduce the state's power in civil society* and encourage a dispersion of collective power in civil society. Corporate law also identifies social norms and institutional arrangements to which corporate officers are expected to exhibit fidelity as they otherwise exercise their business judgment in "private" domains. *This reduces corporate officers' positional power and freedom of contract in civil society* and prevents one-sided exercises of collective power in structured situations.

The larger social significance of the hostile activity of the 1980s was that these changes in corporate control altered how Delaware courts think generally about corporate governance and about how positional power is properly exercised within it. At first, the new market for corporate control altered judges' thinking simply by increasing the number and variety of governance disputes coming before them. As Delaware judges grappled with a changing, growing caseload, they soon found that existing corporate law doctrine no longer oriented them toward broadly consistent rulings. By the late 1980s, many Delaware judges began fearing that their rulings in even major governance disputes were becoming so inconsistent that their institution, the corporate judiciary, was becoming "schizophrenic." As this self-doubt increased and spread to commentaries in major law journals, this "introduced a sizable measure of institutional doubt and angst" into the corporate judiciary and bar.[52] We will see that only in the mid-1990s did Delaware courts *seem*, at least to some legal scholars, to get their sea legs back, to gain some shared understanding of how to proceed in the future.

The wave of hostile takeovers and leveraged buyouts abated in 1989. But the damage had been done. American state courts lost their mooring in once settled principles of corporate law doctrine, and the issue with which we are left today is whether they will remain adrift as an institution or grasp hold of a new mooring.[53] Inconsistent behavior by Delaware courts and the corporate judiciary increases the uncertainties that corporate officers face in today's global economy, thereby affecting another institution that exercises collective power in society: corporate governance structures. The result is reciprocal: The number and variety of governance disputes cast the corporate judiciary adrift; inconsistent state court rulings complicate corporate officers' efforts to govern corporations, thereby setting the stage for future disputes; as state courts handle new disputes in inconsistent ways, this helps to unsettle corporate law doctrine even more.

By the early 1990s, judges were wondering: What institutional arrangements spanning the state and civil society are truly basic to a democratic society, if any? What institutional arrangements cannot be challenged or enervated by changes in corporate governance without altering a democratic society's very direction of change? Correlatively, what institutional arrangements are mere "traditions," once-routine ways of operating that may safely be altered or eliminated altogether?

2

The Turbulence of the 1980s

Over a decade has passed since the last hostile takeovers and leveraged buyouts of the 1980s.[1] More memory today than living experience, it is worthwhile to recall how disruptive this period was both for individuals and for institutional arrangements. It is also worthwhile to trace the sources of disruption. The hostile activity of the 1980s was antedated and fueled by structural changes in the American economy that continue to drive today's corporate restructurings in some part. Equally important, these structural changes reveal why corporate managers today appreciate that the new uncertainties they began experiencing in 1983 are hardly likely to disappear in the foreseeable future, even as the immediate threat of hostile activity waxes and wanes.[2]

I. Structural Change Since the Mid-1960s

Alfred Chandler Jr. points out six developments which began in the mid-1960s that set historical precedent for corporate America, and four merit our attention because they complicated considerably the issues of corporate agency and corporate purpose for American courts.[3] First, American corporations after 1963 changed their rationale for initiating mergers and acquisitions—friendly takeovers—as a means of growth. Rather than merging with other corporations or acquiring new divisions in order to consolidate existing product lines, they began undertaking these transactions in order to move into new product lines, to diversify. From 1963 to 1972, fully 50 percent of all mergers and acquisitions were in unrelated product lines. Thus, corporate officers moved their companies into markets where their existing "organizational capabilities," including management's own experience in operations and strategic planning, did not provide them with any obvious advantages over their competitors.[4]

Second, as product lines multiplied, top managers at headquarters began analyzing operations at their increasingly diversified divisions using quantitative data contained in internal quarterly reports. They no longer attempted to analyze the performance of middle managers running these divisions more qualitatively, on the basis of on-site visits, and as a result, headquarters became increasingly detached from operations. Top managers lost touch with developments at existing divisions and never bothered to gain familiarity with operations at newly acquired divisions. Yet the divisions under their formal control kept growing in number and size. Prior to World War II, only major international corporations had as many as 25 divisions and rarely did the largest national corporations have more than 10. By 1969, however, many corporations routinely operated with anywhere from 40 to 70 divisions. Many *divisions*, in turn, "were often larger in terms of assets and employees" than the original corporation had been in the 1950s.[5]

Third, as headquarters lost familiarity with operations, top managers began treating divisions as if they were independent suppliers of intermediate products under contract. Just as they dismiss some suppliers while signing new contracts with others, so, too, the rate of divestitures began rising relative to that of acquisitions. Starting at one divestiture for every eleven acquisitions in 1965, the rate reached one in two by the mid-1970s. By the mid-1980s, "chief executives of big corporations 'restructured' and 'redeployed' assets by buying and selling midsize divisions as if they were baseball cards."[6] The rising rate of divestitures was driven by a shift in corporate ownership—or, better, in corporations' investment structure.

In the 1950s, large American corporations had financed growth largely by retaining earnings (rather than passing profits along to shareholders as dividends).[7] In the 1960s, they financed mergers and acquisitions by relying more heavily on private placements of debt (often borrowing directly from commercial banks and life insurance companies).[8] By the 1970s, however, they increasingly secured capital by selling shares of stock more widely to the public. Institutional investors (public and private pension funds, insurance companies, and mutual funds) increasingly displaced wealthy individuals and families as the major purchasers.[9] In 1965, for instance, individuals held 84 percent of all corporate stock, institutions 16 percent; by 1990, it was 54 percent to 46 percent.[10] By 1985, block trading accounted for 51 percent of all trading on the New York Stock Exchange. Twenty years earlier, it had accounted for only 3.1 percent.[11] Thus, where entrepreneurs, families, and institutions had earlier been content to receive long-term returns on investments in particular companies,[12] now portfolio managers sought short-term returns in capital markets.

Fourth, beyond the buying and selling of divisions, a new market for buying and selling entire corporations became fully institutionalized for the first time in American history in late 1983.[13] Corporate raiders and buyout specialists could now purchase sufficient shares of stock to gain control over corporations with which they had no previous connection or particular knowledge.[14] In the remainder of this chapter we explore the rise of this new market and begin to identify some of its immediate externalities, its costs and benefits for particular corporate constituents and third parties. In the chapters that follow, we go further, by identifying institutional externalities of changes in corporate governance and corporate control.

II. The Rise of a Market for Corporate Control

1. Junk, Raids, Buyouts

When the first hostile corporate takeover actually took place in the United States is a matter of dispute.[15] Until the 1970s, however, even friendly corporate takeovers, those either initiated or welcomed by a sitting management team, were extremely rare occurrences. In 1966, for instance, there were 100 tender offers for American corporations, large or small; in 1960, only eight.[16]

What is not in dispute is that these earlier transactions, unlike the hostile activity of the 1980s, were not financed with debt, let alone with proceeds from "junk bonds."[17] Junk bonds are corporate securities sold to private investors that are rated below investment grade by standard rating services such as Moody's Investor Services, Standard & Poor's Corporation, and Duff & Phelps Credit Rating Company. A low rating means junk formally carries greater risk for investors than government bonds or investment grade corporate bonds of comparable maturity.[18] Corporations that issue these bonds lure buyers by offering them a higher rate of return, generally 3 to 5 percent higher; thus, when investment grade securities in the 1980s offered yields of 8 to 10 percent, junk's yields were 11 to 15 percent.[19]

The advent of the junk bond driven hostile takeover is not in dispute. In 1982 Drexel Burnham Lambert, a small investment bank, arranged junk bond financing for an unsuccessful bid for Gulf Oil by raider T. Boone Pickens.[20] This failed raid is significant because the types of financing available to hostile bidders determines (a) the speed with which they can act and, as a result, (b) the size of the corporations they can credibly target.[21] Speed of financing allows hostile bidders to punch holes in management's traditional defenses, and thereby to approach shareholders bilaterally with tender offers that management fails to stop or sidestep. Thus, when a market for high-yield securities became institutionalized in late 1983, this effectively institutionalized a new market for corporate control. For reasons that we discuss in section 7 below, junk bond financing simultaneously (a) widened the range of possible takeover targets and (b) enlarged the pool of potential hostile bidders. One of the first corporate raiders, for instance, was Miami financier (and high school dropout) Victor Posner. Once he accumulated a war chest of $1 billion in cash, he could secure additional financing from junk bonds to raid a major corporation as easily as could any blue-chip company with $1 billion in cash that used investment grade securities to initiate a merger.[22]

In addition to being a decade of hostile takeovers, the 1980s was also a decade of leveraged buyouts (LBOs) and management buyouts (MBOs). An LBO is "an acquisition in which the acquirer uses substantial debt (both senior and subordinate [or junk]) to take a business private or to finance a change of corporate control."[23] LBOs may be traced to 1954, when Charles Dyson purchased Hubbard Company, but only in the mid-1970s did the term gain popularity. An MBO is an LBO in which the acquirer is a group drawn from the top management team itself; the management group may also use debt, and may also either take the corporation private or otherwise purchase controlling shares. The first MBO came in 1961 when the management of Anderson-Prichard Oil purchased the company, but MBOs did not become prominent until the 1980s. The first case to go to Delaware courts, for instance, was in 1982.[24]

From the mid-1970s to the early 1980s, Wall Street began making room for buyout "boutiques," the most prominent being Kohlberg Kravis Roberts & Company (KKR).[25] After its founding in May 1976, with $50,000 raised from each of eight investors, KKR was the first to purchase a major publicly held company—three years later.[26] As the junk bond market became firmly established in 1983, leveraged buyouts accelerated rapidly.[27] The sheer number and size of these transactions reveal a cause and effect relationship: In 1981, there were 17 LBOs of publicly held companies valued at a total of $2.16 billion. There were 27 in 1982, 26 in 1983, and then 60 LBOs in 1984 valued at $13.18 billion.[28] By the time KKR acquired RJR Nabisco in 1988, it owned more corporate assets than Texaco, Chrysler, or AT&T.[29] "It defied belief that $50 billion of loans could be orchestrated by a firm so small that all of its employees could fit into a few station wagons."[30]

2. A "Democratization" of Capital?

Six developments in the 1970s and early 1980s—economic, legal, and demographic—paved the way for a junk bond market and, thus, a new market for corporate control.[31] First, the volatility of inflation and interest rates after the oil embargo of 1973 put all investors, and particularly portfolio managers, under enormous pressure to seek yields previously thought unimaginable. When the junk bond market broadened investor access to these high-yield instruments, *it also offered investors relative security.* In junk's early years in particular, its higher rate of return was paid so routinely that the "risk" associated with this new market was considerably *less* than that of investing in the stock market. After all, junk bonds are essentially underwritten commercial loans; unlike a stock dividend, they yield a fixed rate of return biannually.[32]

> Even the least secure of "junk bonds" have more investor-security features than blue-chip common stock. If the issuer gets into trouble and does not pay, the bonds become common stock—either because they have a conversion feature on default or because unpaid debt is the residual claim and acquires working control of the firm by virtue of votes (these instruments have super voting power when payments are in arrears).[33]

Second, the domestic deregulation of business initiated by the Carter administration and then consolidated and extended by the Reagan administration freed American corporations to compete more intensely for investment capital. With interest rates rising, banks charged their corporate borrowers more and, in turn, raised the yields they offered depositors. One result of this upward spiral was that by the early 1980s the average real cost of investment capital in the United States had risen to 10.7 percent, compared to 4.1 percent in Japan. Even worse, the cost of capital for long-term research and development was 10.1 percent in the United States, compared to 2.4 percent in Japan. Given the expense involved in securing long-term loans in particular, American corporations were actually far less leveraged or indebted than either Japanese or German corporations. Even as late as 1987, if Japan's corporate debt as a percentage of its GNP was taken as the standard for 100 percent, then the percentage for Germany was 70 percent, for Canada 65 percent, and for the United States only 42 percent.[34] This was the case even as the percentage in the United States had climbed considerably from where it had been at the start of the junk bond market, at 34 percent in 1983.[35]

A third factor preparing the way for junk bonds and changes in corporate control was the behavior of the bond rating services and major investment banks. Working in tandem, these two Wall Street institutions permitted only 800 American businesses access to the investment grade corporate bond market. Yet there were over 23,000 American companies with sales of $35 million or more, and hundreds of them were starved for capital.[36] The junk bond market offered them a way out of this bind. From 1983 to the end of the decade, 1,800 firms entered the new public debt market, more than doubling the number that had earlier dealt in investment grade securities.[37] Thus, when junk offered buyers a competitive rate of return, many investors were quite willing to take the "risk" of purchasing bonds from American corporations whose only "problem" was more formality than substance, namely their being denied entry to the investment grade bond market.

Fourth, as stock ownership continued shifting from individuals to institutions, one aspect of American deregulation was to liberalize the rules governing managers of public and private pension funds. By permitting these portfolio managers to seek higher yielding investments, lawmakers stimulated competition across all investors, including those still being regulated more strictly.[38] For instance, the new standards permitted managers of public employee pension funds and other fiduciaries to contribute financing to raids and leveraged buyouts, even as they were still prohibited from buying junk bonds. Thus, these money managers were free to sell their shares of corporate stock to raiders, to transfer their proxy votes to block investors, and to invest directly in takeover and buyout *funds*.[39] As examples of these investments, when KKR bought out the Oregon supermarket and department store chain Fred Meyer Inc. for $425 million in December 1981, 40 percent of its financing came from the Oregon State pension fund. None yet came from junk.[40] Washington State and Michigan State pension funds contributed financing to later KKR deals, as did Harvard University's endowment fund.[41]

As pension fund managers moved into these new, higher yielding investments, other investors less restricted by law began exploring the new junk bond market. Thus, among the first purchasers of junk were portfolio managers of insurance companies and savings and loans.

Fifth, increasing flows of international capital, coupled with recent changes in American securities law, attracted international investors to American capital markets. This, too, intensified investor competition in the corporate bond market. A truly global capital market was born, altering first the ownership of American corporations and then the ownership of real estate and other fixed assets. Eventually it touched the American labor force, altering the very nature of employment, training, and education in the United States.[42]

A sixth development preparing the way for junk bonds and changes in corporate control was a broad demographic change in how corporate officers perceived the risks attending debt. By the late 1970s, "the generation of executives who came of age in the Great Depression was beginning to retire. With them disappeared firsthand knowledge about widespread defaults, bankruptcies, and hard times."[43] Thus, the corporate officers being denied access to the investment grade bond market were not only "available" structurally to consider new ways of securing capital; they were also "available" psychologically. We saw above that many institutional investors were also available both structurally and psychologically to assume greater risks in pursuit of higher yields. What was missing was an institutionalized mechanism—a market—to bring these new risk-takers together. The junk bond market turned the trick.

3. Drexel, Milken, and Investment Banks

In 1974, Drexel Burnham Lambert was essentially a second-class Wall Street investment bank. Its revenues totaled only $1.2 million.[44] In 1976, however, it began to underwrite junk bonds. Why was this a possibility, and why did this particular investment bank take advantage of it?

Until recent congressional legislation, in October 1999, banks in the United States were barred from owning stock and operating nationally.[45] In addition, the (Glass-Steagal) Banking Act of 1933 restricted commercial banks to underwriting government bonds, prohibiting them from underwriting even investment grade corporate bonds.[46] Corporate bond underwriting became a preserve of specialized investment banks and underwriting syndicates. These institutions sell corporate securities to their own clienteles of wealthy individual and institutional investors in exchange for a fee.[47] Until 1983, major investment banks—Merrill Lynch, Morgan Stanley, Bear Stearns, Shearson Lehman Brothers, and First Boston—literally monopolized this market. Their monopoly hinged on three factors. First, they had the ear (and confidence) of available investors, who typically knew little or nothing about the securities they were purchasing.[48] Second, the corporations wishing to issue bonds were reluctant to challenge the prestige of the rating services.[49] Third, corporations had no other way to enter a public debt market.

Rather than challenging either the investment banks or the rating services directly, Michael Milken and Drexel deftly sidestepped both institutions.[50] Milken moved Drexel's relatively small clientele of more risk-accepting investors to publicly issued corporate securities that major investment houses were loathe to underwrite, namely those classified as noninvestment grade or junk. With this move, Milken personally created a new securities market, and he did so cautiously, in small, eminently logical steps. At first, he sold only "secondary offerings" to Drexel's clients. These are bonds that corporations issued at investment grade but whose current owners now wanted Drexel, for whatever reason, to re-offer at junk's higher rate of return. As Milken's success in this resale trade became known on Wall Street, Drexel slowly attracted clients from major investment banks. After all, Drexel's clients routinely received a significantly higher rate of return even as the risks involved were slight when compared to those attending other high-yield investments.

By early 1977, Milken's noninvestment grade securities division at Drexel controlled 25 percent of this entire—albeit still nascent and largely ad hoc—market. And Milken was in an ideal position. In the first place, secondary offerings did not have to be registered with the Securities and Exchange Commission (SEC). In the second place, there was no public listing of their changing rates of return. In the third place, the major investment banks continued to shun them. In short, there was as yet no public market for junk bonds; there was instead a rapidly expanding circle of ad hoc exchanges with Drexel and Milken at its nexus.[51] Rather than doing anything illegal or unethical, Milken moved forcefully into secondary bond issues simply by memorizing changing rates of exchange when few others bothered to notice.

By late 1977, Drexel underwrote its first original junk bond issue. Texas International needed capital, and Drexel offered its $30 million in bonds directly to the public (that is, to its own clientele) for a 3 percent underwriting fee. Before the year ended, it underwrote six other new junk bond issues.[52] With this, Drexel literally created a new public debt market. It did so by bearing three responsibilities that major investment houses were unwilling (or too shortsighted) to bear. It located buyers among its own clients. It was prepared to buy the bonds back at cost, thereby assuring their clients and all future investors of their value.[53] If buybacks proved necessary, Drexel was also prepared to bear full responsibility for reselling these issues.[54] In return, Drexel received sizable fees.[55]

The junk bond market grew rapidly after 1977. By late 1983, high-yield securities comprised nearly 40 percent of all outstanding corporate debt in the United States.[56] Indeed, the new bond market looked so secure and enticing that major investment banks began contributing financing to takeovers and buyouts driven by the proceeds from junk. They did so, of course, on their own lending terms. They piggybacked their more secure or "senior" loans, at a lower yield, onto Drexel's junk bond based loans, at their higher yield, under contract provisions guaranteeing them full repayment before any payoff to junk.[57] If a takeover attempt failed, or if a successfully targeted firm later filed for bankruptcy, senior loans were to be repaid *in full*, if possible, before holders of junk received either interest or repayment of principal.[58] Thus, major investment banks were technically keeping the terms of their bonds consistent with their traditionally conservative underwriting policies, and yet they were contributing financing to riskier transactions. After all, even if their loans' seniority guaranteed them repayment priority, failed takeovers or bankruptcies could result in losses of interest and only partial repayments of principal. Of course, aside from expecting interest and repayments, major investment banks also charged an underwriting fee.

Something more important was unfolding, however, than investment bankers learning to live with greater risk on formally traditional terms of investment: Major investment banks were assisting Milken and Drexel directly and indirectly in financing hostile takeovers and buyouts. Hostile bidders used capital raised from Drexel's sale of junk bond issues as collateral when approaching major investment houses for additional underwriting. This was the key ingredient that fueled the hostile activity of the 1980s. As examples, First Boston provided $865 million to help Campeau Corp. acquire Allied Stores Corp.; and Shearson Lehman Brothers offered over $1 billion to Campeau's rival, Edward DeBartolo. Merrill Lynch offered nearly $2 billion to Sir James Goldsmith in his unsuccessful bid for Goodyear Tire and Rubber Co. It offered $650 million to sponsor a leveraged buyout of Borg-Warner to defeat a bid by GAF Corp. And it offered $725 million to sponsor a leveraged buyout of Supermarkets General Corp. to defeat a bid from the Dart Group.[59]

4. The Transformation of Junk: Escalating Risk

The *ultimate* source of capital for hostile bidders was neither Drexel nor major investment banks. It was the anticipated liquidation value of the corporations being targeted. Whenever hostile bidders found themselves in a bind, whenever they became trapped by a tight repayment schedule for their financing, they arranged the resale of their targets' parts.[60] Martin Lipton, a lawyer involved in much of the early hostile activity who became disillusioned as the new market for corporate control seemed to feed on itself, provides the following example: Pantry Pride acquired Revlon with a $1.7 billion hostile bid supported by $725 million in junk bonds. Over $200 million was charged in fees or transaction costs alone. Within one year, nearly $1.4 billion of Revlon's assets was sold to finance the transaction, including: Revlon's Norcliff Thayer, Reheiss and Beecham subsidiaries (for $395 million), Revlon's pharmaceutical business ($690 million), and Revlon's Technicon subsidiary ($300 million).[61]

Legal scholar Mark Loewenstein offers another example, one that illustrates both the risks involved and the enormous yields at stake:[62]

> [W]hen Beatrice Co. was acquired by Kohlberg Kravis Roberts & Co. for $8.2 billion in a 1986 leveraged buyout, KKR estimated that it could realize a profit of $3.8 billion after Beatrice was liquidated. Because KKR and its partners, which included top management of Beatrice, invested $417 million in the acquisition, the estimated return was more than nine times their investment. More than two years after the deal, however, key units of Beatrice remained unsold, and it was reported that the "rosiest" estimate of investor profit at that time was about $382 million.[63]

A tight repayment schedule is not intrinsic to a junk bond market. This became common in the late 1980s only after the new market "matured" and underwent a significant structural change. In early junk bond driven takeovers and buyouts, those before 1986, a typical junk bond issue had "coverage." The underwriter kept on hand nearly twice as much capital as necessary to service the debt. This is why the return on these early securities exceeded all reasonable risk of default.[64] This is also why it was not necessary for the first hostile bidders to resell their targets' parts immediately. Rather, the junk bond market so consistently outperformed investment grade bonds that, ironically, it transferred uncertainty elsewhere—namely, to the two venerable Wall Street institutions running the investment grade market. As more issuers and investors sold and bought junk, their sheer numbers made a mockery of the caution and prestige of rating services and investment banks.[65] More and more influential voices on Wall Street were asking a fundamental question: If these two institutions are so far out of step on this particular investment strategy, why assume their obeisance to other traditional practices is any less out of step?

Milken and Drexel had redefined—had socially reconstructed—acceptable behavior on Wall Street.

By 1988, however, four significant changes in the junk bond market were fully under way (and yet, in themselves, these changes did not restore credibility to rating services and major investment banks).[66] The first change was in the types of ventures junk bonds financed. Through 1986, junk played a direct role in less than 10 percent of all changes in corporate control, hostile or friendly.[67] A full 74 percent of the proceeds from junk bond issues financed internal corporate growth. Another 22 percent financed unopposed acquisitions. Only 3.25 percent financed unsolicited takeovers or buyouts.[68] By 1985, however, junk suddenly played a far different role in the American economy. In the first six months of that year, it helped finance 24.7 percent of all hostile tender offers and 13.6 percent of all successful tender offers, hostile or friendly.[69]

The second change was in the firms floating junk bonds. In 1979, fully half of the firms in the nascent market had sales under $100 million. They tended to be high-growth, innovative firms that preferred to substitute higher-interest, long-term debt for venture capital, a more unpredictable source of financing. By 1988, however, these firms accounted for only 10 percent of the now institutionalized junk bond market. Sixty percent of the market revolved around corporations with revenues exceeding $500 million, and they tended to be low-growth, real estate firms whose margin for error was very thin.

The third change was in the uncertainties and risks attending the junk bond market in general. A typical junk bond issue no longer rested on sufficient capital to service its debt *on the day of its issue*.[70] In order for hostile bidders simply to stay formally on schedule for repayment in the first 24 hours, they had little alternative other than to arrange the resale of target parts *as they initiated* the bidding process. Drexel contributed greatly to this weakening of coverage by providing many hostile bidders with a "highly confident" letter, as opposed to capital. Drexel essentially promised it would raise the capital (and borrowing power) if asked.[71] Until 1988, Drexel's reputation was such that it was rarely asked; when it was, it delivered as promised.

A fourth change was in the expectations and standard operating procedures of Drexel and other junk bond underwriters. In the early junk bond market, Drexel was content with back-end profits tied to corporate issuers' later performance. By decade's end, it demanded (and received) large upfront fees plus overrides (of 20 percent).

5. Pressures on Fund Managers and Corporate Managers

In 1986, all outstanding publicly held high-yield bonds totaled $125 billion, 23 percent of the entire corporate bond market.[72] By the end of 1989, the junk bond market exceeded $200 billion in total value, comprising a full 25 percent of the corporate bond market.[73] By comparison, in 1970 the total was a mere $7 billion.

But who was buying junk bonds? Insurance companies owned 30 percent of all junk bonds and mutual funds another 30 percent. *Private* employee pension funds owned 15 percent, and another 10 percent went to foreign investors.[74] Public employee pension funds, again, were prohibited from investing here.

In considering these investments in context, it is important to recall that in 1986 half of all publicly traded stock was owned by institutional investors[75] and one-third by public and private pension funds.[76] Some of these institutional investors had moved more forcefully into the stock market precisely because they were prohibited from buying junk.[77] Because portfolio managers essentially compete to manage their funds, they are under enormous pressure to maximize profits. Unlike corporate officers, portfolio managers seldom consider broader goals, whether corporate or social, unless a particular fund explicitly instructs them to do so.[78] During the 1980s, their competition for short-term profits, their risk-accepting behavior, began to alter the very ethos of corporate governance in the United States. Corporations were no longer governed unilaterally by top management teams relatively secure in their positions. Rather, corporate officers were now looking over their shoulders for signs of hostile activity. They actively courted approval from institutional investors by endeavoring to maximize share price. More generally, they learned how to live with the greater uncertainty and risk of financing growth with debt rather than retained earnings. The ethos of corporate governance, therefore, no longer revolved around risk-averse financing strategies and long-term planning at headquarters.[79] It now revolved around financing corporate growth with debt, thereby benefitting shareholders and transferring uncertainty and risk to bondholders and corporate officers. This change in ethos continues today.[80]

6. Restructurings: Reverberations of the Market for Corporate Control

What hostile activity revealed for everyone to see was the gap, at a frozen moment in time, between the liquidation value of a target corporation's existing assets and the resale value of its stock. To be sure, knowledgeable investors accept that corporate stock is typically traded at some significant discount of the liquidation value of assets.[81] But the new market for corporate control revealed that this gap was considerably wider than investors had been led to believe by management. It was so wide, in fact, that the uncertainties and risks attending junk bond financed raids and buyouts seemed well worth taking.[82] Indeed, even when uncertainty and risk escalated as hostile bidders arranged the simultaneous resale of target parts, these transactions *remained* enticing because of the sizable returns that were possible.

Aside from the 100 percent increase in the price of Conoco stock in 1981 (see note 17), other examples illustrate why so many investors were willing to live with the uncertainty and risk of hostile activity. CBS shares were selling at $72 in 1984 when Ted Turner presented a bid for the company. Securities analysts then set its breakup value at around $200 a share.[83] As late as 1988, RJR Nabisco shares were selling below $50, but shareholders received $109 after its leveraged buyout by KKR in November of that year.[84]

All of this means that beginning in late 1983, once entrenched (and often arrogant) top management teams suddenly found themselves fighting for their very positions, their careers. In essence, *shareholders' private property began challenging management's positional power for "sovereignty" within corporate governance structures.* Moreover, in addition to hostile bids jeopardizing corporate officers' security, institutional investors and stock analysts increasingly subjected their business decisions to greater scrutiny. Top managers soon reacted accordingly, and continue to do so today: They restructured their firms in an effort both to please (and lull) institutional investors and to preempt surprises, hostile bids.[85] They endeavored to remove the incentives hostile bidders had to approach their stockholders bilaterally with alternative plans and finance strategies. Put differently, corporate officers everywhere endeavored to bring share price more closely into line with the liquidation value of assets.[86]

> If the market price does not fully reflect the firm's value, the managers, faced with a bid, can reveal the news on which the bidder is acting. Investors may evaluate it for themselves. . . . By and large, managers are the mistaken parties—for they have their egos on the line, while professional investors are betting their wallets.[87]

Before 1984, management-initiated restructurings were extremely rare occurrences.[88] In that year, however, they began to proliferate, and they remain prominent today. In just an 18- month period, between January 1984 and mid-July 1985, 398 of the 850 largest corporations in North America restructured.[89] Only 52 of these restructurings were initiated in response to actual hostile activity or credible threats.[90] Actually, even when hostile takeovers peaked, in 1986, they affected only 40 of 3,300 corporate equity ownership transactions; only 110 other transactions were affected by voluntary or unopposed tender offers.[91] Yet throughout the 1980s, 2,300 American companies restructured or were otherwise touched in one way or another by the climate created by hostile activity, and $180 billion was borrowed to finance these transactions.[92] Even after the market for corporate control cooled down, in 1988, restructurings of one kind or another remained a prominent feature of the corporate landscape. They remain favored by institutional investors, other shareholders, and then bondholders as well.

A corporate restructuring can involve one or more of four actions.[93] First, it can entail an overall reduction in the number of managers and other employees. From early 1985 to mid-1986, 89 of the largest 100 American corporations reduced the size of their management teams.[94] Second, a corporate restructuring can turn on an "operational restructuring," a sale of corporate divisions or other assets. In the same 18-month period, nearly a quarter of the largest 850 American corporations restructured in this way.[95] In 1986 alone there were over 1,200 divestitures of corporate divisions and other assets valued at nearly $60 billion.[96] Third, management can restructure by reducing a firm's liquidity directly, by paying higher dividends to shareholders.[97] On average, the premiums paid to shareholders of target companies in hostile transactions during the 1980s increased between 30 percent and 50 percent. Those paid to shareholders of acquiring companies increased 4 percent.[98] Fourth, a corporate restructuring can take the form of a stock repurchase or leveraged buyout by management and its shareholder allies (that is, an MBO).

7. The Lure of Buyouts

During the early and mid-1980s, a typical leveraged buyout was financed 60 percent with secured loans from *commercial* banks. Only 10 percent came from the buying company itself, and the remaining 30 percent came from insurance companies. Indeed, the major problem buyout specialists faced came after they secured commercial loans; insurance companies had a tradition of caution in making these investments and their standard operating procedures slowed everything down.[99] KKR and other buyout "boutiques" were well aware that this gave management too much time. Management could erect traditional defenses and invent new ones (and thereby expand Wall Street's vocabulary, with terms such as poison pill, greenmail, and others). In the mid-1980s, KKR began substituting junk bond financing for the 30 percent from insurance companies, thereby significantly accelerating the takeover process.

Whenever a hostile bidder targeted a firm, the target's management team was always free to consider the option of taking it private itself—to secure outside financing for a management buyout, an MBO. With this, "raider, target, and LBO firm [could] all profit from the outcome." Bondholders might suffer, because new debt could devalue their holdings. Employees might suffer, because many could lose their jobs. Retirees might suffer, because they could lose pension or health benefits. But other corporate constituents stood to gain, and substantially so, particularly major shareholders and the top managers who gained control.[100] In the view of Easterbrook and Fischel and other legal contractarians, all buyouts move capital to where it can be used more efficiently and, thus, can only increase social wealth.[101]

Looking at buyouts in perspective: In 1970, the dollar volume of all such transactions was only $1.2 billion.[102] By 1981, 99 buyouts were carried out, six by KKR alone, with a value totaling $3.1 billion. Then, in 1982, 164 were completed at a value of $3.5 billion and, in 1983, another 230 at $4.5 billion.[103] The first $1 billion LBO ever was carried out by KKR in 1984.[104] A year later there were 18 others.[105] By 1987, major investment banks finally appreciated that buyouts, if not takeovers, were a *fait accompli*. They began financing leveraged buyouts themselves, thereby competing directly with KKR and other "boutiques."[106] They took this step despite the uncertainties and risks attending these transactions because investor return on LBOs was so substantial—often as high as 40 percent to 50 percent once the acquired company was sold.[107] And the typical acquired company was sold within five to seven years.[108]

Consider how profits from LBOs dwarfed those from "traditional" investments, including junk bonds:

> For most of the twentieth century, ordinary stock-market investors earned about 9 percent a year, counting both dividends and capital gains. Even the great growth stocks of the postwar era, such as Kodak, Wal-Mart, or Apple Computer, seldom racked up gains of more than 30 percent a year for long stretches. But to the KKR partners, 30 percent a year *was too low*. Their

standard profit targets called for investors to reap five times their money invested over a five-year span, a profit rate that amounted to about 40 percent a year. And often KKR set its sights on even higher returns.[109]

Also consider the potential profits individual managers might reasonably expect from a LBO or MBO. KKR induced Don Kelly, who had managed the meat packing company Swift, to manage Beatrice by allowing him to buy 10 million shares of Beatrice stock at $5 million. The value of his shares soon climbed to $166 million.[110] Thus, Kelly was "the first big raja that KKR created" among the corporate officers it installed to manage its buyouts.[111]

8. A Decapitalization of Corporate America

Because the debt fueling hostile activity and restructurings exceeded the new equity being invested in American corporations during this period of time, many commentators held that corporate America was being "decapitalized," that its equity base was eroding.[112] In 1984 alone, equity across corporate America shrank by $85 billion, a record figure.[113] To be sure, the ratio of debt to equity in American corporations had been growing gradually since 1962, but at less than 5 percent a year. In one year, however, it jumped from 73 percent (in 1983) to 81.4 percent (in 1984).[114]

From 1978 through 1987, American business bankruptcies increased 150 percent, with a 600 percent increase in Chapter 11 filings.[115] And the numbers kept increasing. In 1989, the number of American businesses filing for Chapter 11 bankruptcy reorganization rose 5 percent to 16,303. In 1990, it rose another 12 percent to 18,282. Corporate bankruptcies peaked in 1991, with 18 billion-dollar companies filing, including Maxwell Communication, Pan Am, and Best Products.[116] Moreover, the asset value of the companies filing rose steadily as well: from $5 billion in 1985, to $12 billion in 1986, $40 billion in 1987, $43 billion in 1988, $72 billion in 1989, and $83 billion in 1990.[117] Corporate bankruptcies finally tapered off in 1993, when 93 companies left bankruptcy and 83 companies entered. Only two of the new bankruptcies, USG Corporation and Evirodyne, were billion-dollar companies.[118]

9. Management on the Chopping Block

There was managerial fat to trim in the 1980s, and, more surprisingly, the situation is not much different today.[119] In 1980, administrative and managerial personnel constituted 10.8 percent of total nonagrarian employment in the United States, as compared to 3 percent in West Germany and 4.4 percent in Japan.[120] Even at decade's end, nonproductive workers were still 30 percent of the total American work force, including manufacturing firms.[121] And these "workers" carry relatively lofty price tags, particularly in the United States. The average annual salary, bonuses, and perquisites (such as stock options) a CEO receives at the 30 largest American companies still typically dwarf those of his or her counterparts in the rest of the industrialized world. In 1990, the figure was $3.2 million for the United States, $1.1 million for Great Britain, $800,000 for France and Germany, and $500,000 for Japan.[122] Towers Perrin, a New York consulting firm, surveyed chief executive compensation (salary, bonuses, company contribution, perquisites, and long-term incentives) at industrial companies with $250 million in sales in 1996, and found the following national differences: Americans averaged more than $850,000; Brazilians and French were next at less than $600,000; then Hong Kong executives at $550,000, Germans and British at $500,000, and Japanese and Canadians at $450,000.[123]

A stock option is an incentive that corporate officers negotiate with boards of directors, namely an option to buy the company's stock at a fixed price over a predetermined period of time. Graef Crystal, a Berkeley economist who studies executive compensation packages, found in 1990 that 274 of 292 major American public corporations awarded stock options averaging $13 million per company. Within this gross figure, some compensation packages in 1990 were particularly lofty: Steven Ross and N.J. Nicholas, Jr. of Time-Warner earned nearly $100 million; Paul Fireman of the British firm Reebok, $33 million; and Leon Hirsch of U.S. Surgical, $15 million. Anthony J. F. O'Reilly, chief executive officer of H. J. Heinz Company, earned $71 million in fiscal year 1991 by exercising his stock options, beyond the $3.6 million he received in cash compensation. With his total earnings included, the entire top management team at Heinz made $86.8 million from stock options in 1991, beyond its $11.1 million in cash compensation.[124]

One irony is that the gap between the compensation of American executives and their counterparts overseas is beginning to close, but not because the rate of compensation in the United States is slowing relative to theirs. Rather, the gap is closing because executives overseas are rapidly adopting the American practice of adding stock options to their compensation package. Towers Perrin found in 1996 that about half of the international manufacturers they surveyed had some kind of long-term incentive bonus or option plan. A year later, the number jumped to over 60 percent. In Germany, 10 percent of companies listed on the DAX offered option packages to executives in 1996; a year later nearly a third did. Japan legalized stock options in May 1997. Within a year, 40 of the more than 3,000 registered companies adopted stock option programs.[125]

The problem Crystal sees with compensation packages in the United States is not simply one of likely excess, as a matter of abstract principle. The problem is one of inaccuracy in general corporate accounting. Management instructs corporate accountants to treat stock options differently from salaries and bonuses. Thus, stock options are neither added to a corporation's compensation expenses nor deducted from its pretax earnings. This means that in 1990 a total of $3.8 billion was missing from the 30 largest American corporations' combined compensation expenses, as reported to their boards. Because this total was not deducted from corporate pretax earnings, it was essentially "skimmed off the top," not unlike the way organized crime syndicates skim gambling receipts before reporting them to the house. Indeed, Crystal notes that if this total had been reported, it would have lowered these corporations' reported earnings by as much as 10 percent.[126]

By the early 1990s, the SEC made it easier for institutional shareholders to challenge management policies and compensation packages at annual meetings. For the first time in 40 years, they enacted proxy rules that allow institutional shareholders to talk among themselves "without having to make cumbersome and expensive proxy filings."[127] As a result of this reform, as well as lessons investors learned in the 1980s, "shareholder activists are promoting a number of measures they say will increase corporate performance through greater shareholder accountability. Most prominent are the elimination of takeover defenses, the curbing of executive compensation and the installation of more independent directors on corporate boards. And they are more likely to approach the managers of under-performing companies to find out what has gone wrong."[128] Management responded accordingly. It provided information not only to securities analysts of lending institutions but also, *for the first time*, to their own institutional investors. Indeed, the voice of shareholder activists became so prominent in corporate governance by the early 1990s that "corporations have changed and are beginning to accept the possibility of a very real partnership with shareholders."[129]

Before a new reconciliation could occur, however, shareholders first had to "go to war" with management. With managerial fat to trim, changes in corporate control extended the threat of layoffs from middle to top management. Nearly half of all *top* managers of *target* firms, for instance, are typically displaced within three years of *any* takeover, hostile or voluntary.[130]

> Within three years of KKR's arrival, the twenty-seventh floor executive suite [of Owens-Illinois' lavish headquarters in Toledo OH] looked gutted. . . . A year before the buyout, Owens-Illinois had boasted 23 vice presidents and a half dozen senior vice presidents. By January 1990, only five executives still had jobs on the twenty-seventh floor.[131]

Still, the brunt of layoffs continues to be borne by middle managers, whom top management earlier treated more like suppliers of intermediate products buried in quarterly reports than as long-term investments in human capital. Easterbrook and Fischel *seem* to dispute this:[132] "Incumbent managers don't pull this trick [of layoffs or wage and benefits cuts] on other workers because the firm's success depends on its reputation for honest and reliable dealing. You can confiscate capital in this way only once, and then only if the firm is shrinking—for it cuts off access to the labor market on equal terms with competitors." Yet Easterbrook and Fischel acknowledge that "exploiting suppliers of human capital makes sense only at the end of a firm's life cycle [and] any given firm may be approaching that end."

The turbulence of the 1980s brought a new forcefulness to top management's earlier quantitative analysis of personnel:

> Also vanishing are lower- and middle-level management jobs involving routine production. Between 1981 and 1986, more than 780,000 foremen, supervisors, and section chiefs lost their jobs through plant closings and layoffs. Large numbers of assistant division heads, assistant directors, assistant managers, and vice presidents also found themselves jobless. GM shed more than 40,000 white-collar employees and planned to eliminate another 25,000 by the mid-1990s.[133]

Yet, with all of the layoffs, total wages paid to nonproductive workers continued to grow after 1984, albeit at a slower rate. Wages paid to productive workers increased only slightly.[134]

With restructurings and layoffs rippling across corporate America, the situation looked dire for many rank-and-file workers by the late 1980s. Journalists began publishing "anecdotal horror stories" about their travails. The watershed came on May 16, 1990, when the *Wall Street Journal* ran its longest news story ever—12 columns—dedicated to workers' experiences.[135] Opinion surveys at the time found that only 8 percent of the voting public believed that hostile takeovers benefitted the economy.[136]

10. The Bubble Bursts: Bankruptcy and Prosecution

The political backlash against hostile activity was informed by passions of the day. Empirical findings were not yet available to demonstrate its larger impact on the economy, one way or the other. These passions first erupted in 1985 when Boone Pickens targeted Unocal Corp. and the company hired Nicholas Brady and Howard Baker to push Congress for anti-takeover legislation.[137] Soon thereafter, takeover lawyer Martin Lipton joined Felix Rohatyn in calling for such legislation.[138] We will see that although Congress never took any such action, appreciating that Presidents Reagan and Bush would likely veto anti-takeover legislation, most state legislatures did. Regardless, events by decade's end unfolded in tight order:

- In February 1989, the Federal Reserve for the first time in history issued guidelines covering loans for highly leveraged transactions. All major banks are now required to report such loans to their shareholders each quarter, and regulators assure them that these loans will receive greater scrutiny.[139]
- By July, Delaware's Chancery Court issued its *Time-Warner* decision (see Chapter 5), and Congress changed tax laws to make LBOs more costly. "[T]he tax system from 1989 onward still favored high-debt buyouts, but in a much less compelling way than before."[140]
- In September 1989, President Bush signed legislation forcing savings and loans to liquidate their junk bond holdings by 1994, and many started selling immediately.[141] The irony was that this effectively eliminated some of their more profitable investments and simultaneously depressed the entire junk bond market.[142] Of all junk bonds issued in 1988, 38 percent failed to pay interest on time.[143]
- On October 13, late in the day, UAL Inc.'s buyout proposal fell through for lack of financing from second-tier banks. Immediately thereafter, the stock market fell 191 points, 7 percent of its value.[144]
- In late 1989, KKR could not sell a $300 million junk bond issue for Beatrice. On December 27, KKR's Hillsborough Holdings Corp., a Fortune 500 company, filed for Chapter 11 bankruptcy in Florida.[145]
- On January 15, 1990 Campeau Corp., owners of Bloomingdale's and other prestige retail stores, filed for Chapter 11 protection. In the same month RJR Nabisco began losing its battle against bankruptcy when Moody's downgraded its junk bonds. It eventually avoided default by turning to equity, a new public offering of stock, and refinancing.[146]

- On February 13, Drexel declared bankruptcy, and on April 24, Michael Milken pled guilty to six felonies. He was later sentenced to ten years in prison and fined $600 million—nearly six times the entire annual budget of the SEC.[147]
- By July, the American economy went into recession, and the two biggest holders of junk bonds went into Chapter 11 bankruptcy: First Executive, an insurance company, and Columbia Savings & Loan. State pension funds survived with few hardships.[148]

Aside from the collapse of the junk bond market, banks reduced their loans to buyout "boutiques" a full 86 percent from 1989 to 1990.[149] The number of leveraged buyouts fell accordingly, to 224 in 1990 (at a value of $15 billion) from 371 in 1989 (at a value of $65 billion). The number of corporate tender offers in 1990 fell to 60, from 152 in 1989 and 208 in 1988. And, of course, the total value of hostile transactions in particular fell even more steeply: from around $127 billion in 1988 to only $45.8 billion in 1989, and then to a mere $11 billion in 1990. The raw number of contested tender offers fell from around 150 in 1988, to slightly more than 100 in 1989, to around 50 in 1990.[150] The total number of completed mergers and acquisitions actually held relatively constant, until 1990, at 3,851, compared to 3,846 in 1989. However, their value fell to $170 billion from $249.7 billion.[151] By 1991, the total number of completed mergers and acquisitions in the United States plummeted 34 percent, for a total value of $142.3 billion, a level that was fully 73 percent below their peak in 1988.[152] By the mid-1990s, however, merger and acquisition activity was again on an upswing, as we will see below.

III. Reflections and Recent Events

1. Why Takeovers and Buyouts Waned

Legal scholar Jeffrey Gordon identifies three events in corporate finance along with changes in corporate law that contributed to the demise of hostile activity.[153] In corporate finance, the three events were: First, the relatively sudden bankruptcy filing of Campeau and Federated Department Stores, which demonstrated that raiders were overstating financial projections. Second, the S&L crisis brought a regulatory clampdown on credit for highly leveraged transactions of any kind. Third, the Milken scandal brought intense public attention not only to insider trading but also to other manipulations in financial markets.[154]

In the law, which we explore at length in later chapters, forty-two state legislatures adopted anti-takeover statutes of one kind or another.[155] In addition, state courts were instructed by Delaware courts' use of extra-economic standards of analysis in resolving major corporate governance disputes. The results were predictable. By August 1998, only 1 out of every 200 changes in corporate control was hostile, a tenth of the proportion in the late 1980s.[156]

2. Structural Context of the New Markets

The impact of the junk bond market and market for corporate control on the American economy is by no means seen as one-sidedly negative.[157] Proponents believe that these markets accelerated four systemic and international changes in corporate finance and corporate behavior that began affecting the American economy earlier, in the 1970s.[158] First, it attuned management more closely to the workings of financial institutions, thereby pushing the American economy closer to Japanese or German models of corporate governance.[159] Second, the market for corporate control made investors more active participants in corporate decision making, thereby pushing American corporations toward a new reintegration of ownership and control.[160] Third, by inducing more managers to become owners and more employees to become investors—through LBOs, MBOs, and other restructurings—the junk bond market and market for corporate control essentially democratized capital:[161] Many more managers and other employees now own their jobs, in the form of an equity stake, than simply rent their jobs, in the form of a wage contract. Moreover, the junk bond market increased management awareness that flexibility and speed in decision making can reap enormous financial rewards. Fourth, the junk bond market in particular permitted smaller, innovative firms to secure longer-term investment capital rather than having to rely more exclusively on venture capital.

John Coffee and other legal scholars, however, see externalities attending these two markets as well as these structural changes. In particular, they see a new acceptance of risk extending across corporate America that disrupts once-settled corporate practices, social norms, and public opinion—and particularly among elites and the upper-middle class (see Chapter 6). Put differently, they see junk bonds, a market for corporate control, and the structural changes preparing public opinion to accept an unusually narrow view of corporations' legitimate place and purpose in American society. This narrow view will be reflected in law when state courts no longer impose public law norms or fiduciary duties on corporate officers and instead only enforce the contracts into which management explicitly enters with suppliers, middle managers, and other corporate constituents.

A new ethos of risk acceptance already permeates corporate governance structures as an institution.[162] This ethos is likely to affect how all other major intermediary associations are governed, including hospitals and universities. As corporate officers and association administrators in the United States live with greater risk in their everyday lives, their personalities adjust accordingly. Ongoing systemic change and a new ethos of corporate governance literally *build* support in existing social norms and public opinion for additional changes in corporate law, judicial practice, and corporate governance.

3. Renascence of the Junk Bond Market

Today's corporate restructurings reflect the fact that a market for corporate control remains in place at least in principle, ever "available" to facilitate new hostile activity. This is why major investment bankers "went into the buyout business for themselves" even as they turned their backs on KKR after the negative publicity surrounding its buyout of RJR Nabisco.[163] This explains, too, why three firms floated new junk bonds issues as early as spring 1991: RJR Nabisco, Chiquita Brands International, and Johnston Coca-Cola Bottling Group. The new junk bond market looked sufficiently sound by spring 1991 that on June 26, the *New York Times* ran a one-column, front-page article informing readers that "a revival is seen for 'junk bonds' as market gains."[164] Two years later business columnist Floyd Norris reported in the *New York Times* (on May 2, 1993) that more money was entering the junk bond fund market than during its previous highpoint, in 1986:

> Junk is back. The first quarter of this year [1993] saw more money than ever put into junk bond mutual funds by investors hungry for yield. The flow, $3.1 billion of it, *just exceeded the former peak, set in the second quarter of 1986.* Then, as now, falling interest rates were causing many investors to take greater risks in search of income. The assets of such funds have risen to $39.4 billion, more than double the level at the beginning of 1991, after the junk bond market crashed. . . . Clearly, investors are bullish on junk. But the money managers who run the funds are even more enthusiastic.[165]

Today, the popularity of junk is spreading globally. By the end of 1996, barely $2 billion of European high-yield debt was traded compared to $250 billion in the United States. A year later, European borrowers issued $4.5 billion and another $4 billion came to market or was in the pipeline during the first quarter of 1998. Estimates for Europe in 1998 were for $12–18 billion of new junk issues, roughly one-tenth of those expected worldwide. Most major European issuers are new telecommunications companies.[166]

Leveraged buyouts are on the rebound as well. By March 1999, a New York investment firm, Independence Holdings Partners LLC, opened a leveraged buyout fund for individual investors. Set at a minimum investment of $250,000, it brought in a total of $50 million. Past funds, geared to larger investors, yielded LBOs' traditional rate of return: 40 percent a year.[167]

IV. Taking Stock: Longer-Term Trends

By 1990, one-third of the 500 largest manufacturers of 1980 ceased to exist as independent entities, employment at Fortune 500 firms fell from 16 million to 12 million, one-third of these firms had received hostile bids, and two-thirds had adopted anti-takeover defenses such as poison pills.[168] As a group, they had reduced their product diversity by half.[169] And these trends continued into the early 1990s: by 1992, three-quarters had downsized during the previous year, nearly the same number had reorganized in one way or another, and one-quarter had divested, merged, or acquired.[170] A cross-section of 2,958 employees in 1992 found that 4 percent had experienced a downsizing and permanent cutback, 20–25 percent had experienced a merger or acquisition that included a reduction in work force.[171] Such restructurings remain profitable for shareholders because they "squeez[e] the organizational slack out of corporate America."[172]

Today economists are only beginning to gather and assess empirical data regarding how the hostile activity of the 1980s affected the economy overall. Yet what they are finding is very similar to what many legal scholars often reluctantly conceded at the time: The cash flow performance of post-merger firms is either mixed or positive, not one-sidedly negative.[173] Thus, a credible case can be made for the economic rationality of takeovers and buyouts, whether hostile or friendly. But how the hostile activity of the 1980s in particular affected individual firms and the economy as a whole remain matters of dispute.

On one side, of 25 cases in which companies were saddled with more than $1 billion in high-yield debt from 1985 to 1989, almost half defaulted on their loans. More than half either filed for bankruptcy or sold off substantial assets.[174] On the other side, one review of empirical evidence finds that takeovers brought economic gains when well-managed firms made bids for poorly managed ones, not the reverse. Hostile activity also added economic value when raiders took control of diversified, inefficient corporations and sold divisions as independent businesses.[175] But these researchers think a system of universal banking could have brought the same economic benefits at less cost, with less disruption.[176]

At this writing, many advanced societies—including the United States—seem primed for new takeover activity, friendly and hostile. Consider the opening two paragraphs and closing paragraph of a July 17, 1994 *New York Times* Sunday business section "Market Watch" column:

> Talk about a blast from the past. The latest Wall Street revival is Dealzapoppin, really big deals, billion dollar deals. Deals like the ones in the '80s. . . . Last week alone, there were big companies buying parts of other big companies, led by Eli Lily's $4 billion purchase of McKesson's PCS unit. There were employees buying their own companies, as UAL's shareholders approved a $4.9 billion recapitalization. There was high drama, as Macy's succumbed to Federated Department Stores. There was even a hostile offer, as Camcast made a run for QVC, scuttling that company's deal with CBS and leaving the latter vulnerable to unsolicited offers. That's not counting smaller deals. Though it is out of fashion to admit it, lots of people are still nostalgic for the Decade of Greed, which even at its worst was great for stocks. Despite the Crash, the S&P 500 ended 1987 up about 2 percent—a modest gain, but still better than this year's slippage of 2.6 percent.[177]

In 1997, 11,119 domestic mergers and acquisitions were announced. A year later, the value of all announced mergers and acquisitions in the United States reached $1 trillion, a total equaling the gross domestic product of Great Britain.[178] Although little of this activity was hostile, hostile bids escalated rather suddenly in 1999, both in number and in total value. And, like the junk bond market, hostile activity has gone global rather than remaining American-based.

> An unprecedented 100 unsolicited bids valued at $364 billion have already been made worldwide, according to Thomson Financial Securities Data. That is triple the total for 1988—the previous record year—and 21 times greater than [1998]. And the largest hostile bid ever was made last week [early November 1999] when Pfizer Inc., the pharmaceutical giant, bid $80 billion for

Warner-Lambert hours after Warner had announced a cordial merger with American Home Products.[179]

There are two major differences between the hostile activity of 1999 and that of 1983–1989. One difference is that stock represented 45 percent of the value of hostile bids in 1999 compared to less than 1 percent in 1988, when cash (that is, debt) represented 63 percent. The other difference is that a typical hostile deal in 1999 did not go to court, did not stimulate shareholder derivative suits (which we discuss at length later), whereas this happened frequently in the 1980s.[180]

Aside from the legal and financing changes that blunted the takeover wave of the 1980s, an additional brake on hostile activity today is simply the rise of high-technology companies. Hostile deals rarely work in the high-tech sector because the most important capital in these companies is their people—who can readily jump ship rather than stand by while their company is "acquired."[181] So out of the eleven unsolicited bids for high-tech companies from spring 1997 to late summer 1998, seven were withdrawn within two months of being announced. One of the few successful hostile takeovers in this sector was IBM's 1995 acquisition of Lotus Development Corp.[182]

Leveraged buyouts continue today, but now comprise only 15 percent of all high-yield offerings compared to 50 percent in the late 1980s. Corporations now use junk bonds more typically to finance expansion as well as friendly acquisitions.

Looking at the economy more generally, from April 1997 to March 1998, the Standard & Poor's 500 stock index recorded an average return on equity of 18.5 percent. This was up from an average rate of 17.9 percent over the previous five years and significantly higher than the 13.7 percent recording during the 1980s.[183]

The point is that the situation today is hardly clear, or predictable. Actually, the signals corporate officers are receiving today from capital markets, from empirical assessments of postmerger performance, and from the corporate judiciary and bar are no less confusing than those they received just before the turbulence of the 1980s began. Takeovers and buyouts are strategies investors and lenders refined during the 1980s in their own positional interests. We just saw that these risk-acceptors were responding, as best they could at the time, to structural changes that began affecting the U.S. economy as far back as the oil embargo and recession of 1973. Because these structural changes continue to affect the U.S. economy, and an increasingly global economy, takeovers and buyouts remain viable investment strategies, as does junk bond financing. *Nothing that happened in the 1980s, whether economic or legal, prevents a new wave of changes in corporate control from sweeping across corporate America.*[184]

Indeed, the junk bond market made a speedy recovery immediately after the bankruptcy of Drexel Burnham Lambert and successful prosecution of Michael Milken. It did so precisely because investors and lenders continue to see junk as a profitable, relatively secure investment. Mergers and acquisitions are again on the upswing. The major difference today is that all corporate transactions, friendly and hostile, are typically financed with what many financial analysts believe are overinflated stocks, not with debt or leverage. Takeovers financed with debt are one mark of shareholders' increasing power in corporate governance structures. Correlatively, the fact that today's takeovers are being financed with stock is a sign that management teams are once again more securely in control of corporate governance.

Coupling an upswing in mergers and acquisitions with a renascence of the junk bond market and a sudden burst of hostile activity in 1999, it is not self-evident how corporate officers will respond to today's uncertainties and risks. The only thing that is clear is what anxious management teams are not likely to do, namely to dismiss out of hand the possibility of floating new junk bonds and instead to rely exclusively on the stock market and investment grade bond market to raise capital. As new junk bond issues increase in number, borrowed capital begins to accumulate. It becomes available for a new generation of hostile bidders to use as leverage to secure additional financing for changes in corporate control. In short, corporate America is likely to face a new wave of hostile takeovers and leveraged buyouts in the future, and other advanced societies are likely to experience a first wave even sooner.

PART I

Overview and Background

3

Contractarians and Imposers

As early as the mid-1970s, legal contractarians were anticipating how shareholders and managers would behave in a market for corporate control. We just reviewed how and why this market emerged in the United States in late 1983. Legal contractarians anticipated this development by analyzing corporations and law in strictly economic terms.[1] Thus, they define corporate governance narrowly, as a mechanism by which suppliers of finance control management and protect their investments.[2] They do not treat corporate governance more sociologically, as an important window in civil society to institutional design.

Contractarianism is part of a larger Law and Economics movement in legal scholarship that endeavors to resolve vexing legal issues by reformulating them in economic terms. Contractarians began proposing in the mid-1970s that if the corporate judiciary adopted this approach in analyzing and resolving corporate governance disputes, two positive results would follow.[3] First, courts would finally encourage managers to maximize shareholder wealth rather than discouraging this by defining "corporate purpose" in more general, social terms. Second, analyzing (and resolving) governance disputes on strictly economic grounds, and in shareholders' interests, would bring greater consistency to state court rulings and thereby increase the integrity of the corporate judiciary as an institution.

Led by Judge Frank Easterbrook, Daniel Fischel, Michael Jensen, Dennis Carlton, Roberta Romano, Bernard Black, Eugene Fama, Ronald Gilson, Reiner Kraakman, Henry Butler, and Larry Ribstein, contractarians increasingly influenced the corporate judiciary through the 1970s and then dominated the debate over corporations and law in the 1980s. We will see that they continue to define the terms of debate today. Consistent with principles of neoclassical economics, contractarians visualize the corporation as a "nexus of contracts," not an intermediary association. In their view, a corporation is a market cluster, an essentially power-neutral, formless site of self-interested negotiations in which constituents enter into and leave transactions in their own interests. Today, this nexus metaphor continues to challenge the courts' much longer standing metaphor of the corporation, as an entity or powerful "person" in civil society with collective interests of "its own."

The significance of today's debate over legal metaphors cannot be overstated. The nexus metaphor orients the corporate judiciary to treat even the largest publicly traded corporation as an essentially passing site of individual contracting, as an inculpable market cluster in civil society. A nexus or market cluster is incapable of affecting institutional design one way or the other. The entity metaphor, by contrast, orients courts to treat a corporation as an intermediary association, a structured situation in civil society that contains positions of trust and positions of dependence. How a major intermediary association is governed can bear centrally on institutional design for two reasons. First, because these positions are more entrenched than passing, directors, top managers, and controlling shareholders exercise positional power over other corporate constituents in a structured situation, not a nexus. Second, corporate officers can exercise their power one-sidedly, in their own positional interests, rather than disinterestedly, in the collective interests of the corporate entity (or in any larger public interest or social interest).[4]

One purpose of this chapter and the next is to explore the promise and limits of contractarians' approach to corporations and law: their metaphor of the corporation (a nexus), their basic unit of analysis (the contract), their approach to corporate governance disputes (shareholder-centered), and their implicit political economic position or view of institutional design (liberal complacency). Another purpose is to consider the promise and limits of today's two major alternatives to this approach: judicial imposing and stakeholder balancing.

Judicial imposers are legal traditionalists who want the corporate judiciary to continue imposing fiduciary duties and public law norms on corporate officers *as mandatory rules*. Stemming from several "schools" of legal theory (see Chapter 4), legal traditionalism faces formidable problems today. Imposers advise judges to continue holding corporate officers to what are essentially social norms of behavior, not to economic contracts alone. But such judicial behavior troubles contractarians because it seems to harm shareholders, and the economy, without yielding any tangible benefits that imposers themselves are able to identify. More important, some judges see the effort to hold corporate officers to social norms and, therefore, to analyze governance disputes even in part by some qualitative standard, as a major source of the corporate judiciary's inconsistency as an institution.

Contractarians are harsh critics of corporate law tradition. Because judicial imposers have so much difficulty identifying the benefits of enforcing mandatory rules of corporate governance, and because everyone, including judges, can see the costs of doing so, contractarians accuse imposers of blindly defending "state paternalism."[5] They accuse them of being hopelessly out of step with basic trends—in the economy and in economics—which everyone else seems to see today and which contractarians saw coming in the mid-1970s.[6] Contractarians are proponents of "contractual freedom" and "governance options"; they are opponents of "political restraint" and "judicial mandates."[7] Thus, they want judges to free management and shareholder majorities from mandatory rules so that these parties may negotiate the rules that will bind them (and other corporate constituents) by contract in court.[8] When judges instead hold corporate officers to their more traditional fiduciary duties to the corporate *entity* (rather than to shareholders more directly, who "own" the entity), this drives contractarians to distraction. If a corporation *is* a passing site of self-interested contracting, as they believe, then how can corporate officers owe mandatory duties to something that literally does not exist, that is simply a "legal fiction" or "convenience" when pointing to a site of contracting?[9]

Balancers enter today's debate over corporations and law at this point. They propose that the participants to the negotiation over voluntary rules of corporate governance not be restricted to management and shareholder majorities but rather be expanded to include at least some stakeholders.[10] At minimum, balancers want state legislatures (and then state courts) either to encourage or compel management to "represent" stakeholder interests in this negotiation. In their view, this will bring balance to the rules governing all corporate constituents voluntarily, by contract. Stakeholder interests, they believe, will countervail the one-sidedness of management positional power and the one-sidedness of shareholder wealth, thereby bringing a more benign equilibrium of positional interests into corporate decision making.

Balancers are proponents of more inclusive contracting, and so are not proponents of legal tradition as such. Unlike judicial imposers, they are not vigilant republicans who defend mandatory rules on principle. Rather, balancers want state legislatures (and then state courts) either to encourage or, if necessary, to compel management by statute to take stakeholder interests into account before making any major corporate decision, particularly any change in control or in governance.[11] Once state legislatures do this—and we will see that by 1988 they did—balancers then affiliate themselves with contractarians.[12] They agree that mandatory rules of corporate governance may then be replaced with contracts. Thus, rather than challenging basic principles of contractarians' nexus of contracts approach directly, in the name of republican vigilance over corporate power, balancers share contractarians' political economic stance of liberal complacency. Only judicial imposers today endeavor to retain some linkage to the Founders' political economic position of republican vigilance, and we will see that they have extraordinary difficulty demonstrating why this matters in today's rapidly changing economy.

We introduce in this chapter and the next some major issues of corporate law and judicial practice that contractarians, imposers, and balancers are debating today and have been debating since the late 1970s. These points of contention reveal why these legal scholars and judges offer different explanations for Delaware court behavior—even as they describe this behavior and the facts at issue in governance disputes in virtually identical ways. Because their descriptions are interchangeable, we can safely think of the norm-based judicial behavior at issue as an empirical fact. In Chapter 5 we explore this "fact" more directly by reviewing major governance disputes of the 1980s and 1990s and how Delaware courts ruled on them. In the chapters following that one, we focus increasingly on the judicial behavior that contractarians, imposers, and balancers have difficulty explaining.

I. Structured Situations and Fiduciary Law

Contractarians anticipated the turbulence of the 1980s as well as today's corporate restructurings by essentially extending their basic unit of analysis—the contract—from markets to corporate governance structures. "[A] contractual approach does not draw a sharp line between employees and contributors of capital."[13] Contractarians felt free to extend economic analysis to corporations because, like neoclassical economists, they are complacent liberals. Their concepts leave no room for the possibility that changes in corporate governance might challenge or enervate the institutional design of a democratic society. Rather, contractarians restate in more specific terms a basic assumption of liberal complacency at the center of neoclassical economics. Economists assume that self-regulating markets simultaneously maximize individual wealth, increase social wealth, and support rather than challenge or enervate institutional design.[14] Contractarians, in turn, assume that when corporate governance is dedicated to maximizing shareholder wealth, this simultaneously benefits society in the same two ways. It *invariably* increases social wealth, and the corporate governance function *invariably* supports the institutional design of a democratic social order.[15]

This assumption of liberal complacency is a credible point of departure in approaching the economic, legal, and social issues surrounding the internal governance of publicly traded corporations. It also offers a clear alternative to corporate law tradition and long-standing judicial practice. Unlike existing law and current practice, contractarians believe that when courts analyze and resolve corporate governance disputes in strictly market-mimicking ways using quantitative standards of analysis alone, harm cannot befall adept individuals, and certainly not society. Thus, as long as corporations maximize share price and shareholder wealth, courts need not concern themselves with either immediate externalities or institutional externalities of corporate power because corporations are power-neutral market clusters, not structured situations or intermediary associations.

Contractarians' liberal complacency, however, reveals two major limitations in any narrowly economic approach to corporations and law. The economic concepts they employ remove from view (a) a central fact of judicial behavior and (b) an equally central fact of corporate governance.

Looking first at judicial behavior, the corporate judiciary does not simply enforce rules that management and shareholder majorities negotiate bilaterally by contract or by consent. It also imposes social norms on directors, management, and controlling shareholders independently of contracts as well as of their consent. As long as corporate officers operate within the legal form of the publicly traded corporation, rather than within the legal form of a close corporation, they cannot ignore or neglect these extracontractual duties even with unanimous shareholder approval.[16]

We may state this point more generally. Within those *structured situations* in American civil society that the corporate judiciary defines as fiduciary relationships, the courts unilaterally place a normative "capsule" around all of the contracts and transactions into which participants may enter, whether voluntarily or not.[17] Thus, individuals who exercise positional power within these structured situations cannot ignore or evade these duties unless and until they leave these structured situations. Fiduciary law, therefore, leaves everyone one and only one option: Enter structured situations and be bound by extracontractual duties, or steer clear of them and enter contracts and transactions in your own interests. Likewise, corporate law leaves all corporate officers one and only one option: Incorporate your business and be bound by the extracontractual duties attending this legal form, or operate your business in some other legal form (and thus do not publicly trade stock and install a board of directors only if you wish).

Having presented a general corollary that follows from the corporate judiciary's fiduciary law tradition, we may state the point of this tradition more specifically. The corporate judiciary normatively mediates how directors, management, controlling shareholders, and all other corporate agents exercise positional power in *corporate* governance *structures*. This normative mediation of corporations' internal governance—a structured situation—is a fact not in dispute. What is in dispute is why the corporate judiciary continues to act in this norm-based way: Why does it enforce mandatory rules? What purpose does this serve? Any theoretical or conceptual approach to the corporation—whether legal, economic, or social—contains an explicit or implicit account of this judicial behavior. Judicial imposers endeavor to account for it explicitly. The accounts contained in contractarian and balancer descriptions of corporations and courts are often implicit; those that contractarians and balancers present explicitly, we will see, are never complimentary to the corporate judiciary.

Turning to a central fact of corporate governance that contractarians' economic concepts remove from view, these concepts downplay the significance of the difference between the investments stakeholders make in corporations and the investments that shareholders make. That these investments do differ qualitatively is also a fact not in dispute. What is in dispute is how best, in light of this, to account for the way positional power is actually exercised within corporations and, most important, whether corporate governance ever carries immediate externalities for constituents or institutional externalities for society. Any theoretical or conceptual approach to the corporation also contains an explicit or implicit account of the positional conflicts that typically arise in corporate governance structures and of the consequences of these conflicts, if any. Here is where contractarians, imposers, and balancers are all most explicit. Here also is where their approaches reveal the clearest points of contention in today's debate over corporations and law.

II. Contracts, Mandatory Rules, Positional Power

1. Are Mandatory Rules Anachronistic or Vital?

The American corporate judiciary not only imposes social norms or extracontractual duties on corporate officers. It does so independently—of legislative statutes, of common law contracts, and of officer and shareholder consent or approval. The most important court-enforced social norms are corporate officers' traditional fiduciary duties of care and loyalty *to the corporate entity*.[18] When judges impose these duties on directors and managers, they are endeavoring to maintain the integrity of the internal governance of the corporate entity, as judges interpret it. They are not endeavoring to facilitate either corporate production or self-interested contracting by shareholders (or stakeholders).[19]

When judges act on the courts' own fiduciary law tradition, they treat corporate officers as *trustees* of the corporate entity. They do not treat them, more narrowly, as *agents* of a principal, the entity's owners. Thus, Delaware law refers to corporate directors as a *firm's* "incorporators," not simply as shareholders' agents.[20] Judges impose nonnegotiable normative standards of behavior on corporate officers because judges are skeptical that directors, management, and controlling shareholders will otherwise act disinterestedly, in the collective interests of the entity. They are skeptical that corporate officers will voluntarily resist acting more one-sidedly, in their own positional interests. They are also skeptical that controlling shareholders in particular will be able or willing to discipline either themselves or management sufficiently in the absence of consistent judicial monitoring.

Legal traditionalists are certain that if Delaware courts in particular ever cease to enforce fiduciary law's norms of disinterested behavior, dire consequences will befall American society. The problem arises, however, when contractarians ask them point blank to identify what these dire consequences are. Traditionalists then falter (see Chapter 7). Contractarians, in turn, react to this uncertainty and vacillation by traditionalists by saying it demonstrates their point. The fiduciary law tradition is anachronistic. It does not serve any purpose—any public law interest—that even its proponents can identify. Ultimately, balancers agree. They simply go further than contractarians in trying to reassure traditionalists. When stakeholder interests are adequately represented in corporate governance structures, they propose, everything will work out for the best even if contract law replaces fiduciary law. This is balancers' version of liberal complacency.

The irony is that all three sets of legal scholars and judges can credibly claim that their views of the corporate judiciary's mission are consistent with corporate law doctrine. In itself, this suggests corporate law spans an unusual, ultimately untenable, mix of concepts. Before we can show why, however, we need to present some corporate law basics.

2. A Morphology of Corporate Law Doctrine

American corporate law revolves around two distinct sets of rules.[21] One set is a "core" of mandatory rules, which contains all of the social norms that the corporate judiciary continues to enforce today. The most important part of the core, as we have said, is the fiduciary duties state courts impose independently on corporate officers, however unevenly. But another part of the core is whatever public law norms state legislatures place in their General Corporation laws by statute. Being social norms, mandatory rules mediate the strictly economic or market-mimicking behavior of corporate agents, whether boards of directors, top management teams, controlling shareholders, or, should the day ever come, powerful stakeholder coalitions. Put more positively, mandatory rules are supposed to encourage disinterestedness in corporate governance and to discourage one-sidedness. Being mandatory, corporate officers cannot alter or suspend either their fiduciary duties to the corporate entity or their statutory duties to the public even with unanimous shareholder (and unanimous stakeholder) approval.

All other rules of corporate law doctrine are negotiable, and can be changed from corporation to corporation. These are the rules contained in a corporation's charter or certificate of incorporation and in its by-laws. The rules in this second set are called "suppletory rules" and "enabling rules." Being negotiable from site to site, these rules can be altered in any number of ways in substance either with shareholder approval (when amending a corporate charter) or by private contract (when top management negotiates agreements with middle managers, long-term suppliers, or other stakeholders). Contractarians and balancers alike want corporate law doctrine to contain only suppletory rules and enabling rules. Contractarians want management to negotiate the most important rules bilaterally with shareholder majorities. Balancers want stakeholder coalitions brought into these negotiations, at least indirectly (through management representation), thereby making them multilateral, more pluralistic. Imposers, by contrast, want *some* core of mandatory rules to remain in place, and particularly corporate officers' traditional duties of care and loyalty to the corporate entity.

A. ENABLING RULES

Corporate law's enabling rules are agreements that corporate constituents negotiate with management in their own positional interests. Some of these rules are bilateral contracts, others are by-law provisions; in either case, enabling rules can be amended or voided at any time with new contracts or by-law changes. By protecting constituent stakes or positional interests, these rules of corporate governance facilitate—enable—participation in the enterprise. Thus, particular bondholders, suppliers, middle managers, and other stakeholders may seek enabling rules that obligate management to protect their loans, intermediate products, human capital, and other "stakes" during major corporate transactions, such as takeovers or mergers. If stakeholders fail to seek such rules, or fail to get management to agree to them, then this whole matter—what is to become of their stakes when the company changes direction—is left open. Management has every legal right to ignore these stakeholders later, when times change and they seek protection belatedly.

Thus, if a particular corporate constituent fails to see to it that a corporation's charter contains provisions that protect its positional interests, or if it fails to protect itself by negotiating a customized contract with management, then this constituent cannot credibly appeal to state courts for protection.[22] It is literally left defenseless, lacking what legal scholars call the "standing" necessary to initiate judicial action (see Chapter 4). Moreover, since enabling rules can be changed at any time by a new contract or by-law amendment, corporate constituents must remain ever-vigilant in protecting their positional interests.[23] Even here, Delaware courts help out. They see to it that by-law changes do not conflict with charter provisions, do not allow directors to entrench themselves, and do not shift the allocation of power between classes of stock.[24]

B. SUPPLETORY RULES

Corporate law's suppletory rules bind everyone, and yet are not mandatory or nonnegotiable. These rules are typically placed in a corporation's certificate of incorporation, its charter.[25] Charter provisions, in turn, must be consistent with a state's General Corporation law and established public policy.[26] Every constituent is bound by suppletory rules in the charter, but each constituent is free at any time to alter by contract how a particular suppletory rule will apply to its position and interests. Each is free to negotiate an enabling rule with management—that is, a contract or a change in by-laws (with director approval and shareholder notice)—that alters how a suppletory rule will apply to it. Suppletory rules remain binding in court, however, until they are *explicitly* altered by contract or by-law change. Thus, these rules are also called default rules. They operate much like default commands in a computer program:[27] A writing program may default all page margins at one inch, but any operator is free at any time to print a manuscript with different margins. But irrespective of what any operator does, page margins of one width or another remain in place; they are never eliminated or voided—whether by action or inaction.

One example of a suppletory rule in state corporate law is the one share–one vote standard for proxy contests at corporate annual meetings. The management of publicly traded corporations is not permitted to waive or void shareholder voting as such; the standard is not an enabling rule that can be voided by agreement. More important in this case, voiding shareholder voting would essentially take a corporation private, thereby changing the legal form—the "computer program"—entirely. It would eliminate an important distinction between a publicly traded corporation and a close corporation, a privately held corporation. Short of doing this, however, officers of publicly traded corporations are permitted, with shareholder approval, to experiment with different ways of allocating proxy votes—whether by types or amounts of shares, or by types of other investments in the corporate enterprise.[28]

State legislatures often place suppletory rules in their General Corporation laws, along with "off-the-rack" or "standard-form" enabling rules of various kinds. Management is free to change suppletory rules with shareholder approval both at incorporation and also later, at "midstream." Midstream changes could involve amending a corporation's existing charter or reincorporating in another state with an amended charter (the cost of which ranges from only $40,000 to $80,000).[29] Far more radically, contractarians want state legislatures (and then state courts) to permit management, again with shareholder approval, to "opt out" of mandatory rules. They advocate "opting out" not only at incorporation but also, even more radically, at midstream (see Chapter 9). For now we simply note that opting out of mandatory rules would mark a fundamental departure from the entire history of corporate law and judicial practice in the United States. Opting out at midstream, moreover, raises constitutional law issues and thereby pushes the envelope of the Contractarian Challenge to corporate law tradition.

C. MANDATORY RULES

Corporate officers are not permitted to adjust, let alone void (or opt out of), corporate law's core of mandatory rules.[30] Mandatory *federal* rules, such as the Williams Act, cover matters of corporate finance and financial disclosure. These rules speak to insider trading, soliciting proxies for annual shareholder meetings, disclosure to shareholders, and the mechanics of tender offers.[31] *There are no federal rules covering the internal governance of corporations; this is a preserve of state legislatures and state courts.*

Thus, mandatory *state* rules cover how corporations govern themselves, including how they may: undertake mergers and acquisitions, engage in parent-subsidiary transactions, and either respond to or defend against hostile takeovers and buyouts. These rules speak to the relative powers *and fiduciary duties* of directors, managers, and controlling shareholders, any public law norms of "corporate citizenship" or "corporate social responsibility" a state legislature expects them to bear, and certain procedures of corporate decision making.[32] The procedures at issue include quorum and notice requirements for shareholder voting and those governing midstream changes of a corporate charter.[33]

Many mandatory rules of corporate governance speak in one way or another to the issue of corporate purpose: What is the legitimate place and purpose of corporations in American civil society? By imposing social norms of behavior on corporate officers, mandatory rules instruct judges to approach at least certain governance disputes with qualitative standards of analysis. They instruct judges not to act more exclusively in market-mimicking ways, namely by applying quantitative standards that draw attention to whether corporate growth (market share) or corporate profit (share price) is being maximized.[34] The questions, of course, are: What are these qualitative standards of analysis? And why exactly should they ever take legal precedence over simply encouraging market-mimicking behavior in corporate governance, over maximizing growth or profits?

When contractarians propose that judges permit management to opt out of mandatory rules with shareholder approval, they draw attention to two central principles of their economic approach to corporations and law.[35] First, they believe corporate law should be enabling wherever practicable.[36]

Because by-law provisions are more readily amended than certificates of incorporation, contractarians see "the very ease of amendment [favoring] stockholders."[37] Second, contractarians also believe judicial rulings in governance disputes should be market mimicking, guided strictly by the same quantitative standards of analysis that, say, investment bankers employ. Judges, they believe, should focus exclusively on the benefits and harms of any disputed corporate transaction that can be priced, and thereby fully recompensed if it comes to that.[38]

These criticisms of mandatory rules follow logically from contractarians' metaphor of the corporation as a nexus of contracts. Common law contracts are enabling rules. The parties to these contracts essentially impose rules on themselves, in their own interests. "Contract means voluntary and unanimous agreement among affected parties."[39]

Despite the simplicity, elegance, and ideological appeal of this view of corporations and law in today's business environment of domestic deregulation and global competition, however, Delaware courts nonetheless resist adopting it outright. Yet their applications of corporate fiduciary obligations seem so "substantially diluted" even to judicial imposers today that these legal scholars acknowledge Delaware courts fail to set clear limits to one-sided behavior by corporate officers or controlling shareholders.[40] Thus, judicial imposers concede that Delaware courts are heavily influenced by legal contractarianism even as imposers appreciate that these courts nonetheless continue to act at times in more traditional ways. Delaware courts continue at times to impose social norms, extracontractual duties, on corporate officers as mandatory rules.[41] This means that Delaware courts continue to analyze, then resolve, corporate governance disputes using qualitative standards, not by acting in market-mimicking ways.

One of the greatest points of contention in today's debate over corporations and law is over how best to account for this extra-economic, norm-based *behavior* by Delaware courts. Imposers have difficulty explaining it, as we noted above, but they ceaselessly ask the questions that at least suggest why such judicial behavior may remain important: Are existing fiduciary duties and public law norms defensible because they serve a public interest? Do significant externalities of corporate power, either for particular constituents or for the larger society, elude pricing and therefore narrow economic analysis? Contractarians Easterbrook and Fischel deny the merit of the first question but acknowledge the merit, not correctness, of the second. Even here, however, they word the issue at stake both conditionally and more narrowly: "If the terms chosen by firms are *both* unpriced and systematically perverse from investors' standpoints, then it might be possible to justify the prescription of a mandatory term by law."[42]

Contractarians respond to imposers' two questions with two assertions that join the issue. First, they assert that existing fiduciary duties and public law norms are hopelessly anachronistic. The corporation is more power-neutral nexus than collective entity, more market cluster than structured situation. Second, they assert that all significant harms of corporate governance are both immediate, for constituents directly involved, and readily priced. Thus, constituents who allege harm by a particular corporate transaction can be fully recompensed if they prevail in court. This means by contractarian accounts that courts may analyze and resolve all governance disputes using the same quantitative standards of analysis that investment bankers employ when they assess corporate performance.

3. A Morphology of "Stakes"

Shareholders' investment in corporations, equity capital, is easily priced, transferable or fungible, and invariant across all shareholders. By contrast, stakeholder investments in corporations vary extraordinarily across stakeholders, often elude pricing and, most important, often become fixed or firm-specific over time. Long-term suppliers, for instance, invest intermediate products and in doing so may over time tailor their own production facilities to meet the particular needs of specific corporate customers. Investments of this kind, unlike equity capital, are hardly transferable or fungible; rather, they are often difficult to sell to others and thereby convert into more liquid assets. The same is true of the investments of all other stakeholders. Managers and other employees invest "human capital" (training and work experience, motivation and creativity) that also often becomes fixed or firm-specific over time. Similarly, residents of local communities invest infrastructure along with an "expectation" (that a corporate neighbor is more long-term enterprise than fly-by-night operation). Localities expect the corporations among them to maintain certain levels of employment, salaries, consumer spending, and tax revenues. Retirees rely on particular corporations to keep their pension funds solvent and to deliver health benefits.

The partial exception among stakeholders is bondholders. Their investment in corporations—loans—can be readily priced, like equity capital; but, like other stakes, loans are more difficult than equity capital to sell at full value and convert into liquid assets. Bondholders ultimately rely on particular corporations to meet repayment schedules and other terms of their loans, and so they also have a greater stake in how corporations are governed internally than do shareholders.

The point of comparing these investments is that it is shareholders who are unusual among corporate constituents, not stakeholders. The nature of their investment understandably leaves shareholders and the contractarians who adopt their point of view with an impression that a corporation is indeed more nexus or market cluster than governance structure. This understandable impression explains why it is not particularly controversial for contractarians to portray shareholders' positional interest in corporations one-dimensionally.[43] Their positional interest is often strictly pecuniary.

However, the "position" that shareholders "enter" when they buy publicly traded stock differs fundamentally from the positions into which all other constituents enter in the same corporations. Whether as bondholders or long-term suppliers, as middle managers or line employees, as retirees or residents of local communities, all stakeholders enter situations that are more structured.[44] They cannot as readily diversify their investment stakes, as if their stakes are part of a portfolio of more liquid assets. Thus, irrespective of the type of contribution that stakeholders make to a corporate enterprise, *their* impression is not one of operating within a market cluster. Rather, their impression is one of operating within a structured situation from which they cannot exit as readily or at little cost. So, upon entering this situation, they have little alternative other than to compete with corporate officers (and controlling shareholders) for power and influence in their own positional interests. They also appreciate, however reluctantly, that this competition can degenerate into trench warfare—and especially when distant shareholders are on the prowl for higher share price at the possible expense of all other corporate constituents.[45] Stakeholders appreciate that corporations perform a governance function, not simply a production function.[46]

Here is where judicial behavior confirms the stakeholder view and, along with it, the entity metaphor. What happens when corporate officers fail to perform the governance function adequately? What happens when they fail to mediate positional conflicts in ways that please not only shareholder majorities but also shareholder minorities? Their decisions and, more important, the corporation's governance structure itself and how officers typically conduct themselves within it can all be subjected to "enhanced scrutiny" by a state court.[47] Thus, when contractarians generalize their basic unit of analysis—the contract—from markets to structured situations, they fail to account fully for corporations' governance function. They similarly fail to account fully for the corporate judiciary's norm-based behavior in analyzing and resolving corporate governance disputes.

In closing this section, we can anticipate some empirically significant factors that come into play in the internal governance of corporations by considering three different levels of analysis at which they appear:

- At a microanalytical level, that of transactions between management and corporate constituents, stakeholders' positional interests differ qualitatively from shareholders' more or less one-dimensional interest in maximizing share price.
- At a mesoanalytical level, that of the corporate entity, certain decisions made by corporate officers can harm either shareholders or stakeholders more than other decisions.
- At a macroanalytical level, that of the relationship between corporate governance and institutional design, certain forms in which the governance function is organized can harm the larger society more than other forms.

III. Alternatives to Legal Contractarianism

1. Limits of Neoclassical Economics: Corporate Power

Contractarians' economic concepts are simplifying in other respects. These concepts simplify the entire issue of corporate or collective power in civil society.[48] Contractarians frequently criticize the power of government in general terms (for instance, when they attack "state paternalism"). But they treat even the largest publicly traded corporation as a power-neutral, formless nexus in which constituents negotiate contracts bilaterally in their own interests.[49] This is why they do not see the point of the fiduciary law tradition today, of courts imposing normative restraints on how positional power is exercised in corporations or in other structured situations in civil society.[50]

Ironically, when economists and contractarians think in more specific terms about particular agencies of government, they do so within and through the same general theoretical approach that discounts the significance of collective power. One stark example is Easterbrook and Fischel's reluctance to concede that Congress exercises collective power, that Congress is an entity.[51] Indebted to public choice theory, they portray Congress—and then all other public agencies, from regulatory bodies to state courts—either as steered internally by strictly self-interested factions or else as reacting to external pressures from interest group coalitions.[52] Given this view of public bodies, contractarians are loath even to entertain the possibility that private commercial enterprises exercise collective power in civil society rather than respond more benignly to pressures from capital markets and investors. "Corporations are a subset of firms. The corporation is a financing device and is not otherwise distinctive."[53] By their account, a corporate nexus is no more capable of exercising collective power, let alone of doing so in harmful ways, than the stock market or the wheat futures market.[54] The same is true, contractarians believe, of all other intermediary bodies, whether universities, hospitals, or professional associations. Thus, even to inquire about whether corporations might act "arbitrarily" in a market society is, in their view, to go over the deep end. Such an inquiry reveals more about the questioner's prejudices and outright superstitions than about economic and social "reality."[55]

Using a framework of concepts that from the outset removes the problem of corporate power in civil society from analytical and empirical inquiry, contractarians cannot see any possible connection between corporate governance and institutional design, let alone one that might be harmful in any significant sense.[56] Given this point of departure, contractarians can be remarkably zealous when calling on legislatures and courts to remove all mandatory rules from corporate law doctrine. Zeal here follows logically from their economic concepts: The only rationale for enforcing mandatory rules is to subordinate shareholders' interest in maximizing share price, and management's interest in entrenching itself, to some putative social or public good. But if corporate power is an oxymoron, and if corporate governance freed from mandatory rules cannot possibly harm society, then mandatory rules are indeed embarrassing displays of "state paternalism." They are devices through which factions within state legislatures or else interest groups pressuring them from the outside push for statutes in their own material interests, even as this distorts corporate decision making at shareholder expense.[57] Or else matters are even worse: Out of personal resentment, the factions and groups take delight in limiting shareholder wealth or, out of populist rancor, they play on the public's unwarranted fear of "corporate power" or "finance capital."[58]

Thus, contractarians do offer an account of corporate law's mandatory rules, but one that traces their origin, not one that identifies their historical or contemporary function.[59] And there is no contractarian account of these rules that is complimentary to the corporate judiciary and bar. Mandatory rules originate in: antiquated tradition (state paternalism); legislative faction (whose members may operate under an illusion that they serve a "public interest"); pressure politics (by risk-averse management teams and their stakeholder allies); resentment; superstition; and rancor. Contractarians' simplicity and disingenuousness in characterizing corporate power is neither an anomaly nor an option within their framework of concepts. To the contrary, simplicity and disingenuousness here is a defining characteristic of any narrowly economic approach to corporations and law.[60]

Still, even as contractarians deny the very existence of corporate power, public or private, another of their central principles holds regardless: Corporations today are rarely unidivisional bureaucracies, and they are hardly insulated from the pressures of capital markets. Rather, they are typically federations of more or less distinguishable divisions and subdivisions, operational units, all of which respond in one way or another to capital markets.[61] Contractarians conclude from this that even if corporations had "power," it would be decentralized in many hands regardless and, for yet another reason, would not pose any particular threat to society.

The problem is that contractarians' nexus metaphor, contract unit of analysis, and liberal complacency about the relationship between corporate governance and institutional design prevent them from appreciating five other, interrelated points about corporations that hold equally well today. First, and consistent with their point about a corporate federation, it is not likely that all corporate divisions, including headquarters, will be organized in the same form. Rather, it is more likely that due to specialization between and then within divisions, different divisions will be organized in different forms.[62] After all, headquarters and divisions are responsible for gathering and processing different types of information, about different sources of uncertainty, which originate in different parts of any corporation's environment.[63] A second point contractarians fail to appreciate follows from the likelihood that divisions are likely organized in different forms. It then becomes a possibility that how positional power is exercised in some headquarters and divisions may differ significantly from how it is exercised in others. With this, it also becomes a possibility that some exercises of positional power may be arbitrary or particularly one-sided, at least at times.[64] We have not established that headquarters or any divisions pose a threat to society, but we are beginning to see why it is legitimate for courts to operate on their traditional premise that distinct entities, and private commercial ones at that, are present in American civil society.

Third, being organized in one form or another, headquarters and divisions contain structured situations by definition. Forms of organization are not necessary at markets or fluid sites of contracting. After all, the wheat futures market is not organized in any form; it does not contain any identifiable structure of authority. By contrast, corporate constituents compete for power and influence within some form, within some identifiable structure of authority. Fourth, given that headquarters and divisions may be organized in one form or another, it is not more "realistic" or insightful to assert or assume that all corporate constituents act, or can act, strictly in their own self-interests. Rather, corporate constituents also act on positional interests that they develop within the forms in which headquarters and divisions are organized. What is in their positional interests at these sites, moreover, may or may not be coterminous with what is in their self-interests as less encumbered individuals.

Fifth, it is a possibility that a particular form may mediate exercises of positional power (and self-interested behavior) short of one-sidedness, whereas other forms fail to have this effect.[65] Thus, a particular form may encourage disinterested behavior in structured situations in American civil society while others fail to do so. To the extent that corporate governance bears at all on institutional design, these issues of form and positional power may allow us to account for corporate law's core of mandatory rules and therefore for judicial behavior.

2. Excesses and Innovations

Actually, legal contractarians go further than neglecting these five points and their possible implications for institutional design. Consistent with their economic concepts, they classify all putative "abuses of power" within corporate governance structures in only two ways. On the one hand, they portray most as short-term mistakes or excesses by corporate officers that are disciplined rather readily, and certainly impersonally, by capital markets, product markets, and labor markets. On the other, they portray all remaining putative "abuses" as innovative corporate transactions and practices that successfully elude market discipline on the merits. These transactions and practices turn out to maximize growth or share price, thereby simultaneously increasing social wealth without self-evidently harming constituents or third parties along the way.[66]

Mistakes or excesses are exposed more readily than are innovative transactions and practices. When a corporation's competitors fail to mimic this first set of putative "abuses" of power by a top management team, and yet these competitors' market share or profits increase whereas the team's does not, this reveals that the team made an error in business judgment. Whether one wishes also to call it an "abuse" of power is a matter of indifference to contractarians. Such behavior is not likely to continue regardless. "Markets that let particular episodes of wrongdoing slide by, or legal systems that use deterrence rather than regulatory supervision to handle the costs of management, are likely to be effective in making judgments about optimal governance structures."[67]

It takes longer, however, to reveal whether the other set of putative "abuses" is truly innovative. When a top management team leads the way in challenging a traditional business practice or a mandatory rule, and thus seemingly abuses their power, their firm's economic performance tells the tale. When firm growth or share price eclipse that of its competitors, and constituents and third parties are not self-evidently harmed or disadvantaged (in ways that elude pricing and full recompense), this reveals that the team's business judgment is basically sound. Backward-looking investment banks or the stodgy corporate judiciary may come down on it, but the team's actions point the way for other innovators. How Milken and Drexel created the junk bond market illustrates this well, and Roe calls for laws to permit greater variation in how financial institutions behave today.[68]

In both instances, whether as excess or innovation, contractarians see all putative abuses of power by corporate entities as ultimately benign in their consequences—both in their immediate consequences for third parties and in their longer-term consequences for the larger society.[69] As long as markets work properly, any problems will be "priced out" as they cause concern to investors.

All the terms in corporate governance are contractual in the sense that they are fully priced in transactions among the interested parties. They are thereafter tested for desirable properties. . . . It is unimportant that they may not be "negotiated"; the pricing and testing mechanisms are all that matter, as long as there are no effects on third parties.[70]

Contractarians have difficulty imagining a profitable, otherwise lawful (that is, contractual) corporate undertaking (a) failing to advance social wealth and therefore (b) failing to support the institutional design of a democratic society. Rather, they see corporate profits underpinning any and all other public goods, however defined. "Within this nation, goals competing with profits are most likely to be sacrificed as profits fall."[71]

This is another way of saying that contractarians are complacent liberals, not vigilant republicans. With their nexus metaphor, contract unit of analysis, and shareholder-centered approach to corporate governance, they are hardly inclined to do legal traditionalists' work for them. Because their central concern is corporate efficiency, not institutional design, they are not inclined to identify norms or institutional arrangements unique to democratic societies that the internal governance of corporations may somehow inadvertently enervate or challenge—whatever these norms or institutional arrangements might be. But this also means that when the corporate judiciary actually does impose social norms of behavior on corporate officers as mandatory rules, norms that exceed their contractual obligations, contractarians cannot explain why this is happening. Yet they can see that courts do this at times, and they can neutrally describe this judicial behavior—much like anthropologists can describe an island people's curious superstitions and rituals without fully appreciating their point.

3. "Norms" of Liberal Complacency: Contracts and Optimal Outcomes

There are only two "norms" or standards of analysis that contractarians believe the corporate judiciary should bring to corporate governance disputes: the norm of Lockean contracts and the norm of Pareto optimal outcomes. Thus, when contractarians observe any governance dispute, they ask only two questions: Did the parties involved enter the disputed transaction or relationship voluntarily? Which way of resolving the dispute would optimize the allocation of resources for the parties involved—that is, which resolution would make each party better off in its own estimation while making no party worse off?[72] We will see that these two norms are favored not only by contractarians but also across the corporate judiciary and bar as an institution. Because of this, we can treat Lockean contracts and Pareto optimal outcomes as twin pillars of today's orthodoxy of liberal complacency.

In eliminating corporate power and the possibility of arbitrariness from their concerns, and in concentrating their attention on whether contracts are voluntary and outcomes are Pareto optimal, contractarians butt up against an empirical state of affairs in the world that neoclassical economists more easily side-step or ignore entirely.[73] Contractarians have to offer *some* account for the *behavior* of Delaware courts.[74] Why do Delaware courts refuse to operate only with the two norms of today's orthodoxy? Why, for example, do they refuse to reduce a corporation's value in a merger or takeover either to its liquidation value or to the price of its stock? Indeed, contractarians are at such a loss to account for this and other norm-based judicial behavior in governance disputes that at times they literally throw up their hands in disbelief, like scientifically trained anthropologists among inscrutable island folk. "It is depressing to see 'earth is flat' reasoning from our premier corporate court."[75]

Any empirically sound theory of corporations and law, however, should enable legal scholars at the very least to account for the judicial behavior before them, and certainly for that of "our premier corporate court." Here, then, is a clear indication that contractarians' economic concepts are indeed simplifying. They fail a basic empirical test. Contractarians can only "explain" the behavior of Delaware courts by proposing that Delaware's judges (a) are somehow "captured" by internal factions or external interests that have it in for shareholders, or else (b) operate independently in a wonderland of superstition, resentment, or rancor. That Delaware judges are upholding a legal tradition vital to a democratic society is not a possibility that contractarian concepts can accommodate. At the moment contractarians entertain this possibility, they cease to be contractarians; they cease to be complacent liberals; they move outside their two norms or standards of analysis and thereby lose their bearings.[76]

Contractarians have no alternative therefore other than to assume or assert that the corporate judiciary is utterly misguided when it worries about corporate power in American society. Yet Delaware courts nonetheless act as if corporate power exists and potentially threatens society. These courts prohibit or rescind certain corporate transactions and changes in corporate governance on the grounds that they cause public harm. They do not do so solely on the grounds that these transactions and changes: violate privately negotiated contracts, are unprofitable, are not Pareto optimal for shareholders, or harm identifiable third parties in ways that cannot be priced and fully recompensed. Any reference to the possible public consequences of private power speaks to institutional design. And any such reference revolves around some qualitative, extra-economic standard for identifying the place and purpose of corporations in American civil society that cannot be reduced to contractarians' two norms.

Contractarians' liberal complacency also reveals why they accord such importance to a market for corporate control and, when doing so, why they pay particular attention to management's role as shareholders' agent. When management erects defenses against takeovers and buyouts, it fails to maximize shareholder wealth. This is an immediate externality of inefficient corporate governance, but one that can be priced and recompensed.[77] Contractarians call attention to these particular breaches of contract only in order to point out that it was once believed that such putative abuses of corporate power eluded the impersonal discipline of self-regulating markets. It was once believed that if abuses such as these were to be corrected, the corporate judiciary had to intervene on shareholders' behalf. Contractarians' point in recalling this is that management nonetheless soon found itself being disciplined rather impersonally by market pressures entirely independently of courts. They also note that this turn of events upended the staid legal literature. Law journals fairly teemed with accounts of "how markets best courts in enforcing contracts [even] between parties have enduring relations," and with charges that the fiduciary law tradition is increasingly irrelevant, an anachronism.[78]

Looking back at the 1980s, contractarians today conclude that the only thing that had prevented management from being disciplined earlier was that dispersed shareholders did not have an opportunity to act on their self-interests with dispatch. Thus, contractarians appreciate that the presence of a robust market for corporate control, one unbridled by "artificial" social norms and legal traditions, supports everything else they are trying to convey about the economic structure of corporations and law:

> Takeovers are a device for limiting the costs of contracting—in particular, for holding down the costs of monitoring and replacing managers. In other words, tender offers control the agency costs of management. *Their existence makes contractarianism on other subjects practical.*[79]

Once hostile bidders offer even a few shareholders opportunities to replace risk-averse management teams with more risk-accepting ones, all shareholders instantly become shark watchers—and all management teams instantly become anxious prey. All managers become attuned to shareholders' interests. Thus, when Kohlberg Kravis Roberts and Company put Don Kelly in charge after buying out Beatrice, he knew his marching orders: "My job has been to constantly evaluate what is good for shareholders."[80]

4

Contractarians and Balancers

Many legal scholars questioned the "realism" of contractarian approaches to corporations and law in the 1980s and many continue to do so today. But, then as now, most appreciate the great merit of contractarians' central point about corporate law's mandatory rules. The new market for corporate control did demonstrate that it is no longer necessary for courts to enforce many statutes and norms once thought to be core doctrines. John Coffee Jr.'s major objection to contractarianism, therefore, is not that it yields methodical criticisms of existing corporate law. Rather, his objection is that contractarians fail to account adequately for the vulnerability of *stakeholders'* positions in corporations. So rather than defending existing law directly, his point is more subtle: Some mandatory rules may remain valuable because the corporate judiciary may potentially use them to hold management and controlling shareholders to their "implicit bargains" with stakeholders, to "enduring relations" that are not technically legal contracts.[1] As Lyman Johnson puts it: "Easterbrook and Fischel conceive of the corporation as a nexus of *bilateral* contracts. Investors stand only in a contractual relationship with the 'firm' (read 'managers' . . .), not with employees, suppliers, customers, or creditors."[2]

What contractarians fail most to appreciate, by this account, is that a corporate nexus freed from all mandatory rules may devolve "naturally" into patterns of governance in which stakeholders are abused, positional conflicts degenerate into trench warfare, and economic efficiency declines. We cannot simply assume that every corporate nexus will develop an equilibrium state of efficient contracting, as if guided by a hidden hand.[3] And we certainly cannot assume that every corporate nexus will adequately protect most stakeholders most of the time.

I. Fiduciary Law and Stakeholders

Until the early 1980s, the American corporate judiciary typically approached the corporation in precisely the way that Johnson and Coffee think is too narrow. From the 1920s through the 1970s, American state courts rarely protected stakeholders' positional interests by (a) intervening into governance disputes on behalf of *shareholders* with standing and then (b) second-guessing business decisions that adversely affected *stakeholders*.[4] Moreover, stakeholders themselves lack "standing" with the corporate judiciary. They cannot bring corporate governance disputes to court in their own positional interests. Thus, when courts intervene into governance disputes on stakeholders' behalf, they always do so indirectly.

We discuss these judicial actions later (Chapter 8). For now, we assert two points without elaborating them. First, courts protect stakeholders at times by holding management more explicitly to its fiduciary duty of loyalty to the corporate entity. Then they leave the details of stakeholder protection to management's business judgment. Second, by holding management to this duty, courts emphasize management's role as the corporate entity's trustee and de-emphasize its role as shareholders' agent. This counterbalances shareholders' influence over management at least somewhat because in corporate law doctrine fiduciary duties trump other legal obligations.[5] With this shift in emphasis, however, the corporate judiciary still defers to management's business judgment; it does not try to second-guess it on stakeholders' behalf. It simply accepts at face value that as management endeavors to identify and advance the entity's collective interests, consistent with its duty of loyalty, it will in one way or another likely take stakeholders' positional interests into account.

Before a market for corporate control emerged in late 1983, state courts often permitted corporate officers of target corporations to defend themselves against hostile tender offers on the fiduciary law ground of exhibiting loyalty to the corporate entity. As long as target boards did not act "solely or primarily" to entrench themselves or management teams and instead credibly claimed they were protecting stakeholders more generally, state courts let defenses against hostile bids stand—at shareholders' expense.[6]

Thus, in the 1970s courts did not concern themselves directly with the immediate externalities stakeholders might suffer at the hands of a management team not yet exposed to a market for corporate control. Back then, courts also had no reason to identify the possible institutional externalities of *changes* in corporate governance. Top management was not yet being challenged by hostile bids, and corporate governance structures were hardly in flux. The corporate judiciary took only two steps in the 1970s in bearing its historical responsibility of seeing to it that corporate power remains broadly consistent with institutional design. First, courts enforced the public law statutes in their states' General Corporation laws. Second, and more important, courts imposed on corporate officers their traditional fiduciary duty of loyalty to the corporate entity.[7] Otherwise, the corporate judiciary permitted every management team to interpret more or less unilaterally what its corporation's purpose was in American society (short of violating basic criminal law and civil law). They did not second-guess these interpretations, whether by compelling management to maximize dividends or by compelling management to protect stake-holders. In the absence of a market for corporate control, many management teams retained dividends to finance growth at shareholders' expense, and to the benefit of many stakeholders.[8]

II. Contractarian Opposition to Stakeholder "Rights"

In this light, contractarians' counterargument to Coffee, to his proposal that courts protect "implicit bargains" that stakeholders believe they made with management, is simple and elegant. They point out that Coffee is making their case for them. Management may do whatever it likes with shareholder approval, but state legislatures must not grant stakeholders standing to bring their own corporate governance disputes to state courts. Nor should courts otherwise encourage management to take stakeholders' positional interests into account when making major corporate decisions. Equalizing stakeholders' legal status with that of shareholders is "artificial," strictly political, not economically sound. This artificial balancing can only convert essentially everyday, fleeting conflicts of interest into more entrenched positional conflicts, and then unnecessary governance disputes.

1. Legal "Standing"

Corporate law grants standing to very few corporate constituents to bring suit in state court over corporate control transactions and governance disputes, and then only under certain conditions.[9] We touch on these conditions in Chapter 5 in the context of discussing major corporate law cases. For the moment, we illustrate standing with five examples:

1. A hostile bidder can join with any shareholder to petition a state court to remove a target corporation's barriers to tender offers, including its merger plans with another firm or its anti-takeover defenses (such as poison pills).
2. Shareholder minorities may bring a "derivative suit" in the name of the corporation itself to redress a breach of fiduciary duty by an officer or controlling shareholder—after first appealing to the corporation's board to handle the matter internally or to bring suit itself.
3. Shareholder minorities of a subsidiary may bring suit in a parent-subsidiary transaction that either discounts their shares or that involves a breach of fiduciary duty by parent management.
4. Former shareholders of a cash-out merger, whether a leveraged buyout or a management buyout, may also bring suit for the same two reasons.
5. Bondholders and other creditors may bring claims of breach of fiduciary duty against a board of directors as a corporation becomes insolvent and the board takes actions that benefit shareholders at bondholders' expense.

With the exception of the last example, stakeholders are noticeably absent from these examples, including top managers and middle managers.[10] Standing in corporate governance disputes is indeed a largely shareholder-centered legal status (for reasons we discuss later). And shareholders have standing primarily to bring "derivative claims" or "representative suits" against directors (and then management), not individual suits. They bring suit *on behalf of the corporate entity*, not on their own behalf as investors.[11] In a derivative claim, shareholders accuse directors and management of breaching their fiduciary duties and thereby harming the corporate entity, not themselves alone. Courts, in turn, treat successful derivative suits as proxies for proper board behavior, not as an opportunity necessarily to increase any return to dissatisfied shareholders.[12] As Wolfe and Pittenger put it, a derivative suit comprises two separate claims for relief in a single legal action: a claim by a stockholder to compel a corporation to protect itself against a fiduciary breach, and a claim by that stockholder on the corporation's behalf to invalidate a contested transaction, one tainted by breach.[13]

Thus, successful derivative actions result in the entity receiving benefits, not shareholders more exclusively, and certainly not the shareholders that initiated legal action.[14] As Easterbrook and Fischel put it, the "dominating characteristic" of derivative litigation is the lack of any link between stake and reward.[15] This is reflected in how these actions are resolved and in the difficulty and expense of bringing them. Courts resolve derivative suits by issuing an order restraining the disputed action and then hearing the case, if possible; or rescinding the disputed transaction later, if possible; or ordering that the corporate entity (including shareholders) be recompensed for losses. Corporate officers may settle derivative suits out of court, but only in quite restricted ways. They can reform their corporation's governance structure, or they can extend to plaintiff shareholders "some other kind of intangible relief" (such as publishing new guidelines that specify how officers may better comply with their fiduciary duties in the future). They may not settle derivative suits, however, by offering direct or indirect material benefits to shareholder-plaintiffs. Moreover, any and all settlements must be approved by Chancery (if filed in Delaware).[16]

In addition, it is neither easy nor inexpensive for shareholders to bring suit. Shareholder-plaintiffs must first make "a demand" to the board to bring the suit itself. If a board decides to dismiss their action, it is both difficult and expensive for shareholder-plaintiffs to go further. State law often requires that they post security for expenses, and they risk liability for lawyers' fees if their action fails.[17]

Given that standing cannot be used directly to protect stakeholders in court, what doctrinal options are available either to stakeholders themselves or to judges who wish to protect their interests? If judges simply broaden management's fiduciary duty of loyalty, they insulate its business judgment from derivative suits that would alter corporate governance in stakeholders' favor. They essentially permit management to do anything it wishes in the name of protecting stakeholders. This is consistent with state courts' longstanding deference to management under what legal scholars call a "presumption of business judgment rule protection." But it is also consistent with management's positional interest in entrenching itself at shareholder expense. Plus, this judicial strategy does not necessarily protect stakeholders; whether it does or not is left to management's discretion.

Is any other doctrinal option available that might protect stakeholders, other than supporting management more fulsomely? Legal scholars generally agree that there is only one other option, and it does protect stakeholders more directly, namely "balancing." To contractarian eyes, however, this option is precisely the artificial turn that will reduce corporate efficiency. It will entrench positional conflicts and foster unnecessary governance disputes, contractarians believe, even if courts remain reluctant to grant legal standing to stakeholders other than creditors.

2. Governance "Representation": Stakeholder Balancing

A full year before the new market for corporate control emerged, some legal scholars reacted to contractarians' criticisms of corporate law tradition in 1982 by proposing a doctrinal alternative to both. They proposed that the corporate judiciary formally recognize stakeholder "rights" to "representation" in corporate decision making, not grant stakeholders legal standing in court.[18] By the mid-1980s, Delaware courts and other state courts began moving tentatively in this direction. And then, rather suddenly, over half of all state legislatures took this step outright. Twenty-nine state legislatures passed "corporate constituency statutes" within months of each other, most explicitly permitting management—thereby encouraging it—to take stakeholder interests into account before responding to hostile bids.[19] Four of these state legislatures went even further, passing statutes that *require* management to do this (see Chapter 8).[20]

Both state-level institutions, therefore, moved toward protecting stakeholders in corporate governance structures largely by default of there being any other way for judges and legislators to try to stem the harms they believed were being done to employees, communities, and others by a market for corporate control. Here is a clear instance where even the most overstated "public choice" understanding of judicial and legislative action looks sound empirically.[21] At the very zenith of hostile activity, and of the voting public's negative reaction to it, state legislatures instructed the corporate officers of companies they incorporated to take into account stakeholder interests when making major corporate decisions. Stakeholders' broader range of positional interests would thereby bring "balance" to corporate decision making. It would countervail shareholders' narrow positional interest in maximizing share price and corporate officers' narrow positional interest in entrenchment.

Today, this third doctrinal option, stakeholder balancing, is precisely what most self-described "legal traditionalists" advocate, not judicial imposing.[22] Balancing is their consensus choice because traditionalists see it as the most practicable doctrinal alternative to: shareholder contracting, management entrenchment, and what we can call judicial "fundamentalism" (enforcing mandatory rules in traditional ways). Contracting would replace mandatory rules with suppletory and enabling rules that serve the interests of shareholders (and management). Entrenchment would broaden management's business judgment rule protection at shareholder expense and would not necessarily benefit stakeholders. Fundamentalism would require a direct defense of the fiduciary law tradition, something imposers to date have been unable to provide. Balancing, by contrast, requires only greater management attentiveness to how stakeholders are likely to be affected by major corporate transactions and, therefore, negotiating suppletory and enabling rules with shareholders accordingly.

What in particular led to balancing becoming *the* doctrinal alternative of choice? In order to account for this, we need to say more about "legal traditionalism" more generally.

III. Traditionalism: Imposers and Balancers

Through the 1970s, many legal scholars encouraged state courts to continue enforcing corporate law's traditional core of mandatory rules—fiduciary duties and public law norms. They opposed early calls by contractarians that courts elevate management's role as shareholders' agent over its fiduciary duties as trustee of the corporate entity. They also opposed contractarians' view that courts simply enforce contracts that management enters explicitly with particular stakeholders, in the normal course of exercising its business judgment. However, the views that these opponents of contracting otherwise had of corporations, other intermediary associations, and the larger social order were hardly similar or, for that matter, "traditional." Rather, the traditionalist camp was, and remains, an aggregation of views, not an identifiable movement or school. Then and now it spans a far broader mix of cultural theories and social theories than the contractarian camp ever has. One result of these internal divisions was that until the option of balancing came into prominence, beginning in 1982, these legal scholars had difficulty offering courts a single, consistently articulated, doctrinal alternative to shareholder contracting.

In the 1970s, the traditionalist camp spanned proponents of three distinct theoretical approaches to corporations and law, and all three remain on the scene today. First, some traditionalists were just that: They wanted courts to maintain the status quo, to enforce all public law statutes and fiduciary duties formally at the core of corporate law doctrine.[23] Second, other traditionalists had loftier goals, those once articulated by the corporate social responsibility movement of the 1960s.[24] These liberal legal scholars (rarely judges) wanted courts to take an even stricter "republican" turn, to impose additional *substantive normative* limitations on corporate behavior.[25] While they rivaled contractarians in their zeal, these fundamentalists never wielded a fraction of contractarians' influence in the corporate judiciary and bar. Finally, still other traditionalists (again, rarely judges) were, ironically, radical legal scholars, proponents of the Critical Legal Studies movement. Like the fundamentalists above, they viewed corporations and most other intermediary associations as for-profit bureaucracies and assumed accordingly that corporate power is rarely benign. They pointed with some specificity to harms corporations cause discrete individuals or groups, but, like liberal proponents of corporate social responsibility, they were uncomfortably vague when referring to the broader consequences of corporate power.[26] One result of their vagueness here is that their prescriptions for change tended either to be unclear or impracticable. Their prescriptions typically hinged not only on altering corporate law and judicial practice radically but also on similarly altering basic American institutional arrangements. Such a position appealed to few judges, legislators, or, for that matter, readily identifiable social movements.

The first set of traditionalists, therefore, had the greatest influence by far within the corporate judiciary and bar in the 1970s. But in the 1980s its influence paled in comparison to that of contractarians. During the early 1980s, as their influence waned rapidly and contractarians' influence rose sharply, these traditionalists came to a great divide. They began offering courts two alternatives to contracting, and this remains the case today.

Melvin Eisenberg,[27] Victor Brudney, Ernest Weinrib, Tamar Frankel, Robert Clark, Deborah DeMott, and Alan Palmiter lead the original group of influential traditionalists, which we call judicial imposers. Imposers encourage courts to continue enforcing at least some remaining public law norms and fiduciary duties. We have seen already, however, that the problems they face are formidable. In the first place, contractarians clearly have exposed significant weaknesses in such traditional judicial behavior. More important, imposers have great difficulty defending at a conceptual level either courts' fiduciary law tradition or state legislatures' public law norms. They are trapped, ironically, in the same dilemma American republicans faced back in the 1830s and 1840s.

As the United States was evolving from an agrarian society to a more commercial society, the republican view of corporations and law still revolved around *substantive normative* beliefs and practices of earlier days, those of the revolutionary generation. Substantive norms emerge from, and remain dedicated to maintaining, a particular way of life, a particular type of society in substance. In this case, the substantive norms of the revolutionary generation were those of yeoman farmers and independent merchants. As such, any law of corporations informed by these norms increasingly obstructed, rather than facilitated, innovative business transactions in a rising commercial society. Something obviously had to give. By the 1830s and 1840s, republican corporate law sounded not only traditional even to tin ears on the bench but anachronistic.

Today, judicial imposers portray corporate law's existing core of mandatory rules as a set of normative duties that corporate officers owe in substance to corporate entities. These duties differ from those of the 1830s and 1840s, to be sure, but they are still substantive norms, developed by the corporate judiciary during the 1950s and 1960s (or earlier). Being substantive norms, by the early 1980s they seemed to be obstructing, not facilitating, innovative business transactions in an increasingly dynamic postindustrial economy. They sounded anachronistic, not simply traditional, and contractarians were indeed zealous in calling this to everyone's attention.

The other influential group of traditionalists supports stakeholder balancing, as opposed to trying to defend mandatory rules more directly. This group is led by William Klein, John Coffee Jr., Jeffrey Gordon, Lyman Johnson, David Millon, Marleen O'Connor, William Bratton Jr., Fiona Patfield, and Eric Orts.[28] These legal scholars promote stakeholder balancing because it is more flexible in its practical application to corporate governance disputes than imposing substantive norms on management as mandatory rules. In other words, balancing offers traditionalists a way out of imposers' republican dilemma without forcing them entirely into the contractarian camp.

For some judges, however, balancing seems a bit radical: It would not only displace shareholder contracting *but potentially displace the fiduciary law tradition* (in favor of public law norms of stakeholder representation that state legislatures place in their General Corporation laws). Balancers want judges to privilege the suppletory and enabling rules that management, controlling shareholders, and *selected* stakeholders negotiate among themselves within each corporation.[29] Moreover, some balancers want to go further. A central debate among them is whether management should take into account only the interests of discrete corporate constituents, or also the interests of local communities and possibly even some broader sense of "the public interest."[30] If these considerations are ever added to balancing, this will move this doctrinal option closer to the idea of corporate social responsibility that liberal legal scholars promoted in the 1960s.[31]

Nevertheless, balancers appreciate that greater stakeholder representation in corporate decision making may harm shareholders and may entrench management. It may encourage corporate officers to forego maximizing share price and instead retain earnings to accommodate other corporate constituents, including middle managers. Balancers also appreciate that greater stakeholder representation in corporate decision making may carry immediate externalities—for constituents whose interests management either refuses to take into account or fails to protect adequately. But they are not concerned that the suppletory and enabling rules that result from balancing may also carry institutional externalities for the larger social order. Rather, when it comes to institutional design, balancers are ultimately complacent liberals, not vigilant republicans.

Balancers assume that when management takes stakeholder interests sufficiently into account, the internal governance of corporations will not otherwise harm the larger society, even if it reduces dividends or share price somewhat.[32] Thus, like contractarians' liberal complacency regarding the consequences of bilateral contracting over rules of governance, balancers assume as an article of faith that greater stakeholder participation in corporate decision making is inherently benign. Because this is a matter of faith, neither contractarians nor balancers support this grand, political economic assumption with empirical evidence or any explicitly articulated theory. Balancers do not ask where multilateral competition for positional power might lead corporate governance structures in substance *or in form*, just as contractarians do not ask where bilateral contracting between management and shareholders might lead. We have more to say about the form of corporate governance structures in later chapters.

Why do some judges take stakeholder balancing seriously, despite its implicit challenge to the courts' fiduciary law tradition? As we just saw, these judges couple stakeholder balancing with liberal complacency, thereby eliminating the issue of institutional externalities from their concerns. With this, judges take this doctrinal option seriously for two related reasons. First, they believe that when corporate law encourages management to consider stakeholder interests, this countervails at least somewhat (a) management's role as shareholders' agent and (b) management's own one-sided behavior. Second, they believe that the contracts and rules of governance that result from balancing are likely to reduce many of the immediate harms of changes in corporate control that troubled judges and legislators in the

1980s. All corporate constituents will be in a better position to protect themselves during takeovers and mergers.

IV. Balancing and Today's Orthodoxy

1. The Promise and Limits of Balancing

Enforcing whatever contracts and rules of governance that result from group competition for power and influence within each corporation will certainly add flexibility to American corporate law. But such flexibility can create three problems for the corporate judiciary that today's two other doctrinal options, judicial imposing and shareholder contracting, do not. First, it is likely that balancing will increase, not decrease, the inconsistency of judicial rulings across courts and across cases.[33] As judicial inconsistency increases, this will raise questions about the coherence and legitimacy of corporate law doctrine. After all, consider what is likely to happen when some state courts lead the way in extending to stakeholders a legal status that begins to rival that of management's role as shareholders' agent. It is likely that (a) other judges and the corporate bar will raise questions about the point of corporate law doctrine, and, more important, (b) the number of governance disputes brought to state courts will increase irrespective of which constituents *today* have standing. The two other problems elaborate why.

Second, stakeholder balancing is likely to complicate corporate decision making, and especially during economic downturns. As management recognizes the interests of some constituents but not those of others, or recognizes some interests in greater part than others, positional conflicts can only increase. In addition, and most notably, when state legislatures (or judges) recognize stakeholder "rights" of representation *at law*, this can only metamorphose at some point into stakeholder standing to initiate legal actions of some kind on their own behalf.[34] After all, how else are individual judges likely to respond when stakeholders claim management is disregarding or abridging what state legislatures (and courts) themselves have held is their due representation in corporate decision making?

Put succinctly, legislative and judicial recognition of stakeholder rights of representation in corporate decision making can only challenge the legal status of shareholders, and then management's presumption of business judgment rule protection. It can only subject the internal governance of corporations, and then judicial rulings in governance disputes, to pluralism, to multiplayer bargaining.[35] With this, an economic institution and a legal institution will be subjected to the same group competition for influence and power that drives legislatures.[36] The problem is that we cannot assume as a matter of faith that group competition within corporate decision making will be any more self-disciplining than that within legislative decision making. We cannot assume that stakeholder balancing in particular will not yield *structures* of governance that either purposefully challenge or inadvertently enervate the institutional design of the larger social order. If we cannot assume this, then a place remains in corporate law doctrine for a core of mandatory rules, and here we already break from today's orthodoxy of liberal complacency. We hold onto *some* connection between corporate law and judicial practice today and the republican vigilance of the Founders and Chancellors.

2. Balancers' Subordination to Contractarians

There is considerable irony, therefore, in treating stakeholder representation even generally as a "traditional" doctrinal alternative to the nexus of contracts approach to corporations and law. Yet the fact that stakeholder balancing is considerably more influential in the corporate judiciary and bar today than judicial imposing is itself revealing. It reveals how successfully contractarians have challenged the status quo, corporate law tradition. As Chancellor Allen put it in 1993:

> The work of [contractarian] scholars has come, I believe, to dominate the academic study of corporate law, even if some of the field's most respects minds remain among the unconverted [Victor Brudney and Melvin Eisenberg are cited]. This work has left academic corporate law far more coherent than it had been and constitutes a substantial intellectual accomplishment.[37]

Chancellor Allen sees that it is contractarians, not imposers, and certainly not balancers, who define the very terms of debate over corporations and law.[38] Particular state courts may at times enforce mandatory rules and thereby still resist shareholder contracting in a market for corporate control. But they are expected to justify such resistance. This expectation is common across the corporate judiciary and bar because the two norms contractarians want judges to employ *exclusively* when analyzing and resolving governance disputes are indeed today's orthodoxy within this institution: Are the contracts in dispute voluntary or "Lockean"? Are the disputed transactions Pareto optimal *for shareholders?* That is, do they increase the private wealth of all shareholders?

Balancing confirms these two norms as today's orthodoxy. It simply amends the second by asking if disputed transactions are Pareto optimal for corporate constituents other than shareholders. Balancers challenge contractarians, that is, only by raising doubts about whether maximizing shareholder wealth is always fair or equitable.[39] Aside from this essentially philosophical issue, which little concerns pragmatic-minded contractarians, balancers otherwise exhibit remarkable fidelity to liberal complacency.[40] Balancers do not challenge today's orthodoxy because they do not, and can not, defend mandatory rules directly, independently of the contracts and rules resulting from group competition within corporate governance structures. They do not and can not identify any public law interest that mandatory rules unambiguously serve. The only questions balancers ask are how far legislatures or courts are prepared to extend stakeholder representation, and how sufficiently each management team bears this statutory or legal responsibility in each corporation.[41]

V. Today's Burden of Proof

Contractarians consolidated today's orthodoxy within the corporate judiciary and bar by challenging recalcitrant judges with the following proposition:[42] If your rulings in major governance disputes are to become more consistent, if the corporate judiciary is to retain legitimacy as an institution, then you have no alternative. You must elevate the principal's (shareholders') legal status over that of its agent (management) *and, certainly, that of other corporate constituents (stakeholders).* This proposition effectively shifts the burden of proof to all legal traditionalists.[43]

Everyone today expects imposers to explain why judges need to enforce existing mandatory rules. Or, alternatively, they expect balancers to explain why legislatures or courts need to place stakeholder representation alongside the legal claims of the principal and its agent. By contrast, few hold contractarians to the same burden of proof. Few call on them to explain why judges need to facilitate, or at least not obstruct, shareholder contracting in a market for corporate control.[44] For instance, Margaret Blair and Lynn Stout hold, on the one hand, that "communitarians" and "progressives" dominate corporate law scholarship today, after two decades of dominance by contractarians. Yet they acknowledge that these legal scholars now operate "within a shareholder primacy model" that short shrifts stakeholders and local communities.[45] Our point is that these critics of contractarianism operate within today's orthodoxy because they fail to defend the courts' fiduciary law tradition directly. Judges or legal scholars who fail here are, ultimately, complacent liberals. By default, they are oriented implicitly by the same two norms that contractarians champion explicitly.

The greater burdens that all traditionalists bear today can be traced in large part to economic events. The hostile activity of the 1980s effectively closed off any likelihood that judges could ever again defer as fully to management's business judgment as they had for half a century, through the 1970s. Thus, the Contractarian Challenge to corporate law tradition not only poses problems in theory for all legal scholars and judges who seek doctrinal options. It has also been institutionalized to some extent in the business environment.

5

Major Delaware Decisions of the 1980s and 1990s

We focus on Delaware courts in this chapter for a straightforward reason: Over 40 percent of the corporations listed on the New York Stock Exchange are incorporated in Delaware, over 60 percent of the Fortune 500, and over 50 percent of the Dow Jones Industrial Average.[1] In addition, most corporations that reincorporate choose in overwhelming numbers to move into Delaware. For the purposes of this chapter we simply assert that Delaware's Chancery Court and Supreme Court wield greater influence in the American corporate judiciary and bar than any other state's courts. They have done so since the 1920s, and no one suggests that any other state's courts, or any set of state courts, is likely to challenge Delaware's dominant position. This begs the question for now of how and why Delaware achieved its dominance, but we will get to this in time (see Chapter 10) as we explain why these courts act at times in norm-based ways rather than market-mimicking ways.

I. Delaware Courts and the 1980s

1. Traditional Standards of Review

Before the market for corporate control emerged in late 1983, Delaware's Chancery Court and Supreme Court classified actions taken by corporate officers in only two ways, as either disinterested or interested. Disinterested actions spanned all exercises of management discretion protected from judicial review by the business judgment rule. In order to retain this judicial "presumption" in their favor, corporate officers simply had to act in ways that did not cause shareholders to allege in derivative suits that they had breached their fiduciary duties of care and loyalty. In the course of normal business activities, this is hardly an issue. But it can be an issue in unusual transactions, in major corporate decisions involving changes of control or changes in governance structure.

In unusual situations, Chancery considered three factors in reviewing business decisions taken or approved by corporate boards of directors. Were the decisions made (a) by independent directors (that is, those having no personal material stake in the transaction), (b) acting in good faith, (c) with due care?[2] An often-cited description of this traditional standard of analysis dates from a 1939 decision by Delaware's Supreme Court (in *Guth v. Loft Inc.*):[3]

> Corporate officers and directors are not permitted to use their position of trust and confidence to further their private interests. . . . [This rule] demands of a corporate officer or director, peremptorily and inexorably, the most scrupulous observance of his duty, not only affirmatively to protect the interests of the corporation committed to his charge, but also to refrain from doing anything that would work injury to the corporation, or to deprive it of profit or advantage which his skill and ability might properly bring to it, or to enable it to make in the reasonable and lawful exercise of its powers.

Actions taken by corporate officers that courts classified as interested were those that failed to meet one or more of the three tests above. With any credible allegation of breach (by a shareholder with standing), Chancery no longer presumed the business judgment rule protected corporate officers from judicial review (when their companies were incorporated in Delaware). Instead, Chancery applied an "intrinsic fairness" or "entire fairness" standard of analysis to the disputed transaction. In applying this standard, Chancery examined the process leading to the transaction and then its outcome or terms. Thus, intrinsic fairness contained two component parts: fair dealing (process) and fair price (outcome).[4] This two-part review includes qualitative considerations of how corporations are governed and how corporate officers conduct themselves within governance structures, not economic calculations of optimality alone.

Consistent with Delaware courts' intrinsic fairness standard, Delaware's General Assembly allowed one exception or "safe harbor" even for formally interested business transactions. It instructed Chancery (and then Delaware's Supreme Court, when hearing appeals) to support these transactions (a) when they were approved by an informed majority of directors or shareholders, or else (b) when Chancery was satisfied they were "intrinsically fair" to the corporation.

This either/or way of categorizing management actions, as disinterested or interested, worked well until the hostile takeovers, leveraged buyouts, and management buyouts of the 1980s brought a tidal wave of new cases before Chancery and then Delaware's Supreme Court on appeal. Hostile tender offers from corporate raiders raised numerous questions in themselves about what qualifies as either disinterested or interested behavior by boards and top management teams: When management defends against hostile activity, is it acting disinterestedly in the collective interests of the corporate entity or one-sidedly to entrench itself? Is the board of directors acting disinterestedly when (a) supporting management defenses, (b) supporting the hostile bidder (who, after all, is offering stockholders a greater return on their investments), or (c) considering how stakeholders, including local communities, might be affected? Is it acting disinterestedly when it does nothing, ignores the hostile offer?

In management buyouts, everything is even more confusing. A subset of senior executives aspires to buy the company they are managing with the goal of either taking it private (and thereby abandoning the legal form of a publicly traded corporation) or else gaining voting control over its publicly traded stock. With this, a top management team and a board of directors face severe conflicts of interest. Management has inside information, and it can also control the timing of the transaction to take best advantage of the corporate entity's valuation in capital markets. The board is placed in a particularly awkward position, one in which it is not clear how it might act appropriately even if it wishes to.[5] After all, the manager buyout group may seek leveraged financing based on how capital markets assess the corporation's breakup value—and yet they are still managing a publicly traded corporation, an entity they do not own. So to whom does a board owe its fiduciary duties: the existing corporate entity, the shareholders who currently own it, or the aspirant ownership team? Some legal traditionalists held that nothing either a management team or a board can do in these situations is truly disinterested, and so proposed that Delaware courts prohibit MBOs outright.[6]

2. A New Intermediate Standard

Our point now is simply to illustrate how complicated matters became for the corporate judiciary in the 1980s. By mid-decade shareholders with standing, as well as hostile bidders teaming up with dissatisfied shareholders, were charging corporate officers with breaches of fiduciary duty in numerous situations that eluded Chancery's earlier standards of intrinsic fairness and business judgment protection.[7] So many different transactions were raising so many new questions about what qualifies as interested or disinterested conduct by corporate officers that Delaware courts faced a stark choice: They could either inquire into the intrinsic fairness of all such transactions, thereby severely restricting management's discretion and multiplying their own case load. Or they could extend the presumption of business judgment rule protection to these new transactions, thereby shielding management from judicial review and leaving it to investors and capital markets to discipline corporate decision making.

The first choice would slow down and discourage so much innovative business activity that it would call into question the corporate judiciary's legitimacy as an institution. The second choice, however, would essentially subordinate fiduciary law to contract law, mandatory rules to negotiable rules. It would also subordinate the corporate judiciary as an institution to the market for corporate control as an institution. Extending a presumption of business judgment rule protection to management's responses to hostile activity as long as management gained shareholder approval would leave courts with the narrow task of simply enforcing whatever outcomes resulted—as contractarians were advising. At most, dissatisfied shareholder minorities might call on courts to remove management defenses against hostile bids, and thereby to intervene into governance disputes in strictly market-mimicking ways. Contractarians were urging this too. Stakeholder balancers, in turn, wanted Delaware courts to see to it that corporate officers took stakeholder interests adequately into account during these transactions.

What Delaware courts ultimately did—and quite pragmatically at first, on a case-by-case basis—was to seek principles compatible with their earlier standards of analysis and their state's General Corporation law that might allow them to deal with these new transactions in consistent ways *on more qualitative grounds.*[8] In its quest for a qualitative standard of analysis covering these new situations, Delaware judges at times supported shareholder contracting, at other times supported management business judgment, and at still other times supported greater stakeholder representation in corporate decision making. After considerable flux, after what *most* legal observers saw as inconsistent, sometimes "schizophrenic," decisions coming out of Delaware, these courts finally began ruling in the early 1990s in ways that at least some observers today believe are relatively consistent (see Chapter 13). They accomplished this by developing an intermediate, qualitative standard of review of contested business transactions called "enhanced scrutiny."[9] This standard, which we discuss momentarily, is at once more abstract and more generally applicable than Delaware courts' earlier, still active, ultimate standard of review, intrinsic fairness.

3. Today's Debate and Where It Leads

What legal scholars are debating today is the new standard's scope of application, its relationship to traditional fiduciary law and mandatory rules, and, most grandly, its implications for defining corporate purpose in today's global economy. Less rigorous and time-consuming than an intrinsic fairness review,[10] enhanced scrutiny nonetheless limits the scope of management's protection under the business judgment rule. It also places *normative* limits on shareholders' self-interested behavior in a market for corporate control. Legal scholars are debating, of course, why Delaware courts are doing this. Contractarians, imposers, and balancers agree that enhanced scrutiny review normatively mediates the behavior of corporate officers and shareholders in order to maintain the "integrity" of the "corporate entity," as Delaware judges understand this, including the integrity of the entity's internal structure of governance. But these legal scholars disagree about why this matters, and even those who believe it does have difficulty explaining what this talk of integrity actually entails in practice. They are uncertain why Delaware courts persist in approaching corporate governance disputes with any qualitative—that is, norm-based—standard of analysis.[11]

We propose in coming chapters that Delaware courts impose extracontractual norms of behavior on corporate officers and shareholders because they implicitly retain a republican view that there is *some* relationship between corporate governance and institutional design. They do not impose such norms with an eye to maximizing corporations' economic performance, or with an eye exclusively to the immediate benefits or costs for management, shareholders, or stakeholders. We will demonstrate that enhanced scrutiny review redefines the very nature of corporate officers' and controlling shareholders' fiduciary duties in governing corporations. In particular, it converts their traditional duties of care and loyalty from mandatory *substantive* normative duties, which invariably become anachronistic as economic change accelerates, to mandatory *procedural* normative duties, which become more vitally important in democratic societies as economic change accelerates.

Our central thesis is that contractarians, imposers, and balancers fail to explain the norm-based *behavior* of Delaware courts because they fail to see this procedural turn in the fiduciary law tradition.[12] As a result, they fail to see *any* connection between corporate governance and institutional design. Failing to grasp this connection, they are left trying to explain this norm-based judicial behavior by examining directly its more immediate effects on corporate performance, or on management, shareholders, or stakeholders, and the explanation does not lie here.[13]

II. Major Governance Cases

The purpose of this chapter is to review the facts, decisions, written opinions, and influential legal commentaries in seven of the most important corporate governance cases to come before Delaware courts in the 1980s and 1990s. In later chapters we explore more fully the central concepts legal scholars employ in explaining this judicial behavior and we offer alternative concepts of our own. We will see that legal scholars broadly agree on the facts and also when describing Delaware court behavior. But they disagree greatly about how best to account for this judicial behavior. More important, we will see points at which legal scholars acknowledge they cannot account satisfactorily for what Delaware courts are doing and, certainly, for why they are doing it. Our task as sociologists is to explain this judicial behavior. In the process, we employ a framework of sociological concepts that identifies specifically when and why the corporate judiciary performs a pattern-maintenance function for the larger society and when and why it fails to do so.

1. Van Gorkom (1985): Shock Waves across Corporate America

In *Smith v. Van Gorkom*, the Delaware Supreme Court imposed a multimillion-dollar *personal* liability on Trans Union Corp's board of directors for breaching their fiduciary duty of care.[14] The court did so despite the fact that the board had approved a cash-out merger that yielded all company stockholders a 40–60 percent premium over the market value of their shares. Here is a clear case, therefore, in which Delaware courts brought some qualitative standard of analysis to a corporate governance dispute rather than relying exclusively on the quantitative standard of whether outcomes are Pareto optimal for shareholders.

This case involved a class action by stockholders of Trans Union Corp.

who originally approached Chancery to rescind the friendly cash-out merger of their company into a wholly owned subsidiary of another corporation. Once the deal had been made, plaintiffs sought damages against members of the Trans Union board, many of whom were outside directors, some "even eminent" directors.[15] The cash-out merger was disputed because Trans Union's CEO, Jerome William Van Gorkom, was nearing retirement at the time and had "initiated, negotiated, and pushed through" the transaction apparently in order to cash out his shares at their highest value. Van Gorkom was indifferent to finding another buyer, but his actions, and certainly their outcome, hardly seemed to breach either the duty of care or the duty of loyalty as traditionally interpreted by Delaware courts. The Trans Union board, however, had approved the transaction in a two-hour meeting without receiving prior notice that its company was about to be merged into another and its shareholders cashed out.[16]

Chancery ruled in favor of defendant directors, holding that they had acted in a sufficiently informed manner and therefore were entitled to a presumption of business judgment rule protection in approving the merger. On appeal by shareholder plaintiffs, however, the Delaware Supreme Court reversed. It pointed out that directors owed fiduciary duties of both care and loyalty to the corporate entity and each duty is of equal, independent significance.[17] This was a new way of interpreting corporate law tradition. In the eyes of the Court, the Trans Union board had approved the merger without keeping itself apprised of the CEO's actions and motives in forcing the company's sale and establishing its purchase price per share. The board had not inquired into the company's "intrinsic value" and was grossly negligent in approving a sale after only a two-hour meeting, without prior notice, and without any crisis or emergency precipitating such a sudden action.[18] Thus, the Court held that for three reasons defendant directors had not taken due care in getting "fair value" for plaintiff stockholders: The board's decision was not the product of an informed business judgment, its later efforts to take corrective action were not effective, and the board was not completely candid with stockholders.[19]

Even legal scholars sympathetic to this Delaware Supreme Court decision fail to see how the board breached its duty of care, given that the outcome indeed seemed Pareto optimal for shareholders. Even these legal scholars question whether the Court "understood what it was doing."[20] Alan Palmiter, for instance, believes the Court was actually imposing a new, "implicit" fiduciary duty on the Trans Union board, a duty he calls "independence." In the case at hand, the Trans Union board had failed to demonstrate sufficient independence from the CEO. But even with this generous interpretation, Palmiter still sees the Delaware Supreme Court's decision leaving judges and legal scholars with a dilemma.

On the one hand, the Court could not credibly cite either the traditional duty of care or the traditional duty of loyalty in challenging the board's behavior, given the way this Court had applied these standards in the past. No one was alleging that directors had breached loyalty, by having a personal, material stake in the disputed transaction. And, until this decision, Delaware courts had treated due care more as formality than fiduciary duty on a par with loyalty, and particularly when outcomes appeared to be Pareto optimal for shareholders.[21] Still, the board had clearly failed to concern itself with Trans Union's future as a corporate entity.

On the other hand, if the Delaware Supreme Court had focused its attention exclusively on the priced outcome of the transaction, as contractarians insist, it would have held in favor of the board. The outcome seemed to be Pareto optimal (at least for shareholders) and, indeed, the board could credibly claim that its action likely maximized shareholder wealth.[22] That it took only two hours for them to achieve this result might merit directors a contractarian award, not a judicial reprimand, and certainly not a personal liability verdict.

When the dust settled, it seemed to many legal observers that Delaware's Supreme Court had punished Trans Union directors for the sort of structural bias that all boards experience, namely a pressure—whether overt or subtle—to acquiesce when a CEO plans and proposes any transaction.[23] As Palmiter would put it four years later, to hold that a board had not exhibited sufficient "independence" from a CEO and top management team is to hold all boards to a standard of behavior that is quite commonly breached all across corporate America. Thus, whatever legal niceties Delaware's Justices may have had in mind when they made this decision, the reaction throughout American boardrooms to their imposing a *personal* liability on directors for breaching a seeming formality, their duty of care, was predictable. Van Gorkom "sent shock waves through the corporate world, raising the specter of directors subject to multi-million dollar personal liability for failure to study mind-numbing merger documents with sufficient care."[24] This decision not only created uncertainty regarding how Delaware courts might interpret fiduciary law in future cases, but also came at a time when the market for insurance for director and management liability was already in turmoil. Insurance was already expensive, sometimes unavailable.[25]

Within a year and a half of the *Van Gorkom* decision, the Delaware General Assembly responded by adding Section 102(b)(7) to its General Corporation law.[26] Thirty other state legislatures followed its lead.[27] Under this Section corporate officers may include in their certificates of incorporation provisions that either limit or eliminate any personal liability directors might bear for breaching their fiduciary duty of care. This Section addresses only the remedy of personal liability, however. It does not prohibit dissatisfied shareholders from bringing derivative claims that directors breached this duty and thereby calling on Chancery either to rescind a disputed transaction or else to find other ways to recompense those who were harmed by it.[28] We will see shortly why this distinction is important. In addition, the new Section does not indemnify directors who breach their duty of loyalty. Loyalty is breached when directors have a personal material stake in a transaction or otherwise: fail to act in good faith, intentionally engage in misconduct, knowingly violate the law, obtain an improper personal benefit, or improperly pay a dividend or approve a stock repurchase.[29]

Even with the Assembly's timely statutory response, however, many directors and managers were hardly reassured in the midst of the hostile activity of the 1980s. "The scope of *Van Gorkom* duties remained unclear, and existed uneasily beside other fiduciary duties imposed on directors in merger situations."[30]

2. *Unocal* (1985): Entering a Domain of Qualitative Analysis

In the early 1980s as today, broad federal law, the Williams Act, regulates the hostile bidding process. State law, however, has sole jurisdiction over how corporations are governed internally, including how they react to hostile activity. Thus, state law mediates how target management teams and boards of directors conduct themselves as they react to raids and buyout proposals. Our point is that however state courts decided to approach hostile takeover situations in the 1980s, their rulings had to remain consistent with the Williams Act, the popular name given to a 1968 federal statute titled Full Disclosure of Corporate Equity Ownership and in Corporate Takeover Bids. Under the Williams Act, a tender offer active for only twenty business days complies with federal law and, therefore, technically merits a response by management. This means that shareholders of a target corporation may technically initiate federal legal action against management on the twenty-first business day if management either ignores the hostile activity or erects defenses against it. The problem, clearly, is that this time

period is too short for target management teams either to defend themselves or to seek and evaluate additional tender offers.[31] The Williams Act,
however, said little about the legality of management defending itself, leaving this whole matter to state courts and legislatures.[32]

Until 1985, Delaware courts treated hostile situations in much the same
way that other state courts did. They, too, failed to distinguish at a doctrinal
level between a target management's defenses and its more routine exercises
of business judgment in friendly transactions. In that year, however, the
Delaware Supreme Court articulated its new intermediate standard of review. In the process it reconsidered the scope of management's business
judgment rule protection, opened a door (however slightly) to stakeholder
balancing, and thereby led many legal observers to believe that Delaware
courts would obstruct, not facilitate, the new market for corporate control.

The Court held in *Unocal Corp. v. Mesa Petroleum Co.* that when a target management team (in this case, at Unocal) responds to an unsolicited
tender offer (in this case, from Mesa's T. Boone Pickens), it enters a qualitatively different legal domain. Within this domain, management's actions merit review, but by a standard intermediate between upholding
everything management does under business judgment rule protection
and scrutinizing everything it does under full or intrinsic fairness review.[33] Stated as doctrine, when management takes action to defeat hostile changes in control and there is no allegation that directors have any
direct personal interest either in the transaction or in management's responses, Chancery will nonetheless apply a flexible, intermediate standard of review when dissatisfied shareholders bring suit. It will also apply
this standard when a board itself unilaterally adopts defensive measures
and dissatisfied shareholders bring suit. By contrast, when a valid stockholder vote approves management or board defenses, the presumption of
business judgment rule protection will remain in place even if some
shareholders are dissatisfied.[34]

In the case at hand, Unocal's board believed Pickens' offer to shareholders, a two-tiered hostile bid, was grossly inadequate and also implied a
threat of greenmail. A greenmailer is a hostile bidder who encourages a target corporation to repurchase his shares in the company at a premium as a
means of inducing him to drop his tender offer. The same repurchasing
plan is not offered to other stockholders.[35] As a two-tiered bid, stockholders
who sold the shares Pickens needed to gain control over the company, the
first tier, would receive cash. But then other stockholders who wished to sell,
the second tier, would be forced to accept junk bonds of equal cash value.

The Delaware Supreme Court agreed with Unocal's board that Pickens was a "raider" with a "national reputation as a 'greenmailer.'"[36]

The Unocal board responded to Pickens' raid by adopting a selective self-tender offer to shareholders, namely one that specifically excluded Pickens. The board told the Court that its objective was either to defeat the inadequate offer outright or else to provide stockholders with a substantially greater amount in investment grade securities, as opposed to junk.[37] To the consternation of contractarians, the Court found both purposes to be valid. More generally, it held that a reasonable response to hostility is one that is fair, just, equitable, and appropriate.[38] The Court noted that a target board need not be a "passive instrumentality" and, indeed, it bears a fiduciary duty to protect the corporate enterprise, including stockholders, from harm. In addition, the Court reaffirmed that every corporation has broad authority to deal in its own stock. But the Court also held that an intermediate standard of review is appropriate in these situations. "Because of the omnipresent specter that a board may be acting primarily in its own interests, rather than those of the corporation and its shareholders, there is an enhanced duty which calls for judicial examination at the threshold before the protections of the business judgment rule may be conferred."[39]

The Court held that if management wishes to retain business judgment rule protection in hostile situations, its defenses must meet two requirements, which would thereafter become known as "the *Unocal* standard." First, a requirement of good faith and reasonable investigation: Management must provide some basis for believing that a proposed change in control endangers corporate policy and the firm's effectiveness "as an enterprise."[40] Second, a requirement of balanced response: Defensive measures must be reasonable and "appropriate" in relation to the threat, with the primary concern being to prevent potential harm to shareholders. As the Court would elaborate in 1995 (in *Unitrin, Inc. v. American General Corp.*): "When a corporation is not for sale, the board of directors is the defender of the metaphorical medieval corporate bastion and the protector of the corporation's shareholders. The fact that a defensive action must not be coercive or preclusive does not prevent a board from responding defensively before a bidder is at the corporate bastion's gate."[41] This would seem to elevate shareholder interests above all others, but we will see in a moment that the Unocal decision is more complicated than this.

When a board meets both requirements, a Delaware court will not substitute its judgment for the board's actions.[42] Since *Unocal*, Delaware courts have cited these requirements, most often when approving defensive actions but eventually when opposing others. For instance, they have op-posed boards offering to purchase the company's own shares and not al-lowing shareholders to accept a hostile bid when that is their preference.[43] But the *Time-Warner* case, which we discuss momentarily, is an example of Delaware courts using the Unocal standard to uphold board actions that fail to maximize shareholder wealth, and through 1990 they never used the Un-ocal standard to oppose board defenses.[44]

Of equal importance, when the Delaware Supreme Court elaborated on the second requirement of the Unocal standard, a balanced response, it *si-multaneously* emphasized the importance of protecting shareholders while opening a door to stakeholder balancing.[45] It called attention not only to a board's responsibility to look after the interests of shareholders but also its responsibility at least to consider the interests of other constituents, includ-ing local communities. It held that as management considers which defen-sive actions to take, it may consider: the inadequacy of the price being of-fered, the nature and timing of the offer, any questions of illegality, the risk of the deal falling through, the relative equality of the securities being of-fered in the exchange, and *the impact on constituencies other than stockhold-ers, including "the community generally."*[46] By 1985, therefore, even Dela-ware's Supreme Court was acknowledging, albeit tentatively, that a "corpo-rate enterprise" is comprised of constituents other than management and shareholders, agent and principal.

Still, the Delaware Supreme Court was also reasserting two doctrinal principles of much longer standing.[47] First, it reasserted that a corpora-tion is more entity than nexus or site of self-interested contracting. After all, there is no reason for a court to permit management to erect defenses against takeovers unless it still attributes to a corporation collective inter-ests of "its own," and thus palpable *qualities* of "firmishness" or "person-hood."[48] Second, the Delaware Supreme Court also reasserted, consistent with management's business judgment rule protection and, it would seem, the fiduciary law tradition, that management and the board are *the corporate agent* responsible for maintaining the entity's viability as a long-term commercial enterprise.[49]

The Delaware Supreme Court simply appended to these two doctrinal principles an additional factor relevant to hostile situations. As manage-ment bears its fiduciary duty of loyalty as corporate agent, it may take into account the "stakes" nonshareholder constituents have in the enter-prise. Management need not restrict itself to maximizing shareholder wealth or, certainly, to maximizing corporate growth (and its own positional power). By making management responsible for the entity's "collective interests," and thereby for considering constituent stakes, Unocal essentially broadened management's discretion under business judgment rule protection. Moreover, by challenging contractarians' claim that maximizing shareholder wealth is the ultimate goal of corporate decision making, it altered the implications of shareholder contracting—beyond opening a door to stakeholder balancing. Unocal began to move Delaware courts outside today's orthodoxy of liberal complacency by bringing some *qualitative* standard of analysis to disputed transactions. It began to pose the issue of corporate purpose, of corporations' legitimate place and purpose in American society, in terms that are more qualitative and institutional than quantitative and immediate, more political economic or sociological than microeconomic.

Once American courts hold that disputed business transactions enter a legal domain that is more normative than economic, judges have little alternative other than to reconsider the merits of their own, independently developed concepts, the fiduciary law tradition. Moreover, some of the corporate judiciary's extraeconomic concepts update the Founders' original concerns about unbridled acquisitiveness and about the need to maintain certain institutional arrangements spanning the state and civil society. The problem is that since the American Civil War each succeeding generation of judges and legal scholars has drifted further and further away from explicitly identifying what these concerns are at a conceptual level. Because legal practitioners have not maintained clear conceptual linkages to the fiduciary law tradition, today's debate over corporate law, judicial practice, and corporate governance remains confined within a remarkably constricting orthodoxy, liberal complacency.

The irony is that this is precisely the type of political economic approach to the issue of corporate purpose, to the relationship between corporate governance and institutional design, that the Founders feared would enervate citizen vigilance and encourage self-indulgence. Yet in the context of today's orthodoxy, when courts try to articulate a broader social vision rather than leaving everything to markets and contract law, they place their own legitimacy at risk.

> Twentieth-century American legal thought has thus placed unprecedented trust in judges and courts. Struggling to discern a theoretical coherence which no longer exists and groping to find a social consensus which informs the future, courts are increasingly having difficulty meeting public expectations. This contemporary crisis results as a consequence of the pervasive

influence of realism as a "habit of thought." Realism's rejection of the declaratory theory of the judicial process encouraged courts to embrace a new activism and accept unprecedented political power. Yet, in proclaiming the relativity of ethical values, realism destroyed the only grounds plausible for justifying and legitimating the exercise of such judicial power in a democratic regime.[50]

In short, as Delaware courts brought a decidedly qualitative standard of analysis to hostile situations after 1985, the country's premier corporate judiciary acted schizophrenically. Its major rulings following *Unocal* illustrate this well. The irony is that *Unocal* also resulted in the Securities and Exchange Commission bringing contractarian principles into its rules governing tender offers: "Unocal's [defensive bid] was a two-tier bid in response to [Boone] Pickens' single-price offer . . . As it turns out, Unocal's offer was value-reducing. Unocal's victory [before the Delaware courts] is the *only* recorded instance of a two-tier offer beating a single-price offer with a higher total value. . . . And Unocal's victory is a freak even for an issuer tender offer, because the SEC promptly amended its rules to prohibit the exclusion feature that was essential to the strategy. Two-tier offers cannot today beat single-price offers with higher total value."[51]

3. *Revlon* (1986): From Balancing to Shareholder Contracting

One year after *Unocal*, the Delaware Supreme Court reconsidered the relationship between shareholder wealth and stakeholder positional interests in *Revlon Inc. v. MacAndrews & Forbes Holdings, Inc.* The *Revlon* case established an important limit to Delaware courts' presuming business judgment rule protection for management *and* their reading of management's duty of loyalty to a corporate entity as a long-term commercial enterprise. The Court held that a board's decision to permit management to negotiate a merger or buyout with a third party constitutes formal recognition that a company is for sale. Legal scholars would say thereafter that such an action constitutes notice that a company has entered the "*Revlon* zone." Once a company is in play, the board's duty under the Unocal standard shifts. Its goal can no longer be to preserve the corporate entity by erecting new defenses. Rather, its goal now is to make every effort to maximize the company's value for stockholders.[52] Within the "*Revlon* zone," management can no longer credibly claim that it bears any extracontractual obligation to the existing entity, or stakeholders, because in this situation all such claims are likely feigned, veiling strictly self-interested behavior by management.[53]

Thus, the Delaware Supreme Court ruled that when Revlon's board terminated an ongoing bidding process for the company by entering into a merger agreement that included certain lock-up and no-shopping provisions, it had breached its fiduciary duty.[54] Contractarians, of course, were overjoyed with this way of looking at hostile situations. They, and many other legal scholars, read the *Revlon* decision as compelling management, at least at some point, to "hold an auction" for a company in order to maximize shareholder return on investment. Contractarians were even more pleased when other state courts followed the Delaware Supreme Court's lead by encouraging sales or auctions at least in certain situations. State courts were finally privileging shareholders' self-interested contracting and Pareto optimal outcomes over public law norms and management's putative duty of loyalty to an entity rather than its owners.[55]

But in coming years it would turn out that Delaware courts were not really identifying "special and distinct '*Revlon* duties'" consistent with contractarians' narrow view of corporate purpose.[56] Rather, they were refining their *Unocal* standard of intermediate review as different situations came before them. When a company is in a hostile situation, as in *Unocal*, Delaware courts use enhanced scrutiny review if dissatisfied shareholders bring suit, as opposed simply to presuming management's behavior is protected by the business judgment rule. In turn, when a company is put up for sale, as in *Revlon*, what initiates an intermediate review "at the threshold" is a plaintiff shareholder who credibly alleges that directors treated one or more hostile bidders on unequal terms, and thereby failed to conduct a fair auction. With this, Delaware courts also suspend any presumption of business judgment rule protection and apply a two-part review that differs only slightly from the *Unocal* standard. First, Chancery determines whether directors properly believed they were advancing shareholder interests. Second, Chancery determines whether a board's behavior, in discriminating between bidders, was reasonable in relation to the advantage it was seeking for shareholders or, conversely, in relation to a threat it saw a particular bidder posing to stockholders before any of them took an interest in this particular tender offer.[57]

At minimum, *Revlon* requires directors to exhibit scrupulous adherence to ordinary principles of fairness so that shareholder wealth is increased. But it does not require directors to hold an auction according to some substantive, standard formula. The primary objective is for directors to conduct a bidding process of one kind or another that benefits stockholders.[58] To this end, a board is free to take any number of steps, including defending against "perceived threats" that surface during the bidding process. Thus, the Court held that a board may adopt a "poison pill" for stock purchase rights in order to defend against one bidder, and then drop this defense when a more suitable bidder comes along.[59]

The Court had first considered whether a poison pill is compatible with presuming business judgment rule protection a year earlier (in *Moran v. Household International*). It held that when there are no credible allegations of bad faith or entrenchment in adopting this defense, such a purchase rights plan is a reasonable reaction to a coercive two-tier tender offer.[60] In its *Revlon* decision, the Court found that Revlon's board took this action in the face of an impending hostile takeover. It acknowledged that this defense "protected stockholders" at a price below the company's "intrinsic value," and yet still approved it. Because a poison pill defense is sufficiently flexible and can be withdrawn at any time, the Court held that it enables a board to consider other tender offers that better serve stockholder interests.[61]

Indeed, the Court also approved lock-up and no-shop clause provisions in general terms, even as it ruled against Revlon's board for the particular ones it adopted. It held that lock-ups ("white knights" that enter a bidding process with support from a target board) are acceptable if they entice other bidders to enter the auction, not if they end an active bidding process.[62] No-shop clauses are more problematic, but a successful bidder who imposes such a condition on a target board can survive enhanced scrutiny review if he demonstrates that his tender offer brings material advantage to stockholders.[63] Since the *Revlon* decision, Chancery has accepted other contractual provisions that alter bidding processes in one way or another, including stock options, expense reimbursements, breakup fees, and requirements that bidders sign confidentiality and standstill agreements.[64] Most important, in its later *QVC* decision, which we discuss momentarily, the Court stressed that *Revlon* does not require both a change of control and a breakup of a company.[65]

With all of this, the *Revlon* decision left state courts with both a practical problem and a new doctrinal issue. The practical problem was that each court had to decide in each case *when* a target management team must acknowledge its company is in play, that is, it has entered the "*Revlon* zone."[66] And irrespective of how a particular court decides this, the *Revlon* decision also left each court with a new doctrinal issue: Did *Revlon* signal that Delaware courts were drifting toward shareholder contracting? Or would *Revlon* prove to be an anomaly as Delaware courts elaborated the second *Unocal* requirement by further legitimating stakeholder balancing or else by supporting management's duty of loyalty to a corporate entity as a long-term commercial enterprise?

The *Unocal* and *Revlon* decisions in 1985 and 1986, however, do not yet fully convey the Delaware courts' schizophrenia during the 1980s. Both *Unocal* and *Revlon* require target boards to treat unwanted bidders with some measure of fairness, but they leave it to Chancery to decide in each case what is a "threat" to a corporate entity and what is a "reasonable action" taken by corporate officers in response to it. But where Chancery had earlier deferred to management's assessment of threats, before 1983 and the rise of a market for corporate control, *Unocal* made it nearly inevitable that it would treat any hostile tender offer as a credible threat. We will see that Delaware courts will eventually replace this essentially substantive normative question with one that is more procedural normative. It will concentrate on whether management acts in good faith and reasonably explores the options available, not on whether the particular decisions it makes can survive review more directly, in substance.[67]

After *Revlon*, Delaware courts at times explicitly subordinated stockholders' private interest in maximizing share price to a putative public interest, namely maintaining the viability of corporate entities as long-term enterprises. At these times, Delaware courts either deferred to management's business judgment or else built on the second *Unocal* requirement by encouraging stakeholder balancing. With the first move, they characterize the corporation as an "entity" or "natural person" whose collective interests are valuable to the larger society, and they hold that corporate officers more or less unilaterally identify and advance these collective interests. With the second, they hold that management can only identify, and then advance, these collective interests by taking constituents' different positional interests into account.[68]

4. *Macmillan* I and II (1988–1989): High Water Mark of Incoherence?

In *Mills Acquisition Co. v. Macmillan Inc.* (1988), Chancery foundered in trying to identify the threshold that triggers a Revlon duty to auction a target company.[69] Seeing this, Delaware courts found it easier to transform *Revlon* from a narrow duty, to hold an auction, to a more general duty, namely to act reasonably to obtain the best value for shareholders in either the short-run or the long run.[70] Edward Rock lists *Macmillan* as the first of three important management buyout (MBO) cases in which Delaware courts most fully established its intermediate standard of review.[71] He also calls *Macmillan* "Exhibit A" in illustrating how management and a board of directors ought not to behave in an MBO.

The management of Macmillan, a publishing house, became concerned about the possibility of being targeted by a hostile bidder.[72] The company's two inside directors, Edward Evans (the chair and chief executive officer) and William Reilly (the president and chief operating officer), respond by seeking absolute control of a restructured company. To this end, they first abet Macmillan's board of directors to: grant them several hundred thousand restricted shares; approve a new employment contract for them that includes golden parachutes and stock options; approve a loan of $60 million that the existing ESOP (Employee Stock Ownership Plan) would then borrow to fund its purchase of one million Macmillan shares; and allow Evans, Reilly, and two other Macmillan employees to replace Citibank as ESOP trustee so that they control all unallocated shares deposited in the Plan. Then, with this done, "management" proposes a restructuring that would give these four people corporate control.

On October 21, 1987, two days after the market crash, an investment group led by Robert Bass discloses it holds 7.5 percent of Macmillan stock. Macmillan management calls a board meeting at which it inaccurately labels Bass a greenmailer (according to Vice Chancellor Jacobs), and the board accordingly treats the Bass Group as a threat to Macmillan and its shareholders. Management forms a special committee of the board to evaluate its restructuring proposal, but Evans and Reilly interview and select the committee's investment banker without disclosing these contacts to the eventual committee. The newly formed committee meets and, with Evans, Reilly, and others in the management group attending, hears a presentation by a representative of investment bank Lazard Freres & Co. which deals exclusively with how to facilitate management's restructuring and how to defeat the Bass Group proposal. Without negotiation, the special committee recommends both measures, the full board approves—but then the Bass Group raises its bid. Chancery condemns both the special committee and Macmillan management as it enjoins the restructuring plan.

Three months later, Macmillan is back in Chancery Court. Evans and Reilly had responded to Chancery's earlier decision (Macmillan I) by abandoning the restructuring plan but then looking for a friendly bidder, namely Kohlberg Kravis Roberts & Company, the premier buyout "boutique." Meanwhile, Robert Maxwell, through Maxwell Communications Corp. (MCC), expresses an interest in acquiring Macmillan, and Macmillan management's response is similar to its earlier one, now aiding KKR and discouraging Maxwell. Maxwell announces an $80 per share all-cash offer on August 12 that tops the Bass Group bid significantly. Evans and Reilly make an unauthorized telephone call to KKR to inform them of MCC's bid, and never disclose the call. Vice Chancellor Jacobs sees this as a breach of fiduciary duty and he questions whether the auction that was held in fact yielded Macmillan shareholders the highest available price. He orders Macmillan to withdraw its poison pill so MCC can proceed with its offer, but Maxwell appeals to Delaware's Supreme Court for even more.

On November 2, 1988 the Court rules in Maxwell's favor orally, on May 3, 1989 in writing, and eventually MCC acquires Macmillan for $90.25 per share. The Court is contemptuous of Evans and Reilly, Macmillan's investment bankers, the board, and the special committee. The Securities and Exchange Commission later charges Evans and Reilly, along with Macmillan general counsel Beverly Chell, with filing a misleading disclosure regarding the ESOP established in the MBO offer.

With *Macmillan* and the other two major MBO cases that Rock highlights, Delaware courts finally established norms covering these especially troubling situations. Rock's account of these norms includes, but is not reduced to, the following five ways to structure an MBO: A special committee should negotiate with management and third parties, retaining its own investment bankers and legal counsel. Counsel should see that managers do not appoint committee members or their investment banker. The committee should issue a press release so others may bid, and provide information to prospective bidders. If bidders enter, the committee should behave in an evenhanded manner rather than favor the management group. And the committee should test the market but need not conduct a *Revlon* auction.[73] More generally, across all major corporate governance disputes, Rock finds that Delaware courts tend to rule against "strong-willed CEOs who dominate directors," boards that allow personal antipathy to interfere with their deliberations, and boards that lean toward management's preferred bidder.[74] Even more generally, Delaware courts focus on process and motive in corporate governance disputes, not on the substantive outcome of management or board action.[75]

5. *Time-Warner* (1989): Again, Qualitative Considerations

The decision that reveals most fully how corporate law suffered from a breakdown of shared meaning in the late 1980s, and also that the relationship between corporations and law is more sociological than narrowly economic, came three years after *Revlon* and less than a year after *Macmillan*. In *Paramount Communications v. Time, Inc.* Chancellor William Allen permitted Time management to block a hostile tender offer from Paramount that was far more lucrative for Time shareholders than its previously arranged merger with Warner Communications.[76] Chancellor Allen ruled in favor of Time managers by reasoning that they not only bear a contractual obligation to Time shareholders but also a fiduciary obligation to maintain the integrity of "Time culture." He came to this conclusion by accepting Time attorneys' arguments that this company's "corporate culture" holds a "distinctive and important" place in American society.[77]

Easterbrook and Fischel see this decision (along with *Van Gorkom*) as the worst examples of Delaware courts' "muddling through."[78] Jeffrey Gordon sees Time-Warner as "one especially important moment of legal change."[79] Lyman Johnson sees it synthesizing at a conceptual level many "discordant principles" in Delaware's anticontractarian decisions both before and after *Revlon*.[80]

One discordant principle is deciding when a corporation enters the *Revlon* zone. In *Time-Warner*, Chancery held that a company is really only put into play when a transaction involves a significant change in its ownership.[81] Thus, if Time Inc. shares were simply to be transferred to Warner shareholders, as the two management teams had planned, then its ownership would remain as dispersed as before.[82] Since neither the ownership *nor governance structure* of Time Inc. was to be altered fundamentally by the transaction, Time Inc. attorneys could credibly claim they never put the company up for sale, and thus never entered the *Revlon* zone. Time Inc. management, therefore, was under no legal obligation to consider the Paramount tender offer at all, let alone to negotiate a sale price that maximized shareholder wealth.

A second discordant principle is Delaware courts' long-standing deference to management under the business judgment rule. The *Time-Warner* decision reasserted that a target management team legitimately rejects the stock market's assessment of its corporation's profitability at a frozen moment in time, if it can demonstrate it is carrying out a viable longer-term plan. Thus, a target management team may legitimately defend itself against a hostile bid by pointing to its company's prospects for longer-term profitability under its continuing stewardship. This is consistent with the first requirement in Delaware courts' *Unocal* standard, namely that management provide evidence that a proposed change in control endangers corporate policy.

Yet a third discordant principle is one attending the other *Unocal* requirement. The *Time-Warner* decision reasserted that the collective interests of a corporate entity may include *qualities* that elude pricing in capital markets,[83] including, in this case, the putative harm society might suffer if the entity's "culture" or "way of life" is needlessly disrupted or altered. Thus, the collective interests of a corporate "person" in American society may not be reducible to immediate externalities for constituents that can be priced (and, therefore, potentially recompensed). Chancellor Allen added an important point to this discordant principle. The qualities at issue here may go beyond management's traditional fiduciary duty of loyalty to a corporate entity as a typical long-term enterprise. These qualities may entail a duty to preserve a particular set of substantive norms—a particular culture or a way of life—distinctive to one such entity. With this, Chancellor Allen took a "European" turn. He moved Delaware fiduciary law toward an organic metaphor of the corporation rather than a metaphor more consistent with either Lockean principles of contracting or Madisonian principles of balancing.[84]

The problem with organic metaphors is they revolve around substantive beliefs putatively shared by corporate officers as well as at least some corporate constituents. We will see in Chapters 11 and 12, however, that it is exceedingly difficult for any observer, including a judge, to recognize when this condition actually holds true, let alone to do so with consistency across cases. Actually, the problem Chancellor Allen faced in *Time-Warner* went beyond efforts to get a handle on the shared substantive beliefs or way of life purportedly animating managers and employees at Time Inc. He could confine these efforts, after all, to the following question: Does Time Inc.'s "corporate culture," which by definition is distinctive to this particular entity, merit judicial protection in a market for corporate control? Put differently: Is the value of this corporate culture to the larger society, in substance, like that of, say, an endangered species or an historical landmark?

But Chancellor Allen went beyond this qualitative issue of "intrinsic value" (both for corporate constituents and for the larger society). He considered at least implicitly another qualitative issue, one far grander, namely whether changes in corporate control can carry institutional externalities, not just immediate externalities. *He considered the argument of* Time Inc. *attorneys that disruptions of "Time culture" might harm American society in some grander sense.* By taking this argument seriously, even if not pinning his decision on it, Chancellor Allen went beyond implicit analogies to endangered species and historical landmarks. He was now operating on some broad, implicit characterization of the direction of change of American society itself. After all, if American society is so robust and dynamic that the disruption of any particular corporation's culture cannot possibly harm it, why worry about "Time culture"? In considering even for a moment that Time Inc., and other corporations, might contribute qualities to American society that are particularly "distinctive and important," Chancellor Allen was endeavoring to identify the possible institutional externalities of a market for corporate control *in directly substantive normative terms*. Any such line of inquiry, of course, falls entirely outside the scope of today's orthodoxy of liberal complacency.[85]

Of the three discordant principles that Time Inc. attorneys raised in calling on Chancellor Allen to support its merger plan and dismiss Paramount's tender offer, legal scholars have been captivated most by the third one. This is the one least developed at a conceptual level and furthest removed from today's orthodoxy.[86] The Time Inc. board and management team was contending that their planned merger was more consistent with maintaining "Time culture" than the more lucrative hostile takeover by Paramount.[87] Chancellor Allen accepted this argument and coupled it with two more familiar doctrinal principles, business judgment rule protection and fiduciary loyalty: "[W]here the board . . . continues to manage the corporation for a long-term profit pursuant to a preexisting business plan that itself is not primarily a control device or scheme, *the corporation* has a legally cognizable interest in achieving that plan."[88] The Delaware Supreme Court did the same thing in upholding his decision on appeal. On the one hand, it held that the Time Inc. board acted "reasonably" when it determined that Paramount's all-cash, all-shares tend offer represented a "threat" other than one of "inadequate value" for shareholders. On the other, it also held: "Directors are not obliged to abandon a deliberately conceived corporate plan for a short-term shareholder profit unless there is clearly no basis to sustain the corporate strategy."[89]

In short, Time attorneys convinced Chancellor Allen and then three Delaware Justices at the very least that the substantive beliefs institutionalized by Time Inc. are unique. They also got them to entertain the idea that this particular corporation's place and purpose within American society are "distinctive and important"—so important, in fact, that this corporation's distinctive qualities merit higher legal status, as a fiduciary duty to this entity, than management's role as shareholders' agent. Time attorneys successfully argued that Time Inc. management bears an extracontractual duty—a true fiduciary obligation—to preserve "Time culture" even should this dampen share price and, presumably, harm some stakeholders.[90] After all, Chancellor Allen did not tie his decision to any promises by Time Inc. management to maintain particular levels of employment or, for that matter, to continue any particular business practices.[91] Nor for that matter did he actually scrutinize details of the Time-Warner merger in order to confirm that "Time culture" was actually uppermost in anyone's mind. Former *Time* magazine journalist Richard Clurman points out, for instance, that "in the actual written agreements between Time and Warner, neither Time journalism nor the editor-in-chief fared well."[92]

In its heyday, *Time* magazine editors and reporters took considerable pride in the company's corporate policy of separating "church and state," editorial divisions and business divisions. Editors and reporters did not justify their journalistic decisions to company management. But this policy was in considerable flux well before 1989, and particularly after Ariel Sharon successfully sued *Time* magazine for slander.[93] As it turned out, the proposed merger with Warner included two major changes in Time Inc.'s traditional church/state policy. The first change was in the requirement that the board approve by a two-thirds vote any significant change in the corporation's governance structure, including any change in the board's editorial committee. This was replaced by a more typical majority rule requirement.[94] The second change was in *Time* magazine's long-standing policy that the editor-in-chief report directly to the Time Inc. board as a whole, not to particular directors or particular committees. Because the role of editor-in-chief was not included explicitly in the merger agreement, everyone knew this meant he would report to the board's editorial committee, no longer the whole board. "As a trade-off for this change, a new entertainment committee of the board was created to 'ensure the creative and artistic independence' of the company, [thereby] implying that journalism and popular entertainment required the same standard."[95]

Chancellor Allen accepted at face value that Time Inc.'s corporate culture is distinctive, however difficult it might be to identify at a conceptual level what its distinctive qualities might be. Moreover, he not only accepted that "Time culture" is unique unto itself, like an endangered species or historical landmark. He also accepted that this corporate culture is "important" within the larger American social order, again however difficult it might be to identify at a conceptual level why it is. These two difficulties explain why Chancellor Allen could not tie Chancery's support of "Time culture" to any particular type of corporate governance structure, including one that actually institutionalized editorial independence at Time Inc. from business management. Instead of moving in this direction, Chancellor Allen took what Jeffrey Gordon calls a broader sociohistorical approach to the merger, "the approach of a constitutional court" that adopts a "social imperative."[96]

A constitutional decision to support the integrity of a particular corporate entity moves as far outside today's orthodoxy as can be imagined. We will see in Chapters 10–13 that, more surprisingly, it is equally inconsistent with the courts' fiduciary law tradition. The *Time-Warner* decision rests on preserving a particular set of *substantive* beliefs, a way of life, literally as an end-in-itself. As it turned out, the substantive beliefs Chancery was supposedly preserving were already inconsistent with corporate practice even at *Time* magazine, the company's flagship publication, let alone with corporate practice across Time Inc. Regardless, Folk, Ward, and Welch say that "[s]everal cases have indicated that a board may properly conclude that potential changes to corporate 'culture' could constitute a threat to the corporation."[97] However, they cite only three cases, all decided in 1989, the first being Time-Warner. The other two are a decision by the Northern District of Illinois (*Newell Co. v. Vermont American Corp.*) protecting Vermont American's corporate culture and a decision by the Delaware Supreme Court (*Shamrock Holdings, Inc. v. Polaroid Corp.*) protecting Polaroid culture.

6. *Technicolor* (1993), citing *Weinberger* (1983): A New Unified Standard?

In *Cede & Co. v. Technicolor* (1993),[98] the Delaware courts were again faced with a situation like the one in *Van Gorkom* in 1985, wherein directors failed to inform themselves before meeting about a proposed merger.[99] To recall, the Delaware General Assembly passed a statute after *Van Gorkom* that permits corporations to protect directors from personal liability for breaches of care, but not necessarily to protect corporations from derivative suits otherwise citing such breaches to contest transactions.[100] Throughout the 1980s, this legislative action seemed to many legal scholars to leave only the duty of loyalty as a truly mandatory rule in Delaware fiduciary law. But in the *Technicolor* decision, Delaware's Supreme Court essentially sidestepped the General Assembly's action at least in part, namely its seeming narrowing of Delaware fiduciary law. The Court explicitly treated violations of care as roughly equivalent to violations of loyalty. This was innovative, suggesting a "broader unification of Delaware fiduciary law" than ever before proposed.[101]

Shareholders of Technicolor Inc. were offered a cash-out merger by MacAndrews & Forbes Group, the parent company of *Revlon* headed by Ronald Perelman (who came to wider public attention in 1999 in a messy divorce proceeding).[102] Perelman initiated contact with Technicolor by asking a company director, Fred Sullivan, to assist him in contacting management. Sullivan informs Technicolor CEO Morton Kamerman of this meeting but, prior to it, he places a purchase order for 10,000 shares of Technicolor stock—which, however, is executed for only 1,000 shares. The SEC later orders Sullivan to pay back $13,700 to Technicolor.

Kamerman meets with Perelman and Sullivan to discuss a possible merger. After several meetings, they agree that if a merger goes through, Sullivan will receive a $150,000 "finders fee" and Kamerman an employment contract making him CEO of Technicolor. Technicolor's investment bank, Goldman Sachs, is asked for a fairness opinion and estimates the value of Technicolor stock to be $20–22 per share. Perelman and Kamerman agree on $23. Two days later Technicolor's nine-member board, which includes Kamerman and Sullivan, meets in special session. Three members have no knowledge of the transaction, and four others have only limited knowledge. Kamerman explains the deal, including his employment contract and Sullivan's fee. The company's outside legal counsel, Meredeth Brown, explains the structure of the merger and reviews documents. A Goldman representative explains orally why $23 is fair. Some directors propose Perelman be approached to try to get more, but they are advised he won't budge. One director asks for other bids, but others chime "a bird in the hand," and there is a unanimous vote.

How and why did Delaware courts subordinate a duty of loyalty in this case to a duty of care?[103] A breach of loyalty did not really apply here and yet both Chancery and the Delaware Supreme Court agreed that the board's behavior was hardly equitable or fair. Regarding loyalty, Chancellor Allen found that two board members, Kamerman and Sullivan, derived personal pecuniary benefits from the merger, but each had also disclosed these interests to the board. Allen held that these conflicts of interest tainted the board as a whole, which he treated as a collective entity.

The Delaware Supreme Court, however, required Chancellor Allen to reconsider his loyalty analysis for two reasons and then also to reconsider the implications of a breach of care. Regarding loyalty, Justice Horsey was skeptical that individual conflicts necessarily taint an entire board. In addition, the standard of loyalty traditionally used in evaluating board behavior under Delaware fiduciary law demanded analyzing conflicts of interest director-by-director regardless, not treating the board as a collective entity. On the other hand, the board's violation of "due care" seemed self-evident. It had not received notice or information about the merger before the special meeting. However, Allen had dismissed these allegations in Chancery because everyone agreed that shareholders "had received more than fair value."

Here is where the Delaware Supreme Court became innovative and worked around the General Assembly's *Van Gorkom* statute. It held that once a breach of due care has been credibly alleged, the burden shifts under Delaware fiduciary law. Defendants (that is, Technicolor's management and board) must now demonstrate the full or "intrinsic fairness" of the contested transaction, in this case, a merger. The Delaware Supreme Court had reasserted this standard back in 1983, two years before *Van Gorkom,* in *Weinberger v. UOP, Inc.,* a freeze-out merger between a parent corporation and a partially owned subsidiary.[104] Because *Weinberger* also "set the doctrinal stage for Delaware's analysis" in *Macmillan* and other MBO cases, it is worthwhile here to review its basic facts and the Court's ruling.[105]

Weinberger involved a cash-out merger between UOP, Inc. and its majority owner, The Signal Companies, Inc.[106] Such a merger forces minority shareholders to give up their shares for cash but allows controlling shareholders to retain their shares. Two years after Signal acquired its position in UOP at $20 per share, Signal management wished to acquire the rest of the company. Two Signal directors, who also served as members of UOP's board, use that company's information to learn that this would be a good investment for Signal at any price up to $24 per share. Signal's senior management proposes a cash-out merger in the range of $20 to $21 per share, "constituting an almost fifty percent premium over UOP's then market price."

UOP's president, a long-time Signal employee and current Signal director, is told of the plan and voices no objection; he considers the price "generous." An investment bank is retained to prepare a fairness opinion, and finds that a $20 or $21 per share price is fair. The Signal board authorizes an offer of $21 per share and the UOP board accepts. UOP shareholders vote approval, including nearly 52 percent of non-Signal held shares. Despite the 50 percent premium for these shareholders, the Delaware Supreme Court finds that Signal's conduct failed the fair dealing requirement of the intrinsic fairness standard. Fairness here, in the words of the Court, "can be equated to conduct by a theoretical, wholly independent board of directors" and, therefore, "arm's length" bargaining between the parties. The Court accepts that approval by a majority of UOP minority shareholders would normally shift the burden to plaintiff shareholders to demonstrate unfairness. But the Court found that in this case approval was "meaningless" because minority shareholders were denied "critical information." The Court remands the issue of fair price to Chancery, and directs Chancery to take into account all factors that investment bankers and other financial analysts would consider relevant.

Again, a full or intrinsic fairness review requires not only fair price (as determined by market value and other relevant financial considerations) but also fair dealing. This second requirement refers to: the timing of a merger or other change of control; how it was initiated, structured, negotiated, and disclosed to directors; and how approvals by a board and a shareholder majority were obtained.[107] With this, Delaware's Supreme Court held that fiduciary law spans not two duties but three: loyalty, due care, and good faith. It held that a credible allegation of breach in any one area simultaneously deprives management of business judgment rule protection and initiates a full review. By dividing fiduciary duties into three parts instead of the first two traditional ones, the Court was ruling that a conscientious director has as much of a duty to be reasonably informed (due care) as he does to avoid conflicts of interest (loyalty) and to act in good faith.

In its *Technicolor* decision of 1993, therefore, Delaware's Supreme Court essentially reasserted this pre-*Van Gorkom* position. In its words, it rejected any "bright-line rule for determining when a director's breach of duty of independence through self-interest translates into evidence sufficient to rebut the business judgment presumption accorded board action."[108] Justice Horsey also agreed with the way Chancellor Allen interpreted the Revlon decision in this light. *Revlon* places directors under a general obligation to be reasonably informed. It does not impose upon them a more specific obligation to sell their companies to the highest bidders.[109] Lawrence Cunningham and Charles Yablon note that the Delaware Supreme Court applied this new, more unified and abstract standard of fiduciary law in another 1993 case (in *In re Tri-Star Pictures*) and Chancery did so as well (in *Orban v. Field*).[110]

7. QVC (1993): Reaffirming *Revlon*? Overturning *Revlon*?

Four years after the *Time-Warner* decision, the collapse of the junk bond market, and a respite in hostile activity, Paramount Communications found itself back in Chancery in fall 1993. This time, ironically, it was arguing that the *Time-Warner* precedent permitted it to close out an unwelcome suitor as it proceeded with its own merger plans. The facts of the new case were that following early discussions in 1990, Martin Davis (chair and CEO of Paramount) and Sumner Redstone (chair, CEO, and controlling shareholder of Viacom Inc.) began in April 1993 negotiating a possible merger informally. During these discussions, Davis learns that Barry Diller (chair and CEO of QVC Network Inc.) is also interested in Paramount, and Davis informs him Paramount is not for sale.[111]

With negotiations completed, including financial advice from both sides (Smith Barney Shearson for Viacom, Lazard Freres & Co. for Paramount), Paramount's board approves a merger with Viacom on September 12. In essence, this transaction would transfer control of Paramount to Sumner Redstone because he was Viacom's controlling shareholder, with about 70 percent of voting shares. Redstone assures Davis he will be named CEO of the merged companies, and the agreement awards Paramount shareholders $69 per share in Viacom securities and cash. The closing market price of Paramount shares on that day, September 12, was $61, already inflated by reports of the impending deal.[112]

In addition, the merger agreement contains provisions designed to seal the deal. It requires the Paramount board to amend its poison pill plan in order to exempt the Viacom merger. The agreement also contains provisions designed to deter competing bids. For instance, Viacom would receive a termination fee of $100 million if Paramount backed out for any reason. Viacom also negotiates a stock option agreement that allows it to buy 20 percent of Paramount at $69 per share if Paramount backs out for any reason.[113]

Before approving the deal, the Paramount board reviews materials provided by management and Lazard Freres concerning valuation and terms, obtains a fairness opinion from Lazard Freres, and is advised by Paramount counsel on how to comply with its fiduciary duties in this situation.[114]

But eight days after the merger is publicly announced, QVC Network Inc. chairman Barry Diller declares that his company will offer Paramount shareholders a cash and stock deal worth $80 a share. It is common knowledge in the industry that Davis hates Diller, a former Paramount manager.[115] When Davis discusses the QVC offer with Paramount's board on September 27, he notes that the market value of the QVC offer exceeds that of Viacom by $18.35 per share as of the previous Friday. He also notes, however, that any deal with QVC would trigger the stock option and termination fee.[116]

The Paramount board nonetheless agrees to consider the QVC offer if QVC provides evidence that it has the financing to consummate the deal. QVC provides evidence and, as both companies line up financing, Paramount's board authorizes its management on October 5 to meet with QVC officials in order to hear what they have to say. This meeting is not held. A month of moves and countermoves follows. QVC files a lawsuit in Chancery to enjoin any contractual barriers to its offer.[117] The Paramount board, meanwhile, approves an amended deal by Viacom on October 24 based on financial advice from Lazard Freres and Booz-Allen & Hamilton on the current relative share values of Viacom and QVC stock for Paramount stockholders.[118]

QVC and Paramount officers finally meet for the first time on November 1. Five days later, the Paramount board accepts a new Viacom deal, offered unilaterally, that exceeds QVC's original offer by $5 a share. Undeterred, QVC raises its cash offer by $5 a share on November 12, the value now standing at $90 a share. Three days later, the Paramount board receives a document summarizing the QVC offer but dismisses it, saying it is "too uncertain" to be taken seriously and not in the best interests of the company.

QVC and a group of dissatisfied Paramount shareholders sue in Chancery to clear the way for it to approach Paramount shareholders directly with its bid. On November 24, Vice Chancellor Jack Jacobs does exactly this,[119] and on December 9 the Delaware Supreme Court supports his decision after hearing Paramount's appeal.[120] Called "the most dramatic case in recent Delaware history," the two-hour oral argument before Delaware's Supreme Court on December 3 was broadcast on *Court TV*.[121] Only hours later, the Court affirmed Jacobs' ruling; six days later it issued a written opinion; and two months after that Chief Justice Veasey released his formal opinion.[122]

Both Delaware courts were highly critical of the Paramount board for two reasons, and both seemed consistent with the earlier *Revlon* decision.[123] First, the Delaware courts pointed out that when the Paramount board failed to take QVC's followup offer seriously, it failed to bear its "fiduciary responsibility to thoroughly analyze the competing bid from QVC." Vice Chancellor Jacobs characterized the Paramount board's rejection of QVC's November 12 bid as "cursory." He insisted that the board had to treat all bidders in an even-handed fashion. "[M]eeting with QVC was the last thing management wanted to do and by skillful advocacy, management persuaded the board that no exploration was required. Those are not the actions of a board motivated to inform itself of all available material information."[124]

Second, the Delaware courts also held that Paramount's board had failed to appreciate that it had put the company into play at the moment it agreed to merge with a company that already had a controlling shareholder, Redstone. This triggered a *Revlon* auction because it gave Paramount shareholders the only opportunity they might ever have to obtain a control premium for their shares.[125] In turn, "the [Delaware Supreme Court] said Paramount had to seek the highest price it could obtain and had to actively consider bidders other than Viacom, its hand-picked partner."[126] However, Vice Chancellor Jacobs had been careful to point out, citing *Technicolor*, that a *Revlon* auction is simply one way Paramount directors had to fulfill their general fiduciary duty of care "to establish that their decision was adequately informed." His major problem with the board's behavior was that it had failed to inform itself adequately about the QVC offer before adopting defensive tactics.[127]

Davis and Redstone had argued all along that they were proposing a strategic merger, not a sale, and that this transaction was consistent with the one approved by Chancery in the *Time-Warner* case.[128] Vice Chancellor Jacobs countered, however, that the two cases differed in one important respect: Paramount ownership was moving from public shareholders to a single controlling shareholder at Viacom Inc. who could later decide to take the company private. As the Delaware Supreme Court later worded this issue: "[I]rrespective of the present board's vision of a long-term strategic alliance, once control passes to Redstone, he has the power to alter that vision."[129]

There is a problem, however, with Delaware courts drawing this distinction between the two mergers. In *Time-Warner*, Chancellor Allen had argued that *even a change of control does not in itself constitute a sufficient trigger for an auction.*[130] And the reason he said this was because a qualitative end was uppermost in his mind, namely preserving the putatively "distinctive and important" place that "Time culture" has in American society, not the quantitative outcome at the center of the *Revlon* decision.

Regardless, Vice Chancellor Jacobs removed Paramount's "poison pill" provision, in place since 1988, which committed Paramount management to flood the market with new stock whenever a raider appeared so as to make the company too expensive to buy.[131] He also removed other obstacles to the company's sale, including consolation payments to Viacom if it were outbid. Vice Chancellor Jacobs' reasoning was:

> The Paramount board is not permitting shareholders to choose between these two alternatives. Rather, by its selective deployment of the poison pill

and other anti-takeover structural devices to favor Viacom and disfavor QVC, the Paramount board would effectively force shareholders to tender into the lower-priced Viacom transaction. Under what fiduciary principle may the board do that? . . . [The circumstances here] implicate the fiduciary and fairness concerns that underlie and inform *Revlon*, *Unocal* and *Macmillan*.[132]

Many early commentators saw Jacobs returning to reasoning at the center of *Revlon*, thereby reducing board discretion in considering qualitative factors, including their entities' collective interests as long-term enterprises. "If someone can, by virtue of making a bid, create an auction, it will certainly take away a good deal of the discretion that boards thought they had."[133] But Cunningham and Yablon pointed out soon after these decisions by Delaware's Chancery and Supreme Court that Chief Justice Veasey rarely refers to *Revlon*. Instead, he emphasizes the importance of Delaware courts bringing "enhanced scrutiny" to any transactions that significantly affect corporate control, as opposed to shielding these transactions under business judgment rule protection.[134] Veasey defined "enhanced scrutiny" as an intermediate standard, and held that in these situations it embodied the intent of both the *Revlon* and the *Unocal* decisions.[135]

The weakness in Vice Chancellor Jacobs' wording is that it follows Easterbrook, Fischel, and other contractarians in attributing to boards a *fiduciary* obligation *to shareholders*, not simply a *contractual* obligation. Such a wording conveys that shareholders' private property is ultimately sovereign within corporate governance structures such that all qualitative considerations may legitimately be subordinated to a priced outcome. This wording moves Delaware courts away from considering explicitly any institutional consequences of how corporate boards conduct their affairs, whether when weighing competing bids or when deliberating over qualitative factors of any kind. It focuses attention more narrowly on whether corporate boards instrumentally facilitate maximizing behavior literally as an end-in-itself.

We will see in the remainder of this volume that the obligation of corporate boards and management teams to deliberate over qualitative factors in particular is a fiduciary obligation. It speaks directly to the institutional externalities of corporate governance and changes in corporate control in any democratic social order. By contrast, the obligation of corporate boards and management teams to maximize shareholder wealth, or to increase stakeholder representation, or to take into account any immediate externality of a particular transaction, are all strictly contractual obligations, not fiduciary obligations.

The strength of Vice Chancellor Jacobs' wording is it emphasizes that in the midst of a change in corporate control, shareholders enter a structured situation; they are not really operating any longer at a site of more fluid contracting, a nexus of contracts.[136] Rather, their property interests become more like stakeholders' positional interests, an analogy that Easterbrook and Fischel and other contractarians would oppose vehemently. Yet during a change in corporate control, shareholders nonetheless do enter a structured situation. They have little alternative other than ultimately to trust a management team's and a board's business judgment. The issue for the courts is how management teams and boards best exercise this discretion:

> For if it may be assumed that directors may, in certain instances, exercise a power to choose what premium the shareholders will receive in a change-of-control transaction, then those directors, as fiduciaries, must be deemed to have assumed the duty that accompanies the power.... That duty is to do for shareholders what the shareholders would otherwise do for themselves—to choose the best premium-conferring transaction that is available in the circumstances. Fairness requires no less. What is at risk here is the adequacy of the protection of the property interest of shareholders who are involuntarily being made dependent upon the directors to protect that interest.[137]

During a change in corporate control, Vice Chancellor Jacobs argued, "Directors must satisfy the court of the reasonableness of their actions before those actions will merit the protection of the business judgment rule."[138] To his credit, this wording moves Delaware courts away from trying to plumb corporations' "intrinsic value," a dubious notion that orients judges to treat corporations as if they are historical landmarks or endangered species. The question, of course, is how do corporate judges know when managers are acting reasonably—other than in terms of whether they maximize share price?

The importance of the *QVC* decision is that it establishes firmly an intermediate standard for analyzing whether directors breach their fiduciary duties, an "enhanced scrutiny" standard. This standard does not specify any particular action managers and directors must take, such as the once-believed *Revlon* duty to auction their companies. Rather, it requires managers and directors more generally to act in informed ways during takeovers as they seek what Delaware courts call "the best value reasonably available to the stockholders."[139] Thus, this standard is more flexible than that in *Revlon* but more stringent than that in *Time-Warner*. Cunningham and Yablon see it establishing a new "unified standard" in Delaware fiduciary law.[140]

PART II

Sources of Judicial Drift

6

Why Contractarians Fail to Explain Judicial Behavior

The conceptual fissures latent in corporate law doctrine meta-morphosed into full-blown doctrinal crisis beginning in 1985. We saw in Chapters 3 and 4 that contractarians' criticisms of existing doctrine have considerable merit. But we have just seen that Delaware courts nonetheless resist adopting an economic approach to corporate governance disputes outright. Why they resist is a mystery to contractarians, but how such norm-based judicial behavior affects corporate performance seems self-evident to them. They believe that qualitative analyses of corporate disputes lead to inconsistent rulings and this, in turn, only works to management's advantage and shareholders' disadvantage. Corporate officers already operate on their long-standing positional interest in entrenchment. When they see Delaware courts upholding defenses against hostile bids and less frequently requiring auctions, corporate officers will conclude that they are less likely to have their defensive actions reviewed and possibly rescinded by Delaware courts than their efforts to maximize shareholder wealth at stakeholders' expense.

Mark Loewenstein found in 1989 that up to that point the Delaware Supreme Court had never used the Unocal standard to declare a defensive action unreasonable in relation to any threat posed by a hostile bid.[1] Two years later, Easterbrook and Fischel were hardly more sanguine. Examining the substantive outcomes of Delaware court rulings up to 1991, they concluded that "our premier corporate court" is "muddling through."

> Muddling through . . . has the virtue of conserving judges' information costs. It also creates an odd set of incentives for managers. If they adopt shark repellent provisions and so scare away bidders, they face no risk of liability [as in *Unocal*]. If, however, they sell the firm, they may be mulcted in damages for getting "only" 50 percent over market rather than the higher price the court supposes they might have had [they cite the *Van Gorkom* case]. If they commit themselves firmly (beyond the possibility of

argument to a corporate plan), they may block bids that entail a change of plans [as in *Time-Warner*]; if they are flexible and seek out handsome opportunities for investors, they may be deemed to have put the firm on the block and will be compelled to raffle it off [as in *Revlon*]. Even dedicated managers, faced with such choices, may be expected to adopt devices that save their skins at some expense to investors.[2]

Delaware court behavior is a major source of contention and controversy not only among contractarians but across the corporate judiciary and bar as a whole. We offer our own explanation for it beginning in Chapter 10. For now, we summarize where the corporate judiciary stands today in light of the decisions we reviewed by presenting a typology of general doctrinal options currently available to American state courts.

- Courts can portray the publicly traded corporation as a market cluster, a power-neutral site of self-interested contracting. This nexus metaphor is incompatible with the fiduciary law tradition and any effort to impose mandatory rules on corporate officers. It leads either to shareholder contracting (in *Revlon*) or to stakeholder balancing (in the second *Unocal* requirement).
- Courts can portray the corporation as a long-term economic enterprise that, for whatever reason, merits judicial protection in a market for corporate control. We will see that this endangered species or national landmark metaphor (implied in the *Time-Warner* decision) retains some linkage to the fiduciary law tradition, but one that is untenable in a global economy.
- Courts can portray the corporation as a site of structured situations containing positions of trust and positions of dependence. This intermediary association metaphor (implied in all of the other decisions we reviewed) falls centrally within the fiduciary law tradition. Here courts endeavor to identify the structured situations that merit judicial monitoring while also trying to convince skeptics that norm-based interventions into private governance disputes uniquely serve some public law interest.

We pointed out earlier that contractarians define the terms of today's debate over corporations and law. They want judges to cease using fiduciary rhetoric when describing management's putative obligations to the corporation, its "artificial" or legally defined role as trustee of an entity. Instead contractarians want judges to transfer this rhetoric to management's obligations to maximize shareholder wealth, its "natural" or economically sounder role as agent of a principal.[3] But for whatever reason, Delaware courts cling to one or the other metaphor of the corporate entity. Before we begin explaining why, we prepare the way in this chapter by identifying specifically where and why contractarians fail to explain this norm-based judicial behavior. In the next chapter we do the same with judicial imposers.

There are two fundamental problems with the way contractarians in particular conceptualize corporate governance. One is that their economic concepts would expose courts to new doctrinal crises. The other problem, more important for our purposes, is contractarians acknowledge that their economic concepts fail to yield any reasoned or constructive rationale for Delaware court behavior in most major corporate governance cases.

I. Living with Doctrinal Crisis

Contractarians' alternative to corporate law and judicial practice is simple and straightforward: Courts should declare that *the* legitimate place and purpose of corporations in American society is to maximize shareholder wealth. By defining corporate purpose this narrowly, contractarians pose a clear, credible alternative to ongoing judicial practice. We just saw that Delaware courts continue to operate with some broader definition of corporate purpose. As long as they impose *any* social norms on corporate officers *as mandatory rules* of corporate governance, they operate on the basis of some traditional—that is, precontractual—approach to corporations and law. These courts' norm-based behavior also means that Delaware judges are less sanguine than contractarians about the externalities of a market for corporate control. They still operate with assumptions or ways of thinking about corporations that are, in one way or another, more consistent with republican vigilance than liberal complacency.

1. A Thought Experiment

One way of analyzing corporate law and judicial practice today, as well as any reform of them, is to take seriously each of the three elements of contractarians' version of liberal complacency: Maximizing private wealth automatically increases social wealth and supports institutional design. Rather than following contractarians and other complacent liberals in assuming as a matter of faith that both corollaries follow necessarily from the premise, like falling dominoes, we can treat each element as an independent variable of empirical study. Each offers social scientists a different standard by which to analyze corporate behavior in any modern society. Each also offers social scientists a different standard by which to analyze corporate law and judicial practice.

These empirical uses of liberal complacency come into view when we ask, in thought experiment, what would happen if the corporate judiciary adopted contractarians' proposed approach to corporate purpose without reservation? One obvious answer is that a contractarian court would find itself in doctrinal crisis whenever *successful* efforts to maximize shareholder wealth nonetheless failed, and failed unambiguously, to increase social wealth. Any clear failure here would in three ways reduce the capacity of a contractarian court to bring coherence to corporate law and consistency to judicial practice. First, judges would not be able in the face of this development to treat today's orthodoxy as a matter of faith. They would have to offer reasons—either empirical evidence or an explicitly articulated theory—for why the dominoes must fall, and very soon at that. Second, judges would also not be able to analyze corporate behavior, including governance disputes, exclusively on the basis of whether outcomes are Pareto optimal for shareholders. Because this quantitative standard favors shareholders over all other corporate constituents, its legitimacy in a context of declining social wealth would hardly seem self-evident. Its legitimacy would have to be defended with reasons.

Third, when maximizing shareholder wealth fails readily to increase social wealth, this would compel a contractarian court to account explicitly for at least some of the immediate externalities of corporate behavior—at least those that can be priced. Judges, presumably, would account for why social wealth is not increasing in terms of harms being done to other constituents, including local communities. Going further, were steady increases in shareholder wealth to fail to increase social wealth for an extended period of time, this might even compel a contractarian court to consider that certain changes in corporate governance or in corporate control can carry institutional externalities for the larger society. Ultimately, these economic developments might reveal harms being done to the institutional design of a democratic society in particular. Here a contractarian court would falter entirely. Its orthodoxy of liberal complacency and framework of economic concepts do not countenance the possibility that *institutional* externalities can attend increases in shareholder wealth.[4] The full effects of such externalities, after all, would invariably include qualities that elude pricing. Here is where a contractarian court could only muddle through, could only persist in substituting liberal complacency for methodical inquiry and analysis.

2. Implications of Our Thought Experiment

Our thought experiment brings into view a problem legal contractarians face at a conceptual level, one that they share with neoclassical economists. They cannot simply assert *a priori* or, as legal scholars put it, *ex ante* that in fact the interrelationship between shareholder wealth and social wealth is invariant.[5] Rather, this is self-evidently a variable. Any interrelationship in practice, whatever it is, requires explanation, and particularly when any gap between private wealth and social wealth persists or widens rather than rapidly closes. We can illustrate the problem contractarians face in this regard by considering just two of the many anomalies of the takeovers and buyouts of the 1980s and of restructurings today.

One anomaly is that these changes often simultaneously increase shareholder wealth and corporate debt. The latter, in turn, reduces the taxes corporations pay at local, state, and federal levels.[6] This is the case in part because interest payments on corporate debt are tax deductible whereas dividend payments on corporate stock are not.[7] As one example, RJR Nabisco's tax fell to $60 million in 1988, two years after KKR & Company acquired it in a leveraged buyout. In 1987, its tax had been $893 million.[8]

The other anomaly is related and more central to our concerns. Many corporate boards and top management teams in the 1980s responded to the new market for corporate control by borrowing heavily whenever they wished to finance growth projects or long-term plans. They no longer withheld dividends. Corporate lawyers then correctly predicted that bankruptcy law would become their new growth practice.[9] Our point is that it is hardly self-evident that corporate bankruptcies increase social wealth even when assets are moved elsewhere and eventually used relatively more efficiently. *Easterbrook and Fischel concede this.*[10] Having considered two specific ways in which maximizing shareholder wealth might not necessarily increase social wealth, and thereby establishing that this interrelationship is a variable, we can now turn to a broader, more sociological way of challenging liberal complacency.

II. "Cultural Change": Risk and Gambling

French sociologist Pierre Bourdieu proposes a principle that begins to speak to broader social issues surrounding today's debate over corporations and law. When struggles over power and status are "fought out within the dominant fraction of the dominant class, [they] are inseparable from conflicts of values which involve the participants' whole world views and arts of living."[11] With this principle in mind, we propose at least tentatively that a broad cultural change can attend sudden increases in private wealth. Change at a cultural level, in turn, can just as well obstruct or dampen, rather than facilitate or encourage, the overall wealth of nations. The relationship here too is a variable. Being a qualitative effect either way, the relationship between cultural change and social wealth eludes economic concepts regardless. It eludes economic concepts even when the qualitative effect of cultural change is widespread, spanning not only elite and upper-middle-class constituents of American corporations but also members of the same class and status groups working in American hospitals, universities, and other major sites of professional practice.

1. Management's Situation Today

The first place to look for empirical evidence of cultural change affecting elite and upper-middle-class Americans, of course, is in the everyday lives of *top* managers. Corporate managers today operate within an environment of uncertainty that is now structured or institutionalized, no longer passing. This environment of uncertainty stands in sharp contrast to the world in which they lived before the oil embargo and recession of 1973, then the hostile activity of the 1980s, and now today's corporate restructurings and intensifying global competition. Notwithstanding how contractarians interpret the rulings of Delaware courts, top managers today endeavor ceaselessly to assure institutional investors and other informed "market watchers" that they are minimizing agency costs (thereby preempting potential raids and buyouts).[12]

This means that top managers today live with a dual threat looming over their positions and careers that did not affect their world before 1983, and was literally unimaginable before 1973.[13] On the one hand, they live with the threat of a change in corporate control or, at the very least, the threat of closer scrutiny of their performance by institutional investors, both of which can jeopardize their positions and careers. On the other, they also live with the threat of bankruptcy or, at the very least, the threat of closer scrutiny of their performance by investment bankers, both of which can also jeopardize their positions and careers.[14]

In short, corporate officers cannot avoid making a fundamental business decision that only first preoccupied them, and rather suddenly, at the onset of the market for corporate control: whether to finance corporate growth by retaining earnings or by borrowing. What is new is that irrespective of the choice they make, the decision cannot remove or ameliorate the additional uncertainty with which they operate regardless. On the one hand, if they finance growth by borrowing, they increase the possibility of bankruptcy, and then of (a) losing their positions and (b) possibly being held personally liable for errors of judgment.[15] On the other, if they retain earnings, or in other ways fail to maximize share price, they increase the possibility of converting once passive institutional investors into active owners. They also risk encouraging takeovers or buyouts, and thereby converting individual investors too into active owners. Since nearly half of all *top* managers are dismissed within three years of any takeover or buyout, hostile *or friendly*, this decision also places their positions and careers into jeopardy.[16] Even short of a change in corporate control, institutional investors may publicly criticize financing schemes that they believe fail to minimize costs and maximize profits. Any such public criticism, in turn, simultaneously encourages others to scrutinize management's behavior.[17]

Corporate officers who might prefer personally to return to their earlier, more risk-averse mode of governing corporations, when they were more sovereign and could routinely finance growth by retaining earnings, appreciate that this door has been closed to them. The environmental pressures they face today are now firmly institutionalized. Their world is one of a steady, secular escalation and accumulation of uncertainties and risks. Seeing this, Charles Calomiris and Carlos Ramirez call for changes in U.S. legislation so that "universal banks" may form, and thereby bring greater predictability to the relationship between corporations and financial intermediaries, and also bring greater expertise to oversight of corporate governance.[18]

2. A Typology of Elite Risk

Uncertainty is a quality of the conditions in which individuals operate in their everyday lives. Thus, it can increase or decrease considerably in the course of anyone's business career. Risk, in turn, refers to how individuals respond to these conditions, and particularly as everyday uncertainties escalate and accumulate.[19] Are they willing to put their own wealth or careers into greater jeopardy? Are they willing to put the corporations that they manage or the intermediary associations that they administer into greater jeopardy?

In exploring the overall "cultural impact" of the hostile activity of the 1980s and then restructurings today, it is not necessary to string together wrenching vignettes about how these changes, and threats of change, disrupt the lives of everyday people. It is sufficient to consider how a market for corporate control forever altered the everyday lives even of prominent Americans.[20] By the time the wave of hostile activity crested, in 1989, it increased considerably the uncertainties with which elite and upper-middle-class Americans live every day. As a result, it altered how they think about taking risks with their careers, inherited wealth, and family legacies.

Even Americans who inherit great wealth or hold the loftiest corporate positions are now more willing to take risks than at any time since the 1920s. Indeed, we may distinguish three types of risks they take: First, they take *personal and positional risks* when they *purposefully* place their careers or livelihoods into greater jeopardy than their counterparts did in the 1970s. Second, they take *corporate risks* when they *purposefully* place their corporations' futures into greater jeopardy than their counterparts did in the 1970s. Third, and most important, they take *institutional risks* when their exercises of private power in structured situations *inadvertently* enervate institutional arrangements unique to democratic social orders.[21]

3. The Social Psychology and Culture of Elites

In today's business environment, corporate managers find themselves in a structured situation in which they are allowed little alternative other than to take greater personal and positional risks than their counterparts did in the 1970s. Indeed, the narrow margins within which they sometimes operate and compete push them at times to outright gambling.[22] Put differently, the positional interest top management once had in risk-averse behavior has been overlaid in the past 15 years by a new positional interest. Top management has developed a positional interest in more risk-accepting, often risk-seeking, behavior. As a result, top managers routinely put their corporations, positions, and careers at greater risk today than their counterparts ever entertained in the 1970s when they surveyed the "active options" before them. This is the case because there is no strategy of long-term corporate growth—other than fulsome leveraging—that is likely to reduce scrutiny from one quarter or another, whether from institutional investors, creditors, or today's raiders. Since the option of developing, then acting with consistency on, a longer-term plan is no longer available to most top management teams as an "active option," top managers are driven by default to seek shorter-term, manifestly *visible* results, that is, results that are readily priced. This is why Calvin Morrill reports that corporate managers today evince an attitude of "nihilism," not one of "loyalty."[23]

Here, then, we find a specific link between changes in corporate governance, the social psychology of managers, and broader cultural changes affecting elites and the upper middle class more generally. Ongoing, impersonal structural changes altering the management *position* are consolidated at both social psychological and cultural levels as younger managers interact with each other and with other elites and as new managers are recruited into these positions. These structural changes are consolidated at a social psychological level by a secular change in corporate officers' subjective willingness to take risks with their positions, careers, and corporations. They are also consolidated at a broader, cultural level by a secular change in the orientation of elites and the upper middle class toward risk-taking, toward putting their careers, statuses, and family legacies on the line.

Research and theory in the sociology of the family is controversial today because, at least in part, the family clearly seems to be less valued as an institution even by the upper class and middle class.[24] We propose that the controversy stems in large part from the fact that it is difficult for sociologists to grasp this larger, cultural trend by looking directly at family research. We propose that sociologists stand back from the fact that only one-quarter of American households contain two adults and at least one child. They should explore more methodically how the upper class and middle class take greater risks across a whole range of personal and positional resources, the family being only one set of such resources among many others.[25]

When corporate officers today seek immediate, priced results, they are doing more than endeavoring to increase their positional power within corporate governance structures. They are endeavoring to reassure themselves subjectively—social psychologically—about their own status and personal worth, both within and outside the company. "[S]mall win strategies often manifest themselves as [their only opportunity for] 'managerial free agency.'"[26] Moreover, because the management position is now exposed structurally to greater threats of bankruptcy, more intrusive monitoring, and the possibility of hostile transactions, individual managers are less reluctant personally to extend uncertainty to other employees, including retirees. Whenever their companies become financially "troubled," they "trim costs where they can." Thus, "benefits of all types for all employees, past and present, have become fair game."[27]

Still, it is one thing for sociologist Calvin Morrill and other ethnographers to document that individual managers often hunker down to "small win strategies." It is also consistent in this light for Barbara Noble and Milt Freudenheim of the *New York Times* and other journalists to report that retirees face new uncertainties.[28] Going further, we may fairly propose in the same light that today's uncertainties extend from corporate governance structures as an institution to the family as an institution. Indeed, John Coffee and other legal scholars go even further, proposing that corporate officers are prone to gambling.[29]

How has management's earlier positional interest in risk-averse behavior evolved not simply toward accepting risk but toward being willing at times to gamble? We first provide some basis for believing that there is some connection between risk and gambling, and then we answer this question directly.

Daniel Kahneman and Amos Tversky demonstrate through experiments that when any individual's performance meets or exceeds his expectations for success, his aspiration level, he prefers risk-avoiding strategies. But when the same individual's performance falls below this level, he is then willing to gamble in an effort to return as quickly as possible to the level of success he finds subjectively acceptable.[30] One implication of this experimental finding carries an irony for contractarians' faith that the relationship between private wealth and social wealth is invariant. Even as shareholders' greater preference for risk *successfully* transformed the internal governance of corporations, as contractarians wished, we cannot assume with them that this necessarily reduced corporate agency costs overall. Rather, these changes in corporate governance may have increased agency costs, and considerably so, because so many individual managers now gamble at times to meet loftier aspiration levels. Thus, we cannot assume as a matter of faith that corporate officers' efforts to maximize shareholder wealth necessarily increase social wealth. Whether they have or not is an open, empirical question, the answer to which will likely vary from economic sector to economic sector and also likely vary over time within each sector.

What is clear is that as management finds itself operating within conditions of greater uncertainty, we can predict that individual managers will respond to this social psychologically by becoming more "available" to take risks as aspiration levels rise to new levels for all managers. This may account for the "nihilism" that Morrill observes. In the first place, more top managers today may fear subjectively that their performance will be found wanting by investors (and their analysts) than possibly at any time since the Depression.[31] In the second place, these same individuals are not necessarily yet personally comfortable with the new conditions that have been imposed upon them by ongoing structural changes in the economy and in corporate governance. They are not necessarily yet as personally comfortable as many investors may be with risking their own positions and careers to meet today's aspiration levels. Rather, many may experience today's uncertainties social psychologically as a burden from which their condition allows no escape—other than to exit or to gamble everything at times.[32]

When corporations leverage or take on debt when they either divest divisions or acquire new ones, *investors* become more willing to take additional risks. They, too, develop a new positional interest. In turn, *creditors* react in precisely the ways Oliver Williamson and other transaction cost economists predicted they would under these conditions: They demand either higher interest rates for their loans or, more typically, seek greater protections from default in the event of a bankruptcy or takeover.[33] Thus, creditors, too, develop a new positional interest—which, in turn, directly reduces the security of retirees' pension funds.

It is safe to say that when top management extends its condition of escalating and accumulating uncertainties to other corporate constituents, the positional conflicts that result reverberate across the social order—as waves of immediate externalities.[34] At the very least, such intracorporate jostling for advantage and protection suggests that a larger secular social change may well be under way. After all, *if* there has been a secular decline in managerial and employee loyalty and, thus, in the motivation and creativity these constituents contribute to corporate team activities, then this increases agency costs. This reduces social wealth. Our point is that we cannot assert or assume that a condition of escalating and accumulating uncertainties somehow increases social wealth automatically. This, too, is an open, empirical question, and again the answer will likely vary across sectors and over time.

What Coffee found in the mid-1980s is that the aspiration levels of each major corporate constituent had already risen.[35] The result today is not some social psychological fad or intermittent panic. Rather, the result is a corporate governance function being performed by managers who react personally and positionally to new conditions of uncertainty. They react personally by becoming "available" social psychologically to take risks. They react positionally by becoming willing to extend uncertainty to other constituents. And all of this—the structural changes and the reactions to them—is firmly institutionalized by ongoing domestic deregulation and global competition.[36]

With this as a backdrop, we can now consider some evidence that many corporate financial managers in particular are moving from strategies that are risk-accepting to others that amount to outright gambling. Indeed, corporate finance gambling is itself now institutionalized in its own markets, its own industries. As one example, Floyd Norris reported in 1992 in the *New York Times* that commercial banks and other financial institutions are swapping interest payments (as well as swapping currencies).[37] For example:

> In a simple swap, one party agrees to pay the other's fixed-rate payments on, say, a $100 million loan—the "notional principal amount" . . . —while the other agrees to pay variable rates. . . . If one party defaults, the other resumes making its own interest payments or buys a new swap to replace the old one. The maximum loss is the cost of the new swap.

Norris goes on to discuss the implications of this new market, and of its new trade association, the International Swap Dealers Association (my emphasis is added):

> Used properly, the risk of an interest-rate swap for a bank is not very different from the risk of making a loan. . . . But swaps and other financial innovations *can also be used to place huge bets on the markets.* And [E. Gerald] Corrigan [the president of the New York Federal Reserve Bank] seems to be worried that those bets may be made, and lost, before top management, or regulators, realize what is going on. . . . "[S]ome of the specific purposes for which swaps are now being used may be quite at odds with an appropriately conservative view of the purpose of a swap, thereby introducing new elements of risk or distortion into the marketplace." Is he right to worry? That's the problem with how secret this market has been. For outsiders, there is no way to be sure.

In 1990 all swaps outstanding totaled over $2 trillion.[38] The swap market in interest rates alone was nearly $800 billion in 1991, up from around $200 billion in 1988. Announcements by Proctor & Gamble as well as Paine Webber Group in the mid-1990s illustrate well how such gambles can affect a corporation's bottom line, and thus managers' positions and careers.[39] In

April 1994, Proctor & Gamble took "a one-time pretax charge of $157 million to close out some derivative positions—two interest rate 'swap' contracts it had made in the United States and Germany." The company disclosed this loss only because it was "material," it reduced company profits or assets by 5 percent or more. Losses from "derivative trades" that do not reach or exceed this percentage may legally be hidden.[40] In July 1994, Paine Webber Group spent $180 million "to bail out a mutual fund battered by its holdings of the highly technical and often risky Wall Street securities called derivatives."

> The rescue effort comes on top of $88 million already spent by the big brokerage firm to reimburse investors burned by what was advertised as a safe and secure mutual fund. The bailout, at $268 million, may be the largest ever in the rapidly growing mutual fund industry. It is the latest and sharpest example of the way Wall Street wizardry can go wrong—and how such problems can hurt ordinary Americans. It also raises fears about what would happen if such a fiasco occurred at a firm that could not afford to cover investors' losses. The money from the bailout announced yesterday will not go directly to investors. It is intended to shore up the value of the fund in an effort to stem its losses.[41]

III. What the Debate over Corporations and Law Is Ultimately About

Economists are as uncertain today as legal scholars were during the 1980s about whether a market for corporate control actually increased social wealth in the 1980s, and whether it is likely to do so today. Journalist George Anders anticipated this a decade ago: "[A]s thousands of companies were tugged through buyouts in the 1980s, economists periodically tried to assess the net gain or loss to society at the end of it all. . . . No sweeping answers emerged; none is likely to. Merely deciding what amounts to corporate 'success' or 'failure,' the economists quickly discovered, is a surprisingly slippery task."[42] Economists define corporate wealth as (a) a firm's immediate profit and return to shareholder equity, or (b) a firm's expected net present value of likely future profit, or (c) a firm's market value generally.[43] But as Marshall Meyer puts the matter, "[organization] performance is either a moving target, the parameters of which always change, or a fixed target, the parameters of which are known only partially."[44]

Still, as contractarian Daniel Fischel correctly insisted early in the decade, anyone who offers illustrations of how maximizing private wealth purportedly jeopardizes social wealth must do more than this.[45] The critic must do at least two things: First, the critic must demonstrate that economic or legal reform is both desirable and practicable. Second, the critic must demonstrate that the reform, whatever it is, actually requires some change in existing corporate law, in current judicial practice, and in ongoing corporate governance.

Fischel also correctly points out what is not involved in today's debate, namely a clash between competing ideals of unbridled laissez-faire and omniscient regulation.[46] Still, how Fischel phrases what is involved is significant. He says that what is needed is a sustained, methodical inquiry into *the implications* of different, practicable *institutional arrangements*. What Fischel means by this is that the respective flaws and uncertainties that attend any proposed institutional arrangement must be kept fully in view. Presumably this means that neither contractarians nor traditionalists legitimately bracket such flaws and uncertainties from their concerns at the outset, at a conceptual level.

Finally, Fischel is surely correct that today's debate between contractarians and traditionalists is not simply an academic exercise. Rather, it weighs heavily on the thinking and decisions of Delaware judges as well as on the actions taken by state legislatures, state and federal agencies, Congress, and the Supreme Court. And this debate is distinct in one key respect from how sociologists and political scientists typically study corporations and other complex organizations.[47] Unlike most social scientists, even legal contractarians find that they cannot characterize the relationship between private wealth and social wealth without addressing in one way or another the *direction* of change of the larger society, including changes in institutional arrangements spanning the state and civil society.[48] Unlike Fischel's candor in the passage above, however, most legal contractarians typically keep the issue of corporate purpose at arm's length and, by extension, the issue of whether changes in corporate governance carry any possible institutional externalities. In turn, judicial imposers and stakeholder balancers also fail to offer judges a suitable conceptual framework with which to address this empirical but decidedly normative or qualitative issue methodically.

7

Why Imposers Fail to Explain
Judicial Behavior

Having identified some general limitations in legal contractarianism, we can now consider some problems legal traditionalists face. Proponents of judicial imposing defend corporate law's core of mandatory rules. But limitations in the ways they approach corporations and law come into view when we pose a sociological issue: What if judicial deference to management under the business judgment rule, coupled with continuing judicial enforcement of management's duty of loyalty and other mandatory rules, not only permit management to pursue goals other than maximizing shareholder wealth? What if this also permits management to exercise positional power in one-sided ways in corporate governance structures? More specifically, what if management does not simply endeavor to entrench itself and thereby reduce the uncertainties it faces? What if management, to this end, exercises positional power in ways that enervate the institutional design of a democratic society?

We will see in this chapter that the few occasions when imposers address this sociological issue, they treat it as one of corporate purpose, of identifying specifically the legitimate place and purpose of corporations in American civil society. And here is where they falter. They fail to draw the analytical distinctions they need (a) to defend existing mandatory rules even in part, and therefore (b) to address the issue of corporate purpose methodically, with specificity.[1] This dual failure explains why most traditionalists today advocate shareholder balancing, no longer judicial imposing. They substitute balancing and today's orthodoxy of liberal complacency for methodical inquiry into corporate purpose and therefore for any direct defense of mandatory rules consistent with the fiduciary law tradition and republican vigilance.

To recall, where contractarians see the corporation as a power-neutral site of contracting, imposers see it as a battleground of positional conflicts. Imposers fear that if courts cease requiring corporate officers, including controlling shareholders, to exercise positional power in relatively disinterested ways, then "traditional norms" that disciplined directors within boardrooms in the 1970s will wither away naturally under today's global economic competition. What do they have in mind? When sociologists and other social scientists study corporate boards, they typically concentrate on the class backgrounds and current political, economic, and social affiliations of individual directors, particularly outside directors.[2] They also call attention to interlocking directorates and corporate lobbying of Congress.[3] They say surprisingly little about how corporate boards, and then top management teams, actually conduct their affairs as a distinct institution, as part of a governance structure.[4]

Michael Useem's ethnography and Jay Lorsch's questionnaire-based study are the most important exceptions in the sociological literature, but partial exceptions at best.[5] Each sociologist moves briefly and tentatively from the backgrounds and affiliations of individual directors to the positional interests that separate inside directors, who are members of the management team, and outside directors, who manage other corporations or are otherwise employed independently of management. They also find that certain *institutionalized norms* mediate how all directors conduct themselves within boardrooms. Michael Useem finds, for instance, that directors consider it "an egregious impropriety if they used one board position to promote another company's interests."[6] Useem ends this promising line of inquiry, however, without addressing two issues central to it: First, how, if at all, do norms institutionalized within or around boardrooms affect a corporation's governance structure? Second, how, if at all, do state courts support these norms that caught Useem's attention? Jay Lorsch, in turn, finds that directors "don't see themselves as pawns of management," yet operate within constraints that "include their own available time and knowledge, a lack of consensus about their goals, and the superior power of management, particularly the CEO-chairman."[7]

Judicial imposers appreciate that directors and management teams are far more capable of abusing their positional power than Useem and Lorsch report. After all, they are familiar with the *Macmillan* case and hundreds of others like it in which directors and CEOs conducted themselves in questionable ways. This is why they believe that when contractarians propose that corporate officers be permitted to opt out of mandatory rules of corporate governance with formal shareholder approval, contractarians bear a burden, namely to answer at least three questions:

1. What is the compelling economic or legal rationale for replacing all mandatory rules with suppletory and enabling rules?
2. Why increase the vulnerability of corporations (and then the larger society) to positional conflicts, to entrenched intracorporate power struggles?
3. Most important, can contractarians really assume *a priori* that rules of corporate governance that shareholder majorities formally approve will carry only benign consequences for the larger social order?

These questions, and particularly the third, expose a major gap in contractarian concepts: These legal scholars are free to use the contract as their basic unit of analysis, if they wish. But this conceptual decision does not permit them, or anyone else, to assume anything about how changes in corporate governance will or will not affect the larger social order. It certainly does not permit them without argument to substitute liberal complacency here for a two-century long tradition of republican vigilance.[8]

Imposers operate with a similar blind spot at a conceptual level, however. They are free to defend existing mandatory rules, if they wish. But this decision does not permit them to assert, or assume, that basic institutional arrangements will necessarily be harmed if most mandatory rules are replaced by contracts, by suppletory and enabling rules.[9] Traditionalist Ernest Weinrib is blunt in pointing to the source of this weakness: "The vagaries of judicial determination of these difficult problems [of corporate purpose] is in large measure the result of the failure to develop reliable conceptual instruments."[10] The collective failure of judicial imposers is that they lack concepts with which to defend existing mandatory rules directly. The concepts they need are those that reveal unambiguously the public law interest that these rules uniquely serve.[11] Karl Kaysen is both blunt and accurate when saying "ideas about the public good and desirable society are fuzzy" in both legal scholarship and social science.[12]

In Chapters 10–13, we draw analytical distinctions designed to replace "fuzziness" here with rigor, with a way of identifying institutional design that contractors, balancers, and imposers can recognize in common. These concepts preserve a linkage to the fiduciary law tradition and, more important, they open a way to accounting for Delaware courts' norm-based behavior in resolving corporate governance disputes. With this, we demonstrate that there really is a third doctrinal alternative available to the corporate judiciary today—other than shareholder contracting and stakeholder balancing. This doctrinal alternative not only accounts for recent rulings by Delaware courts but also yields predictions regarding what these courts are likely to do in the future—even as we cannot predict how the American economy will change in coming decades.

I. Eisenberg v. McChesney: The Issues Joined

The two most respected defenders of mandatory rules are Melvin Eisenberg and Victor Brudney. For his part, Eisenberg debated the future of mandatory rules with contractarian economist Fred McChesney in a 1989 *Columbia Law Review* symposium devoted to opting out, an issue we explore in Chapter 9.[13] Should management be permitted, with shareholder approval, to opt out of mandatory rules at incorporation, and then possibly later, "at midstream," by amending corporate charters? That this debate was acrimonious is not surprising. That the debaters essentially talked past each other, with each too readily shifting the burden of proof to the other rather than first responding directly and positively, is more surprising, and disappointing. It is also revealing. It reveals the shaky conceptual foundation upon which legal traditionalism in particular stands today, and why, in turn, even Delaware courts at times in the 1980s drifted by conceptual default toward a nexus of contracts approach (particularly in the *Revlon* decision). It also reveals why stakeholder balancing, not judicial imposing, is today's most influential alternative to shareholder contracting (see Chapter 8).

For his part, Eisenberg informs McChesney that courts still enforce a core of mandatory rules, a fact that no one denies but contractarians cannot really explain.[14] Since McChesney and other contractrarians propose replacing mandatory rules with either suppletory or enabling rules, Eisenberg correctly notes that this position is more a "normative" prescription than a neutral description of existing law and current judicial practice. He calls on McChesney to pursue two lines of analysis in light of this. First, he wants him to identify the mandatory rules that he would replace. Second, he wants McChesney to demonstrate that these changes will indeed maximize shareholder wealth, increase social wealth by improving corporate performance, and otherwise not harm American society.[15]

Instead of responding directly, McChesney turns the tables on Eisenberg, in effect saying: You provide me with some standard or "guidance" by which I might determine whether any rules of governance currently imposed on corporate officers should remain mandatory. Only with this, McChesney continues, can we together identify the true limits of corporate law's existing core.[16] And McChesney's point is well taken. Simply acknowledging that certain rules of corporate governance remain mandatory fails to demonstrate that their current scope of application is irreducible, nonnegotiable. Why not assume the opposite, that their current scope can be reduced, possibly dramatically, without jeopardizing orderly relations of economic and social exchange within and around corporate America?[17]

Eisenberg, in turn, never proposes a standard by which to analyze the scope of existing mandatory rules.[18] But, then, he had little reason to approach the general issue of opting out in this way. He had only two choices, actually, and neither worked to his advantage. One choice was to assert an absolutist defense of all mandatory rules. The problem here is that contractarians had already so influenced the corporate judiciary, and a market for corporate control had already so disrupted traditional practices of corporate governance, that this tack was too extreme to appeal any longer even to judges still inclined to support legal tradition in principle.[19] Eisenberg's only other choice, however, was to take up McChesney's challenge, to identify in one way or another which mandatory rules are vital (in any sense) and which are either overextended in scope or negotiable. The reason Eisenberg had little to gain in doing this, however, is that whatever conceptual basis or qualitative standard of analysis he proposed in drawing this distinction, contractarians could use it against him and other judicial imposers. They could use it to show that judicial applications of public law norms and fiduciary duties often fail to meet this standard, whatever it is.[20] Again, consider Easterbrook and Fischel's point that Delaware courts "muddle through" rather than operate in any consistent way.

Eisenberg ended up ignoring McChesney's inquiry. With this, however, he failed to establish that narrowing the current scope of existing mandatory rules will somehow invariably harm publicly traded corporations in the United States, let alone harm other intermediary associations and the larger social order.[21] Many legal scholars otherwise inclined to resist the Contractarian Challenge to corporate law tradition nonetheless argue persuasively that courts have been overextending fiduciary duties for years.[22] The courts treat many more principal-agent arrangements today as if they are fiduciary relationships than they did in earlier decades.[23]

Eisenberg's only "response" to McChesney's inquiry is one we can reconstruct for him, using his article "The Structure of Corporation Law." This article preceded the Eisenberg-McChesney exchange in the symposium on opting out, and McChesney's comments were in part responses to it. This

60-page article may be the single most impressive defense of corporate law tradition in the literature. For this reason, McChesney took every opportunity to push Eisenberg as hard as he could as he responded to this article because, if he could get Eisenberg to concede any major points to contractarians, other traditionalists would see this and surely follow. In this article Eisenberg acknowledges that the legitimacy of corporate America as an economic institution rests most generally on three *normative* beliefs widely shared across American public opinion.[24] One American belief is that because shareholders are a corporation's owners and, regardless, are bearers of residual risk, they should ultimately determine corporate policy. Another is that corporate management is adequately monitored and restrained by self-regulating markets. The third American belief is that the most optimal way to govern any corporation is for a board of directors, elected by shareholders, to appoint a top management team that, in turn, takes responsibility for daily operations.

The problem Eisenberg faced in responding to McChesney, in light of the way he characterized American beliefs in his article, is obvious: None of the three "shared norms" just noted is consistent with judicial imposers' defenses of existing mandatory rules or, for that matter, with their harsh criticisms of a nexus of contracts approach.[25] To the contrary, all three "shared norms" are consistent with basic principles of neoclassical economics.[26] Thus, Eisenberg failed even before his debate with McChesney began to identify any social norms that self-evidently support legal traditionalism, judicial imposing. In short, legal traditionalists need a framework of concepts that (a) identifies the social norms explicitly or implicitly informing the behavior of Delaware courts and, of equal importance, that (b) establishes why these social norms, and the rules of corporate governance presumably reflecting and supporting them, are nonnegotiable.

II. Can Self-Regulating Markets Restrain Management?

Traditionalists defend mandatory rules because, ultimately, they do not believe self-regulating markets restrain *management* sufficiently from abusing its positional power within corporate governance structures.[27] Victor Brudney accounts as clearly for this "market failure" as any legal traditionalist ever has. He does so by proposing that a contractarian approach to corporations and law boils down to a quite cynical line of reasoning regarding how markets putatively restrain management (a line of reasoning Easterbrook and Fischel indeed pursued six years later).[28] When dispersed investors "contract" with a board and management team to exercise business judgment on their behalf, as their agent, they implicitly grant them countless opportunities to shirk, self-deal, and otherwise abuse their power as agents. Investors grant corporate officers these opportunities, however, only up to that point at which these agents' excesses come to the attention of capital markets. When this happens, institutional investors in particular realize that agents' abuses of power leave investors with only two alternatives, namely (a) to sell their shares, at a price that by this time may have fallen substantially, or (b) to monitor management more actively, as owners.[29]

Brudney's point, again, is to trace fully the practical implications of contractarians' critique of mandatory rules. Constrained only by markets and investor incentives, corporate officers who are not somewhat prudent, who do not act somewhat discreetly as they advance their own positional interests, run the risk of converting passive investors into active owners, into bosses. Once the situation degenerates this far, investors are likely to demand considerably greater accountability from corporate officers, including a more transparent governance structure.[30] Indeed, they may go further, replacing these corporate officers with more obedient, disciplined agents.

But this "cynical" line of reasoning does not end here. Once investors replace the board and management team, the new corporate officers may in time endeavor to "buy back" some of the discretion owners had seized from their predecessors. They accomplish this by being sufficiently disciplined and discreet over time that this eventually lulls owners, who begin to feel that they may safely return to their much preferred role, namely that of passive shareholders.[31] With this, owners regain the discretionary time that any principal seeks in the first place when hiring an agent to work in its interests.

Having surveyed the logical implications of substituting market discipline for mandatory rules, Brudney concludes that what effectively restrains any board and management team from excessively one-sided behavior, by contractarians' account, is, ultimately, a game of chicken—not a legislature's or a court's "paternalistic" protections.[32] The point of his allegory, like Eisenberg's point when replying to McChesney, is that thinking about the internal governance of corporations in this way stretches the meaning of "contract" beyond recognition. A game of chicken between management and investors does not speak even to the immediate externalities of corporate governance, to how stakeholders might be harmed as management acts excessively and investors eventually react. Thus, Brudney, like Eisenberg, believes he broadens the debate over corporations and law sufficiently to present a credible defense of mandatory rules by bringing these externalities more explicitly into view. He asks: How might directors, managers, and controlling shareholders alike be restrained from needlessly harming stakeholders?

The problem, however, is that this question does not lead logically to a defense of corporate law's core of mandatory rules. It leads logically only to legislative or judicial support for stakeholder balancing. With such legislative or judicial action, courts would then accede to whatever balanced outcomes or rules of governance emerge from group competition for power and influence within each corporation. In its own way, this process replaces republican vigilance with pluralist drift, a variation of today's orthodoxy of liberal complacency consistent with contractarians' general critique of mandatory rules.

Like Eisenberg, therefore, Brudney fails to identify any larger social consequences of corporate governance that lead logically to a direct defense of existing mandatory rules. He fails to identify explicitly any institutional externalities of corporate governance or changes in corporate control. Two questions, however, *begin* to bring this into view: First, how is the game of chicken between management and investors likely to affect the way positional power is exercised within corporate governance structures and other structured situations in American civil society? Second, how are these exercises of positional power likely to affect the expectations of elites, the upper middle class, and the larger American public?[33] James Boyd White at least alludes to the type of conceptual framework Eisenberg, Brudney, and other traditionalists must have in mind when they warn judges about the "excesses" of shareholder contracting in the absence of mandatory rules and consistent judicial enforcement of them.

III. Corporate Social Responsibility Today

1. Corporate Sharks, Corporate Citizens

James Boyd White is a legal scholar influenced by the corporate social responsibility movement of the 1960s who opens his defense of mandatory rules provocatively by saying he is certain of one thing. Corporate law and the judges who enforce it in traditional ways do not *reduce* the issue of corporate purpose to whether management maximizes either shareholder wealth or corporate growth.[34] White elaborates this point by also asking us to engage in a thought experiment: What would it mean if law and judicial practice actually did this? It would mean, he contends, that courts treat "the corporation as a kind of shark that lives off the community."[35]

Given that Delaware courts and the entire fiduciary law tradition do not treat corporations as sharks, White proposes we identify at least somewhat more accurately how they in fact do think about the place and purpose of corporations in American society. A first step in this direction is to appreciate that corporate law continues to revolve around an entity metaphor, not a nexus metaphor. In itself this means corporate law and courts do not treat the corporation as an inculpable market cluster but rather treat it as a "collective citizen," an unusually powerful person in civil society who, accordingly, is to be held legally responsible for its behavior. Part of corporate purpose, therefore, involves law and judges seeing to it that most actions taken by these powerful persons are, at the very least, broadly comparable to most actions taken by other, less powerful persons in civil society. We expect law and judges to see to it that the behavior of most people most of the time broadly supports, not purposefully or inadvertently undermines or weakens, institutions and organizations in civil society that "make meaningful economic and social activity possible."

White concludes his thought experiment with a rather vague phrase, to be sure, but his general way of thinking about corporations and law differs fundamentally from that of contractarians.[36] Judges (and the public) reasonably expect all people in American society, including the most powerful, to conform broadly to certain *social norms* even as they otherwise act in aggressive ways in self-regulating markets. For example, we expect everyone, including corporate entities, to obey the social norms codified in basic criminal law and basic civil law. We expect even the most self-interested among us to be sufficiently self-disciplining that their behavior does not needlessly disrupt "meaningful economic and social activity" as such.[37]

2. Substantive Norms and Procedural Norms

For all of its promise as a point of departure in revealing the social norms within which corporations and courts operate today, a fundamental problem nonetheless runs through White's account, beyond the vagueness of the phrase we noted above. His shark/citizen dichotomy, while suggestive, moves his discussion too far conceptually, too quickly. It moves his discussion from a seemingly enforceable standard of improper corporate conduct (the shark that disrupts meaningful economic and social activity) to a vague, decidedly unenforceable, standard of proper corporate conduct (the responsible citizen). Yet both standards are equally unenforceable. The corporate judiciary cannot use White's first qualitative standard *directly* to prohibit profitable or growing corporations from acting like disruptive sharks (for instance, by moving headquarters or operations to different locations). It certainly cannot use White's second qualitative standard *directly* to compel unprofitable or declining corporations to act like responsible citizens. The corporate judiciary cannot rely primarily on either of these standards because both are *substantive normative standards* of proper and improper corporate conduct. Our thesis is that it is inherently difficult—ultimately impossible—for different courts to enforce such standards with consistency across cases and over time in modern societies.

Aside from enforcing basic criminal law and civil law as mandatory rules, courts have difficulty enforcing substantive norms of corporate governance with consistency *as mandatory rules* when an economy is dynamic rather than static, and a society is culturally heterogeneous rather than homogeneous. This is precisely why so much of American corporate law doctrine has given way over the decades to contract law, enabling rules. American courts had difficulty enforcing substantive norms of corporate governance even in the 1830s, during the transition from a yeoman economy to a commercial society. And they came up against the same problem again, from the 1970s to the 1980s, during the transition from owner passivity to shareholder activism. In both cases, the corporate judiciary faced the problem that, say, the family judiciary would face if it tried, either in the 1830s or 1980s, to enforce table manners, another substantive normative standard of behavior. Would different courts, hearing different cases, at different times and places, really enforce this standard in similar ways across families? Or would judicial enforcement vary so much that this would call into question the legitimacy of such law, and of the courts themselves?

For the same reasons that the family judiciary cannot enforce table manners with consistency, the corporate judiciary cannot *directly* apply either of *White's* two qualitative standards of analysis to corporate governance disputes with consistency. Rather, *at best*, it can apply these standards *indirectly*, by first applying and remaining *always* oriented primarily by some different standard. One such standard is the *quantitative* analysis contractarians champion, namely determining first whether a disputed corporate transaction maximizes either share price or market share. *As* the corporate judiciary analyzes and resolves governance disputes by first deciding this, it can then also try to instruct corporate officers regarding substantive norms of corporate citizenship, if it wishes. Another standard the corporate judiciary can enforce directly in consistent ways is qualitative. But this standard brings a *procedural normative analysis* to corporate governance disputes, namely whether corporate officers exhibit fidelity to certain procedures as they exercise their business judgment. *As* the corporate judiciary first analyzes and resolves governance disputes in this way, it can then also try to instruct corporate officers regarding substantive norms of corporate citizenship, if it wishes.

We present the kind of qualitative analysis we have in mind in Chapters 11 and 12. Our point now is simply to assert that the *social norms* within which corporations and courts operate today are more procedural mediations of corporate governance than direct, substantive limitations of corporate performance. By contrast, White's two qualitative standards wrongly convey that the opposite is the case, or that it can possibly be again. We conclude this chapter by exploring two reasons why the corporate judiciary cannot enforce substantive norms directly, including White's two qualitative standards.

A. ELITE SOCIALIZATION

In the first place, courts can enforce substantive norms directly with consistency only when these norms are already widely shared, when most individuals have already internalized these standards of conduct as their own personal beliefs. This often happens with the substantive norms contained in basic criminal law and civil law.[38] The problem is that few other substantive norms are shared as widely, and certainly not table manners—or how corporate officers are to conduct themselves within governance structures. Only beliefs that individuals internalize during primary socialization are truly substantive norms for them, quite literally the personal beliefs by which they conduct their everyday affairs.[39] But, aside from basic criminal law and civil law, these beliefs are just that—personal. They are matters of personal taste, personal cultivation. Every person's substantive normative beliefs are his or her most basic sense of what conduct is normal or acceptable, moral or laudable, in certain situations. We cannot assume that these beliefs are generally shared across any occupational group, including corporate officers.

Our point is that corporate officers (and other American elites) were raised and socialized in different ways, not similar ways.[40] As one example of how diverse their socialization experiences have been, the alumni of elite preparatory schools (who themselves are hardly socialized similarly) account for no more than 10 percent of the members of corporate boards of directors.[41] This percentage shrinks considerably when this base figure is brought to the total membership of top management teams. This means it is safer for us to assume that corporate officers have internalized different substantive norms as personal beliefs than to assume the opposite. It also means that corporate officers are more likely to value different qualities in their own lives and in social life generally than the same qualities.[42]

With this in mind, we can identify two very different bases of solidarity in any group (occupational, residential, or voluntary), whether comprised exclusively of elites or spanning other economic categories of people. Groups exhibit solidarity when their members share material or positional interests. Or, alternatively, groups exhibit solidarity when their members share personal beliefs.[43] The first basis of group solidarity is common in corporate America and elsewhere in economic and social life. Corporate officers often act in common when (a) they seek outcomes whose value for anyone in their position can be priced (or otherwise measured), and when (b) they can act strictly instrumentally or in market-mimicking ways to maximize these priced outcomes. Group solidarity here hinges on whether members indeed act in ways that markets conclude are efficient, and each member can analyze team success independently by monitoring priced outcomes all along the way. Because all ends-in-view are priced or otherwise measurable, members can also analyze independently whether their team's activities are becoming more efficient over time. This remains possible even when members otherwise hold heterogeneous personal beliefs about any and all qualities that elude pricing. Any market society fairly abounds with groups that operate primarily in this way, and corporate divisions and subdivisions are hardly exceptional here.

By contrast, the second basis of group solidarity, members sharing personal beliefs, revolves around a quite different combination of ends and means. Here members seek outcomes whose value for anyone in their position includes qualities that, as such, elude pricing (and any other ready measurement). In addition, members cannot maximize these outcomes by simply acting instrumentally. Rather, their first task is simply to keep the qualities they value in *collective* view. Since pricing and markets cannot help them here, they develop symbols, rituals, and norms of behavior that signal to themselves, to anyone in their position, that they are indeed working together, acting toward the same end. In these kinds of situations, members have to construct, then constantly maintain, their own shared understandings of (a) what the qualities are that they value, and (b) how best to coordinate their collective efforts to attain (or preserve) these qualities over time. Such concerted behavior, such group solidarity, may often be habitual or ritualistic, but it is always norm-based, never strictly instrumental.

Our point is that any group whose members are attaining or preserving qualities that anyone in their position would value is by definition not acting in strictly economic or market-mimicking ways. By definition, they are not employing the most efficient means to maximize priced outcomes, which is what market-mimicking behavior ultimately entails. Rather, the group and its members are exhibiting fidelity to symbols, rituals, and norms that keep valued qualities in collective view.

Examples of valued qualities that individuals in general only attain or preserve through norm-based behavior, never instrumental behavior alone, include: personal cultivation, raising children "properly," and developing a friendship. One cannot become cultivated or develop "taste" simply by acting instrumentally, say by purchasing certain pieces of art or music selections in certain styles.[44] One cannot raise children "properly" in strictly instrumental ways, say by keeping them regimented in day care and schools. Presumably, one cannot cultivate friendships in strictly instrumental ways, say by offering acquaintances material inducements alone. More relevant for our purposes, an example of a valued quality that corporate officers can only attain or preserve through norm-based behavior is that of maintaining "*meaningful* economic and social activity." Whatever this phrase means, White's thought experiment aptly reveals that such activity cannot be kept in collective view simply by maximizing shareholder wealth or corporate growth.

B. RECOGNIZING QUALITIES IN COMMON

This leads us to the second reason why courts cannot enforce substantive norms of behavior directly with consistency—rather than indirectly, by primarily applying quantitative standards of analysis or else by primarily enforcing fidelity to procedures. It is safe to assume that corporate officers typically experience great difficulty establishing and maintaining a shared or interpersonal understanding of those qualities that anyone in their position would have a stake in attaining or preserving (let alone establishing and maintaining a shared understanding about how best to accomplish this). It is sociologically unsound to assume the opposite. The governance disputes that we reviewed in Chapter 5 bear this out. More generally, even members of the same economic class, and even members of the same status group, typically fail to maintain such an understanding among themselves.[45] Sociologists' descriptions of the personal beliefs of elites and the upper middle class in France and the United States bear this out.[46]

Robert Bellah and Michele Lamont demonstrate independently that personal beliefs are hardly commensurable, or settled, even within this very narrow category of people. Other sociologists find that elites experience extraordinary difficulty simply transferring to their own children a shared understanding of the qualities putatively valued by anyone in their position. Peter Cookson and Caroline Persell find, for instance, that elites rely on a "total institution" to instill such a world view, a boarding school, and even with this the results are notoriously uneven.[47]

More generally, French social theorist Pierre Bourdieu reminds us that personal beliefs regarding matters of taste and cultivation are not "a gift of nature," something any class or status group can take for granted. Rather, they are "a product of upbringing and education" within what Bourdieu calls a "habitus," a distinct location in time and space.[48] Precisely because he appreciates that "taste" and "cultivation" are "imponderable[s] of practice," Bourdieu insists their acquisition is always local, always a product of intense, concentrated effort. Elites in Normandy are hardly likely to share the understanding of valued qualities with which elites in Paris operate (unevenly among themselves); and elites in Indianapolis are hardly likely to do so with elites in New York. Add to regional differences other factors that differentiate elites even at the same geographic locations and we find heterogeneity stemming from ascribed factors and from what sociologists call functional differentiation. The ascribed heterogeneity of an economic elite stems from its members' differences in religion, ethnicity, gender, region, and general family background. The functional differentiation of an economic elite stems from the different career trajectory members typically experience within and across occupational fields, such as banking, manufacturing, high technology, foreign trade, retail commerce, entertainment, and the arts.[49] Members of the "same" economic elite perform different tasks at different times in their careers in different "fields." Their expectations in their careers and their outlooks about life generally therefore differ accordingly, including the qualities that *anyone* in *their* position values. This is why Bourdieu sees cultivation being tied to some particular "habitus," to some particular "system of dispositions."[50]

We can illustrate our point about elite heterogeneity with another thought experiment. Consider what would happen if we gathered 100 elite or upper-middle-class parents from different regions of the same country and asked each of them to state what they believe is the best or preferred way to raise their own children. It is very possible that we might hear 50, 70, or even 100 different answers. Any parent's view of how best to raise his or her own child is very much a lived matter, a matter of substantive belief. The same result is likely, of course, if we asked 100 elite or upper-middle-class residents to identify the qualities they believe mark a "desirable" neighborhood, "gourmet" cuisine, or "high culture" in music or art.

For that matter, consider the following description of efforts taken by university presidents to define "academic freedom" in substantive terms at the height of the McCarthy era in the United States—*when they shared a positional interest*, when consensus here really mattered *to anyone in their position*:

> On February 15, 1953, twenty-five presidents of America's most prestigious universities met in New York City and attempted to define academic freedom. . . . The minutes of the meeting reveal that the presidents dealt mainly with the practical problems of Communist professors and congressional investigations. But they also recognized the need for a general statement on the nature of academic freedom, something that would, as one president put it, "induce feelings of confidence and respect in the minds of thoughtful people." But the more these men discussed the matter, the more elusive it became. Each president, it seemed, had his own definition. One claimed that academic freedom "was broader and more inclusive than civil rights." Another insisted that it should "offer no more freedom than the Constitution." And a third considered it only "a special shield under which a professor could speak within his field." Significantly, the final product of these deliberations, issued at the end of March, was not a definition of academic freedom but a response to the issues raised by congressional investigations and Communist Party members. It mentioned academic freedom only in passing, and then only in quotation marks, as the necessary—but undefined—prerequisite for what the [Association of American Universities] called intellectual "free enterprise."[51]

If heterogeneity marks the substantive beliefs of university presidents regarding academic freedom, and those of elite or upper-middle-class residents regarding art, imagine how much more heterogeneity we will find among individuals in the same occupation coming from different class, ethnic, religious, and regional backgrounds. This is why sociologist Anselm Strauss insists that each and every instance of orderly behavior in social life is a product of "negotiation."[52] For Strauss, this remains true irrespective of whether we find a particular "negotiated order" at the level of a small group (including a family) or at the level of a large organization or institution (including a corporation, or a division). This is also why sociologists Ralph Turner and Lewis Killian insist that "emergent [substantive] norms" can be found not only within every group but also at sites of the most fleeting interactions, including demonstrations, panics, and even milling crowds.[53] Emergent norms are just that: temporary, spontaneous, not permanent, settled.

3. White's Norms and Commitment to a Way of Life

With these sociological findings in mind, we can return to White's way of characterizing corporate purpose and mandatory rules. His entire argument in favor of mandatory rules rests on the ability of judges to apply two different substantive normative standards of analysis simultaneously to the behavior of corporate officers, and to do so in consistent ways across courts and across cases. First, judges must apply in consistent ways to corporate officers a qualitative standard of proper behavior that is directly substantive normative, like good table manners. One court-enforced substantive norm today is Delaware courts' "belief that the market price of a firm's stock is not (necessarily) its 'real' or 'intrinsic' value" and therefore that corporate officers can be held responsible for identifying their firms' "real value."[54] Considered in light of our earlier discussion, Easterbrook and Fischel's objection to holding corporate officers to such a standard of conduct in disputed corporate transactions is well taken:

> Current law on takeovers . . . reflects a devotion to intrinsic value that has as much empirical support as the proposition that hurricanes are caused by witches. *Even if there were an intrinsic value, the courts could not identify it*—could not, in other words, separate managers who are right that the price is too low from managers who just believe that the price is too low. Judicial inability to separate one from the other, to identify the "best" strategy to maximize investors' wealth, is a fundamental premise of the business judgment rule.[55]

All *substantive* norms of corporate governance are like this notion of "intrinsic value." They compel courts to draw fine distinctions when analyzing corporate officers' behavior and this cannot be done with consistency across cases and across courts.

Second, judges must do more than hold corporate officers to substantive norms in consistent ways if they are to enforce mandatory rules in the way that White envisions. Judges must also establish and then maintain among themselves a shared understanding of the "meaningful economic and social activity" that merits protection in a market for corporate control. This marks another, even grander, qualitative standard of corporate conduct that is directly substantive normative. After all, White is assuming that judges can identify in common when a particular corporation (or division) is acting in substance like a disruptive shark and when it is acting in substance like a responsible citizen—*independently of all quantitative standards of analysis.* If judges were to rely primarily on quantitative standards to guide them here, this would render White's distinction between corporate sharks and corporate citizens irrelevant, strictly rhetorical. The issue of corporate purpose could in principle be left to product markets and capital markets, independently of the corporate judiciary and its mandatory rules.

White is assuming judges can establish, and then operate broadly within, a literal consensus regarding which particular ways of life in American communities, or in corporate cultures, merit judicial protection in a market for corporate control. *He is assuming this because there is no other reason to define corporate purpose directly in terms of a substantive normative standard of proper and improper corporate conduct.* Yet we have seen the dilemma that judges faced historically whenever they tried to enforce such standards over time. After all, behavior by corporate owners that was considered sharklike in a yeoman republic became generally acceptable, indeed institutionalized, in a commercial society. In turn, behavior by shareholders that was considered sharklike in the 1970s became generally acceptable, indeed institutionalized, by the late 1980s and early 1990s.

Yet White is assuming judges today can do better, can identify in common whether and when future changes in corporate governance and corporate control either broaden or narrow that set of "meaningful activities" to which they must hold corporate officers through mandatory rules. At the very least, judges must agree that the qualities of life (the substantive norms) they are maintaining by enforcing mandatory rules in corporate governance disputes are more important to the larger society than corporate officers' market-mimicking behavior, than increasing either market share or corporate growth.[56] But White himself is reluctant to identify what this way of life is, what these qualities are. His phrase "meaningful economic and social activity" is the best he can do, and this can hardly orient judges toward consistent rulings across particular cases. Any effort by him or anyone else to identify directly in substance the "activity" he has in mind is more likely to reveal the identifier's own prejudices than to bring into view any overarching consensus, any truly institutionalized set of substantive norms of corporate conduct. Worse, any effort taken by judges to attain or maintain "meaningful economic and social activity" by imposing substantive norms of behavior on corporate officers directly as mandatory rules transforms corporate law. Such judicial activism transforms corporate law from a regime of enforceable social duties into a regime of unenforceable social aspirations.[57]

At most, therefore, White demonstrates that contractarians' quantitative standard of corporate governance cannot account for the scope of corporate law norms or for the scope of judicial interventions into corporate governance disputes. But this is a fact not in dispute. What is in dispute is how best to account for the corporate judiciary's *norm-based* behavior, the *qualitative* standards of analysis that it brings to governance disputes. The way in which White accounts for this fact does not directly refute or challenge contractarians' thesis that existing mandatory rules are anachronistic in today's deregulated domestic economy and increasingly competitive global economy. Rather, White's account confirms this thesis.

However, a limitation in any contractarian approach to corporate purpose comes into view once we bring a threshold of *procedural* norms to White's effort to identify disruptive corporate sharks (but not otherwise to identify responsible corporate citizens). This same step also begins to move us beyond the conceptual limitations we identified earlier in Eisenberg's and Brudney's traditionalism. In Chapter 11 we explore the second basis of group solidarity. We draw a distinction within the relationship between (a) qualities whose value eludes pricing for anyone in a corporate officer position and (b) the symbols, rituals, and social norms that can keep such qualities in collective view. We show that otherwise heterogeneous corporate officers can exhibit behavioral fidelity to procedural norms, even as their personal beliefs and positional interests otherwise differ. Similarly, otherwise heterogeneous judges can enforce such behavior with consistency across cases and over time.

8

Legislative Action
Stakeholder Balancing and Its Limits

Contractarians convert the sociological issue of corporate purpose into a narrower economic issue—how to maximize investor wealth. This removes from view many immediate externalities of corporate governance, namely, harms done to stakeholders that elude pricing. It also removes from view all institutional externalities, harms done to institutional design. Imposers employ more traditional legal concepts yet fare little better in addressing this sociological issue.

Unlike contractarians, imposers are preoccupied with defining corporate purpose more broadly and with drawing attention to how changes in corporate control can "disfigure" or otherwise harm "society." They fail, however, to *identify* institutional externalities of corporate governance. They fail to establish any specific connection between corporate governance and institutional design and, because of this, they then have difficulty accounting for why Delaware courts continue to enforce mandatory rules. Appreciating that this failure weakens considerably the case for mandatory rules of corporate governance, many "traditionalists" now dedicate themselves to what they acknowledge is a second-best option: They explore how to decrease the immediate harms changes in corporate control cause to stakeholders. Thus, most traditionalists today are self-labeled "communitarians" or "progressives," that is, champions of stakeholder balancing. They no longer endeavor to defend directly the courts' fiduciary law tradition.[1] However, stakeholder balancing complicates the other responsibility of the corporate judiciary, identifying *the* agent legally responsible for what a corporation does, and it fails to bring greater clarity to the issue of corporate purpose.

One purpose of this chapter is to describe the rise and steady institutionalization of stakeholder balancing since the mid-1980s. A second purpose is to begin to clarify the issues of corporate agency and corporate purpose. Still, we must do more than clarify these two issues if we are to account for the norm-based behavior of Delaware courts and then predict what these courts are likely to do in coming decades. Our sociological concepts need to bring into view doctrinal options that are: practicable in today's global economy, legally enforceable, consistent with Delaware court behavior as an institution,[2] and consistent with existing social norms and public opinion. If our concepts fail to point to such options, legal scholars will rightly question whether we are offering a more accurate description and explanation of Delaware court behavior.

I. Again, the Issue of Corporate Agency

1. Agency and Agency Relationship

We may appreciate how difficult it is for judges at times to identify *the* corporate agent by first considering why treating the corporation as a nexus, a power-neutral, formless market cluster, is often more appealing than treating it as an entity with collective interests of "its own." As any public choice theorist would anticipate, judges often have difficulty answering the following question in consistent ways: In which respects, if any, is the corporate "entity" itself an actor?[3] That is, in which respects does this legal "person" (a) make decisions in "its" own "collective interests" (in any sense) and, as a result, (b) bear legal responsibility for "its own" behavior? Whenever a judge agrees with public choice theorists that this way of thinking is anthropomorphic,[4] the judge assigns corporate agency (and legal responsibility) to some identifiable position within the corporation.[5] A judge holds particular corporate positions—directors, managers, controlling shareholders—legally responsible for what a corporation does (as opposed to holding the individuals in these positions personally liable for what a corporation does). The judge attributes legal responsibility to an identifiable corporate agent.

But why would a judge assign legal responsibility in this way? And why do judges often disagree about who the agent of a particular corporate action is? When judges face the issue of corporate agency directly, they come up against a conceptual dilemma. We may appreciate it by comparing how sociologist Anthony Giddens defines *agency* to how economists Michael Jensen and William Meckling define *agency relationship*. Giddens defines agency as the "capability of doing things."[6] Persons are able to do things, of course, and criminal court and civil court judges often hold convicted persons responsible for their own behavior. For Jensen and Meckling, however, an agency relationship is "*a contract* under which one or more persons (the principal) engage another person (the agent) to perform some service on their behalf."[7] The parties to a contract contribute to a joint enterprise or team activity that, in turn, can do things—through an agent.

Precisely because the corporation is such a complex team activity, however, the law has always treated it as a rather peculiar "entity" or rather peculiar "agency relationship." Thousands of individuals, hundreds of groups, scores of distinct divisions and subsidiaries contribute capital, intermediate products, labor, and managerial skills to it.[8] Rather than the values of these contributions being self-evidently comparable, or readily priced, their values differ enormously and often elude pricing in some part. Employees, for instance, vary considerably in their motivation, managers in their dedication, and long-term suppliers in their quality control; all may vary even more in the creativity they typically bring to team activities. This means that constituent "stakes" in team success (however defined) can differ enormously.

Going further, consider what happens even after judges decide that, for whatever reason, a corporation is too complex a team activity for them to keep agency (and legal responsibility) unified. Judges then make two other decisions, and each is just as political or normative as the one they just made. First, they identify, or try to delimit, the positions that potentially can be held legally responsible for a corporation's behavior, as its agents. In effect, they decide which positions exercise sufficient control over a corporation's concentrated wealth and collective power to be able to get things done in its name.

Second, judges also identify, or again try to delimit, the types of legal claims that may be made against the corporate entity, or its agents, as it and they go about their legitimate business activities. Are judges to hold a corporate entity or its agents broadly responsible for serving some greater good, which legal scholars call a public law interest? Or are they instead to encourage the entity and its agents to maximize either growth or share price? Or, alternatively, are judges to hold the entity and its agents responsible for protecting, if not maximizing the values of, the "stakes" that nonshareholder constituents have developed in the corporation's success (again, however defined)?

Unlike most investors, but much like top and middle management, all stakeholders have a positional interest in increasing their relative power and influence in corporate decision making.[9] Stakeholders have a positional interest, that is, in increasing their share of control over a corporation's concentrated wealth and collective power to that point where *they* are able to get things done in its name.[10] Their ceaseless competition for positional power is structurally induced, much like that between the presidency and Congress or that between political parties. Indeed, this explains why the corporate judiciary does not grant stakeholders standing to bring legal claims against managers and directors in the name of the corporate entity for putative breaches of fiduciary duty, whereas it grants standing to the poorest shareholder. Stakeholders are more likely than shareholders to use standing as a weapon, to threaten to bring derivative suits as a means of extracting governance concessions from management.[11]

Regardless, those stakeholders who gain sufficient control over corporate wealth and power to be able to get things done in its name are available, at least in principle, to be treated by courts as corporate agents. This way of thinking about corporate agency begins to reveal the conceptual dilemma judges face today:

- When does a judge declare that an entity itself is a "person," with interests of "its own," who thereby bears legal responsibility for "its own" behavior?
- When does a judge declare that one constituent—whether a board, a top management team, a middle management team at a division, a controlling shareholder, *or an outside bidder*—is *the* corporate agent, who thereby bears legal (not personal) responsibility for a corporation's behavior?
- When does a judge declare that corporate officers either may or must take into account the stakes of non-shareholder constituents—of at least some identifiable set of stakeholders—before they legitimately act as *the* corporate agent?
- When does a judge acknowledge that a corporation is such a complex team activity or "instrumentality" that he or she cannot keep corporate agency unified in any of the ways above? When does a judge *divide* corporate agency (and legal responsibility) and therefore acknowledge that corporate decision making is more pluralistic or multilateral than unilateral (management-dominated) or bilateral (shareholder-driven)?[12]

2. Why Corporate Agency Is So Elusive

It is not possible for judges to escape the conceptual dilemma we just presented. This is not possible because neither the unity nor divisibility of corporate agency (and legal responsibility) is a quality intrinsic to the corporation as such. The corporation, after all, was not present with the persons who populated Hobbes' or Locke's allegorical state of nature.[13] Only "natural persons" are bearers of precontractual, thereby inalienable, rights in Anglo-American legal and political tradition. Lacking rights "by nature," American judges did not recognize a corporation's "right" to accumulate capital without limit until 1875. They did not acknowledge a corporation's "right" of free speech for another century. In short, the American corporate judiciary has always been reluctant to take seriously any organic, European view of corporate bodies that elevates the legal standing of a team—including a family—over the "natural rights" of its members, let alone of a team's "owners."[14]

Going further, it is also not possible for American judges to escape the conceptual dilemma above by settling the issue of corporate agency on strictly economic grounds, independently of the legal and political tradition just noted. This is not a possibility because the priced outcomes of self-regulating markets do not demonstrate unambiguously that any one type of agency relationship, or governance structure, is superior economically.[15] Contractarians appreciate this, and yet try to simplify matters by reducing the analysis of agency relationships and governance structures to a single issue, namely whether one reduces agency costs more than another:

> [T]here is no right relation among managers, investors, and other corporate constituents. The relation must be worked out one firm at a time. A change in technology . . . will be reflected in changes in the operation or governance of corporations. To understand corporate law you must understand how the balance of advantage among devices for controlling agency costs differs across firms and shifts from time to time. The role of corporate law at any instant is to establish rights among participants in the venture. Who governs? For whose benefit? Without answering difficult questions about the effectiveness of different devices for controlling agency costs, one cannot determine the appropriate allocation of rights.[16]

The empirical problem contractarians face when they propose reducing judges' conceptual dilemma to an economic, quantitative analysis of agency costs is that this adequately accounts only for a quite limited range of Delaware court decisions in major corporate governance disputes. The disputes for which it accounts are those in which judges are certain that an agent's behavior did not carry any externalities whatsoever, whether for stakeholders or for the larger social order. When courts are uncertain about this, contractarians' narrow standard of analysis—minimizing agency costs—fails to account for judicial behavior either historically or today.

In short, whether judges divide corporate agency (and legal responsibility) or instead keep it unified is a quintessentially political—and normative—decision. In turn, how they conceptualize the corporation itself, whether as entity or nexus, whether as intermediary association or commercial enterprise, whether as long-term enterprise or fly-by-night operation, whether as citizen or shark, *hinges on how they interpret social norms of the day and the direction of social change.* After all, corporate law doctrine in the United States, as in any other country, is ultimately a product of judges' ongoing efforts to keep corporate power broadly aligned with social expectations (which, of course, change over time). Legal scholar George Dent captures the implications of this well: "Even apart from the different costs of capital, comparisons between American and Japanese corporations are hazardous because of the tremendous cultural differences between the two countries."[17]

3. Corporate Agency Today: An Overview

We showed in Chapters 3 and 4 that conceptual fissures latent in corporate law doctrine began bubbling to the surface in the mid-1970s. At first, judges saw corporate law's untenable mix of concepts no longer helping them to address in consistent ways the issue of corporate purpose. If a corporation's legitimate place and purpose in American society is not *solely* to maximize its owners' wealth or "its own" growth, then what other specific, legal responsibilities do we expect it to bear (other than not to violate basic criminal law and civil law)? Many judges in the 1970s still had residual concerns about the possible institutional externalities of corporate power. On the one hand, they were still imposing traditional fiduciary duties on management, that is, duties of "equitable conduct" or "disinterested behavior." But on the other hand, they were having difficulty identifying the public law interest this serves. Again, they failed to identify any specific connection between corporate governance and institutional design. Thus, the more important trend of the mid-1970s was that judges were increasingly deferring to management, under business judgment rule protection, to address the issues of both agency and purpose, as management saw fit. They deferred to management's interpretations of each corporate person's collective interests and, by default of any clear legal restrictions, of corporations' legitimate place and purpose in American society more generally.

By the end of 1983, however, everything began getting more complicated. Raiders and buyout specialists began challenging management's position as *the* corporate agent. They began offering competing interpretations of the corporate person's collective interests, one that indeed narrowed the issue of corporate purpose to that of maximizing share price in capital markets. In this context, traditional corporate law concepts no longer helped judges to address in consistent ways even the issue of corporate agency, let alone the thornier issue of corporate purpose. Is *the* corporate agent a target management team, or a hostile bidder? And should either "agent" be encouraged or compelled by law to protect the stakes of non-shareholder constituents? Conceptual fissures once latent in corporate law tradition now blossomed into full-blown doctrinal crises.[18] Who ultimately controls a corporation's assets, positions, and collective power? How may they control them? In whose interests may they exercise control? How may they pass control to successors?[19]

Today's judicial inconsistency does not end with these questions. We may add two other complicating factors to the mix. First, judges and legal scholars operate more broadly today than in the past within the orthodoxy of liberal complacency. Thus, they are generally less concerned now than they were from the mid-1970s to the early 1980s about whether changes in corporate control and changes in judicial behavior might carry institutional externalities or potentially harm the larger society. Second, the corporate judiciary as an institution nonetheless operates uneasily within this orthodoxy. As an institution, it is less certain today than it was before the mid-1970s about how generally to characterize American social norms, the direction of change of American society in today's global economy and, therefore, corporations' ultimate legal responsibilities in this society.

> Surely part of the explanation for the definition of corporation doctrine and its central place in business law generally lies, not in practical vocational concerns, but rather in ideological ones. This doctrine and this arrangement express tacitly a vision of the social order that holds sway over legal and business elites.[20]

Will Delaware courts in particular learn to operate more comfortably within today's orthodoxy by acting more explicitly on the assumption that social change in the United States is inherently benign? Or, given the turbulence of the 1980s, today's restructurings, and whatever competitive pressures corporate America experiences in coming decades, will Delaware courts endeavor in some way to update their own fiduciary law tradition?

Will Delaware judges acknowledge explicitly that the institutional design of a democratic society in a global economy is never self-regulating or autopoietic, that changes in corporate governance can have institutional consequences? Will they acknowledge explicitly that they perform what social theorist Talcott Parsons called a pattern maintenance function for American society?

II. Dividing Corporate Agency

1. Three Crises of Authority and Legitimacy

The new market for corporate control suddenly heightened shareholder expectations, turning once passive investors into active owners (prompted by raiders and buyout specialists). Shareholder acquisitiveness in turn initiated at least three dramatic changes in the rules of the game in corporate America.[21]

First, shareholder acquisitiveness challenges the authority and legitimacy of management's business judgment. The 30–50 percent yields that shareholders received from raids and buyouts were a startling shot across management's bow. Today, shareholders have every reason to believe that even management teams that seem on the surface to govern disinterestedly often make decisions in their own positional interests, at shareholders' expense.[22] The management compensation packages we reported at the end of Chapter 2 are not definitive evidence that something is wrong, but they hardly support an assumption that managers act disinterestedly, or that they are somehow inherently self-disciplining. Second, shareholder acquisitiveness weakens the authority and legitimacy of the corporate judiciary and corporate law doctrine. The same returns on raids and buyouts revealed that many agency costs failed to come to the attention of state courts in the absence of a market for corporate control.[23] Shareholders today have every reason to believe that judicial enforcement of management's fiduciary duties of care and loyalty to the corporate entity—rather than to the entity's owners—fail adequately to restrain management from advancing its own positional interests. Finally, shareholder acquisitiveness weakens the authority and legitimacy of corporate governance structures as an institution. Shareholders today have every reason to believe that if they wish to protect their investments, they had better find new ways to monitor corporate decision making.[24]

2. From Neoclassical Economics to Contracting and Balancing

Increasing challenges to management, corporate law doctrine, and corporate governance structures altered the corporate judiciary in three interrelated ways. First, and ironically, it weakened in judges' eyes the explanatory power of neoclassical economics. Fundamental tenets of neoclassical economics held that product markets, capital markets, and labor markets generally orient management to maximize profits even in the absence of a market for corporate control.[25] Second, evidence that markets had earlier failed shareholders led many judges to attribute a certain *moral* quality to shareholder acquisitiveness. Shareholder efforts to maximize their return in the new market for corporate control seemed a measured response to management's entrenchment and one-sidedness. It seemed to improve corporate governance and, more grandly, to serve a public law interest of sorts. Indeed, many judges believed that shareholder acquisitiveness in the new market for corporate control could potentially resolve the two crises of corporate law doctrine for them. After all, courts could now treat shareholder majorities as *the* corporate agent, at least during changes in corporate control. They could also declare, at these times, that *the* corporate purpose is indeed to maximize share price.[26] Third, courts became receptive to doing more than simply permitting shareholder majorities to challenge management by accepting hostile bids, and thereby essentially opting out of management's putative fiduciary duties to the corporate entity. They became receptive to increasing stakeholder representation in corporate decision making and, therefore, to dividing corporate agency. We saw this in the Delaware Supreme Court's *Unocal* decision.

Looking at each change in turn, institutional investors in particular no longer accepted economists' earlier treatment of corporate governance as an insignificant "black box." They no longer assumed that self-regulating markets otherwise adequately protect their interests. As a result, they no longer believed it is more rational for them to enjoy the discretionary time of passive investing than to dedicate at least some additional time to more active ownership. Institutional investors now saw the internal governance of corporations as a battleground, a *structured* situation in which they had to be willing at times to engage management and stakeholders alike in trench warfare.[27] Aside from being designed to diminish the everyday conflicts of interest of any team activity, corporate governance structures are also designed to contain one-sided exercises of positional power and, therefore, positional conflicts unique to the management-corporation. Institutional investors now appreciated that in the absence of a robust market for corporate control, and aggressive raiders and buyout specialists driving this market, management much prefers to finance growth or acquisitions by retaining dividends (thereby harming shareholders). It prefers not to do so by borrowing (thereby transferring uncertainty and risk to bondholders and management itself).

The revelations of the new market for corporate control came at a time when management's performance was already being widely questioned. The global competitiveness of American corporations was declining, a troubling trend that began in 1973 with the OPEC oil embargo and subsequent energy crisis. In the midst of social turmoil in the aftermath of Vietnam, an alarming surge in inflation, less predictable exchanges rates (the United States had just abandoned the gold standard), and freer international trade, Americans learned that their automobile industry was bloated, incapable of reacting effectively to global competitors. The American electronics industry was nearly pushed to extinction, and the American steel industry was reeling. Even IBM was having problems.[28]

In this context of general, widespread disillusionment with management performance, judges had little reason to defer any longer to its business judgment. They had no reason to operate on the assumption that management's interpretations of a corporation's collective interests were any more disinterested, or far-sighted, than alternative interpretations being offered to shareholders by hostile bidders. Growing skepticism about management's business judgment in turn increased judges' uncertainty about the general relationship between corporate governance and social wealth. Judges began to question whether *management's* interpretations either maximize private wealth *or increase social wealth.*

Still, as the new market for corporate control disrupted many local communities, state legislatures became increasingly reluctant simply to adopt contractarians' sanguine portrayals of what the new market can accomplish in the complete absence of statutory regulation. Thus, 29 state legislatures passed statutes by 1988 that encouraged management to consider stakeholder interests before making any major corporate decision, including any change in corporate control. Four of these state legislatures passed statutes compelling management to do this. Thus, these states broadened business judgment rule protection beyond management's unilateral interpretations of a corporation's collective interests without otherwise revamping corporate law doctrine. They began essentially to divide corporate agency rather than keeping it unitary.

3. Constitutional Balancing

Powerful legal precedents instructed corporate judges to support the new legislation rather than oppose or resist it. In the past, whenever state courts intervened into a new governance dispute, they had the option of transferring or dividing corporate agency and then adjusting corporate law doctrine accordingly. For instance, in the 1920s, when courts moved to the doctrinal approach to the corporation that is still in place today, they transferred corporate agency from shareholder-owners to professional managers. They recognized management as agent and shareholders as principal and bearer of residual risk. At the same time, courts further divided corporate agency, at least formally, when they held that boards of directors are responsible for mediating disputes between management and shareholders.[29]

Other divisions of corporate agency came with developments in statutory law and common law. Federal statutes hold portfolio managers, indenture trustees, institutional investors, and other financial intermediaries responsible for *corporate* activities within selected areas *independently of management's bidding*.[30] State statutes in turn address which actions taken by corporate divisions may adversely affect suppliers, customers, or local communities; which corporate policies may adversely affect shareholders and bondholders; and, for that matter, which corporate policies may adversely affect management or other employees. When any constituent with legal standing initiates a suit in the name of "the corporation" to alter decisions made by managers or directors, they are in essence claiming to be the corporate agent in this area.

The U.S. Supreme Court also provided precedent for further dividing corporate agency. It had adopted balancing a half-century earlier as a central method of constitutional law analysis. The Court abandoned the effort to keep constitutional law tied to nonnegotiable duties designed to serve a greater good, however defined. It began assuming that the "public interest," whatever it is in substance, will come into view as the Court "balances" the rights and claims of an ever-expanding pool of litigants and claimants.[31] Thus, by the 1930s and the New Deal, the "identification, valuation, and comparison of competing interests" became an explicit standard of *constitutional* interpretation.[32] Legal pragmatism supplanted the last vestiges of legal formalism, and a new "age of balancing" was inaugurated.[33] Today, federal and state courts alike routinely balance competing claims not only in constitutional law cases but also in administrative law cases. In both areas of law, courts no longer endeavor to define the "public interest" independently.[34] Yet only some degree of independence here permits the courts as an institution to mediate—simultaneously to overarch and stand between—competing claims as truly disinterested, relatively apolitical bodies.[35]

III. Today's Impending Doctrinal Alternative

Corporate agency had already been divided, therefore, well before a market for corporate control cast into doubt the relevance of mandatory rules of corporate governance. Of equal importance, balancing had already been institutionalized in other major areas of the law. Seeing this, critics of contractarians' shareholder-centered approach to corporations and law began proposing that the corporate judiciary follow these precedents more explicitly. They called on the corporate judiciary to encourage stakeholder balancing as a means of identifying more accurately (a) a corporate entity's collective interests as well as (b) corporations' legitimate place and purpose in American society more generally. They no longer believed that imposing mandatory rules on management (or other corporate agents) necessarily ensures that it will act disinterestedly on an entity's behalf, let alone act in ways that serve any greater good.

Nearly two years before the market for corporate control emerged, therefore, William Klein called on judges to abandon their century-long effort to keep corporate agency unified.[36] He proposed that judges literally remove from corporate law doctrine the metaphor of *the* "corporate person"—*the* independent "entity" and *the* corporate "agent"—and declare at a doctrinal level that corporate agency is divisible.[37] By 1982, therefore, the corporate judiciary was already on the brink of injecting principles of American pluralist politics into the internal governance of corporations and, with this, into corporate law doctrine. It was already acknowledging that questions about corporate agency and corporate purpose could, in principle, be left to whatever "balanced" outcomes emerge from multilateral negotiations between managers, shareholders, and stakeholders.

1. Balancing's Appeal in Principle

Klein's central concern in 1982 remains legitimate today. Neither management's nor institutional investors' interpretations of a corporate entity's collective interests, or of corporations' legitimate place and purpose in society, necessarily increases social wealth sufficiently. Rather, management and institutional investors may each so devalue the "stakes" of other constituents that social wealth suffers, even as shareholder wealth or management power increase.[38] This begins to explain why many judges today believe there is little to lose in enforcing state statutes that either encourage or require stakeholder balancing. When Klein raised this issue in 1982, his position appealed immediately to many traditionalists on two conceptual grounds.[39]

First, stakeholder balancing has a Madisonian ring to it. In *Federalist Papers* (Number 10), James Madison proposed that the "cure for faction" is to broaden the political arena (from the state level to the federal level) in order to increase the number of organized interests competing for power and influence. The "faction" of greatest concern to Madison was a zealous majority, or, alternatively, any well-organized group that wields great power or influence.[40] Madison's Virginia Plan proposed transferring greater power to the federal level than did the Articles of Confederation in order to broaden the arena of political competition. This appealed to Madison because it would convert every state-level power bloc into just another contender for national power.[41]

The second appeal of stakeholder balancing is that it broadens management's business judgment rule protection rather than discarding or radically altering it. Thus, balancing leaves the courts with at least one mooring of corporate law doctrine even as it lends support to contractarian calls to eliminate another—mandatory rules. Balancing replaces this second mooring with whatever suppletory rules and enabling rules stakeholders negotiate with management, then shareholder majorities, within each corporate entity. Once state legislatures encouraged or mandated balancing by statute, judges sympathetic to this option no longer needed to hold management to its fiduciary duty of loyalty to the corporate entity in order to protect stakeholders, including local communities.

In addition, by 1982 judges also had two practical reasons for accepting this half-a-loaf arrangement. First, they needed to respond in one way or another to the conceptual fissures riddling corporate law doctrine. They fully appreciated that judicial imposers failed to identify the public law interest that mandatory rules serve. Second, judges were hardly willing simply to declare management *the* corporate agent, *the* interpreter of a corporation's collective interests. Presuming business judgment rule protection this narrowly would make the corporate judiciary appear out of touch with changes clearly taking place in the American economy and in corporate governance structures. Again, corporations were increasingly seen more as federations of divisions and subdivisions than as centralized hierarchies.

Corporate decision making was seen less as a product of top-down chains of command than as a product of shifting coalitions within an identifiable (albeit federalized) structure of authority. Within this structure, finance managers (and institutional investors) in particular offer one interpretation of a corporate entity's collective interests, informed by one narrow set of positional interests.[42] Moreover, finance managers and institutional investors rarely act unilaterally. They typically form coalitions with managers specialized in other areas and, at times, with selected sets of stakeholders. As Coffee would put the matter by 1990:

> The public corporation is less a series of bargains or contracts [as contractarians say] than a series of coalitions that are less stable, less enforceable and less predictable than contracts. Outcomes are determined less on the basis of legal rights than through coalition politics. Because coalitions tend to be short-lived, this means that the locus of power and authority within the corporation is less certain, and control shifts more unpredictable, than traditional theory implies.[43]

By 1982, and in particular regarding Klein's call for reform, judges therefore appreciated that there was really no compelling obstacle, doctrinal or practical, to their broadening the presumption of business judgment rule protection to accommodate the interests of at least some stakeholders. These judges were prepared to counter contractarians' formidable challenge to defenders of mandatory rules by asking: What possible harm can befall American society if we act explicitly on trends already under way in corporate decision making? Why should we grant management and shareholder majorities sovereignty or prerogative in interpreting a corporate entity's collective interests and purpose in American civil society?[44] Does a top management team, even with shareholder approval, really ever have the same degree of unilateral control over corporate behavior that any individual typically has over his or her behavior?

2. Balancing in Practice: Legislatures Take Action

It turned out that state legislatures, not state courts, took the lead in implementing this alternative doctrinal approach to corporations and law. Some state legislatures had tried in the 1970s, albeit haltingly, to promote balancing, to encourage management to pay greater attention to stakeholder interests when making major corporate decisions. However, courts in Delaware, California, New York, and elsewhere still resisted these legislative initiatives. Most important, the U.S. Supreme Court routinely declared unconstitutional the few state anti-takeover bills that passed into law, as undue restrictions on interstate commerce and as violations of the Williams Act.[45]

In late 1983 and with the onset of a new market for corporate control, however, state legislatures tried again with a second generation of anti-takeover statutes. By 1987, the U.S. Supreme Court ruled on their constitutionality in *CTS Corp. v. Dynamics Corp.* The Court, we must keep in mind, lacks the authority to rule in corporate governance disputes, or to hear these disputes on appeal. This is a jurisdiction of state courts alone. The constitutional issue for the Court was not the substance of any particular corporate governance dispute but rather two related issues. Does the Williams Act comprehensively regulate the takeover bidding process, such that it bans any obstruction of hostile activity by state legislatures? Do new anti-takeover statutes obstruct interstate commerce?[46]

In earlier years the Court treated the Williams Act as comprehensively regulating hostile transactions, and thus ruled that state legislative restrictions on raids and buyouts were incompatible with its 20-day rule for tender offers. As late as 1982 (in *Edgar v. Mite Corp.*), the Court invalidated an Illinois statute by ruling that states may not hold up tender offers because they are essentially acts of commerce.[47] In the context of increasing hostile activity during the 1980s, many state legislatures after the *Edgar* decision shifted their focus from the takeover bidding process to how corporations defend themselves. Thus, rather than trying to subject any acquisition of corporate stock to reviews by state agencies, they turned to corporate "internal affairs," their traditional jurisdiction.

By the mid-1980s, management's primary defense against takeovers was the poison pill, which makes it more expensive for hostile bidders to purchase controlling shares of stock. This did not violate the Williams Act, but it was not clear how the Court would rule on its implications for commerce. At this same time, state legislatures began passing control-share statutes: When a hostile bidder acquires 20 percent of shares, the "disinterested shareholders" remaining are required to vote on whether to allow the new controlling shareholder to vote his block. In 1986, Indiana passed such a statute and a federal district court declared it unconstitutional (in *Dynamics Corp. v. CTS Corp.*).[48] CTS appealed to the U.S. Supreme Court, where Indiana attorneys successfully presented three related arguments in support of their state's statute: Their statute enhances "shareholder autonomy"; whatever delays it might cause are a small price to pay for this; and this goal is also clearly consistent with the intent of the Williams Act.[49] The key for the Court was that state law, not federal law, is sovereign in corporate internal affairs. As long as state legislatures pass laws directed to how the businesses they incorporate are governed, and do not obstruct the affairs of "foreign corporations"—those incorporated elsewhere—they do not run afoul of either the Williams Act or the commerce clause.[50]

This decision was the first by the U.S. Supreme Court to uphold a state anti-takeover statute since 1896, when states began adopting General Corporation laws, and it opened the floodgates to a second generation of anti-takeover statutes.[51] State legislatures began passing statutes that called for supermajority shareholder approval of hostile bids, longer waiting periods (which the Court now held the Williams Act allows), approval by "disinterested" shareholders or directors, ways of assessing "fair value," and, most important, "corporate constituency statutes" that effectively institutionalize shareholder balancing.[52]

Contractarian Roberta Romano sees the *CTS* decision reducing the pressure on Congress to take action against takeovers in the 1980s, a move that the Reagan and Bush administrations opposed and surely would have vetoed.[53] And no major takeover statute did come out of Congress during the entire decade. Contractarian John Kozyris sees this decision elevating form ("shareholder autonomy") over substance (management entrenchment). It is not that Supreme Court Justices failed to appreciate that many state statutes would favor target management teams and disfavor hostile bidders. Rather, the Justices recognized that state legislatures are free to favor management in myriad ways, if they wish, by adjusting their General Corporation laws accordingly.[54] It is up to Congress to stop them, not the Court.

State legislatures' most important reaction to the layoffs, benefit cuts, salary reductions, and other harms being done to employees, retirees, and local communities was to pass what legal scholars call "corporate constituency statutes." Beginning with a Pennsylvania statute in 1983, these laws formalize stakeholder rights of representation within corporate governance structures and, with this, open a door to new suits of one kind or another entering state courts.[55] State legislatures often combined these statutes with other anti-takeover provisions that explicitly prevented management from adopting shareholders' greater preference for risk unilaterally. Such legislation, of course, drove contractarians to utter distraction, to the point of questioning whether state competition for corporate charters really benefits the economy.[56]

Today, 42 states offer corporations some form of statutory protection against takeovers:[57]

- Twenty-nine states have "corporate constituency statutes" which either encourage or require management to consult stakeholders before agreeing to any takeover.[58]
- Twenty-seven states prohibit certain "control share" transactions.
- Twenty-eight states prohibit certain business combinations.
- Twenty-five states have "fair price" statutes, which either require a supermajority shareholder vote after a takeover or else that a "fair price" be offered to shareholders who did not participate.
- Twenty-four states permit shareholder rights plans or "poison pills," which allow shareholders to purchase shares at a discount either before or after a takeover, thereby raising the costs of takeovers.
- Six states have anti-greenmail statutes, prohibiting corporations from purchasing shares from anyone holding more than a specific percentage of outstanding shares (usually 3–5 percent) unless a majority vote of disinterested shareholders approves or else all shareholders receive the same offer.
- Two states have cash-out statutes, which require a purchaser of a controlling interest to buy all remaining shares at a price that reflects the premium paid for control.
- Two states have disgorgement statutes, which recover profits made within short time periods by "speculators" or "greenmailers."

For present purposes we look exclusively at corporate constituency statutes, and then in the next chapter at contractarians' reaction to them, because these laws bring stakeholder balancing into states' General Corporation laws.[59] The 29 states that used Pennsylvania's pathbreaking 1983 statute as their model essentially encourage management to consider stakeholder interests before making any major changes in corporate control.[60] In these states, management only legitimately identifies and advances the collective interests of a corporate entity when it explicitly considers the interests of stakeholders.[61] Management is thereby prohibited in the companies incorporated by these states from acting more unilaterally—whether (a) on its own interpretations, positional interests, or business judgment or (b) on shareholders' wish to entertain raids and buyouts. Thus, in these states, neither controlling shareholders nor top management teams alone are *the* corporate agent.[62]

This doctrinal alternative to shareholding contracting and judicial imposing of mandatory rules fundamentally redefines the issue of corporate agency. Corporate agency is now a legal status that particular state judges may pass from constituent to constituent depending on various factors. What is even more important for our purposes, judges may divide corporate agency among constituents that either have (a) legal standing to bring suit or (b) *statutory rights of representation by management in major corporate decisions*. Eric Orts is enthusiastic about this, calling balancing a "community of interests model" on a par with how corporations are governed in Europe and Japan.[63] Yet, like fellow balancer William Bratton, he also notes that it may usher in a new era of corporatism, an entrenchment of positional interests.[64] John Kozyris and other contractarians take a more jaundiced view, saying this doctrinal option amounts to giving management unilateral power at shareholder expense. "If recent trends continue, virtually all major corporations will be transformed into fortresses in the near future."[65]

IV. Limits to Dividing Corporate Agency

The judges who substitute stakeholder balancing for shareholder contracting (and, of course, for unilateral managing) are breaking new ground in corporate law doctrine. They are operating with a doctrinal approach to corporations and law that no longer instructs courts, on one public law ground or another, to reassign corporate agency (and legal responsibility) to one discrete corporate constituent or, at most, to an identifiable, delimited set of corporate constituents. They are instead operating with an approach that instructs courts in principle to extend the rhetoric of constitutional rights to any number of corporate constituents.

For this reason, however, balancing cannot ultimately compete successfully with contracting, with greater shareholder sovereignty in corporate governance, as a practicable doctrinal option.[66] We can see why by thinking again about balancing in constitutional law. Here, courts emphasize the importance of extending individuals' rights of judicial "standing"—their rights to bring legal claims in response to public and private encroachments that harm them—and individuals' legislative rights of representation. Brought unmediated to the internal governance of corporations, this principle challenges corporate law and judicial tradition in three related ways.

First, as we have noted, such constitutional rhetoric opens the way eventually to removing all legal limits on dividing corporate agency. Second, it challenges management's business judgment in corporate governance structures without transferring management's earlier responsibility for the corporation's future to any readily identifiable corporate agent. Third, it ironically subordinates all *economic*, quantitative standards of analysis, including maximizing share price or maximizing growth, to a new *extra-economic, qualitative* standard of analysis. The new standard is breadth of constituent representation in corporate governance. Moreover, this standard implies that at some point stakeholders will gain legal standing, at the very least to initiate claims in court over encroachments of their statutorily authorized "right of representation."[67] This moves balancing far beyond contractarians' version of liberal complacency, the faith that private wealth and social wealth are inherently interrelated. It moves balancing into some extra-economic, decidedly normative domain.

1. Systemic Pressures and Judicial Interventions

Stakeholder balancing can only exacerbate the three crises of authority and legitimacy we discussed earlier in this chapter. We can appreciate why by standing back from today's debate over corporations and law and considering more generally what any corporation's purpose is in any modern society, whether a fully institutionalized democracy, a limited government, a formal democracy, or an imposed social order. Irrespective of whether a corporate entity is a commercial enterprise or a nonprofit organization, it is a complex team activity pressured by unrelenting systemic forces of modern life to perform two tasks. First, it is pressured to organize at least somewhat efficiently one small part of a society's productive capacity. Second, and to this end, it is also pressured to administer at least somewhat effectively—to "monitor"—the conduct of its personnel or team members. These systemic pressures are more readily evident in market societies, to be sure, but they are hardly absent from planned economies, particularly in today's global economy. All team leaders in all societies are driven by the same systemic pressures to see to it that, at the very least, their team merits continuing control over its part of their society's productive capacity. As neoclassical economists Alchian and Allen put the matter:

> The contractual organization within the team differs in socialist and free-enterprise economies; but in both economies the technical physical productivity advantages of team production are sought, providing the metering

and detecting of team-member performance can be made sufficiently cheap and effective.[68]

One mark of corporate success in market societies is the share price of publicly traded stock.[69] Another is market share. But these are only two marks among many others, some of which include: capitalization, research and development, diversification, recruitment and training of middle and top managers, and cultivation of employee loyalty and commitment.[70] Moreover, all of these marks of corporate success are approximations at best: "Realistically speaking, we must recognize that modern business firms—even the largest—are unable to calculate their marginal revenue and marginal cost. They cannot determine their optimum price and output with nice exactitude. Yet, the day's work must somehow get done."[71]

Our point in calling attention to today's systemic pressures is that state courts and state legislatures in the United States really have no reason to intervene into the internal governance of private commercial enterprises on behalf of any particular constituent *except on some extra-economic, qualitative ground*. Systemic pressures "evaluate" commercial enterprises independently and relentlessly on narrowly economic (or quantitative) grounds regardless. Klein pointed this out in 1982 when he advocated that courts intervene into corporate governance disputes in order to increase stakeholder notice and representation in major corporate decisions. He saw that "the allocation of control [over a corporation's actions] reflects the bargains made as to the other [extra-economic] elements as well as the underlying economic realities those bargains reflect and create."[72] That is, Klein saw that the internal governance structures of commercial enterprises essentially "balance" extra-economic considerations (of whatever kind) against economic calculations regarding when (and how) to act in market-mimicking ways.

Thus, corporate governance structures "balance," in practice, how management, shareholders, and stakeholders interrelate their positional interests, coordinate their specialties, diversify their investments, and otherwise exercise their discretion or business judgment within their respective spheres of authority.[73] Consider, however, what this means for the corporate judiciary in particular. It means courts cannot determine from the outside whether one corporate governance structure's balancing of these factors is superior to another's. Notwithstanding Easterbrook and Fischel's wish to focus judicial attention exclusively on whether agency costs are increasing or decreasing in any corporation, courts cannot identify even this simply by comparing profits, dividends, growth rates, or any other priced outcomes either within or across a sector of the economy. Rather, each and every priced outcome of each and every corporation reflects how its governance structure is currently balancing economic and extra-economic factors as its constituents respond to uncertainties in its environment, both quantitative and qualitative, that may well be unique to it. Thus, each corporate governance structure, in its own way, may advance a corporation's domestic profitability and global competitiveness more efficiently and effectively than any alternative.[74] If, by enforcing mandatory rules, courts restrict unduly the full range of governance options from which management may select with shareholder approval, they may unnecessarily jeopardize corporate profitability and competitiveness rather than self-evidently facilitate it.[75]

Contractarians see this line of argument as justifying their call for opting out, for permitting management to replace mandatory rules with suppletory and enabling rules approved by shareholder majorities (see the next chapter). Yet this line of argument carries at least four implications, not just one. First, each corporation is exposed to a unique set of uncertainties, originating from a unique set of sources.[76] Second, not all uncertainties that a corporation faces are readily measurable or "priced." Rather, many are qualitative, including the degrees of effort and creativity that managers and other employees dedicate to their respective team activities. Third, and following from the first two implications, there is no "objective" measure of a corporation's governance function, although there may be different "objective measures" of its analytically distinguishable production function.[77] No one can gauge definitively the degree to which a given governance structure already deals efficiently and effectively with the unique combinations of quantitative and qualitative uncertainties facing a particular corporation at a particular time.[78] Fourth, corporate constituents adjust governance structures in countless ways as they respond in their own positional interests to changes in these combinations of uncertainties. Which of these adjustments actually contributes to profitability and competitiveness is anyone's guess.[79]

2. Balancers' Qualitative Standard

One irony of the 1970s and early 1980s is that the U.S. Supreme Court, which had moved constitutional law toward balancing four decades earlier, tried for a time to support state court resistance to dividing corporate agency. It did so by ruling that management, not shareholder majorities and certainly not coalitions of stakeholders, is ultimately responsible for any corporate entity's survival. The Court held that management bears this responsibility even when its policies fail to maximize share price or market share or, for that matter, fail to meet any other quantitative standard of corporate performance. Thus, the Court kept corporate agency unified, but at an extraordinarily high price. It was asserting that management may subordinate its role as shareholders' agent to that of meeting qualitative standards of corporate performance that management, and state courts, need not identify explicitly. By the mid-1980s, this brought state court judges face-to-face with a very practical problem: How far were they willing to go in elevating management's freedom to exercise its business judgment above all quantitative standards of efficiency and effectiveness, but short of endangering the corporate entity's survival?[80] Correlatively, how could they recognize, *on the basis of an unidentified qualitative standard* (reflected in mandatory rules), when a particular management team no longer exercises its business judgment responsibly or disinterestedly?

Fortunately or unfortunately, the hostile takeovers and leveraged buyouts of the mid-1980s resolved this practical problem on contractarian grounds, at least for a few years. The market for corporate control no longer permitted judges to focus exclusively on management's interpretations of a corporate entity's collective interests, and particularly when they clearly failed to maximize share price. When state legislatures drafted corporate constituency statutes, they used stakeholder balancing—along with *a now identified* qualitative standard of corporate governance—to mediate unilateral managing, shareholder contracting, and all quantitative standards of corporate performance. The new standard was breadth of stakeholder representation within corporate governance structures.

The problem is that these state corporate constituency statutes bring pluralism into the governance of corporations without offering judges any guidance regarding how far they might go in dividing corporate agency. Because these statutes have not yet been tested in courts, no one knows how state courts will interpret them or how entrenchment-minded management teams or boards of directors might use them.[81] The statutes are so vague regarding what directors and other corporate officers are supposed to do that some legal scholars say they impose "multi-fiduciary" duties on management and leave it at that.[82] George Smith and Davis Dyer add that shareholder activism of the mid-1990s has not somehow displaced stakeholder claims; rather, these claims "continue to pile up."[83] Stakeholders can claim at any time that restructured corporations renege on implicit contracts.[84] Freeman and Evan want all stakeholders to have voting rights, like shareholders; in effect, they are already pushing balancing from stakeholder representation to stakeholder standing.[85]

The question today is on what constitutional, doctrinal, or statutory ground may a judge ever restrict or delimit the number of stakeholders who seek representation in corporate decision making and then standing in court? After all, as judges across state courts extend rights of representation to stakeholders beyond the financial intermediaries already covered by federal statutes, on what grounds can particular judges then deny any stakeholder representation? Klein's list of "participants," other than managers and shareholders, who invest capital or services in corporations is instructive:[86] promoters, investors, and negotiators of particular ventures; semi-residual claimants of royalties, licensing fees, or percentage leases; fixed claimants such as lenders, trade creditors, lessors, and rank-and-file employees; and distributors and franchisers. Moreover, this list is hardly exhaustive; it was Klein's opening salvo. He eventually called for judges to extend the same protections to suppliers, customers, and residents of local communities. Lawrence Mitchell calls for courts to extend judicial protection to bondholders based on "community values of fairness and decency."[87]

Again, on what constitutional, doctrinal, or statutory grounds may a particular judge deny a corporate constituent representation, even as the ongoing process of constituent competition for power and influence eventually yields the kinds of decision making logjams that at times riddle Congress and state legislatures?[88] At some point in this process, near or far, constituent competition can only jeopardize share price and other economic standards of corporate success.[89] Oliver Williamson and Janet Bercovitz see three main costs in broadening stakeholder representation either on boards of directors or in management teams.[90] First, it invites opportunism, or each constituent endeavoring to extract additional concessions at strategic times during decision making. Second, instead of seeking private contracts to protect their stakes, constituents will expect equitable treatment, thereby distorting the allocation of corporate assets. Third, constituent representation reduces management accountability, giving managers an "excuse" as they advance their own positional interests more one-sidedly than in the past.

In short, should courts become "unable or unwilling" to delimit the "universe of interest" on a board or in a top management team, they will substitute drift for direction, group competition for mandatory rules.[91] This result is likely because the very idea that courts might resiliently restrain group competition later, on the basis of some unambiguous public law ground, has long been lost from the Supreme Court's institutional memory

Contractarians' facility in using constitutional (and common law) rhetoric to place defenders of mandatory rules on the defensive means that in the late 1980s they had the means to go much further than demanding the *status quo ante* in corporate law. They had the means to call into question the legitimacy of *any* law of corporate *entities*. Contractarians could at any time initiate a radical re-reading of corporate law's first principles, the corporate judiciary's fiduciary law tradition itself. Thus, beginning then and continuing today, contractarians insist that fiduciary law properly understood, what they call "*the* fiduciary principle," *facilitates* maximizing behavior, not normatively mediates it.[18] It applies to management's role as shareholders' agent, not to management's role as trustee of a corporate entity. Whatever fiduciary duties management owes, it owes to shareholders, not to an entity that shareholders own.

4. Blurring Fiduciary Law and Contract Law

Contractarians' way of characterizing fiduciary duties sounds compelling even as it runs counter to two centuries of American corporate law precedent. It sounds compelling to the corporate judiciary and bar in particular because since the 1950s state and federal courts have been taking two steps that effectively dilute the "interdicting power" of the fiduciary law tradition.[19] First, they have been bringing fiduciary rhetoric to more and more agency relationships as they simply enforce agents' contractual obligations to principals. With this, they fail to restrict their use of fiduciary rhetoric to *structured* situations in which authorities (in positions of trust) exercise positional power over subordinates (in positions of dependence). Second, because the manner in which agents conduct themselves in typical agency relationships poses no threat whatsoever to the larger society, courts end up transferring fiduciary rhetoric to what are essentially breaches of contract, namely harms agents cause to principals or third parties. With this, courts lose sight of the central point of the fiduciary law tradition: To identify structured situations in which exercises of power between positions of trust and positions of dependence—exercises of positional power—do indeed carry consequences for institutional design.[20]

Our point is that all courts, including the corporate judiciary, have been bringing extra-economic considerations of fairness or equity to disputes in which this is not only unnecessary but also inappropriate, and thereby confusing. As a result, even the corporate judiciary has had more experience identifying the immediate externalities of agency relationships, and then often mislabeling them as breaches of fiduciary duty. It has far less experience identifying the institutional externalities of structured situations, exercises of positional power that indeed challenge or enervate basic institutional arrangements spanning the state and civil society. And, as we just noted, constitutional rhetoric blurs the distinction between structured situations in civil society and agency relationships rather than drawing attention to it.

Anyone adversely affected by an agency relationship is essentially a stakeholder in it, if not its principal. And here, identifying and recompensing the immediate externalities of an agent's behavior for a principal or stakeholder, is where fiduciary rhetoric may be replaced entirely with contract law. Courts may simply enforce suppletory rules and enabling rules, disregarding all extra-economic considerations of fairness or equity. Contractarians appreciate this, and they also appreciate the significance of the two steps courts have been taking in diluting fiduciary law more generally. Their goal is to accelerate the demise of fiduciary law, and thus of corporate law's core of mandatory rules, by promoting the second step and encouraging courts to stop taking the first step. They want courts to reign in their use of fiduciary rhetoric by applying it exclusively to management's contractual obligations *to shareholders*.

Thus, contractarians bring fiduciary rhetoric to management's role as shareholders' agent.[21] With this, they quite purposefully mislabel an essentially contractual obligation as a fiduciary duty, a mandatory rule of corporate governance. They mislabel a simple agency relationship as a fiduciary relationship. This confuses everything, of course, because fiduciary law *traditionally* has *always* normatively mediated contractual transactions and agency relationships in certain structured situations, namely those containing positions of trust and positions of dependence. Fiduciary law *never* instrumentally facilitated principals' self-interest. Thus, to call management's contractual obligation to maximize shareholder wealth a fiduciary duty of corporate governance is like calling a horse a saddle. In an age in which few ride horses, you might get away with it, and contractarians likely will.

Contractarians were given a license to misapply fiduciary rhetoric in the 1990s because the corporate judiciary clearly misapplied the same rhetoric from the 1950s through the early 1970s and continues at times to do so today. Back then, when corporate governance followed well-worn patterns and corporate America led the advanced economies, the corporate judiciary had little reason—and in any event no opportunity—to identify the possible institutional externalities of *changes* in corporate governance. But this also meant that two generations of Delaware judges and other state judges lost sight of the central thrust of the entire fiduciary law tradition, dating from fourteenth-century England: Management's fiduciary duties *to the corporate entity* are ultimately designed to guard against these externalities—harms done to institutional design, not harms done to shareholders or stakeholders. Having lost sight of this, the corporate judiciary back then interpreted management's fiduciary duty of loyalty to the corporate entity quite literally. They misapplied fiduciary rhetoric by treating the corporate entity as a long-term commercial enterprise. They interpreted management's "duty of loyalty" as a non-negotiable obligation to preserve a corporate entity as a long-term commercial enterprise, even if at times at shareholders' expense.

We see this interpretation still in the *Unocal* decision and even more dramatically in the *Time-Warner* decision. The corporate judiciary did not keep their use of fiduciary rhetoric confined to an understanding of the corporation as an intermediary association. Here management's fiduciary duties stem from the fact that it exercises positional power in a structured situation and, thus, that it can do so one-sidedly. Whether it does so on its own behalf—or on shareholders' behalf or at shareholders' expense, or on stakeholders' behalf or at stakeholders' expense—is less important than whether it indeed acts one-sidedly.

We will see in the next four chapters that the only justification for fiduciary law in today's global economy, and thus for mandatory rules of corporate governance, is whether such law and rules help courts to identify and then mediate one-sided exercises of positional power in structured situations, including in corporate governance structures. This legal tradition cannot be justified if it is read as encouraging courts to support management in preserving corporate entities as long-term commercial enterprises at their owners' expense.

II. "Mid-Stream" Opting Out: Contract Radicalism

In the context of ongoing, at times sudden, economic and legal changes during the late 1980s and early 1990s, it was surprisingly easy for contractarians to strike a radical pose when criticizing anti-takeover legislation. They argued ever more explicitly, and stridently, that supporting by statute management's putative duty to preserve the corporate entity as a long-term commercial enterprise is counterproductive in numerous ways: It is indefensible economically; "artificial" politically; ungrounded doctrinally; and inconsistent with social norms supporting domestic deregulation. Thus, two centuries of corporate law tradition in the United States notwithstanding, and over five centuries of fiduciary law tradition in England, contractarians argued persuasively that court-enforced mandatory duties to corporate entities are illegitimate elements of existing corporate law and contemporary judicial practice.

Contractarians are so opposed to mandatory rules that they want management to be free to "opt out" of them, with shareholder approval, both at incorporation and "at midstream."[22] Lucian Bebchuk, a sympathetic critic of this stance, points out that contractarians have been so successful in challenging corporate law tradition that the case for opting out at incorporation, once unthinkable, now seems unassailable.[23] This in itself marks a sea change in American corporate law scholarship, if not yet in judicial practice. It reveals how successfully contractarians have used constitutional principles of individual rights and private property to consolidate today's orthodoxy of liberal complacency in corporate law scholarship. They have successfully used constitutional principles to call into question the most fundamental point of the corporate judiciary's fiduciary law tradition and to challenge any lingering republican concerns that Delaware courts in particular may have about corporate power.

Opting out at incorporation can credibly claim some conceptual affinity with Locke's allegory of the rise of legitimate government out of a state of nature. At incorporation, after all, managers, shareholders, and stakeholders alike can all be portrayed as unattached individuals in an eminently unstructured situation much like a "state of nature." When they agree independently to participate in a new corporate venture, they implicitly accept unanimously the terms of governance contained in its certificate of incorporation. We can credibly say they have contracted freely, voluntarily. They certainly did not self-evidently alienate any of their "natural rights" in their persons or property.[24]

By contrast, opting out at midstream is more problematic. This is difficult to reconcile with Locke's allegory and, thus, would seem more difficult to promote with constitutional rhetoric.[25] In four ways at least, midstream changes of corporate charters (and governance structures) clearly exceed any analogy to a social contract in a state of nature.[26] First, and most obviously, changing an existing charter is not like entering a social contract and establishing government; it is more like changing regimes. Second, most corporate constituents are hardly unattached individuals, and thus are not necessarily motivated solely by their own personal beliefs and interests. Most are stakeholders. They occupy positions in a structured situation and thus act on the basis of positional interests that may diverge considerably from their personal beliefs and interests as unattached individuals. Thus, some constituents may accept midstream charter changes because their stakes in the corporation are vulnerable to management's (or controlling shareholders') exercises of positional power. Clearly, the constituents of an existing corporation are hardly operating in a state of nature.

Third, shareholders are the only constituent whose investment or "stake" is sufficiently transferable that they can withdraw it on short notice and thereby escape most immediate externalities of midstream changes.[27] Fourth, midstream changes require approval by shareholder majorities regardless (and so are likely to advance shareholders' interests, which is why contractarians favor them), but few are likely to secure unanimous shareholder approval, to say nothing of unanimous stakeholder approval.[28]

Easterbrook and Fischel are well aware that factors such as these complicate midstream opting out. They nonetheless insist that midstream changes are consistent with both basic norms of liberal complacency. These changes, they point out, are likely to be Pareto optimal in their outcomes (for shareholders) and, more surprisingly, they insist that these changes also do not ultimately violate the norm of Lockean or voluntary contracting. Easterbrook and Fischel support this seemingly counterfactual assertion by taking two distinct steps. First, they devalue the legal (that is, contractual) status of all stakes in corporate enterprises that may be recompensed only partially at midstream.[29] This may sound callous, but we should recall that this is consistent with how the corporate judiciary treated stakeholder interests until the mid-1980s and how corporate law doctrine characterized their interests prior to the new anti-takeover legislation. State courts and corporate law doctrine recognized the legal status of shareholders' private property, as the principal, and management's positional power, as the agent, not of stakeholders' firm-specific investments or sunk costs.

Easterbrook and Fischel's second step is to call attention to a point they believe is self-evident: Legislative and judicial protection of constituent "stakes" is like any other display of governmental paternalism. It stifles robust economic competition and thereby "artificially" reduces social wealth. This is self-evident to them because, *with legal traditionalists*, they believe that when state courts bring qualitative standards of analysis to corporate governance disputes as mandatory rules, this delimits everyone's freedom of contract *in substance*.[30] Thus, Easterbrook and Fischel believe corporate law's mandatory rules "artificially"—paternalistically—delimit the range of charters, provisions, and governance structures from which management may select with shareholder approval both at incorporation and midstream. They then add a leap of logic to their call for greater contractual freedom: Because opting out of mandatory rules at midstream would clearly end governmental paternalism in corporate law, then everyone must agree, with them, that this is more Lockean or "natural" than the status quo.[31]

Irrespective of the precariousness of this leap, as well as the controversy of their first step in the eyes of balancers, Easterbrook and Fischel's two-step argument in support of opting out effectively puts judicial imposers on the defensive. It does so by seemingly demonstrating that midstream changes are consistent with both norms of the orthodoxy that balancers and imposers share with contractarians. This is why contractarians assert with such confidence that a robust market for corporate control renders mandatory rules irrelevant. The only thing this market leaves state courts (and state legislatures) to do, in their view, is to increase the rigor of the procedures through which management customizes charters and governance structures from corporation to corporation with shareholder approval.

For their part, Easterbrook and Fischel want procedures that ensure all shareholders are kept fully informed about midstream changes, not just shareholder majorities.[32] They also want supermajority votes of approval by shareholders over two successive annual meetings.[33] Once every shareholder receives the same information and agrees twice by supermajority votes, they then see no good reason—doctrinal or practical—for judges to stop management from replacing any and all mandatory rules, federal or state, with suppletory rules or even enabling rules.[34] Thus, Carlton and Fischel call for opting out of all insider-trading rules.[35] Easterbrook wants opting out of management's fiduciary duty of loyalty to the corporate entity—the most traditional mandatory rule and corporate law's window to social norms and institutional design.[36] Roe wants to move this laissez-faire approach from the internal governance of corporations to contractual relationships between corporations and financial institutions. He wants law to permit more variation, including allowing the rise of "universal banks," but not law that necessarily encourages concentrated ownership and, therefore, more intrusive intervention by institutional investors into corporate governance.[37]

With these calls for reform, contractarians are assuming that an optimal allocation of capital across an economy is the sole standard by which to define corporations' legitimate place and purpose in American society and, therefore, by which to analyze the success of corporate law and judicial practice.[38] They are neglecting the possibility that some mandatory rules comprise the core of corporate law doctrine in the United States for other, equally sound, practical reasons. Whether or not judicial imposers and other legal traditionalists today can successfully identify and articulate these reasons is a separate issue. Cass Sunstein puts this matter well in the context of discussing administrative law, not corporate law:

> Courts have . . . demanded a showing of a sharp and clear relationship between regulatory measures and particular, identifiable, real-world harms— even though regulatory statutes frequently attempt to counteract environmental or other risks that are merely probable or systemic. Courts have also misunderstood the systemic effects of regulatory programs, effects that make the incidence of regulatory benefits and burdens far more complicated than they might at first appear.[39]

Put more specifically, the very existence of a distinctively Anglo-American tradition of fiduciary law suggests the possibility that some mandatory rules may codify vital practical limits to the drift of corporate governance options, limits that uniquely support a democratic society. It suggests that England's Chancellors as well as America's Founders may have seen more clearly than do today's traditionalists what these vital practical limits are. After all, traditionalists' vision is clouded by today's orthodoxy, by their own feverish swimming upstream against liberal complacency. Traditionalists' vision is further distorted by the Contractarian Challenge to corporate law tradition and today's ongoing overextension of constitutional and contractual rhetoric from individuals to corporate entities. Today's orthodoxy and these other two developments did not fetter the vision of Chancellors and the Founders. Rather, liberal complacency became salient in American legal thought and judicial practice only at the turn of the twentieth century.[40] England's Chancellors and America's Founders did not share the faith of complacent liberals and, certainly, did not have to contend with it as the orthodoxy of their day. To the contrary, they were moral philosophers and classical political economists. They were attuned to the possible institutional externalities of concentrated private power and of unbridled "appetites," including economic acquisitiveness.[41]

III. Qualities of Corporate Entities: Substantive and Procedural

Judges and legal scholars today actively debate only three doctrinal approaches to corporate agency—unilateral managing, bilateral contracting, and multilateral balancing.[42] Judicial imposers read fiduciary law as a tradition of substantive normative analysis designed to reveal when management defenses of an entity as a long-term commercial enterprise merit judicial support in hostile situations. They do not read it more strictly as a tradition of procedural normative analysis designed only to reveal when an entity's governance structure merits judicial support on a public law ground and then, of course, what this public law ground is. Thus, what eludes judicial imposers today are the full implications of particular procedural normative qualities of corporate entities as governance structures—structured situations—in civil society. This distinction between procedural normative analysis and substantive normative analysis opens a way to explaining Delaware court behavior in the 1980s and 1990s and then also to predicting these courts' behavior in coming decades.

When imposers, and Delaware courts, read fiduciary law as a tradition that has anything to do with protecting corporations as long-term commercial enterprises, the ridicule they receive from contractarians is reasoned. This is why imposers such as Eisenberg and Brudney react so defensively to this ridicule, and so unconvincingly. This is also why former traditionalists beat a hasty retreat to their second-best option of promoting stakeholder balancing. They no longer endeavor to defend directly any such substantive normative analysis of corporate officers' fiduciary duties. But with their turn to balancing they concede nearly everything to contractarians at a doctrinal and conceptual level.[43] In particular, where contractarians focus judges' attention on increasing shareholder wealth, balancers propose there is no limit in principle—constitutional, doctrinal, or statutory—to how far courts might divide corporate agency once management's business judgment is called into question. The only limit is practical, namely the number of stakeholders who press management for representation and how successfully they do so.[44]

Thus, traditionalists-turned-balancers ask the following question about corporate purpose, consistently with today's orthodoxy of liberal complacency: How might corporate law and judicial practice help simultaneously to maximize private wealth, protect the stakes of other constituents, and thereby increase social wealth? This question already brackets from view the fact that a corporation is not only a commercial enterprise, whether long-term or not. A corporation is also an intermediary association that performs a governance function. It contains an important structured situation in American civil society in which positional power can be exercised one-sidedly rather than disinterestedly. Thus, these "traditionalists" fail to pose the following question: How, if at all, does corporate law and judicial practice keep the internal governance of corporations at least broadly aligned with institutional arrangements spanning the state and civil society that are unique to democratic societies as opposed to limited governments, formal democracies, and imposed social orders?

This second question moves the issue of corporate purpose and institutional externalities from background to foreground. It poses a lingering challenge to today's orthodoxy because it reestablishes some linkage to the Founders' republican vigilance and the corporate judiciary's fiduciary law tradition. The question builds on this heritage because the issue of corporate purpose and institutional externalities reminds everyone that an alternative metaphor of the corporation remains available to the courts, namely the metaphor of the corporate entity.[45] It also reminds everyone that this metaphor remains more consistent with existing corporate law and judicial tradition than managing, contracting, or balancing shorn of mandatory rules. But we will see in the rest of this volume that when judges and legal scholars persist in linking the entity metaphor directly to a substantive normative analysis of corporate governance disputes, they do indeed render the fiduciary law tradition anachronistic.

When judges and legal scholars tie the entity metaphor directly to a substantive normative analysis of corporate governance disputes, they propose that certain corporate enterprises contribute unique, substantive qualities to the larger society that merit judicial protection in a market for corporate control. This is what happens when they read management's fiduciary duty of loyalty to the corporate entity as if it encompasses an obligation to ensure the survival of a long-term commercial enterprise even at shareholders' expense. We saw this in the *Unocal* and *Time-Warner* decisions. Judges extend legal protection to management's defenses of a particular corporation in much the same way that they protect historical landmarks or endangered species from commercial use or development. They propose that certain substantive qualities that particular corporations putatively contribute to the larger society are so self-evidently "distinctive and important" that the "intrinsic value" of these entities cannot be fully priced in capital markets.

By contrast, when judges and legal scholars tie the entity metaphor to a procedural normative analysis of corporate governance disputes, they propose that all corporate governance structures are, by definition, structured situations. All corporate governance structures contain positions of dependence and positions of trust in civil society, and the relationship between these positions can become so one-sided that exercises of positional power become abusive. The issue then becomes when do certain structured situations qualify as fiduciary relationships and when do they qualify simply as agency relations that may be regulated by contract law in the absence of mandatory rules of private governance? Our point now is that the only possible quality of value for the larger society of structured situations that qualify as fiduciary relationships is procedural normative, never substantive normative. The quality is how the relationship between positions of dependence and positions of trust is governed, how positional power is exercised between them. It is not what the people in these positions happen to value personally in substance, the substantive qualities they are keeping in collective view in these positions.

IV. Again, the Courts' Doctrinal Options Today

The corporate constituency statutes of the 1980s pushed state courts toward dividing corporate agency. A multilateral approach to corporate agency, moreover, leads inexorably to a new way of posing the issue of corporate purpose. After all, when state courts draw management's attention to stakeholder interests rather than to mandatory rules of corporate governance, they lose their only independent, qualitative standard by which to identify, then mediate, externalities of corporate power in consistent ways. They also lose the quantitative standard contractarians favor, namely Pareto optimal outcomes for shareholders. The courts drift. They approve whatever transactions or rules of governance emerge from each corporate governance structure after a management team considers how various constituents are likely to be affected. With this, the courts essentially ask: What is corporations' place and purpose in American society today, other than to increase profits or growth and broaden representation?

Today, therefore, state courts have essentially three doctrinal options available to them when considering issues of corporate agency and corporate purpose. Judges draw in particular on the second and third options:

- Judges can presume business judgment rule protection for management's more or less unilateral interpretations of the entity's collective interests. They thereby declare that the place and purpose of corporations in American society are ultimately whatever management teams decide. With this, they support management discretion as far as shareholders in particular are willing to tolerate. This is the option the corporate judiciary inherited from the 1970s (and that can be traced much further back).
- Judges can adopt a nexus of contracts approach, declaring that the place and purpose of corporations in American society are ultimately to maximize share price. With this, they support opting out and a market for corporate control as far as management and other stakeholders are willing to tolerate. This is the option that Delaware courts exercised in the *Revlon* decision.
- Judges can adopt Madisonian principles of balancing by holding that a corporate entity's collective interests and corporations' place and purpose in American society are both reflected in whatever outcomes are Pareto optimal for major constituents. With this, judges support stakeholder representation as far as both management and shareholders are willing to tolerate. This is the option that the Delaware courts considered in *Unocal* (and then *Credit Lyonnais*), that 29 state legislatures exercised in the 1980s, and that the U.S. Supreme Court affirmed at least indirectly in *CTS Corp.*

We saw in Chapter 5, however, that Delaware courts have also exercised yet a fourth doctrinal option, one that simultaneously retains strengths of the other three while removing some major weaknesses of each. Unlike contracting and balancing in particular, this fourth option also moves outside today's orthodoxy of liberal complacency. It retains linkages to the courts' fiduciary law tradition and, thus, the Founders' republican vigilance:

- Judges can maintain the integrity of a particular form of organization within corporate governance structures, one that uniquely mediates positional power short of one-sidedness and thereby encourages disinterested decision making. With this, judges can support management discretion, shareholder contracting, or stakeholder balancing, but only on the basis of a qualitative standard of analysis of governance disputes that they continue to enforce as a mandatory rule. This is the option at least implied by the *Time-Warner* case, found in even more subdued form in *QVC*, but that runs centrally through the *Weinberger, Van Gorkom, Macmillan*, and *Technicolor* decisions.

Still, for two reasons judges and legal scholars have not identified this fourth option explicitly at a doctrinal level. First, any reference to mediating private power, and then to institutionalizing disinterested decision making, hinges on some qualitative standard of analysis. This clearly moves beyond today's orthodoxy of liberal complacency. Second, judges' failure to identify this qualitative standard of analysis explicitly is interrelated with judicial imposers' failure to update the fiduciary law tradition at a conceptual level. As a result, even when judges exercise this doctrinal option, they fail to instruct management teams (or legal scholars) explicitly about what they are doing and, even more, why they are doing it.

PART III

Corporate Law and Judicial Practice in a Global Economy

10

America's Constitutional Court for Intermediary Associations

Some contractarians and some traditionalists see the Delaware courts as deliberative bodies that sometimes act on a broad social mandate. They see Delaware's Chancery and Supreme Court as this country's constitutional court for corporate persons. More cynical legal scholars in both camps look at the same judicial behavior and see an extended exercise in strategic rivalry. Delaware, after all, reigns supreme in states' competition to charter major corporations and it is also the greatest accumulator, by far, of franchise fees as a percentage of any state's total revenues. What everyone acknowledges is that Delaware judges are quite prepared at times, for better or worse, for reasons of principle or reasons of strategic plan, to articulate a broad social vision. Delaware judges are prepared to speak broadly on occasion to the issue of corporate purpose as they rule on particular governance disputes. Moreover, everyone also acknowledges that the rulings and written decisions of this state's courts carry greater influence across the corporate judiciary and bar than those of any other state, California and New York included. Thus, if any state's courts are ever to stake out a political economic position that is closer to republican vigilance than to liberal complacency, *and then also to influence the corporate judiciary and bar as an institution*, it will be Delaware's.[1]

Because the United States has gone through nearly two full decades of flux in corporate law and judicial practice, Delaware courts are more influential today, not less. Through the 1980s, corporate law no longer rested on settled doctrinal principles, and particularly ones speaking directly and in one voice to the corporate judiciary's grand issues of agency and purpose. Given the drift, at times schizophrenia, that Delaware courts experienced during this decade, their decisions today that speak forcefully to these issues carry considerable influence nationally. Everyone knows that the prestige of Delaware courts (to say nothing of this small state's revenue base) rests on whether the positions they take on agency and purpose maintain their hard-won reputation for sophistication and prescience.

In short, if the corporate judiciary and bar as an institution is to resist drift today, whether toward shareholder contracting or toward stakeholder balancing, it will be Delaware courts that institutionalize (if not necessarily initiate) resistance. Put differently, even if Congress or the Supreme Court or some administrative agency were to develop a new doctrinal rationale for resistance, it would still need the support of Delaware courts in order to institutionalize this rationale across the corporate judiciary and bar.[2] America's corporate judiciary is a decentralized, national network of relatively self-referring, deliberative bodies (or, again, strategic competitors). This network's collective reasoning is not easily altered by Supreme Court decisions, let alone congressional statutes, state statutes, administrative decrees, rulings by most state courts, or, certainly, articles published in major law journals.[3] But the decisions and written opinions that carry the greatest influence across the entire network are those that Delaware judges either issue or confirm.[4]

I. Delaware's Dominant Position

Delaware has dominated state competition for corporate charters since the 1920s, and no state, including California, poses a credible challenge to its influence in the area of corporate law. Delaware collects over $200 million in franchise taxes from the businesses it incorporates. This figure represents slightly over 17 percent of the total tax revenues that this state collects annually.[5] No other state raises such a significant portion of its total tax revenues from charters.[6]

Over 40 percent of the corporations listed on the New York Stock Exchange are incorporated in Delaware, as are over 60 percent of the Fortune 500, and over 50 percent of the Dow Jones Industrial Average.[7] Most corporations that reincorporate choose, in overwhelming numbers, to move into Delaware. Fewer than 8 percent of all businesses that reincorporate leave Delaware, and 80 percent of this small set reincorporate in the state of their principal place of business. Their home state, after all, is where laws might better protect their particular business, where they often wield greatest influence in a state legislature, and where franchise taxes are lower.[8]

Delaware's franchise tax rate for incorporated businesses is higher than that of any other state.[9]

Of the 255 corporations that made the decision to reincorporate from 1982 through 1994, 226 or fully 89 percent moved into Delaware.[10] A business can reincorporate in Delaware literally overnight. A *typical* incorporation in Delaware takes 24 hours; for an additional fee, it can be completed the same business day. By comparison, it takes four to six weeks to reincorporate into New York, and three to four weeks into Connecticut, another small state.[11]

New Jersey had the initial advantage in chartering corporations in 1888, when it passed the nation's first General Corporation law. Delaware entered the competition soon thereafter but made little headway against New Jersey until 1913. In that year, New Jersey Governor Woodrow Wilson successfully lobbied the legislature to amend its General Corporation law with the "Seven Sisters Act," effectively outlawing trusts and holding companies. Delaware resisted making such a move.[12] The more general point is that state competition for corporate charters has affected corporate law and corporate governance in the United States far longer than has a market for corporate control, and Delaware has bested its competitors for over 70 years. By 1969, Delaware was incorporating businesses at a rate of 800 per month, by 1993 at a rate of nearly 4,000 per year.[13]

Still, this begs an obvious question: Why have so many companies incorporated in Delaware, and why do so many reincorporate there? Management makes these decisions, of course, and so one possible answer is that management sees Delaware law serving its positional interests. However, shareholder majorities must approve these decisions. Is it really likely that dispersed shareholders all around the country, voting independently on management decisions in thousands of instances spanning hundreds of industries, are concurring so frequently in management decisions that harm their interests? We answer these questions in two steps. First, we present some of the advantages Delaware has developed in competing for corporate charters. Which of them favor management and which of them favor shareholders will hardly be self-evident. Second, we present four major explanations that legal scholars have provided for Delaware's dominant position of long standing. It will also not be self-evident, after considering all four explanations, that Delaware law favors either management or shareholders.[14]

Our thesis in this chapter is that Delaware courts are deliberative bodies, not more narrow-minded strategic competitors. Because this state has dominated its rivals for charters for over 70 years, Delaware judges have considerable latitude. They can operate with relative independence and disinterestedness as corporate law specialists. On the one hand, they are not driven by *any* identifiable interest group pressures (whether from management or from shareholders) nor by *any* identifiable policy concerns (whether to favor management or to favor shareholders).[15] On the other hand, they could not turn to these groups or to any particular policy preference in search of authoritative guidance or even general orientation regardless. They cannot rely on the opinions or interests of others to serve somehow as a proxy for their own decision making in difficult cases, for their own careful reasoning in written opinions that all interested parties are free to evaluate and criticize.

We will see in coming chapters that Delaware courts are exemplars of a collegial form of organization, a form also found in certain corporate boardrooms and certain corporate governance structures. Rather than defining this form here, we simply assert for now that four points follow from approaching Delaware courts as deliberative bodies, rather than as strategic competitors. First, Delaware judges fully realize they are expected *always* to give sound reasons for their decisions. Exceptions do not go unnoticed, nor are they casually tolerated by interested parties or observing legal scholars. Second, their commitment to sound judicial reasoning, in turn, orients them *institutionally*—cognitively, in their own positional interest—to endeavor to act with consistency across cases and over time. This is particularly true when a rapidly changing business environment presents them with governance disputes whose complexity or unusualness throws them off course for a time. Their institutional orientation and positional interest drive them, again strictly cognitively, to *seek* consistency or, at least, to avoid fragmentation, unexplainable breakdowns in reasoning. Third, in meeting both expectations in so many cases, Delaware judges have become corporate law specialists. More than other state judges, who hear governance disputes more infrequently, Delaware judges develop a pride of craft in this area of the law. Fourth, and most important, in meeting both expectations with a specialist's pride, Delaware judges consider, however implicitly at times, whether there is a possible relationship between corporate governance and institutional design. This is why we think it appropriate to perceive them as environmental agents who uniquely perform a pattern maintenance function for American civil society. This is also why we think it appropriate to think of Delaware as this country's constitutional court for powerful corporate persons.

II. The Delaware Advantage: Code, Courts, Services

The advantages Delaware has over other states in incorporating and reincorporating businesses include a responsive legislature, a flexible General Corporation Code, courts specialized in corporate law cases, a mass of case law precedent, an efficient Secretary of State Office, and efficient private corporate service companies.[16] Delaware's General Corporation Code is liberal. It gives corporate managers great flexibility in conducting their business affairs, with shareholder approval. For instance, Delaware's case law standard of corporate officers' fiduciary duty of care, the "gross negligence" standard, is "the least restrictive standard of care" of all states that potentially rival Delaware for charters.[17] More generally, provisions in the Delaware Code lay out practical, off-the-rack ways of dealing with problems. Corporate officers are free either to adopt them or to vary them in terms of how they will be applied to their company.[18]

Aside from being flexible, the Delaware Code is also periodically amended by the General Assembly, which since 1967 has been under the supervision of the Section on General Corporation Law of Delaware's Bar Association. The amendment process makes it difficult for pressure groups, other than the Delaware Bar itself, to change the Code in their own narrow interests. Any proposed Code revision first goes to the Section, which carefully studies it in subcommittees.[19] In point of fact, the Section itself develops and drafts most proposed Code amendments. In any case, changes that are approved in subcommittees are sent to the Section Council, then to the Executive Committee of the Bar Association, and finally to the state's two-house General Assembly. In the Assembly, the Delaware Constitution requires a supermajority two-thirds vote of both chambers in order to revise the Code.[20] With rare exceptions both chambers rubberstamp Bar Association proposals.[21]

Given the flexibility of its Code and its Assembly's responsiveness to changes in the business environment, the actual meaning of Delaware's General Corporation law is largely a product of case law. Judicial decisions in hundreds of specific governance disputes, and particularly those in the most unusual, complex, and controversial ones, comprise the substance of Delaware law. This is why the late Ernest Folk, and today Rodman Ward and Edward Welch, and all other legal commentators, refer constantly to Delaware cases, and particularly to recent cases, as they describe and explain Delaware's General Corporation law.[22] It is not possible to explain what the Code means without presenting the reasoning of Chancery and the Supreme Court in numerous cases.

All corporate law cases in Delaware are filed in Chancery Court, which is currently composed of one Chancellor and four Vice Chancellors (until 1978 there were two). All appeals from Chancery go to the Delaware Supreme Court, which is composed of five Justices (whereas most state supreme courts have seven, and the U.S. Supreme Court has nine). All Delaware judges—whether those serving in Chancery, the Supreme Court, or the Superior Court, Delaware's general court—are appointed by the governor, with State Senate confirmation, for 12-year, renewable terms. This makes Delaware judges broadly responsive to elected officials and yet considerably independent from them.[23] Appointment rather than election, however, also increases the influence of Delaware's Bar Association in these judicial selections.[24]

Delaware's Constitution provides that no more than 50 percent of all state judges (spanning all three courts) may be drawn from the same major political party.[25] Aside from this formality, however, the nomination process "is largely divorced from party politics in practice."[26] The Executive Committee of Delaware's Bar Association appoints a nominating commission to screen all candidates and submit a list to the governor, from which he or she makes appointments.[27] The commission is required to submit at least three nominees for each vacancy unless it agrees unanimously to submit fewer.[28] This happened in 1994 when the commission refused to renominate Justice Andrew Moore for another 12-year term to the Supreme Court and instead submitted one name, Vice Chancellor Carolyn Berger.[29] Moore had a reputation at the Bar for humiliating the lawyers appearing before him.[30] Most appointees to Chancery and the Supreme Court are experienced, respected practitioners of Delaware corporate law. Those who lack experience in this area are soon socialized into its "peculiar practices" as a result of the high degree of collegiality on the Delaware bench.[31]

Delaware's Chancery Court gained a national reputation for expertise in corporate law cases early in the twentieth century and since then has developed the largest "well-reasoned" body of corporate precedent in the country—and the world.[32] The same is true of precedent covering hostile activity in particular. As Easterbrook and Fischel have observed, "Delaware has by far the most developed body of case law on tender offers."[33] Being a court in equity, not in common law, Chancery has no jurisdiction over criminal cases or tort cases seeking damages.[34] Since 1971, Chancery has also been relieved of family court matters.[35] By contrast, other states use various judges, drawn from courts of general, common law jurisdiction, to hear corporate law cases—in the midst of dockets filled with myriad criminal or civil cases.[36]

Delaware's Supreme Court, like all state supreme courts, is a general appellate court. Thus, it hears appeals not only from Chancery but also from Delaware's common law court, the Superior Court. The Supreme Court's docket is divided roughly evenly between criminal and civil cases (207 and 249 respectively in 1995). Its corporate cases are a minority of the civil half but "have an obvious prominence."[37]

Since Delaware limits corporate litigation to Chancery and then, on appeal, to the Supreme Court, this means that these two courts are the only state courts in the United States with truly specialized expertise in corporate law cases.[38] It also means that these judges have a positional interest that differs significantly from the interests of other state judges. Thus, Donald Wolfe and Michael Pittenger describe Chancery's "role" as "the nation's principal forum for the resolution of internal corporate governance disputes."[39]

Being a court in equity, not in common law, Chancery is not permitted to conduct jury trials (and a litigant in equity has no right to jury trial). Indeed, Chancery rarely operates in a formal courtroom setting. It typically operates as a tribunal or forum, as do appellate courts (state and federal Supreme Courts included) which otherwise combine equity and common law procedures.[40] And Chancery values its time and that of the lawyers who argue before it. It does not require an opening brief or memorandum with a motion, but its guidelines are strict for those who wish to do so. "Without express permission of the court, no opening or answering brief may exceed fifty pages and no reply brief may exceed thirty pages, in each instance exclusive of tables of contents and citations."[41] The Chancellor and Vice Chancellors also operate like appellate judges by presenting reasons for their decisions both orally and in writing;[42] hence, the large body of precedent in Delaware corporate law cases. "[T]he Chancellor and Vice Chancellors have been called upon more frequently than their counterparts in the [common] law courts to articulate the basis for their decisions in written opinions."[43] Unlike appellate courts, however, Chancery is authorized, as a court in equity, to exercise all of its business, if it wishes, in chambers; it may elect to hear cases of consequence in open court.[44]

Being a court in equity, not in common law, Chancery may assume jurisdiction over a case "regardless of whether [this] issue has been raised by the parties" actually involved.[45] Chancery's jurisdiction is any right to equity or fairness that is not traditionally recognized at common law or that can not receive an adequate remedy at common law.[46] Chancery maintains dockets in Delaware's three counties (New Castle, Kent, and

Sussex), and cases may be brought in any county irrespective of where the parties are located. The Chancellor assigns cases to himself or a Vice Chancellor on a rotating basis, with consideration given to the cases already pending before each.[47]

The Delaware Supreme Court typically works in three-justice panels, not *en banc* (as a court of the whole).[48] Under the Court's Internal Operating Procedures, the three panelists do not discuss cases until after hearing oral argument; thus, they act like jurors. Case assignments are rotated to discourage development of specialties.[49]

Quite unlike the U.S. Supreme Court, Delaware's Supreme Court rarely issues separate or divided opinions on appeals from Chancery, even on deeply controversial issues.[50] They do so in only 3 percent of reported cases, whereas this figure is 70 percent for California's Supreme Court.[51] Thus, all of the Delaware Supreme Court's hostile takeover cases in the 1980s and early 1990s were decided unanimously.[52] There are costs for a panelist who dissents from colleagues. Any panel disagreement automatically initiates an *en banc* hearing, as does any case in which a Delaware precedent may be overturned, any capital case, and any case in which two Justices vote to hear *en banc*. This means, therefore, that a Justice can dissent only if he or she is willing to force a full court hearing, and then to continue adhering to a dissenting position. When this happens, the Court does not tell the parties why it is rehearing.[53]

Aside from a Chancery court specialized in corporate law matters, and then a Supreme Court similarly specialized in hearing appeals, Delaware's office of the Secretary of State is also specialized, in this case in maintaining all corporate records. In addition, private corporate service companies work closely with this office, particularly in filing papers that deal with takeovers.[54]

What, then, is the Delaware advantage? Other states can duplicate its Code. What they can not duplicate are Delaware's public and private services. And they can not guarantee that their own courts of general jurisdiction will follow precedents of Delaware's courts in equity.[55] For instance, Nevada is in second place, far behind Delaware, in receiving reincorporations, but up to 1995 a case had not yet gone to its Supreme Court testing the standard of directors' fiduciary duty of care contained in its Code.[56] Moreover, consider what would happen if a state, such as Nevada, were to try to challenge Delaware more directly by establishing a specialized court dedicated to hearing corporate cases, and if its legislature instructed this court explicitly by statute to follow Delaware precedent. It would still take considerable time for the new court to develop the local judicial expertise and specialized bar now found uniquely in Delaware, and even longer for the state's Supreme Court to do so hearing appeals.[57]

Thus, Delaware's dominance today is self-reinforcing. Being so dominant, this reduces the costs for lawyers who decide to specialize in Delaware corporate law (as opposed to other state corporate law). Once they do, they then have strong incentives to advise their corporate clients either to remain in Delaware or to move to Delaware. Thus, every year Delaware adds more franchise tax receipts, more legal precedents, and more judicial and legal expertise.[58] What typically happens today is that Delaware's General Assembly and courts take the lead in adapting corporate law to changing times, and then most other states eventually follow their lead. The General Assembly acts far more quickly than Congress in reversing what it perceives to be undesirable judicial decisions. For instance, under the watchful eye of the Delaware Bar, which clearly has a positional interest of its own in keeping Delaware corporate law up to date, the General Assembly responded to the *Van Gorkom* decision by statute within a year and a half of the Supreme Court's decision.[59]

III. The Market for Corporate Charters

1. Four Explanations for Delaware's Dominance

Having presented advantages Delaware offers to corporations whose officers are shopping for a charter state, we can now turn to legal scholars' four major explanations for why Delaware fares so well in a "market for corporate charters."[60]

A. INSTITUTIONALIZING MANAGEMENT SOVEREIGNTY

Beginning with William Cary in 1974, many legal traditionalists once offered a "race to the bottom" explanation for why so many major companies incorporate in Delaware. They held that state competition for corporate charters can only favor management, not dispersed shareholders, and certainly not other stakeholders.[61] Management, after all, ultimately decides where to incorporate. Since it is likely to decide this in its own positional interests, management will select a state whose General Corporation law makes it difficult for shareholders (and stakeholders) to challenge its discretion. As a result, these legal scholars held that Delaware incorporates nearly half of all major companies precisely because its General Corporation law has always led the way in protecting and broadening management's positional power within corporate governance structures.[62] They also held later, against contractarians, that the competitive pressures of self-regulating markets fail to counterbalance the obstacles that Delaware's General Corporation Law presents to shareholders (and stakeholders).

Although initially appealing, because of this explanation's simplicity and conspiratorial tone, "Cary's proposal found no footing" and it misunderstands "the economic structure of the corporation and of corporate law."[63] For example, "progressive" legal scholar Douglas Branson categorized all 66 corporate law opinions of the Delaware Supreme Court from 1974 to 1987, beginning the year Cary published his race to the bottom thesis. Branson's empirical study revealed that "in over 55 percent of the published decisions" shareholders predominated, not management.[64] In addition, Cary's proponents today face the problem that decisions by Chancery and Delaware's Supreme Court over the past quarter century "established ever more precise and demanding principles of fiduciary conduct"—something that management hardly advocated or preferred to happen. "By endeavoring to promote the interests of all corporate constituencies without unduly favoring management or the stockholders, the Delaware courts further enhanced Delaware's status as a highly respected corporate litigation forum."[65]

B. INSTITUTIONALIZING A CURIOUS MIX: BALANCING AND MARKET-MIMICKING RULES

Beginning with Judge Ralph Winter in 1977, many legal contractarians (including Barry Baysinger and Henry Butler, Frank Easterbrook and Daniel Fischel) presented the opposite view, a "race to the top."[66] They held that each certificate of incorporation is a contract into which constituents enter freely, in their own interests. Delaware incorporates more major companies than any other state because its General Corporation law attracts not only management but also shareholders and, then at least indirectly, stakeholders. Contractarians are convinced, of course, that what is good for shareholders is ultimately good for society. It follows for them that any corporate certificate and General Corporation law that favors shareholders broadly serves all other corporate constituents.

Contractarians are also confident that self-regulating markets unencumbered by "state paternalism" not only increase corporate efficiency but also price out "charter-mongering," any bottlenecks in state competition for charters. Thus, contractarians see this competition ultimately reflecting, and augmenting, hidden hand outcomes of capital, product, and labor markets, not "artificially" distorting them. When firms operate under a legal regime that places "artificial obstacles" in the way of maximizing share value, these firms will be outperformed by those operating under a legal regime that does not.[67] "Just as the business judgment rule leaves to capital markets the punishment of errant managers, so the Constitution leaves to markets the discipline of errant states."[68]

The problem is that neither Cary nor Winter really explained how Delaware *maintains* its dominance in a market for charters. Other legal scholars endeavor to do so by focusing their attention on the "swing vote" in the charter market, the reincorporating trade.[69] Why do firms typically move into Delaware rather than shop around?

c. INSTITUTIONALIZING NORMS THAT (SOMEHOW) ENHANCE EFFICIENCY

Lucian Bebchuk, Robert Clark, John Coffee, Robert Gordon, and other legal scholars who do not share contractarians' unbounded faith in self-regulating markets offer a more recent, revisionist explanation for why Delaware is such an appealing place to incorporate or reincorporate. They point out that Delaware's General Corporation law has not abolished all mandatory rules. This must mean its General Assembly and courts continue to believe that existing public law norms and fiduciary duties contribute—somehow—to corporate domestic profitability and global competitiveness. Management, in turn, must believe these lawmakers and judges have good reasons for keeping mandatory rules in their Code. But how can court-enforced *norms* of corporate behavior (which bring a qualitative standard of analysis into governance disputes) possibly *facilitate* maximizing behavior (which would seem to hinge exclusively on economic, quantitative outcomes)?

These revisionist legal scholars hold that corporate governance structures do not typically institutionalize strictly market-mimicking behavior. They institutionalize their constituents' collective efforts to advance more qualitative goals, including that of good governance, of either preventing or resolving positional conflicts before they become governance disputes.[70] The seeming "inefficiencies" of the qualitative factors contributing to good governance have not self-evidently harmed these corporations' domestic profitability and global competitiveness. To the extent they have not, then to this same extent shareholders opting out from Delaware's mandatory rules might. By substituting suppletory rules and enabling rules for these mandatory rules, shareholders might end up approving certificates of incorporation (or by-law changes) that entrench positional conflicts and increase governance disputes—thereby, ironically increasing agency costs at least in the short term. True, as shareholder majorities act in self-interested ways in adjusting corporate governance structures to respond to rising agency costs, they might "in the long run" hit upon suppletory and enabling rules that reverse this trend. But the point these revisionist legal scholars are making is we cannot expect shareholder opting out to accomplish this in a more foreseeable future, and this is the only "future" that really counts for shareholders (or contractarians).

D. INSTITUTIONALIZING DELIBERATION REGARDING CORPORATE PURPOSE

Roberta Romano, Jonathan Macey, and other contractarians offer a revisionist explanation of their own for Delaware's success, but the irony is this explanation moves them outside today's orthodoxy of liberal complacency and, therefore, beyond the economic concepts they employ in making it. They point out, against fellow contractarians as well as the revisionists just discussed, that Delaware's General Corporation law is not the most optimizing by any standard, quantitative *or qualitative*. Its Code has always included, and continues to include, all sorts of "inefficiencies." These legal scholars contend, however, that managers decide to incorporate in Delaware for reasons that are simultaneously institutional and strategic, not more narrowly economic.

Managers believe, and company shareholders and stakeholders seemingly agree, that for all of the inefficiencies attending incorporating in Delaware, these inefficiencies are counterbalanced by the sophistication of this state's Chancery Court, Supreme Court, and corporate bar. As one journalist put it in the early 1990s:

> [L]awyers for QVC and Viacom Inc. . . . will have the advantage of arguing before what many experts consider the most knowledgeable judges in the country on corporate law. Because more major American companies by far are incorporated in Delaware than in any other state, Delaware has built an enormous body of case law. Because of such an arrangement, said Joel Seligman, a professor of law at the University of Michigan, "with complex corporate issues, you can be more confident that the judges understand what is going on."[71]

The legal scholars who offer this fourth explanation for Delaware's success are also explaining this state's general influence across the corporate judiciary and bar. They hold that managers and shareholders alike appreciate that Delaware's corporate judiciary and bar committed itself long ago to keeping its Code and corporate law doctrine broadly responsive to changing uncertainties in the economy. Easterbrook and Fischel concede the merits of this view even as they (a) open their concession by emphasizing that Delaware's standard charter is also largely "enabling" (rather than "directive"), and then (b) close their concession by accounting for Delaware's sophistication in terms of a pecuniary payoff:

> [Delaware's] success comes from its enabling statute, its large body of precedents and sophisticated corporate bar, and its credible commitment to be receptive to corporate needs because of the large percentage of its state revenues derived from franchise fees and taxes.[72]

What falls outside this narrow, economic understanding of what Delaware courts are doing is what falls outside a nexus of contracts approach to corporate law and economic concepts more generally: Managers and institutional investors recognize that Delaware courts are truly deliberative bodies. These courts do not respond to interest group pressures, but rather deliberate over the governance disputes coming before them. As they do so, they at times place the particular issues of particular cases into larger social context, that is, institutional context. Thus, Delaware judges at times bring their own informed sense of the direction of ongoing social and institutional change to their analyses of major corporate governance disputes.

Easterbrook and Fischel cannot call attention to this element of judicial *behavior* because deliberation over qualities, including institutional design, falls outside the scope of application of their economic concepts. Using the same concepts, the best contractarian Romano can do is contend, more narrowly, that Delaware law "reduces the cost of doing business" when corporations are engaged in, or are planning to initiate, unusual or aggressive transactions.[73] She holds that firms reincorporate in Delaware when they are planning an initial public offering of stock, a merger and acquisition program, or anti-takeover defensive tactics—all of which increase the likelihood that dissatisfied shareholders will bring derivative suits to court. When management becomes anxious about this, "specific characteristics of the legal regime become important, such as a comprehensive, well-developed case law, which facilitates the ready availability of legal opinions on specific transactions, and clearly specified indemnification rules" that protect corporate officers from personal liability.[74] Thus, Delaware dominates state competition for charters, in Romano's view, because it has proven, whereas New Jersey for instance has not, that it will not "welch" in guaranteeing the terms of its General Corporation law over time.[75]

2. Implications of the Fourth Explanation

Consider what this fourth explanation for Delaware's success means, whether stated narrowly as Romano has done, or more generally as our proposition that Delaware courts are willing at times to explore the relationship between corporate governance and institutional design. First, it means managers and institutional investors accept that Delaware courts have decided, for whatever reason, not to adopt a nexus of contracts approach outright. Second, it means they accept that Delaware courts have decided, again for whatever reason, to enforce as mandatory rules some remaining public law norms and fiduciary duties.[76] Managers and institutional investors accept these seeming "inefficiencies," presumably, because they believe that when governance disputes affecting them are decided in Delaware, the arguments presented and the issues at stake will be understood. They also believe, again presumably, that Delaware courts continue to enforce mandatory rules for a reason. When Delaware judges no longer believe this reason holds true, they will adjust their rulings accordingly. In short, managers and institutional investors are confident that Delaware judges will not for long impose norms of behavior on them that are needlessly constricting, let alone paternalistic or anachronistic.

For their part, Delaware courts endeavor ceaselessly, and quite purposefully, to cultivate this general perception of their sophistication and prescience among elites. This means Delaware judges are quite aware that they cannot issue rulings in major governance disputes that are widely perceived across the corporate judiciary and bar, and elites, to be extreme or indefensible. As *New York Times* business columnist Floyd Norris stated in the early 1990s:

> It is a historical curiosity that Delaware is where virtually all major companies are incorporated. The continuation of that depends on the state's judiciary being perceived as expert in corporate law, which it clearly is, and reasonably friendly to management, who in most cases make the decision on where to incorporate. It also helps to have clear law, something that the muddle over takeover law decisions in the last decade has not provided. A cynical view of Delaware is that it vacillates between protecting shareholder rights—*Revlon* and *Macmillan*—and management prerogatives—*Unocal* and *Time-*

Warner—without making anyone angry enough to leave and deprive the state of an important business.[77]

Clearly Delaware judges were not pleased with this perception of their "pride of craft" in the late 1980s and early 1990s. And just as clearly they had a positional interest in bringing consistency to their rulings and, with this, greater coherence to corporate law doctrine.

Traditionalist Melvin Eisenberg points out that because Delaware controls a huge share of the charter market and also offers many other amenities to the companies it incorporates that other states cannot match, its courts long ago lost any strong pecuniary incentive to curry management's favor in particular.[78] To the contrary, with its specialized Chancery and Supreme Court, Delaware is unique among American states. Its judges may address even the most controversial governance disputes in relatively statesmanlike ways. They may defend remaining mandatory rules by considering what we call the institutional externalities of changes in corporate governance, the harms that these changes can do to institutional design. They are less compelled than judges in other states to confine themselves to the immediate externalities of particular governance disputes, the harms done to discrete shareholders or stakeholders.[79]

Delaware judges are less insecure than judges in other states to speak directly to the broad issue of corporate purpose when they feel basic institutional arrangements can be challenged or enervated by any new trend in how corporations govern themselves internally. However, they are not sufficiently secure to speak to this complicated issue in ways that informed observers and elites think are extreme, peculiar, or inconsistent. Thus, they will speak to the issue of corporate purpose when they are relatively confident they can do so on the basis of general principles that they are prepared to enforce with consistency across cases, and thereby enhance their reputation for sophistication. They will not do so when they believe they will draw credible criticisms and, with this, precipitate any serious reexamination of their success and reputation.

IV. Deliberation and Pattern Maintenance

For all of the seeming inconsistencies of Delaware court rulings across the 1980s, this state's body of case law precedent offered litigants greater predictability in complex or controversial corporate law disputes than case law in any other state.[80] As hostile activity increased across the decade, Delaware's specialized judiciary offered litigants who were facing new uncertainties and risks an even more solid mooring: An assurance that the judges hearing their case would understand the issues involved and the arguments being presented by both sides. When David Skeel offers three explanations for the Delaware Supreme Court's "unanimity norm," which held true even during this turbulent decade, he simultaneously supports our thesis that Delaware courts are deliberative bodies that at times explore the relationship between corporate governance and institutional design.

Skeel's first explanation for why Delaware Supreme Court decisions are typically unanimous is that it speaks with one voice in order to maintain its reputation as the leading arbiter of corporate law issues in the United States.[81] Delaware Justices are aware that many observers and elites find considerable irony in the fact that five judges in one of the smallest states in the country hear most appeals affecting the largest corporations. Thus, they are more concerned about their Court's reputation than are, say, Justices of the U.S. Supreme Court.[82]

The second explanation is an interest group or public choice account that Skeel accepts only in part. Because interest group pressures change over time, any such account would seem to challenge the view that Delaware offers corporate officers and their lawyers predictability. Here, however, the public choice account is that the "unanimity norm" of the Delaware Supreme Court benefits the corporate bar, a "discrete community of interpreters" in Delaware and selected New York law firms who invest considerable time and human capital mastering Delaware law. Judicial unanimity serves this community's interests by obscuring how and why Delaware corporate law doctrine is developed, especially in difficult cases. The "doctrinal uncertainty" that results benefits a specialized corporate bar because managers, shareholder litigants, and other legal practitioners have to rely on its interpretations and explanations of what is going on.[83]

Skeel sees a twofold problem with this explanation of the unanimity norm. On the one hand, the benefits the corporate bar may receive from any such additional uncertainty "are not enormous" because corporate law is sufficiently complex regardless. On the other hand, and more important, the unanimity norm carries significant costs for each Justice. This runs directly counter to the way public choice theorists account for how and why public officials act. In the first place, the unanimity norm often drains Justices' time because, to maintain it, they have to rehear cases *en banc*. In the second place, and more significantly, the unanimity norm reduces each Justice's opportunities to develop an individual reputation.[84] Public choice theory does not easily explain this. It hardly revolves around situations in which individuals exhibit fidelity to a commons rather than behaving more self-interestedly; it revolves instead around situations in which putatively collective action is actually driven by self-interested behavior. Contractarian Roberta Romano is also skeptical that "lawyers' interests" dominate the Delaware Code or dictate what Delaware judges do, albeit for a different reason.[85] She believes Delaware's Code benefits shareholders (not management), and her reason for skepticism follows from this: She sees no evidence that Delaware judges are "siphoning rents" to the corporate bar at shareholder expense.[86]

So Skeel's preferred explanation for the Delaware Supreme Court's unanimity norm is a third one, namely, there is a "moral dimension [to] Delaware corporate law." And this factor brings us back to the fourth explanation above for Delaware's success in the market for corporate charters as well as to our own thesis about these courts being deliberative bodies organized in a collegial form.[87] Delaware Justices focus on whether corporate officers perform their fiduciary duties—that is, their normative, extra-economic duties to corporate entities. They do not focus more exclusively on whether they more formally meet the letter of Delaware's General Corporate law. If these Justices are to be effective as "moral arbiters," then their own unanimous agreement about what fidelity to fiduciary law means and entails is vital. Moreover, on the rare occasions when Justices write separate opinions, this sends a powerful signal that corporate law *norms* are being reinterpreted.[88]

Lawrence Cunningham and Charles Yablon support this view independently and our thesis more directly. They propose that the "primary reasons" why Delaware courts sought "a unified standard" for reviewing governance disputes in hostile situations during the late 1980s and early 1990s were "internal considerations of coherence and legal craft." These courts were not driven to this goal by interest group pressures of any kind, including those stemming from Delaware's Bar or, certainly, from prominent legal academics. Indeed, if Delaware courts wished to foster uncertainty, and thereby "create" work for a specialized bar, why seek a unified standard? There is also little evidence that Delaware courts were otherwise seeking to make life either easier or harder for management, or controlling shareholders, or hostile bidders.[89]

The evidence, as Cunningham and Yablon read it, points to an explanation they present in conditional form: Delaware judges "could turn out to be uniquely concerned with the internal consistency, coherence, and justifiability of Delaware corporate law." Moreover, as judges in equity, "they must also be concerned that the rules they are applying lead to fair and consistent results."[90] The point of this explanation is that the apparent fragmentation of Delaware court rulings after the *Revlon* decision likely troubled Delaware's judges, both professionally and personally. These judges were not likely pleased that many informed observers and practitioners were seeing mere formal distinctions separating their rulings in major governance disputes, formal distinctions that a specialized bar could school corporate officers in trying manipulate. For instance, corporate officers other than those at Paramount Communications might try to feign a merger and then claim a *Time-Warner* defense against a hostile bid.

Against the views of legal academics and journalists (recall Frank Norris quoted earlier) that Delaware court rulings in the 1980s were either "fragmented" or tied strictly to "formal distinctions," Delaware judges themselves kept insisting that *all* of their rulings express the same standards, not different or competing standards.[91] Their professional and personal mission going into the 1990s, therefore, was to convey these standards in ways that removed doubt.

Edward Rock goes further. He sees Delaware courts monitoring and sanctioning a "surprisingly small, close-knit community," namely corporate officers of large, publicly traded corporations and their lawyers. Rather than drawing formal distinctions between cases, Delaware judges' written opinions are "morality tales," corporate law "sermons." Rather than laying down tightly circumscribed rules of behavior, Delaware judges endeavor to instruct the members of this community about how they should conduct themselves in unusual situations, including during challenges to their control.[92] Rock thinks it mistaken, therefore, to treat Delaware corporate law as if it is driven by a quest for consistency in substantive outcomes and thereby tied to rules corporate officers can treat as formalities as they otherwise act strategically or one-sidedly to attain certain outcomes.[93] Rather, Delaware corporate law revolves around "fact-intensive, normatively saturated descriptions of manager, director, and lawyer conduct, and of process." None of this can be reduced to, or summarized in terms of, fixed rules.

Delaware corporate law is designed to instruct corporate officers about how to exhibit fidelity to general norms, and this is why Delaware judges bring *qualitative* standards of analysis to governance disputes. Thus, "concepts of independence, good faith, and due care" exceed all "rules or algo-rithms."[94] We will see in the next three chapters that the flexibility, yet pre-dictability, of these qualitative standards of analysis lies in the following dis-tinction: These standards rest on procedural norms of behavior and im-plicit references to a form in which the governance function (what Rock calls process) is organized. They do not rest on substantive norms of be-havior and references to the content of corporate officers' decisions or the content of the outcomes of particular governance disputes. Thus, Rock is correct when he says Delaware judges look more to process and motive than to substance. But he errs when he says there are no "mandatory rules" to guide corporate officers.[95]

At the same time, Rock also acknowledges a modified interest group ex-planation (as did Skeel). The Delaware General Assembly responds to pres-sures from the corporations it charters, and this indeed sets an outer limit to what Delaware courts can do. Delaware judges are not legal academics who are free to espouse any theory of law they wish. So Delaware judges in-tervene normatively into corporate governance disputes only with "the ac-quiescence of" the Delaware Bar, the General Assembly, and, especially, the companies Delaware incorporates.[96] We can add to this that during the 1980s only 8 percent of voters viewed hostile takeovers in a positive way, and this made it easier for interest groups opposed to these transactions to lobby all state legislatures.[97]

We will see in time that, consistent with this view of an "outer limit" which Delaware courts (and other state courts) cannot exceed without rais-ing doubts about their reputation, there is a more credible explanation for what Delaware courts were doing in the 1980s and are doing today. They were and are performing a pattern maintenance function for the larger so-ciety. Delaware judges act not only with an eye to their own legal crafts-manship, as Cunningham and Yablon correctly propose. They also act with an eye to institutional design (and their own reputation and national legit-imacy). This explanation is more credible because few corporations of any size, let alone the nation's largest ones, are physically present in Delaware (DuPont being the notable exception). The large number of businesses that this state incorporates, therefore, means that no management team, and no identifiable coalition of management teams, has the clout to drive a bill through the Delaware Bar and General Assembly. Why?

Delaware's corporate clientele *includes targets and hostile bidders alike.* Delaware has no favored state industry, other than the "corporate law in-dustry" itself. Being a small state, it is also cheap for insiders or outsiders—

including institutional investors and other shareholder groups—to lobby the Delaware Bar and General Assembly. Finally, the Bar itself represents diverse professional interests within the broad area of corporate law. It is not dominated by any identifiable set of interests.[98] This general, relative independence from all narrow interest group pressures explains why Delaware resisted adopting a corporate constituency statute in the 1980s or any other significant anti-takeover legislation, despite vigorous lobbying by management.[99]

V. Economic Orthodoxy? Or Updated Fiduciary Law?

In the late 1980s, Delaware courts were poised at a crossroads.[100] They could have focused their attention on identifying those changes in corporate control that harm discrete stakeholders, as immediate externalities. With this, they would have broadened business judgment rule protection to permit management to reduce, if not eliminate, these harms. Depending on how far they traveled down this road, Delaware courts would have either supported unilateral managing or divided corporate agency, thereby supporting stakeholder balancing. Either way, they would have lost their current (albeit often tenuous) mooring in existing mandatory rules. Delaware courts were reluctant in earlier decades to move down this road, but by the late 1980s it seemed at times they were reconsidering its merits.[101]

Alternatively, Delaware courts could have plumbed how much support there was in social norms and elite opinion for opting out, for facilitating shareholder contracting in a market for corporate control. Would American elites (and the general public) accept bringing shareholders' greater preference for risk more forcefully into corporate governance structures? Or would American elites (and the public) remain concerned about how changes in corporate control affect employees, retirees, local communities, and others?

> Which is it to be? A virtuous relationship with world capital or a vicious one? Much depends on the implicit social choices buried within political [and legal] decisions about the strength of the public's will and the thickness of its wallet.[102]

Delaware courts did indeed move rather steadily down this second road during the 1980s. This was particularly true of its Chancery Court, until 1989.[103] But they moved down this road largely by conceptual default: They

were less impressed with stakeholder balancing than with shareholder contracting. They appreciated that balancing is traditionalists' second-best alternative, that judicial imposers fail to update the fiduciary law tradition at
a doctrinal or conceptual level. This failure more than anything else left
Delaware judges with little choice other than increasingly to operate within
today's orthodoxy of liberal complacency. Thus, when they drew attention
to immediate externalities of changes in corporate control, they typically
focused on those that can be priced (except in the *Time-Warner* case).

Still, what distinguishes Delaware courts from the rest of the corporate
judiciary is that its judges at times break out of today's orthodoxy. This is
precisely what drives contractarians to distraction.[104] Delaware judges break
out whenever they consider the possibility that particular changes in corporate control (a) might carry some *qualitative* value for the parties directly
involved that, for whatever reason, merits judicial protection; or else (b)
might carry *institutional* externalities for the larger society. However, like
judicial imposers, Delaware judges do not draw this distinction explicitly.
Failing to do so, the substance of their rulings in these cases permits contractarians to read into their behavior that they are exploring only the first
possibility above. That is, contractarians see Delaware courts at times protecting substantive qualities that corporations putatively contribute to the
larger society, as if certain corporations are akin to historical landmarks or
endangered species. These critics genuinely do not see that Delaware courts
are at times treating corporations more sociologically, as intermediary associations *whose governance* bears on institutional design. This account of
Delaware court behavior eludes contractarians because it too moves too far
outside the scope of application of their economic concepts and equally far
outside today's orthodoxy. When Delaware judges explore this second possibility—that certain changes in corporate governance can harm the larger
society—contractarians can only explain this as a sign of their confusion,
their "muddling through."[105]

Unlike other state courts with less experience analyzing and resolving
major corporate governance disputes, Delaware courts are uniquely positioned to avoid drifting toward contracting or balancing. They are uniquely
positioned to keep their standards of analysis linked in some part to the corporate judiciary's fiduciary law tradition. After all, these are courts in equity,
not in common law. The problem, again, is they receive precious little support from judicial imposers as they act at times in "statesmanlike" ways, as
they at times perform a pattern maintenance function for the larger society.
Instead, this is when they hear forceful, often brutally cutting criticisms

from contractarians and balancers alike.[106] Contractarians in particular press Delaware judges hard to return to the fold, to today's orthodoxy. They want Delaware judges literally to reduce the issue of corporate purpose to that of agency costs, to harms done to shareholders that can be priced and recompensed.[107] This means Delaware judges are under enormous pressure to articulate their social vision, whatever it might be, in terms that can be reconciled with liberal complacency and economic concepts.

Despite these pressures, Delaware courts nonetheless at times raise the possibility that certain changes in corporate control, and in corporate governance, may carry institutional externalities for the larger society. They raise this issue, however implicitly, because they face another set of pressures, equally compelling though more subtly brought to bear on them: All informed observers expect them to take the lead in speaking to the issues of corporate agency and corporate purpose for the corporate judiciary and bar as an institution. Irrespective of whether Delaware judges wish to take this lead or not, everyone looks to them to do so by interrelating corporate law doctrine and their own rulings with existing social norms.[108] In the words of Chancellor Allen in 1987: "This court, being a court of equity, tries to bring to its function the most sensitive regard for the moral sentiments that lie below the surface of legal rules."[109]

This more general responsibility borne by Delaware courts qualifies them as an environmental agent that performs a pattern maintenance function for the larger society. And this carries an important implication for contractarians in particular. Contractarians know full well that they will fail truly to reform corporate law until they demonstrate to the satisfaction of Delaware judges that there is significant support for shareholder opting out in existing social norms.[110] Only when Delaware judges are sufficiently certain of this can we expect them to substitute enabling and suppletory rules for corporate law's mandatory rules. More particularly, only then can we expect them to substitute contractarians' two norms—Lockean contracts and Pareto optimal outcomes—for fiduciary law's relational norms, those norms mediating how power is exercised between positions of trust and positions of dependence in structured situations.

> Before prevailing doctrine is reformed, there must be a substantial failure of congruence between social norms and legal doctrine. . . . Of course, this conception of the interplay between norms and law bespeaks a tremendous faith that, over time, consensus in a free society will congeal around only those ideals and practices that, in the stubborn residue of our arational and asocial selves, we regard as timelessly decent and just. Moreover, to admire the cau-

tious dynamics of the common-law process regardless of its inherent flaws may simply be to reveal one's own root norm—a conservative preference for incremental change from time-tested traditions. This preference, however, seems predominant, if only by virtue of the continued and thriving functioning of our legal regime and widespread assent to its method and force.[111]

Everything ultimately hinges on whether Delaware judges eventually affiliate themselves without reservation to today's orthodoxy or whether they establish a more unambiguous linkage to the fiduciary law tradition. As long as they retain any such linkage, they at times interrelate how they read corporate law with their understanding of social norms broadly institutionalized across American society. This, too, qualifies the Delaware judiciary as an environmental agent that performs a pattern maintenance function. It is a particularly influential interpreter of existing social norms. Delaware courts endeavor: (a) to preserve broad public trust in corporate America as an institution, (b) to preserve the institutional integrity of the corporate judiciary, and (c) to preserve their own reputation and stature within this decentralized network of deliberative bodies. All of these goals or ends-in-view are qualities, not economic measures or priced outcomes. As Delaware judges keep such qualities in mind, in their own institution's positional interests, they quite literally socially construct an understanding of the norms spanning elites and the wider public. They do not try to anticipate how existing social norms, or elites' understanding of them, are likely to change, whether next year or in coming decades. After all, if they guess wrong, this can only tarnish their reputation, and their institution's status.[112]

This is why Lyman Johnson says that the corporate laws Delaware courts articulate "are socially loaded vessels."[113] This is why Jeffrey Gordon says the Delaware Supreme Court "tries to map the powerful feelings of an historical moment onto the law . . . [and that it operates at times on] a socio-historical impulse that seeks to restrict the domain of the market in corporate law."[114] Economists and legal scholars may not be able to identify the qualitative ends at stake in the issue of corporate purpose in theory, at a conceptual level. But everyone acknowledges which courts will speak to this issue for the corporate judiciary and bar in practice.

11

Beyond the Failures

A Threshold of Procedural Norms

When contractarians assume or assert that maximizing share price automatically increases social wealth and supports institutional design, they are complacent liberals. When balancers assume or assert the same two consequences follow automatically from broadening stakeholder representation in corporate decision making, they are complacent liberals. Both sets of judges and legal scholars collapse the three component parts of today's orthodoxy rather than treating each as a distinct empirical variable. Each part, however, informs a quite different empirical inquiry into corporate governance: First, when empirically do governance structures either maximize share price or sufficiently represent stakeholders? Second, when empirically do governance structures that meet either the first, quantitative standard or the second, more qualitative standard increase social wealth? Third, when empirically does the internal governance of corporations either challenge or enervate institutional arrangements unique to a democratic social order?

We saw in Chapters 3, 4, 6, and 9 that contractarians and economists explore only the first part of today's orthodoxy. They draw inferences about the second and, given their version of liberal complacency, they assume the third part as a matter of faith. We saw in chapters 4 and 8 that balancers treat all three parts more casually still. They add a concern about stakeholders to how contractarians define private wealth; but they then typically make the same inferences about social wealth; and, because they operate with their own version of liberal complacency, they assume any institutional consequences of stakeholder balancing are inherently benign. We showed in Chapter 6, however, why it is possible for private wealth to vary from social wealth. This in itself calls liberal complacency into question. But we acknowledged that demonstrating that this is a possibility is hardly sufficient to undermine contractarians' and balancers' criticisms of mandatory rules.

When we focus attention directly on the third part of today's orthodoxy, we lose the luxury of assuming or asserting as a matter of faith that unilateral managing, shareholder contracting and stakeholder balancing can never harm institutional design. We instead see an empirical variable, one worthy of disinterested inquiry on its own terms. Our point in the previous chapter is that Delaware courts, as courts in equity, do indeed see the third part of today's orthodoxy as a variable, and they analyze and resolve governance disputes accordingly, often implicitly to be sure but at times explicitly.

Delaware courts, after all, bring *qualitative* standards of analysis to corporate governance disputes when they enforce mandatory rules, and particularly when they identify breaches of fiduciary duty. This is a fact not in dispute. What are in dispute are two issues. First, what are the qualitative standards that these courts are using? Second, what purpose do these standards and mandatory rules serve, if not that of maximizing shareholder wealth or corporate growth?

I. The Purpose and Standards of Delaware Court Behavior

Looking at the question of purpose first, we propose that Delaware judges act in norm-based ways, rather than market-mimicking ways, because they assume there is *some* relationship between corporate governance and institutional design. This in itself moves them outside of today's orthodoxy. As judges sitting in equity, not exclusively in common law, they assume that when corporations are governed in "inequitable" or "unfair" ways, this harms the larger society *even if the transactions that result otherwise increase private wealth and social wealth*. Delaware judges also assume, as judges sitting in equity, that it is *their* unique responsibility to prevent corporate entities from harming society. The question now is how do they define or portray these harms, and when and how do they analyze and resolve governance disputes with this in mind either implicitly or explicitly?

As the "premier corporate court" of the United States, Delaware's Chancery and Supreme Court are uniquely stewards of the relationship between corporate governance and institutional design. By contrast, all other state judges can neglect this responsibility because their courts, including those in California, New York, and New Jersey, wield considerably less influence across the corporate judiciary and bar. Actually, these judges are largely unaware of this responsibility regardless because, as we showed in the previous chapter, they are considerably less familiar with the corporate judiciary's fiduciary law tradition. The same is true, of course, of Justices of the U.S. Supreme Court.

Whenever the internal governance of corporations challenges basic norms institutionalized in the larger society, this draws attention uniquely to the rulings of Delaware judges. Such attention can always potentially escalate into challenges to their national status and legitimacy because the latter is entirely out of proportion with this state's size and direct contribution to the economy This means Delaware judges have a unique positional interest in monitoring the relationship between corporate governance and institutional design. Thus, aside from considering how best to resolve the particular disputed transactions that come before them, on the merits, Delaware judges at times also consider a larger issue. Implicitly or explicitly, they consider whether their decisions in particular cases may permit new *patterns* of corporate governance to become established that are capable of enervating institutional design. Will permitting corporate officers to govern a corporation in a certain way establish a model of corporate governance that can enervate institutional design? This broader, "constitutional" concern about institutional design, we propose, is what ultimately moves Delaware judges from market-mimicking behavior to norm-based behavior, from applying quantitative analyses to corporate transactions to applying qualitative analyses to corporate decision making.

A "constitutional" concern informs Delaware court behavior because Delaware judges realize that their rulings in particular governance disputes can uniquely either facilitate or obstruct ongoing changes in the internal governance of corporations across the country. All of the cases we reviewed in Chapter 5 illustrate this. When Delaware judges accept or tolerate, rather than criticize, the particular ways in which important corporate decisions were made in the disputes they hear, they convert these specific decision making processes, and the specific governance structures framing them, into general models. With a favorable Delaware court ruling, *all* other top management teams are then free, in principle, to experiment with these processes and structures if they wish (and if their situations permit).

Our point is that Delaware judges criticize particular corporate transactions at times because they do not want to see the processes and structures through which they were carried out becoming models of corporate governance. They do not criticize them because they believe the priced outcomes of these particular transactions seriously harm shareholders, stakeholders or, for that matter, corporate entities. All of the cases we reviewed in Chapter 5 also illustrate this. Many of the transactions in dispute either benefitted shareholders or would have benefitted them, at times handsomely. Whatever harms they caused or might have caused to the corporate entity or any of its other constituents were hardly self-evident, let alone egregious in any sense. Yet Delaware courts rescinded these transactions, or supported defenses against them, or otherwise criticized corporate officers' behavior.

By contrast to this way of explaining Delaware court behavior, as a product of Delaware judges' unique positional interest in monitoring the relationship between corporate governance and institutional design, contractarians try to explain the same judicial behavior by focusing on the priced outcomes that particular decisions carry for shareholders. Given this narrow focus, they then logically conclude that these decisions are inconsistent in substance and often harm shareholders economically. This is a fair and credible description of these decisions' economic results. The problem is that this narrow focus can not yield any positive explanation of Delaware court behavior (see Chapter 6). It results either in proposing some conspiracy theory (interests behind the scenes unduly influence Delaware judges) or in resorting to name calling (Delaware judges are superstitious, unscientific, or otherwise muddle headed).

As complacent liberals, contractarians justify their narrow approach, and then negative accounts of Delaware court behavior, by rejecting outright the idea that there is, or can be, *any* relationship between corporate governance and institutional design in a market society. They do not believe it is possible for any changes in the internal governance of corporations to affect the larger society in one way or the other, let alone do so in ways that are "harmful" in any meaningful sense. Contractarians assume this, however, even as they see, as do all other informed observers, that Delaware courts are courts in equity, not courts in common law. As such, Delaware judges operate within a fiduciary law tradition that *explicitly* instructs them *not* to analyze and resolve corporate governance disputes this narrowly, with an eye exclusively to the harms being done immediately to particular constituents. Observers agree that Delaware courts bring *some* broader set of concerns into their rulings, and that these concerns are extra-economic—both qualitative and normative. This is reflected in Delaware judges' continuing practice of holding corporate officers to extra-economic norms of behavior as mandatory rules. After all, it is not possible to read the *Van Gorkom* decision or decisions in *Macmillan, Time-Warner, Technicolor,* and *QVC* without appreciating that broader, qualitative concerns entered the picture in one way or another. More generally, it is not possible to read the fiduciary law tradition in any other way, from the fourteenth century to today.[1] Again, issues in dispute are what these broader concerns or social norms are and how, if at all, qualitative analyses and mandatory rules address them.

Turning from the purpose being served to what these qualitative standards of analysis are, we can now identify specifically a major source of the inconsistency of Delaware court decisions across the 1980s and 1990s. When Delaware courts consider the broader consequences of accepting rather than criticizing particular decision making processes and governance structures, they have brought and continue today to bring two very different *qualitative* standards of analysis to governance disputes.

One qualitative standard is substantive normative and its potential scope of application is expansive. Here Delaware courts consider whether substantive qualities of particular corporate entities merit judicial protection in a market for corporate control. This is reflected in their references to "intrinsic fairness" in transactions and to "intrinsic value" in mergers or takeovers. Such terms are ontological. They invite qualitative analyses that are directly substantive normative. More grandly still, when Delaware courts apply such analyses to governance disputes, they substitute a putative relationship between substantive qualities of corporations and substantive qualities of American society for any identifiable relationship between corporate governance and institutional design. They typically do this implicitly, but in the *Time-Warner* case they did so explicitly. They assume changes in corporate control can harm particular entities in substance and, more grandly, can breach social order in substance, can disrupt an American way of life. This assumption, we will show, obscures rather than identifies institutional externalities, when the internal governance of corporations challenges or enervates institutional design. Instead of revealing unambiguous institutional externalities of corporate governance, this assumption leads to vague criticisms of corporate sharks, corporate hegemony, management mean-spiritedness, and social disfigurement.[2]

The other qualitative standard of analysis that Delaware courts also employ is procedural normative. Its scope of application is far narrower, yet this analysis too falls entirely outside today's orthodoxy. Instead of focusing on whether contracts are Lockean and outcomes are Pareto optimal, Delaware courts consider implicitly or explicitly whether particular decision making processes and particular governance structures would challenge or enervate institutional design if they became models, if other top management teams adopted them in whole or part. We saw this in particular in the *Weinberger, Van Gorkom, Macmillan,* and *Technicolor* decisions. Any references to the substantive qualities of corporate entities (and to an American way of life) now enter the picture only indirectly at best, through the mediation of deciding first on procedural normative grounds whether governance structures are acceptable models. This narrow yet qualitative analysis, we will show, reveals a specific relationship between corporate governance and institutional design in democratic societies in particular.

II. A Threshold of Procedural Norms

In Chapter 7, we explored in general terms how substantive norms differ from procedural norms when we discussed White's metaphors of corporate shark and corporate citizen. Now and in the next chapter we explore how differences in applying a substantive normative analysis to governance disputes and applying a procedural normative analysis account for Delaware courts' inconsistent behavior in the 1980s and 1990s. We will see in the last chapter how this also allows us to predict what Delaware courts are likely to do in the future, even as we cannot predict what will happen in the economy in coming decades.

Courts of any kind—whether criminal, civil, family, constitutional, or corporate—can only enforce laws with consistency when the laws themselves display eight procedural normative qualities (irrespective of what they require in substance of those subjected to them). Consistently enforced laws: apply generally to violators, do not contradict each other, and are publicized, prospective, clear, relatively constant, possible to obey, and congruent with the actual conduct of those enforcing them.[3] A shorthand way of characterizing this procedural normative approach to law is to say that consistently enforced laws are clear and possible to obey. They are clear at least to those trained in the law, and compliance with them requires typical or common effort, not unusual or heroic effort. This shorthand description encompasses the other procedural normative qualities because retroactive laws, unpublicized laws, laws frequently changed and laws not applied to all violators are simultaneously unclear and impossible to follow even with heroic effort. By bringing this *threshold* of procedural norms to today's debate over corporations and law, we can begin to explain the behavior of Delaware courts as well as account for the broader evolution of American corporate law since the 1890s.

1. Formal Democracy, Limited Government, Democratic Society

Lon Fuller, the Harvard legal theorist who first identified the threshold standard of consistently enforced law, held throughout his career that this is what ultimately distinguishes democracies from authoritarian regimes.[4] Authorities' *behavioral* fidelity to the threshold is more vital to democracy than their fidelity to any formalities of government, whether regularly held elections, competing political parties, or even basic First Amendment freedoms. After all, voters can grant authorities the power to enact laws that are unclear or impossible to obey; they can vote "freely" to subject themselves to arbitrary rule. The same is true of a political party or of citizens exercising their freedoms of speech and assembly. A party can mandate encroachments against the threshold and citizens can then speak and assemble to acclaim them. Thus, Fuller insisted that the relationship between consistent law enforcement and institutional design is more fundamental to democracy than the relationship between formalities of government and institutional design. Put succinctly, officials' behavioral fidelity to the rule of law is more basic to democracy than whether all, most, or any officials are elected and how voters otherwise react to officials' conduct.

Again, Fuller used his procedural normative approach to law as a threshold standard to distinguish democracy from authoritarianism in general. But this threshold is a much finer qualitative standard of analysis than this, drawing our attention to two other distinctions. One is between formal democracy and limited government, and the other is between limited government and democratic *society*. By drawing these two distinctions explicitly, we begin to see that the threshold also reveals a *specific* relationship between corporate governance and institutional design in democratic societies in particular. Corporate governance, after all, is simply private rule enforcement overseen by courts, rule enforcement in an identifiable, delimited set of structured situations in civil society.[5]

We begin by identifying formal democracy more specifically. Unlike a classic authoritarian regime, a formal democracy institutionalizes regularly held elections, competing political parties, and general First Amendment freedoms—reflected, for instance, in the presence of a relatively independent press. However, formalities of democratic government may remain in place while public authorities or private elites rely increasingly on force, intimidation, and manipulation to maintain order in civil society. As the case of Mexico before the recent election of Vicente Fox well illustrates (in the eyes of many area specialists), formal democracy is quite compatible with what we call an imposed social order.[6]

With this in mind, we can turn to the first of our two distinctions. Limited governments differ from formal democracies in that, beyond institutionalizing formalities of government, they institutionalize rules of *public* governance that are clear and possible to perform. Thus, courts (or, in Europe and Japan, administrative agencies) are able to enforce these rules with consistency and, in the process, to instruct public officials about what the rules (and judicial practice) require of them. This *quality* of public governance and judicial monitoring is unique to *the institutional design* of limited governments. Like formal democracies, limited governments are compatible with imposed social orders, as not only Japan illustrates (in the eyes of many area specialists), but as do many Western democracies as well. Consider, for example, the problem of corruption in Italian civil society and, more generally, the susceptibility to arbitrariness of "corporatist interest intermediation" across Western Europe.[7]

In turn, Fuller's threshold standard also points to how democratic societies differ from formal democracies and limited governments. Democratic societies maintain formalities of democratic government and also share the quality of public governance and judicial monitoring that is unique to limited governments. But then they go a step further. They also institutionalize rules of *private* governance for major intermediary associations that are clear and possible to perform. Here courts (or administrative agencies) endeavor ceaselessly to enforce these rules with consistency, and thereby to instruct corporate officers and association administrators (in universities, hospitals, and elsewhere) about what the rules (and judicial practice) require of them. This additional *quality*, of consistent rule enforcement and judicial monitoring within and around private governance structures, is what ultimately distinguishes *the institutional design* of democratic societies from that of formal democracies and limited governments.[8]

2. Democratic Society and Fiduciary Law Tradition

In short, democratic societies are marked not only by formalities of government and consistent rule enforcement in and around the state but also by consistent rule enforcement in and around at least certain structured situations in civil society. We propose that the structured situations that matter most here are those found in intermediary associations, not those found in other organizations or, certainly, those found in primary groups (such as families, neighborhoods, and local schools and communities). Put bluntly, it matters more in democratic societies how corporate officers exercise their positional power within governance structures than how restaurant owners exercise theirs over waiters and kitchen staff, how parents and neighbors exercise theirs over children, or how teachers exercise theirs over students. Thus, it is more important for courts to hold corporate officers to the threshold of procedural norms, if courts wish to support the institutional design of a democratic society. Restaurant owners, parents and neighbors, and schoolteachers may impose a vast range of substantive norms of behavior on those subject to their rule in the complete absence of any procedural normative mediation without this enervating the institutional design of *any* modern society. But if corporate officers are permitted to do this within corporate governance structures, this enervates the institutional design of democratic societies in particular.

We propose that this is the central point of the entire fiduciary law tradition, namely, extending consistent rule enforcement from the state to powerful private entities in civil society. Put differently, the central point of this distinct legal tradition is to encourage disinterested behavior, and discourage one-sided behavior, by anyone who occupies a position of trust in a structured situation, whether in government or in civil society.[9]

The problem that the history of fiduciary law poses for us today, however, is that English chancery courts during the Middle Ages and then American chancery courts in the newly independent country tried to encourage disinterest by imposing substantive norms of acceptable behavior on barons and then corporate officers. As Fuller would predict, they enforced these norms unevenly at best. We add that they also never really identified the public law interest that such interventions into the internal governance of manors and corporations were supposed to serve. Many informed observers first in England and then in the United States, upon seeing the inconsistency of chancery court rulings and the vagueness with which Chancellors justified them, became troubled that fiduciary law's norms of "equity" or "fairness" amounted to nothing more than each Chancellor's whim or fancy.[10] Chancery court rulings seemed to reflect each Chancellor's subjective impression of what is acceptable and unacceptable governance in manors and corporations. Contractarians explain Delaware court behavior in much the same way today.

Against this historical backdrop of uneven enforcement of substantive norms of private governance, we propose that for over a century Delaware courts in particular have been steadily substituting procedural norms of private governance for fiduciary law's more traditional substantive norms. Our thesis in accounting for the behavior of Delaware courts over the past two decades in particular, therefore, is that these courts moved even more forcefully in this direction in the 1980s, but at first unevenly, and then in the early 1990s with increasing steadiness. The problem is that this procedural turn is ongoing, not yet completed. Delaware courts today can either proceed with it or revert to interpreting corporate officers' fiduciary duties in more traditional, that is, substantive normative ways. The choices they make here, we believe, hold the key to: explaining the behavior of Delaware courts, identifying the relationship between corporate governance and institutional design today, and predicting what Delaware courts are likely to do in coming decades irrespective of what happens to the economy.

III. Qualitative Analyses of Governance Disputes

1. The Contingency and Vulnerability of Democratic Society

When rules of any kind become unclear or impossible to obey, those subjected to them cannot anticipate cognitively—either individually or interpersonally—what authorities will expect of them next. Authorities, in turn, are similarly confused about what the courts (to the extent that courts monitor their behavior at all) are likely to think of their own behavior. Everything comes down to a precarious, interpersonal dynamic: How authorities feel at any moment in each situation, the impression that those subject to the rules make on authorities in each situation, and what if anything courts ever do in response to citizen complaints. After all, unclear rules or rules that are impossible to obey do not offer authorities any guidance in distinguishing types of behavior.[11] Authorities are free to exercise their positional power however they wish, including in their own one-sided interests.

In imposed social orders, the conditions that allow individuals simply to recognize cognitively what rules require of them and of authorities are absent in both public and private governance structures; everyone is in principle subjected to arbitrariness both by the state and by intermediary associations in civil society. In formal democracies, the conditions extend only to formalities of government and basic First Amendment freedoms, not to how authorities otherwise conduct themselves in civil society; everyone is still in principle subjected to public and private arbitrariness. In limited governments, the conditions now extend to public governance structures but not yet to private ones; everyone is in principle subjected to arbitrariness within and by intermediary associations.

Finally, only in democratic societies do courts also *endeavor* to extend the conditions present in public governance structures to certain structured situations in civil society. *This process is inherently asymptotic and contingent in every democratic society.* It is never completed, extended to all structured situations in civil society. Moreover, any gains courts make in extending these conditions into civil society can always be reversed, at times quite suddenly.

2. Corporate Governance: Two Levels of Rule Enforcement

More than any formal democracy or limited government, any democratic society is institutionalized only partially and always in eminently mutable stages or steps (from type of intermediary association to type of intermediary association, from economic sector to economic sector). Its institutional design is singularly vulnerable to direct challenge and, even more, to enervation. We can appreciate why by considering how the threshold standard of consistent rule enforcement applies to the internal governance of corporations. Fuller's threshold standard allows us to make this move, from public governance to private governance, because it applies with equal force to how positional power is exercised and rules are enforced in any structured situation, public or private. The threshold identifies the conditions under which individuals in *any* structured situation *are able to recognize cognitively* and thus in common or interpersonally, what *any* rules require of them and of the authorities enforcing the rules. These conditions reveal a general *qualitative* standard, a bright-line threshold, by which to *begin* analysis of how corporate officers exercise positional power in any governance structure.

The threshold standard applies to corporate governance at two levels of rule enforcement, and it is exceedingly vulnerable to challenge or enervation at each level. One level is that of charters, by-laws and contracts, the suppletory and enabling rules of corporate governance. Are these rules sufficiently clear and possible to perform that they can guide corporate officers toward enforcing them in consistent ways within corporate governance structures? The other level is more important for our purpose, that of identifying the relationship between corporate governance and the institutional design of democratic societies. This is the level of fiduciary law norms (and public law statutes), the mandatory rules of corporate governance. Are these *social norms* of equitable or fair behavior sufficiently clear and possible to perform that they can guide the corporate judiciary toward enforcing them in consistent ways across courts and governance disputes?

We propose that fiduciary duties are sufficiently clear and possible to perform when judges interpret these social norms *primarily* as a procedural normative standard of acceptable corporate governance. With this procedural turn, they interpret fiduciary duties only secondarily, if at all, as a substantive normative standard of a corporate entity's "intrinsic value" or of a transaction's "intrinsic fairness." With this procedural turn, judges can also identify and keep in collective view a clear, qualitative relationship between corporate governance and institutional design.

By contrast, if they interpret fiduciary duties more directly as a substantive normative standard of intrinsic value and intrinsic fairness, they are endeavoring to identify and keep in collective view some particular valued qualities of everyday life, first within selected corporations and then in the larger society. They are assuming some putative relationship exists in substance between these valued qualities. However, they invariably allude to this relationship in vague terms because *any* such putative relationship between corporate entities and societies is hopelessly anachronistic in a global economy (see the next chapter). If courts did try to identify such a relationship specifically, this would indeed reveal muddled thinking on their part or, worse, their unjustified favoritism of particular interests at particular times. Thus, courts monitor the substantive "harms" that changes in corporate control putatively cause "society" always implicitly, always with dazzling metaphors (such as the corporate shark) whose import sounds vital or ominous but whose meaning eludes interpersonal understanding and consistent enforcement. As they act in this way, they also obscure rather than reveal what we propose is the specific, readily identifiable procedural normative relationship between corporate governance and institutional design in democratic societies.

Judges can only enforce social norms of corporate governance with consistency when judges as well as corporate officers can at least recognize cognitively what these social norms typically require of anyone subject to them. This threshold standard of consistent rule enforcement holds true irrespective of whether judges are imposing fiduciary duties (and public law statutes) on corporate officers as mandatory rules, or corporate officers are imposing provisions of charters, by-laws, and contracts on corporate constituents as suppletory rules and enabling rules. The threshold standard draws judges' attention in particular to *how* corporate officers, in positions of trust, exercise their positional power over others, in positions of dependence, in structured situations. Then judges consider only secondarily, if at all, the economic or other substantive outcomes of corporate officers' decisions and actions.

3. Mandatory Social Norms of Institutional Design and Corporate Governance

In short, one mandatory social norm of corporate governance *in democratic societies* is the threshold standard of consistent rule enforcement. This threshold is easily breached, but breaches are cognitively self-evident to *any* corporate constituent or judicial observer because it marks a bright-line duty borne by anyone in a position of trust in a structured situation in a democratic society. A *mandatory* social norm of corporate governance is not, and cannot be, any substantive standard of equitable corporate decision making or any economic standard of optimal corporate performance. A substantive standard of equitable corporate decision making never provides judges (or corporate constituents) with a bright-line threshold of acceptable and unacceptable corporate governance. Breaches of such a standard are never cognitively self-evident to any and all participants and observers. In turn, an economic standard of corporate performance is just that; it does not speak directly to corporate governance at all. It never suggests that there is any relationship whatsoever between corporations and society, let alone pointing to a specific relationship between corporate governance and institutional design.

The procedural normative threshold of consistent rule enforcement is *one* mandatory social norm of corporate governance in democratic societies, and Delaware courts at times *do* impose this social norm on corporate officers. Unlike more traditional interpretations of corporate officers' fiduciary duties, this threshold standard of corporate governance is uniquely *part* of these societies' institutional design. There is a second, related mandatory social norm of corporate governance in democratic societies and, thus, a second part of these societies' institutional design: The presence of *collegial* formations within the boardrooms and governance structures of corporations and other major intermediary associations. A shorthand way of characterizing collegial formations is that they are deliberative bodies.

Consistent with taking a procedural turn in interpreting corporate officers' fiduciary duties and the relationship between corporate governance and institutional design, the collegial *form* of organization is what uniquely *institutionalizes* public and private authorities' ongoing *behavioral* fidelity to the threshold of consistent rule enforcement *at particular sites of decision making*. The collegial form also uniquely *institutionalizes* ongoing deliberation and ongoing disinterested behavior at these same sites, public or private. This is not true of the three other forms of organization that are available to public or private authorities today: the bureaucratic form, the formally democratic form, and the patron-client form.

We discuss the collegial form and the other three forms of organization at greater length in the next chapter. For now we begin by providing a provisional definition of collegial formations and then asserting some implications of the presence of the collegial form in boardrooms and corporate governance structures. After we demonstrate the relevance of this concept for describing and explaining Delaware court behavior in the next section, we elaborate further on our provisional definition.

Collegial formations are distinct sites of governance or decision making at which participants deliberate and otherwise act in relatively disinterested ways (rather than exercising their positional power more directly). In deliberating and acting disinterestedly, members of collegial formations *at the very least* exhibit behavioral fidelity to the threshold of consistent rule enforcement. After all, when members breach any one of the eight qualities of consistent rule enforcement (by, for instance, failing to inform others about what they are doing and to offer reasons for their behavior), they simultaneously enervate deliberation and act one-sidedly rather than disinterestedly.

We assert that the presence of the collegial form within boardrooms and corporate governance structures uniquely institutionalizes deliberation and disinterested behavior by corporate officers at least at these identifiable sites. In turn, corporate officers learn within collegial formations how to exhibit fidelity to the threshold standard of consistent rule enforcement more generally, and thus how to govern corporations in ways that support rather than enervate the institutional design of a democratic society. The absence of collegial formations in corporate governance structures means corporate officers are learning the opposite lesson, namely, how to govern corporations in ways that breach the threshold standard. Thus, we also assert that keeping collegial formations present in private governance structures, and ever asymptotically extending their presence, is a *second* ultimate mandatory social norm of corporate governance in democratic societies.

More important for present purposes, we show in the next section that

Delaware courts at times also impose this social norm on corporate officers. Indeed, we show that they impose this social norm *more often, and more directly,* than they enforce corporate officers' general fidelity to the threshold standard of consistent rule enforcement. When Delaware courts endeavor to institutionalize consistent rule enforcement within and around corporate governance structures, they hold corporate officers first and foremost to the qualitative standard of making their major corporate decisions within and through collegial formations, deliberative bodies. Holding corporate officers to this qualitative standard of corporate governance as a mandatory rule, in turn, encourages corporate officers more generally to exhibit behavioral fidelity to the threshold of procedural norms as they enforce suppletory and enabling rules of corporate governance outside of existing collegial formations.

We propose, therefore, that keeping rules of corporate governance clear and possible to perform *over time* invariably comes down to institutionalizing deliberation and disinterested behavior within corporate governance structures, at the very least in boardrooms. It comes down to establishing and then maintaining the collegial form because only its presence, not the presence of any other form of organization, *normatively* mediates management's behavior short of unilateral decision making and one-sided exercises of positional power at least at certain sites. Thus, as two equally vital parts of institutional design, corporate officers' fidelity to the collegial form and then to the threshold standard of consistent rule enforcement are nonnegotiable social norms of corporate governance in democratic societies. Stated differently, both are *mandatory rules* of corporate governance *because* they stem from institutional design, not solely because they stem from the fiduciary law tradition as such. Enforcing *these* mandatory rules cannot be attributed to the whims or subjective impressions of particular sitting judges, or to the pressures organized interests bring to bear on legislatures and courts, or to anachronistic legal tradition.

IV. Procedural Analysis and Substantive Analysis by Delaware Courts

To demonstrate that the collegial form and threshold standard are not simply thought experiments on our part but rather inform the behavior of Delaware courts, often implicitly but at times more explicitly, we can reconsider in this light the cases we discussed in Chapter 5. In the process, we also show that Delaware courts continue to bring substantive normative standards of analysis to governance disputes. This, we believe, accounts for the seeming inconsistency of their rulings across the 1980s and 1990s, and it also accounts for their failure to justify explicitly their continued enforcement of mandatory rules.

1. Evidence of an Ongoing Procedural Turn

In *Van Gorkom*, the Delaware Supreme Court reprimanded Trans Union directors for not being "completely candid" with stockholders about a merger plan. This can be read as a breach of the procedural norm that authorities act in public ways, if they wish to instruct others prospectively about what to expect. What is more significant, the Delaware Supreme Court was most concerned that directors had not taken sufficient care in becoming familiar with the merger plan, and instead were being too obeisant to their CEO. Legal scholar Alan Palmiter proposed that the Court was holding Trans Union directors to a duty of independence (from the CEO and management), but he questioned whether such a rule is possible to obey.[12] We propose that the Court held directors personally liable because they failed truly to deliberate and thereby to maintain a collegial form of organization in the boardroom.

In *Unocal* and *Revlon*, the Delaware Supreme Court held that it would bring an intermediate standard of review to corporate officers' behavior in hostile situations because of the "omnipresent specter" that they may act in their own positional interests rather than disinterestedly on behalf of the corporation and its shareholders. We propose that the Court is saying that in hostile situations it is understandably difficult for corporate officers to establish and then maintain a collegial form of organization in boardrooms and elsewhere in a governance structure. When their own positions and careers are in jeopardy, it is difficult for corporate officers (or anyone else) to leave their fate to a deliberative body. Yet the Court is saying it will review corporate officers' behavior in these situations precisely in order to see whether and how directors deliberate over the transactions at issue and whether corporate officers otherwise act in disinterested ways. It will not allow corporate officers to act unilaterally either in their own or shareholders' positional interests. It will certainly not allow corporate officers to institutionalize such one-sidedness by organizing boardrooms and corporate governance structures in some other form that obstructs deliberation and discourages disinterested behavior.

In *Macmillan*, our account of Delaware court behavior is clearest of all. Management established a "special committee" to evaluate its own buyout plan as well as a hostile bid from the outside, but management selected the committee's financial advisors and otherwise acted in one-sided ways. The Delaware Supreme Court held that the committee needed greater independence from management and also needed to act in a more evenhanded manner. Again, we propose that the Court was telling the board, then its committee, to establish and maintain a collegial form, to deliberate and to act disinterestedly. The Court appreciated that shareholder wealth or corporate growth may be maximized when directors permit corporate officers to act on interests that they fail to disclose or publicize. And the Court certainly appreciated that contractarians are prepared to accept such behavior as a general model of corporate governance.[13] But the Court is saying that breaches of the threshold standard, in particular the procedural norm that corporate officers inform directors and then shareholders regarding what they are doing, compromises directors' deliberations. Such behavior by corporate officers is hardly disinterested. It encroaches against the integrity of the collegial form in boardrooms and, if allowed to go unchecked, will ultimately encourage (or at least permit) all other top management teams to organize their boardrooms in some other form.

In *Technicolor*, the Delaware Supreme Court cited its *Weinberger* decision of 1983 in which it reprimanded management for denying a shareholder minority critical information (again a breach of the procedural norm regarding authorities acting in public ways). The Court called for "fair dealing" by the Technicolor board, including "arm's length" negotiation with outside bidders and, thus, independence from management. We propose that the Court saw that the special committee was not organized in the collegial form, that directors failed truly to deliberate, and on this procedural normative ground it blocked two changes in control that were potentially Pareto optimal for shareholders.

Our point overall is that Delaware courts in the *Van Gorkom, Macmillan,* and *Technicolor* decisions in particular insisted that corporate officers establish and then maintain collegial formations, deliberative bodies, in boardrooms (and, by implication, elsewhere in corporate governance structures). Delaware courts insisted that directors truly deliberate as formal equals over the *qualitative meaning* as well as priced outcomes of corporate officers' behavior. Our point is that collegial formations are not sites at which directors take marching orders in a chain of command (the bureaucratic form), take perfunctory majority votes acclaiming corporate officers' behavior (the formally democratic form), or exhibit personal fealty to the corporate officers who supported their directorships (the patron-client form). *None of these alternative ways of organizing boardrooms would have survived Delaware court review in the three cases we just noted.*

2. Evidence of Residual Ontological Analysis

We just showed that Delaware courts intervene into governance disputes at times in order to support deliberation in boardrooms and disinterested behavior elsewhere in corporate governance structures. We interpret this as evidence of an ongoing procedural turn and, more specifically, as evidence of an effort to maintain the integrity of the collegial form at least in boardrooms. We propose that this is important because when corporate officers are willing to obstruct rather than facilitate directors' deliberations, they are essentially endeavoring to organize boardrooms and the rest of the governance structure in some other form. In turn, this same behavior means corporate officers are already "available" to act one-sidedly outside the boardroom. They are already "available" to breach the threshold of procedural norms in their own positional interests as they "enforce" other rules of corporate governance. Thus, we propose that Delaware courts support corporate collegial formations as a first line of defense in maintaining the relationship between corporate governance and institutional design unique to democratic societies.

However, Delaware courts have taken this procedural turn unevenly at best because the fiduciary law tradition emerged historically not with procedural norms of disinterested behavior and equitable outcomes uppermost in Chancellors' minds but rather with substantive norms of disinterested behavior and equitable outcomes. Residual elements of this ontological tradition are reflected still in Delaware judges' references to the "intrinsic value" of corporate entities and the "intrinsic fairness" of corporate transactions. Thus, in *Van Gorkom*, the Delaware Supreme Court pointed out that Trans Union directors had a duty to seek "fair value" and "intrinsic value" for their company. In *Time-Warner*, Chancery held that Time Inc. occupied a "distinctive and important" place in American society, and thereby merited judicial protection in a market for corporate control on this substantive normative ground. In *Technicolor*, the Delaware Supreme Court said it wanted proof of a transaction's "intrinsic fairness" and, worse, it said explicitly that it was not holding the board to any "bright-line rule" for independence from management. Here in particular, we propose, the Court was mixing a substantive normative analysis (intrinsic fairness) with a procedural normative analysis. Establishing independence from management means to deliberate (rather than one-sidedly to support any other constituent) and, therefore, to organize the board in a form that both supports and institutionalizes deliberation.

In *QVC*, the Delaware Supreme Court similarly mixed both types of qualitative analysis. It ruled that a board must treat all bidders in even-handed ways, and directors must be motivated to inform themselves about important transactions. A board need not hold a *Revlon* auction but it must seek "the best value reasonably available to the stockholders." We propose that any process of genuine deliberation by directors entails becoming informed and, therefore, results in exploring the options available. Referring more directly to a substantive norm of behavior (best value) rather than a procedural norm (establish and maintain the collegial form) only confused matters and made consistent enforcement more difficult in future cases.

Even worse, Delaware courts themselves impose duties on corporate officers (or hostile bidders) that are unclear or impossible to obey as putative mandatory rules of corporate governance. Thus, when rules covering takeovers or buyouts set conditions that make it impossible for these actions to succeed, such rules clearly allow managers (or judges) to block all hostile tender offers, or selectively to permit certain ones to proceed. This is how management's poison pill defense works. Management keeps these defenses in place to rebuff hostile bidders it prefers not to engage, but is free to remove them for preferred bidders. Unless Delaware courts identify when poison pill defenses are inappropriate in principle, as a general rule, they leave management with more than business judgment rule protection. They leave management with the opportunity to exercise positional power in one-sided ways, ways that entrench its power rather than serve any identifiable corporate purpose. Correlatively, when putative mandatory rules make it impossible for managers to defend themselves against any hostile activity, this clearly leaves shareholder majorities with the opportunity to displace any management team at any time. This is how a normatively unmediated market for corporate control operates, and it leaves shareholders with the opportunity to exercise positional power in one-sided ways. Our point is that impossible mandatory rules of any kind are more than displays of state paternalism; they are challenges to institutional design. They place everyone in jeopardy.

When Delaware courts hold that corporations have some "intrinsic value" that eludes pricing in capital markets, they are trying to enforce an ontological standard of corporate governance, of corporate "integrity." But such a standard is both unclear and impossible to meet. Delaware courts' *ultimate* justification for enforcing mandatory rules in *these* ways is their putative fidelity to a legal tradition as a literal end in itself.[14] In the process, however, they fail to identify institutional externalities of corporate governance today. They fail to identify any relationship between corporate governance and institutional design, let alone one unique to democratic societies. Thus, they fail to demonstrate that *any* rules of corporate governance are mandatory because they stem from institutional design rather than from legal tradition alone.

Informed shareholders (and stakeholders) must be able to recognize cognitively, with judges, when corporate officers either bear or breach their fiduciary duties, if these duties are to have any traction in practice. They must also be able to recognize cognitively when corporate officers either comply with or breach public law statutes, charters, by-laws, and contracts. If shareholders (and stakeholders) are unable to recognize breaches of rules of corporate governance cognitively, with judges, then they will also be unable to recognize cognitively when corporate officers act one-sidedly and increasingly organize boardrooms and governance structures in forms that discourage deliberation and disinterested behavior. This means, for example, that rules of corporate governance cannot require hostile bidders (as in the *Time-Warner* case) to conform to any particular corporation's "culture," as defined directly in substance by its management team. They may be required, by contrast, to maintain elements of a particular corporation's governance structure that some believe help to preserve its "culture" (see the next chapter).

3. Again, the Importance of Today's Ongoing Procedural Turn

Fuller appreciated how easily consistent law enforcement can give way to one-sidedness in formally democratic societies. He saw, for instance, that the case-by-case approach to violations of law adopted by some American regulatory agencies often results in enforcement that breaches the threshold of procedural norms. By privileging too directly the particular settlements that agencies negotiate with the entities they regulate, this approach often tolerates inconsistency. Likewise, when the corporate judiciary accommodates too directly the suppletory and enabling rules that emerge from unilateral managing, shareholder contracting, or stakeholder balancing, it also often tolerates inconsistency. Like regulatory agencies, state courts can keep these decentralized processes of rule-making broadly aligned with the institutional design of a democratic society only if they hold all rules of private governance, at the very least, to the threshold standard *as a mandatory rule.* When they fail to do this, rules of private governance can become one-sided or arbitrary—even if inadvertently. They then enervate institutional design—even if inadvertently.

In order for judges to analyze corporate governance disputes in consistent ways, and then possibly to resolve then in consistent ways, at least some standards of corporate governance must apply generally to all corporate officers in all publicly traded companies. This, in turn, already brings a *qualitative* standard of analysis to any corporate governance dispute. Consistent rule enforcement and the presence of collegial formations in boardrooms and elsewhere are not automatic or "natural" outcomes of self-interested behavior by shareholders in a market for corporate control. They are not automatic or "natural" outcomes of stakeholders' competition for power and influence in corporate governance structures. Clearly, they are not automatic or "natural" outcomes of managers' unilateral decision making. Moreover, the benefits of consistent enforcement and collegial organization are qualitative and institutional. These benefits are not readily priced or, for that matter, readily evident (or appreciated) by most constituents (or the general public).

After all, keeping rules clear and possible to perform and maintaining the integrity of collegial formations is not necessarily economizing. These are not instrumental means to quantifiable ends. This is norm-based behavior, not instrumental behavior. As such, consistent rule enforcement and collegial organization will not necessarily improve corporate performance. It will not necessarily result in maximizing either shareholder wealth or corporate growth. To the contrary, corporate officers' one-sided exercises of positional power through bureaucratic or patron-client formations might well yield these results.[15] This is why norm-based behavior within private governance structures is not somehow institutionalized automatically across all sectors or industries of an advanced society. Such behavior is not institutionalized in any sector or industry independently of quite purposeful efforts by judges to support it. The contingency of these efforts *exposes uniquely to empirical study the institutional externalities of changes in corporate control and changes in corporate governance in democratic societies.* The corporate judiciary mediates the institutional externalities of corporate power when it enforces mandatory rules of corporate governance that hold corporate officers, at the very least, to the threshold of procedural norms within boardrooms and other collegial formations. When this relationship between courts and private governance structures holds in practice, the corporate judiciary advances an unambiguous public law interest in two ways. First, it helps to maintain interpersonal cognition of at least certain mandatory rules among corporate constituents who are otherwise oriented by different, often competing, positional interests. Second, it instructs corporate constituents more generally about how to recognize, and then possibly to restrain, one-sidedness elsewhere in corporate governance *and elsewhere in society*. Here courts and private governance structures broadly support citizen vigilance more generally, a clear linkage to the Founders' political economic position of republican vigilance.

There is of course a corollary to this broader, institutional contribution of the corporate judiciary: When the corporate judiciary subordinates its mission of keeping private governance structures broadly aligned with institutional design to any other mission, it simultaneously narrows the "interdicting power" of corporate law's mandatory rules. With this narrowing, corporate law accedes to liberal complacency. It advances only private law interests and, at most, may compel corporate officers to reduce the immediate externalities of changes in corporate control. It no longer endeavors to identify, let alone to mediate, the institutional externalities of corporate governance.

Standing back, we can rephrase in the terminology of this volume Fuller's general point about the procedural normative integrity of law, now applied to the mandatory, suppletory, and enabling rules of corporate governance. Rules of corporate governance that support the institutional design of a democratic society survive the following *qualitative* analysis: Neither the rules nor their enforcement, whether by corporate officers or by courts, encroach against the threshold standard. And now we can state specifically the relationship between corporate governance and institutional design. Only when this condition of consistent rule enforcement actually holds true, when the threshold standard is actively upheld, can judges in different state courts *possibly* establish and maintain among themselves a shared understanding of what the corporate judiciary is doing as an institution. Such an interpersonal understanding among judges is a prerequisite for corporate officers *possibly* to understand what the mandatory, suppletory and enabling rules of corporate governance require of them. After all, only when an interpersonal understanding spans judges can judges then possibly extend this understanding first to corporate counsel and then to corporate officers, other corporate constituents (including shareholders), and the wider public of elites.[16]

Because other putative mandatory rules, more traditional or ontological readings of fiduciary law norms and public law statutes, cannot be enforced in consistent ways, contractarians' effort to replace *these* mandatory rules with suppletory rules and enabling rules is both economically sound and morally laudable. The public law statutes that republican legislatures placed in their special corporate charters in the nineteenth century could sustain shared understanding for only one generation because they largely delimited what corporate officers could do *in substance* even as economic conditions were changing.[17] Fuller's procedural normative approach to rules of corporate governance allows us to explain why these public law statutes began giving way, as early as the 1830s. His approach also reveals why these statutes gave way even more, and "rather suddenly," when New Jersey developed the first standard charter or General Corporation law in 1888.

As the first transformation began, republicans' once-shared vision of the particular way of life they wished to preserve with their public law statutes first dimmed among their successors and then splintered into disparate visions.[18] This happened because the material interests and personal beliefs largely shared by the Founding generation steadily eroded during the 1830s and 1840s. Even during this early period of economic and social change, the relative positions of elites in American society (their wealth, power, and status) were increasingly exposed to challenges, to greater competition. Thus, the very meaning of the substantive limitations that republicans had so self-righteously placed on corporations became subject to competing interpretations. Their zeal gave way to their successors' uncertainty. When do particular corporations contribute sufficiently to the "general welfare" so that they may then dedicate more of their constituents' time and resources to increasing their owners' wealth? When do particular corporations, to use White's later terminology, act sufficiently like responsible citizens even as they become increasingly committed to maximizing private wealth?

This breakdown of interpersonal understanding eventually extended to judges' and elites' general sense of the larger significance of these public law statutes, of their relationship to institutional design. Instead of these substantive limitations remaining widely perceived as serving any unambiguous public law interest, more and more judges and elites began seeing them favoring particular interests alone (see note 10). This absence of elite and judicial consensus here (or on much else) continued for a century, and it accounts too for a central fact about the evolution of the American corporate judiciary since the 1920s. The corporate judiciary has become increasingly reluctant as an institution to delimit in substance *what* corporate officers may aspire to accomplish in their positional interests or in the collective interests of corporate entities (as they interpret them). The trend of change since the 1920s has been one of steadily removing more and more substantive normative limitations on corporate power from corporate law doctrine. Thus, courts have been unwilling for over half a century to declare that the corporate agent *must* maximize shareholders' dividends, *must* compete for market share, *must* maintain certain employment levels, *must* retain a research and development division (or any other division), or *must* advance any other *substantive* end. By the 1980s, contractarians simply called on courts to accelerate this trend. In this way they anticipated and then helped to legitimate the new market for corporate control.

The problem today is certainly not that this trend continues, and at times accelerates. The problem is that opting out, as contractarians are promoting it, would effectively eliminate all mandatory rules, including the corporate judiciary's enforcement of the two social norms we just showed stem from institutional design.

For two related reasons, the American corporate judiciary cannot any longer impose substantive normative limitations on how corporations are governed as mandatory rules. The first reason is that all such limitations likely reduce a modern economy's domestic productivity and global competitiveness. These limitations needlessly stultify strategic planning within corporations.[19] The second reason is that courts cannot enforce these limitations with consistency regardless. In a rapidly changing economy and society, substantive norms are incapable directly of establishing and maintaining interpersonal recognition across judges, outside the mediation provided by the procedural turn we discussed above. It goes without saying that corporate officers and then the elite public cannot apprehend substantive norms cognitively, as a bright-line threshold. They cannot anticipate prospectively the types of corporate decision making that are "intrinsically fair" or the types of transactions that yield "intrinsic value." Thus, they cannot distinguish corporate citizens from corporate sharks on this basis.

Courts can "enforce" substantive limitations on private commercial activity only when the constituents directly involved decide, for whatever reason, to impose these limitations on themselves. This is precisely why Easterbrook and Fischel and other contractarians are so persuasive when they insist that much of corporate law is better left to suppletory rules and enabling rules than tied any longer to mandatory rules. Yet even if contractarians got their wish, courts would still be called on at times to enforce "contracts," the terms of transactions into which constituents entered voluntarily in their own positional interests. And courts would still experience enormous difficulties interpreting what "contracts" require when their terms cannot be converted into priced outcomes. In these cases, judges are called on to identify each constituent's qualitative contributions to a team activity, such as its effort, dedication, creativity, or "team loyalty." As judges endeavor to hold each constituent to the promises it made to the team, they soon find that the "rules" or "contractual provisions" in question, while suppletory or enabling, are still unenforceable.[20]

V. Two Mandatory Rules of Institutional Design

1. Procedural Norms and Private Governance

The threshold standard and collegial form comprise a bright-line standard of consistent rule enforcement and yet not a thought experiment or counterfactual baseline. Rather than requiring excellence or heroism from judges or corporate officers, it is not a particularly lofty standard for anyone to meet. Quite ordinary people meet this standard every day as they enforce rules of one kind or another. Yet, equally ordinary people also fall short of this standard as they enforce rules. It is, therefore, a practicable standard by which to draw sharp distinctions between governance structures, both public and private.

With one exception, corporate officers are free to act in any way they wish as they endeavor to maximize either share price or corporate growth, or, for that matter, as they endeavor to entrench themselves. The exception comes into play when shareholders challenge their behavior in court by credibly alleging that they breached their fiduciary duties by acting one-sidedly in their own (or others') positional interests. With this, top managers have to be able to convince a court of two things: They kept the board of directors informed about what they were doing, and the board acted fairly or disinterestedly, not as a pawn of a self-aggrandizing management team. We have seen that Delaware courts at times require such evidence from managers. Corporate officers have to convince these courts, that is, that the corporation's governance structure affords other constituents some opportunity to protect and advance their positional interests.

Most important, we can account now for the fact that the American corporate judiciary has always imposed *social norms* of behavior on corporate officers, that is, fiduciary duties. Courts impose fiduciary duties on corporate officers today because they still appreciate that corporate governance structures are indeed structured situations in civil society in which positional power can be exercised one-sidedly rather than disinterestedly. The corporate judiciary does not yet treat the corporation as an inculpable nexus or market cluster. Thus, it imposes fiduciary duties on corporate officers with an eye to protecting more than the positional interests of particular shareholders and other constituents. The Delaware courts in particular at times impose fiduciary duties on corporate officers with an eye to protecting "society."

2. Procedural Norms and Institutional Change

We propose that changes in the internal governance of corporations and other major intermediary associations account in larger part for differences in the direction of institutional change across advanced societies today than in earlier decades. All advanced societies, after all, are likely to keep in place formalities of democratic government, even when their most basic institutions change in ways that diverge dramatically from each other and from their own past practices. Indeed, it is likely that the last step taken as an advanced society steadily loses the institutional design of a democratic social order will be for its elites to suspend the formalities of democratic government.

What largely accounts for differences in advanced societies' directions of institutional change, therefore, is whether consistent rule enforcement is institutionalized first within and around the state and then also in civil society, within and around the governance structures of major intermediary associations. When any advanced society, including the United States, fails sufficiently to extend consistent rule enforcement into civil society, it can remain a formal democracy and limited government while courts (or administrative agencies) tolerate increasing one-sidedness in structured situations in civil society. It can remain a formal democracy and limited government as its social order otherwise becomes more imposed. As courts (or administrative agencies) increasingly permit those who occupy positions of trust to exercise power in their own positional interests in private governance structures, this transition is under way. Intensifying competition in self-regulating markets does not somehow mediate this transition automatically, as if guided by a hidden hand. Thus, contractarians cannot simply assert that all existing mandatory rules be replaced with suppletory and enabling rules.

The more fundamental question, however, is: Are economists and contractarians willing to acknowledge in principle—at a doctrinal level—that one-sided exercises of *private* power can enervate basic institutional arrangements in the United States as much as one-sided exercise of public power? At the moment they acknowledge that this is a possibility, they cease to be complacent liberals. They also move outside the scope of application of their economic concepts. They acknowledge that "opting out" of all mandatory rules is not inherently benign. They begin to accept the possibility that corporate governance may carry institutional externalities for the larger social order.

Our distinction between procedural normative mediations and substantive normative limitations begins to move the debate over corporations and law forward. It does so in four ways, ranked in increasing importance.[21] First, it helps to explain why traditionalists have been talking past economists and contractarians for nearly two decades (Chapter 7). Second, it helps to explain why corporate law lacks coherence and why judges issue rulings that Chancellor Allen calls schizophrenic: The courts are not capable of enforcing substantive limitations or other aspirations in consistent ways, yet such norms remain parts of corporate law's existing core of mandatory rules.[22] Thus, our conceptual distinction demonstrates that economists and contractarians have a point. As it stands, parts of the existing core are both economically impracticable and legally unenforceable.

Third, our conceptual distinction also helps to identify intractable problems that contractarians face at a conceptual level. Contractarians wrongly assume that all existing mandatory rules are substantive norms, thereby unenforceable aspirations. They assume this because they see correctly that judges fail to enforce the existing core with consistency. Yet one irony here is that the scope of application of contractarians' neoclassical concepts is too limited for them to conclude this. Their concepts do not permit them to advocate shareholder opting out from all existing mandatory rules, and thereby to assume without argument that institutional externalities can never come into play. Their neoclassical concepts bracket this issue from their concerns at the very outset.

Fourth, our conceptual distinction between procedural normative mediations and substantive normative limitations allows us to see why traditionalists ultimately contribute to corporate law's declining coherence and to courts' accelerating drift toward contracting and balancing. Actually, it reveals that traditionalists contribute to both processes in three ways. In the first place, traditionalists follow contractarians in treating all existing public law norms and fiduciary duties as if they delimit in substance what management and shareholder majorities can do. With this, contractarians easily demonstrate that in a dynamic, global economy, such limitations are aspirations at best, not enforceable duties. In the second place, traditionalists fail to acknowledge that some mandatory rules are indeed legally *unen-forceable*, economically *im*practicable, and also fail to advance any identifiable public law interest. In the third place, and worse, traditionalists fail to see that the fiduciary law tradition can be read, at least in part, as an ongoing effort by (English, then American) courts since the fourteenth century to institutionalize the threshold standard of consistent rule enforcement in civil society. By contrast, state legislatures' public law norms have always revolved around efforts to preserve some particular way of life in substance. These norms are responses to the demands of particular coalitions of interest groups at particular moments in time.

We propose that the only publicly defensible purpose any mandatory rules of corporate governance ultimately serve in a market society, and that any qualitative analysis of governance disputes ultimately serves, is to support institutional design, a qualitative end. The purpose cannot be to maximize corporations' economic performance, whether their share-price or their market-share, a quantitative end. Enforcing extra-economic *norms* of corporate governance as mandatory rules and analyzing governance disputes using *qualitative* standards of analysis cannot possibly be the most efficient means to maximize corporate performance in market societies. By contrast, strictly market-mimicking behavior by courts might be.

This is the point that contractarians fail to appreciate at a conceptual level, and that traditionalists fail to make with sufficient specificity. The collective failure of contractarians here in particular explains why Easterbrook and Fischel can be so glib when dismissing the significance of all mandatory rules, even as they correctly challenge Delaware court efforts to identify corporations' "intrinsic value" in substance. As one example of their glibness, they do not consider the possibility that when corporate officers develop habits of bribing officials overseas, these habits may be difficult, if not impossible, to stop at the American shoreline.[23] This, too, is an empirically researchable issue, not something we can assert *a priori*, one way or the other.

This gives us a way of evaluating contractarians' criticisms of corporate law tradition. If we find that corporate purpose, maintaining a certain relationship between corporate governance and institutional design, is not and cannot be served by applying a particular standard of analysis or by enforcing a particular mandatory rule, then this standard and this rule are indeed anachronistic, as contractarians believe. The standard and the rule needlessly hamper corporate performance. In addition, if we find that corporate purpose is not and cannot be served by applying *any* qualitative standard of analysis or by enforcing *any* mandatory rules, then this validates the Contractarian Challenge to corporate law tradition. It confirms that Delaware courts have no reason to resist applying only quantitative standards of analysis to governance disputes as they enforce contracts alone, as they act in market-mimicking ways. We just showed, however, that there is a qualitative standard of analysis and two social norms that stem from institutional design, and we showed that Delaware courts do at times employ this analysis and enforce these social norms as mandatory rules.

Contractarians would indeed eliminate substantive social norms of corporate governance from fiduciary law and public law statutes as well as most procedural social norms, including the two we discussed in this chapter.[24] Eliminating these from judicial analyses of governance disputes is a practicable option in a democratic society, however, only if there is in fact no relationship whatsoever between corporate governance and institutional design. This is what contractarians are assuming, and often explicitly. This assumption of liberal complacency eliminates the ultimate rationale for having any state courts sit in equity. It eliminates the ultimate rationale for corporate officers bearing any fiduciary duties or mandatory rules to an entity, as opposed to bearing only contractual obligations to shareholders, the entity's owners. Indeed, these points follow logically, as corollaries, from contractarians' proposal that courts enforce contracts alone, not mandatory rules. They are assuming that disputed corporate transactions do not and can never entail breaches of social order, only breaches of contract at most.

12

Time-Warner and Institutional Externalities

From Culture to Form

One-sided exercises of positional power can increase in frequency and broaden in scope across corporate America even as shareholder wealth is increasing. One-sidedness can also increase as stakeholder representation is broadening, and, arguably, as social wealth is increasing. Today's orthodoxy holds true empirically, however, only when corporate governance structures in fact mediate one-sidedness as they simultaneously maximize private wealth and increase social wealth.

All of the decisions we discussed in Chapter 5 speak to the issue of corporate purpose—What is the legitimate place and purpose of corporations in American society?—but only one does so explicitly, the *Time-Warner* decision. By refusing to facilitate a hostile takeover that was clearly Pareto optimal for Time Inc. shareholders, and possibly most stakeholders, Chancellor Allen explicitly challenged today's orthodoxy of liberal complacency. He raised the specter that this proposed change in control might harm not only a particular corporate entity but also the larger society. He challenged today's orthodoxy by extending judicial protection not to stakeholders, consistent with the earlier *Unocal* decision, but rather to a corporate entity's "culture." This is a substantive quality whose value to corporate constituents and the larger society, whatever it is, clearly eludes pricing or economic measurement.[1]

Consider again how distinctive *Time-Warner* is compared to *Unocal* and *Revlon*, the two most influential decisions that preceded it. *Unocal* rests on the doctrinal principle that management's business judgment is ultimately sovereign within corporate governance structures, as long as its defenses are proportionate to any challenge to its control. A Madisonian provision was also added, permitting management to erect defenses with an eye to reducing harms to stakeholders. *Revlon*, in turn, rests on the doctrinal principle that once a corporation is put up for sale, it becomes a nexus of contracts. The will of shareholder majorities becomes sovereign. Courts no longer legitimately hold management to a fiduciary duty of loyalty to a corporate entity as a long-term commercial enterprise.

These two decisions may well be at odds with each other, but the different doctrinal principles that inform each nonetheless share two important characteristics in speaking to the issue of corporate purpose. First, they each fall easily within today's orthodoxy of liberal complacency and, therefore, readily inform judicial practice. Second, and related, they each focus judges' attention on immediate externalities, on whether changes in corporate control harm management and stakeholders or shareholders. Neither *Unocal* nor *Revlon* orients judges to consider in any way whether changes in control and in governance structures might also harm the larger social order.[2]

Time-Warner was the first major decision to bring the issue of institutional externalities to the foreground (without, of course, using this term). The problem is that it did so implicitly and in an uncertain way. The *QVC* decision continues this practice. By contrast, decisions in *Macmillan* and *Technicolor*, and what they say in retrospect about principles central to *Van Gorkom* and *Weinberger*, reveal more clearly the difference between bringing a procedural normative analysis to governance disputes and a substantive normative analysis.

What is intriguing about the *Time-Warner* decision, therefore, is that Chancellor Allen employed a substantive normative analysis rather than taking the procedural turn we presented in the previous chapter. As such, he implied there is some identifiable relationship between substantive qualities of corporations and substantive qualities of the larger society *and* that this relationship merits judicial protection in a market for corporate control. He did not employ a procedural normative analysis and thereby endeavor, more narrowly, to identify any relationship between corporate governance and institutional design. The *Time-Warner* case in particular reveals that Delaware courts are struggling to find a terminology with which to express what are essentially republican concerns about the possible institutional externalities of changes in corporate control and corporate governance. As courts in equity, this is their unique responsibility as an institution.

Our thesis is that the *Time-Warner* decision illustrates the pitfalls of substantive normative analysis in general. As it stands, *Time-Warner* orients judges to enforce managers' fiduciary duties to a corporate entity that is no longer defined *either* as a long-term commercial enterprise *or* as a set of structured situations in civil society that contains positions of trust and positions of dependence. It orients them instead to enforce fiduciary duties to a corporate entity defined *as a unique "culture," way of life, or set of substantive qualities.* By treating corporations in this way, *Time-Warner* rests on some implicit qualitative standard for analyzing not only governance disputes but also a social order's direction of change.

Can Chancellor Allen or legal scholars identify the types of corporate cultures that merit judicial protection? Indeed, why should courts protect "distinctive and important" corporate cultures or *any* substantive qualities of corporations in a market for corporate control? Is it the case that certain corporations merit legal protection literally as an end in itself? Here the analogy is to endangered species and historical landmarks. Or is it the case, more consistent with tenets of American pluralism and a "population ecology" approach in the sociology of organizations, that courts are interested in preserving a certain range of corporations in American civil society?[3] Here the analogy is to a "population" or "pool" of corporations that society putatively needs either to preserve a "way of life" or else to compete effectively in a global economy.

With both analogies, the assumption or assertion is that certain substantive qualities of corporations are needed to maintain institutional arrangements truly basic to society, either culturally or economically. In both cases, the *qualities* at issue (those of the corporate population and those of the larger society) are not narrowly economic or readily priced but rather more intangible, more norm-based.

We identify a conceptual problem at the center of *Time-Warner* by showing that Chancellor Allen drew only one analytical distinction in his ruling instead of two. In addition, he drew his distinction implicitly and, therefore, tentatively. Chancellor Allen distinguished implicitly between priced outcomes and qualitative consequences of changes in corporate control. This moved his ruling toward the "devotion for intrinsic value" that Easterbrook and Fischel rightly ridicule. He failed to draw a second analytical distinction, one within the category of qualitative consequences. On the one hand, some qualities of corporations are reflected (presumably) in constituents broadly sharing a set of substantive beliefs, as the (putative) source of their solidarity. These qualities draw our attention to corporate cultures, and they open a way to asserting that changes in control can disrupt these shared beliefs and, therefore, carry consequences that elude pricing. The question still remains, however, whether anyone can demonstrate there is some relationship between the presence of certain substantive qualities of corporations, rather than other substantive qualities, and the direction of change of the larger social order.

On the other hand, other qualities of corporations are reflected only in whether their governance structures institutionalize corporate officers' behavioral fidelity to the threshold standard of consistent rule enforcement that we discussed in the previous chapter. These qualities are procedural normative and draw our attention to the *form* in which corporate governance is organized. We proposed in the previous chapter that there is indeed a relationship between the presence of a collegial form of organization in corporate governance structures and the institutional design of a democratic society. Our thesis is that we can demonstrate that this second relationship holds true in practice whereas no one can demonstrate the first holds true. The institutional design of a democratic social order hinges on whether the collegial form of organization is present in corporations and other major intermediary associations, not on whether certain corporate cultures are present in civil society.

I. Deliberation and Disinterest

To the extent that corporate officers deliberate together in a governance structure over the interpersonal meaning or significance of any valued qualities, they refrain from exercising positional power more one-sidedly in their own positional interests. They act more disinterestedly than self-interestedly. The same is true when other constituents deliberate together in a particular division, including a research division. We can put this point more positively. Deliberation in particular and disinterested conduct more generally are found only where corporate officers institutionalize a shared expectation that at certain sites everyone will provide reasons for the corporate strategies they propose.[4] The reasons corporate officers offer each other are adopted, disputed, or rejected on the merits, as everyone endeavors to establish and maintain some interpersonal understanding regarding what they will do next, including how they will keep the qualities that they value in collective view. Sites of deliberation are not present when corporate officers advance corporate strategies more unilaterally, by issuing commands, offering material incentives, or appealing directly to colleagues' substantive beliefs (for example, by pressuring the recalcitrant to be "team players").

1. The Collegial Form

Unlike three other forms of organization that corporate officers may adopt—the bureaucratic, the patron-client, and the formally democratic—the collegial form is present at sites of decision making and governance in which corporate officers engage actively in two practices. First, it is found where corporate officers deliberate over the meaning and significance of qualities, whether in their corporations or in their environments, whose value *for anyone in their position* is meaningful or significant. Second, and related, the collegial form is found where corporate officers also deliberate over how best to keep such valued qualities in collective view over time. When corporate governance structures contain collegial formations, corporate officers keep valued qualities in collective view, therefore, not by exhibiting fidelity to substantive beliefs or rituals directly but rather by exhibiting fidelity to the threshold standard we presented in Chapter 8. Worded as a formal definition:[5] Collegial formations are deliberative bodies in which members exhibit fidelity to procedural norms as they endeavor (a) to identify in common those qualities which are meaningful or significant for anyone in their position and (b) to understand in common how best to keep these valued qualities in collective view.

2. Positive Externalities of Collegial Formations

Only the collegial form uniquely *institutionalizes* deliberation and, more generally, disinterested conduct within corporations and other intermediary associations. All other forms of organization permit directors, managers, and controlling shareholders to substitute threats, material incentives, or appeals to substantive beliefs for a giving-and-taking of reasons. Deliberation and disinterestedness are only possible at sites in which corporate officers, who elsewhere do exercise positional power more one-sidedly, are oriented *cognitively* by institutionalized procedural norms to substitute reasons for commands, payoffs, and appeals.[6] Only the collegial form of organization institutionalizes their fidelity to procedural norms at three levels simultaneously: At the level of governance structure, collegial formations institutionalize a site-specific suspension of one-sided exercises of positional power. At a social psychological level, they institutionalize corporate officers' shared cognitive recognition, not an internalized belief or personal faith, that a giving-and-taking of reasons typically replaces all exercises of positional power at these sites. And at a social or institutional level, collegial formations institutionalize corporate officers' fidelity to the threshold standard of consistent rule enforcement institutionalized *only in democratic societies, not limited governments, formal democracies, or imposed social orders.*[7]

These three consequences of the presence of collegial formations in corporate governance structures are interrelated. Outside of this particular form of organization, a management team can only recognize meaningful or significant qualities in common when a CEO or one faction imposes its view on all others, its social construction of the corporation and its environment. This often happens in corporations (and other intermediary associations) *in all societies.* What happens uniquely in at least some corporations and major intermediary associations in institutionalized democracies, however, is that such imposed understandings are replaced by those arrived at in relatively disinterested ways through deliberation.

In this light, we can reconsider Useem's ethnographic finding of the early 1980s that the behavior of outside directors in American and British corporate boardrooms is more disinterested than self-interested.[8] Useem believes this reveals empirical evidence that outside directors share substantive beliefs and, more grandly, that these beliefs, much like good table manners, span an "inner circle" of elites, an elite culture.[9] Yet disinterested behavior within American and British boardrooms is not empirical evidence that directors share a social psychological quality, a shared personal faith regarding how "gentlemen" properly conduct themselves at these sites. Rather, it is evidence of the presence of an institutional quality, a particular form of organization found uniquely in at least some corporate governance structures and many more boardrooms in democratic social orders. Useem found evidence that boardrooms are often organized in a collegial form in the United States and Great Britain wherein one-sided exercises of positional power are unacceptable cognitively. Such behavior is unacceptable not because it is "ungentlemanly" in the eyes of those "in the know," an inner circle, the faithful. It is inappropriate because any instance of one-sidedness breaches a threshold standard that even the most boorish director *or outside observer* can recognize cognitively, *including any judge in any state court.* Consider in this light how Delaware courts reacted in *Van Gorkom, Macmillan, Technicolor,* and *QVC* when it was credibly alleged, in essence, that corporate officers breached the collegial form.

With this in mind, we add to our earlier discussion of procedural norms an empirical, falsifiable proposition: When institutional arrangements spanning the state and civil society fail to orient courts to support the presence of collegial formations in corporations and other intermediary associations, civil society lacks *institutionalized* sites of deliberation and disinterested behavior. Instead, civil society only contains sites at which rituals and practices of bureaucratic, patron-client, and formally democratic formations are present in various combinations. Such sites are found in all advanced societies, including the most imposed social orders. Ultimately, they all facilitate corporate officers' one-sidedness, their self-interested behavior. None of these sites supports ongoing deliberation over valued qualities because none mediates exercises of positional power short of one-sidedness *by its very presence* in boardrooms and corporate governance structures.

3. Negative Externalities of Alternative Formations

We may appreciate why this is the case by considering briefly in turn each of the formations corporate officers may substitute for collegial formations.[10] First, corporate governance structures within all societies are often organized in the bureaucratic form, as are many boardrooms. Bureaucratic formations institutionalize top-down chains of command that, at best, instrumentally implement CEOs' interpretations of their corporations' collective interests. Within these formations, each member follows orders—including interpretations of interpersonal meaning—in a strict chain of command.[11] It is suicidal to do otherwise. This means that a bureaucratic governance structure is consistent with the business judgment rule and the courts' approach to corporate agency and corporate purpose in the 1970s. Bureaucratic formations are found frequently in Japan and East Asia generally, and they are hardly absent in Europe, the United States, and Great Britain. Consider again what Delaware courts found in *Van Gorkom*, and then in *QVC*.

Second, corporate governance structures within all societies, and many boardrooms as well, are also often organized in the patron-client form. Patron-client networks institutionalize personal alliances of trust and dependence that, at best, instrumentally implement interpretations of corporations' collective interests by coalitions of managers, possibly along with selected stakeholders and institutional investors. Within these networks, each member exhibits fealty to his or her network of trust and dependence.[12] It is suicidal to do otherwise. Power struggles between networks can extend across a governance structure and, because this essentially divides corporate agency, the patron-client form is consistent with today's drift toward stakeholder balancing. Patron-client networks are found frequently in Europe and across the Southern Hemisphere, and they are hardly absent in the

United States, Great Britain, and East Asia.[13] Consider again what Delaware courts found in *Macmillan*, and then in *Technicolor*.

Third, corporate governance structures are rarely organized anywhere in the formally democratic form, even as this always remains a possibility in practice.[14] Formally democratic formations institutionalize majority rule, in the case at hand rule by management majorities or shareholder majorities. This happens rarely in practice because members of management teams rarely vote as formal equals. This formality is more common in corporate boardrooms, however, and it is rife in congressional committees and floor votes. That it does not institutionalize (nor at all encourage) deliberation or disinterested behavior is self-evident. For their part, shareholder majorities typically acclaim most decisions made by top management (or by hostile bidders), just as congressional majorities typically acclaim most decisions made by political party leaders.[15] When on occasion a shareholder majority effectively challenges a sitting management team, this is typically a product, or reflection, of divisions within the team itself, just as breakdowns in congressional majorities typically reflect divided party leadership. Only recently has it become more possible in the United States for such a challenge to be a product of dispersed shareholders' independence, of their collective deliberation as owners.

4. Why Researchers Overlook Both Externalities

Again, our thesis is that the collegial form, institutionalized sites of deliberation and disinterested behavior, will be found rarely and infrequently in corporations and other intermediary associations in limited governments, formal democracies, and imposed social orders but will be found in significant numbers in democratic societies. Collegial formations are not as widely present in civil society when institutional arrangements spanning a state and civil society fail to orient courts (or, outside the United States, administrative agencies) to sanction one-sidedness in corporate governance structures and in other structured situations in civil society. Mexico again provides a convenient example because it combines formal democracy with an imposed social order. Cross-national research establishes that patron-client networks pervade the Mexican government and civil society. Stemming from the presidency and other high-ranking offices of the governing political party, these networks fan out both horizontally across provinces, and vertically across the class structure. What researchers often fail to appreciate, however, is that patron-client networks pervade not only the Mexican civil service. These networks also displace deliberative bodies and sites of disinterested behavior within Mexico's corporations and other intermediary associations, including its universities and sites of professional practice.[16] This is why even though Mexico holds regular elections and retains a market economy, its institutional arrangements enervate, not broadly support a democratic *social* order. Dealing with Mexico's entrenched patron-client networks, and the corruption they tolerate and often encourage, will be Vicente Fox's most formidable challenge.[17]

There is a more ironic reason why researchers often fail to appreciate the institutional externalities of Mexican intermediary associations. They fail to appreciate the broader, institutional benefits of the presence of collegial formations in the United States and other relatively democratic social orders. This oversight is common in the social sciences because it originates at a conceptual level.[18]

This explains why Useem failed to appreciate that he had found empirical evidence of the presence of collegial formations in boardrooms. Like other social scientists, he is influenced generally by Max Weber's economic sociology and approach to organizations and, therefore, he studied directors and the "inner circle" with Weber's ideal type of bureaucracy in mind. Treating corporations at the outset as federations of bureaucracies, rather than as federations that might contain collegial formations, he could only account for directors' disinterested behavior by attributing it to how they were socialized and trained as elites. Following Weber (and Emile Durkheim), he treated the fact that directors typically act disinterestedly in boardrooms as evidence that they share a culture and social psychology as elites which mediates their one-sided behavior. He failed even to consider that their disinterested behavior might be a product of organizational form, which the corporate judiciary supports by analyzing and resolving corporate governance disputes consistently with institutional design.

Contractarians similarly fail to consider this same possibility because they approach the study of corporations at the outset with another ideal type that removes it from view, that of a nexus, a *formless* site of self-interested contracting. With this, they fail at the outset to appreciate that corporations are intermediary associations. Corporations contain structured situations, structures of authority as well as positions of dependence and trust, all of which are organized in *some form*. The ideal type of a formless nexus makes it impossible for contractarians to identify when and where corporate officers, who otherwise do compete directly for power and influence, deliberate over the interpersonal meaning and significance of qualities affecting anyone in their position.

Returning to Useem, we can now see why he overlooked three implications of his important empirical finding, even as the first two were central to his own research concerns. First, he failed to see that disinterested behavior by outside directors is likely a product of organizational form and institutionalized procedural norms, not of directors' socialization and substantive beliefs as individuals. When this form is not present, this behavior will not be in evidence, as the *Macmillan* case and others well illustrate.[19] Second, Useem failed to appreciate that the presence of collegial formations in boardrooms and corporate governance structures is contingent everywhere in the world, including in the United States and Great Britain. Their presence is never an automatic product of elite socialization or any national or elite culture. Third, and most important for our purposes, Useem also failed to appreciate that American (and British) courts extend judicial protection to collegial formations in boardrooms and corporate governance structures.

II. Deliberation: Valued Qualities within a Range

Irrespective of the unique institutional benefits corporate collegial formations contribute to democratic societies, domestic and global markets nonetheless pressure directors, managers, and controlling shareholders to maximize either share price or market share as instrumentally as possible. These pressures are part of the *systemic* forces of modern social change that Weber called "rationalization." They make it impracticable for managers to establish and maintain collegial formations across an entire governance structure. Corporations, after all, are not salons or legislatures, talking clubs. Yet something else is equally clear. Useem's finding and the way Delaware courts describe how directors behave when these courts uphold their decisions documents that some American *boardrooms* are nonetheless organized in the collegial form, despite all systemic pressures to the contrary *and often despite an absence of collegial formations elsewhere in the governance structure.* Delaware court rulings in *Macmillan, Technicolor,* and *QVC,* as well as earlier rulings in *Weinberger* and *Van Gorkom,* also document that these courts expect to see this form framing corporate decision making during changes in control.

Our point is that notwithstanding Weber's correct characterization of systemic pressures, corporate collegial formations remain present and do not noticeably jeopardize the domestic profitability and global competitiveness of corporate America. The issues, then, are: Under what conditions is it economically practicable for corporate officers in any modern society to adopt and maintain the collegial form? And under what conditions do courts extend judicial protection to these formations in ways that are both legally enforceable and economically practicable?

1. Conditions of Deliberation

It is practicable economically under two related conditions for corporate officers to institutionalize their own deliberation and disinterested behavior in corporate decision making. One condition is when corporate officers believe, for whatever reason, that they can best advance their own positional interests, as well as the corporate entity's collective interests, by taking the following step: By keeping certain valued qualities in collective view, as opposed to reacting more immediately and exclusively to market pressures and priced outcomes. The related condition is that keeping valued qualities in collective view is only possible when corporate officers successfully symbolize, socially construct, their meaning and significance *for anyone in their position*, even as corporate rituals, corporate cultures, and all other substantive normative practices change over time.

Taking both conditions together, once corporate officers decide, for whatever reason, to keep valued qualities of any kind in collective view, one option they have is to act ritualistically. A corporate culture is relevant here. It is reflected in constituents' behavioral fidelity to rituals, substantive norms of behavior. It is also reflected in constituents believing as a matter of faith that fidelity to these rituals bears some relationship to maintaining a corporate culture, to keeping certain valued qualities in collective view. Thus, constituents of Time Inc. presumably exhibited fidelity to certain company rituals in the belief this bore some connection to keeping "Time culture" in collective view. Were they no longer to believe this, they would either adopt other rituals that they believed better reflected their sense of what "Time culture" means or they would abandon the effort to keep these once-valued qualities in collective view.

Another, more practicable option corporate officers have in trying to keep valued qualities in collective view is to deliberate over the interpersonal meaning and significance of these qualities (and over how best to keep them in collective view). When they deliberate, they are by definition not yet acting more ritualistically, nor are they yet acting in any one of three other ways.[20] First, directors and other corporate officers are not deferring more immediately to a CEO's view of a corporate entity's collective interests (as typically happens in a bureaucratic form). Second, they are not substituting the will of a shareholder majority or manager majority (as would typically happen in a formally democratic form). Third, directors and other corporate officers are not rubberstamping the interpretations of any coalition of manager patrons and stakeholder dependents, or any "balanced" outcome of positional conflicts between stakeholders (as typically happens in a patron-client form).

2. Within Range: Valued Qualities for Anyone in a Position

Still, only qualities-in-view that fall within a certain range can sustain ongoing deliberation and, therefore, disinterested behavior anywhere in a corporate governance structure. This range spans a minimum and maximum distance from the priced outcomes corporate officers can maximize by acting strictly instrumentally, whether in market-mimicking ways or one-sidedly in their own positional interests.

At the minimum pole of this range, the qualities-in-view must be sufficiently complex in their meaning or significance for anyone in corporate officers' position that they can indeed *sustain* ongoing deliberation. This is clearly the case with many of the product lines of publishing and entertainment companies, including Time Inc. (and, for that matter, Warner Communications as well as Paramount Communications). This is also the case with many of the product lines of high-technology corporations, which engage in what Robert Reich calls high-value production as opposed to high-volume production, the more routine production of traditional manufacturing corporations.[21] It is also the case when deciding how to react to merger proposals or takeover bids in ways that Delaware courts would approve rather than rescind.

This is the minimum range for deliberation because advances in technology or information processing often make it possible to replace earlier deliberations over the interpersonal meaning and significance of qualities with simple measures of quantities, with now identified factors of production that corporations can purchase or produce in high volume. Once such a replacement becomes technically possible, there is no longer any sound economic reason for corporate officers to deliberate over these "qualities."

The only reason for their doing so is normative, to continue their fidelity to rituals because they believe this bears some connection to maintaining a corporate culture. Short of this, there is every economic reason for corporate officers to deal with these "qualities" in more strictly instrumental ways, *organized in some other form.*

This is a basic tenet of Weber's understanding of rationalization, and of what he called "bureaucratization." When any product's complexity falls below this minimum range, for instance, corporate officers understandably respond to systemic pressures accordingly. They readily substitute instrumental behavior for deliberation. This is what happens when television executives, for instance, discover a "formula" that increases the chances of program success. Corporate officers adopt a bureaucratic form of organization in which questions about meaning are either ignored or else answered unilaterally, by decree. Alternatively, they may operate within a patron-client network in which questions about meaning are either ignored or else answered unilaterally after a power struggle between networks of patron managers and client stakeholders. Rarely will they operate by majority rule, in which questions about meaning either are ignored or answered unilaterally by a shareholder or management majority.

At the maximum pole of the range, however, the valued qualities corporate officers endeavor to keep in collective view, whether through deliberation or rituals, cannot be so complex or intangible that their interpersonal meaning or significance for anyone in their position is esoteric. When this happens, their meaning or significance can sustain interpersonal recognition and understanding only among the faithful. Only votaries of a particular "corporate culture" can identify (or, more likely, feign identifying) the "intrinsic value" of these qualities, or the connection between these qualities and what corporate officers are doing (presumably) to keep them in collective view.

There are two key factors at this maximum pole: First, does corporate officers' ongoing deliberation, or constituents' ritualistic behavior, bear any credible connection to keeping the valued qualities in question in collective view? Second, can anyone in corporate officers' position, particularly judges but also institutional investors and hostile bidders, also recognize and understand this connection in common, interpersonally?[22] When these questions cannot be answered positively, the putative relationship between means and ends is severed, beyond already being norm-based or extra-economic. Not only do the ends elude pricing, because they are qualities, but the means by which they are presumably being kept in collective view—deliberation or fidelity to rituals—elude interpersonal recognition and understanding.

3. Beyond Range: *Time-Warner*

We can illustrate the importance of this maximum pole, and how deliberation differs from ritual, by recalling how Chancellor Allen's *Time-Warner* decision exceeded it. It is not possible for corporate officers, or for observing judges and other interested parties, to identify "Time culture" directly, let alone whether and when these valued qualities are being kept in collective view. What they can identify is constituents' fidelity to rituals. Then they decide whether there is any connection between this behavior and "Time culture." Or, more readily, they can identify whether corporate officers deliberate within collegial formations (over the interpersonal meaning and significance of valued qualities of any kind). They can identify this by observing whether corporate officers act disinterestedly, exhibit fidelity to procedural norms, at these sites. Then, similarly, they decide whether there is any connection between their deliberations in collegial formations and "Time culture."

Whether either ritualistic behavior or deliberation takes place in a corporation is one empirical variable. Whether there is any connection between either type of behavior and "Time culture" is another empirical variable.

Our point is that when corporate officers exhibit behavioral fidelity to the threshold standard of consistent rule enforcement at any site, they can credibly claim that their governance structure contains collegial formations, sites of their deliberation and disinterested behavior. They cannot claim this when they (and other constituents) exhibit fidelity to rituals. In turn, they can also credibly claim that *they* are endeavoring actively to keep valued qualities of one kind or another in collective view that have interpersonal meaning or significance for anyone in their position, including any hostile bidder. There is no other practicable reason for organizing any part of corporate governance structures in the collegial form other than to keep valued qualities of some kind or another in collective view. Whether corporate officers call the valued qualities over which they are deliberating "Time culture" or something else is irrelevant. What is relevant is that *in the absence of their own behavioral fidelity to the threshold standard at particular, identifiable sites of corporate governance, they cannot credibly claim they are actively endeavoring to keep any valued qualities in collective view.*

This brings to the fore an important logical distinction, one Chancellor Allen failed to draw because he failed to appreciate explicitly the institutional benefits of corporate collegial formations and instead focused too directly on the putative social benefits of a corporate culture. The presence of collegial formations within corporate governance structures does not guarantee that corporate officers' interpretations of their entities' collective interests will be widely accepted by constituents. But the absence of these formations does guarantee two things. First, it guarantees that these interpretations, whatever they are, are (a) bureaucratic decrees, (b) products of management power struggles, or (c) preferences of management or shareholder majorities. Second, and more important, the absence of collegial formations also guarantees that courts lack any credible public law ground for extending judicial protection to these interpretations in hostile situations. Thus, if collegial formations were not present at Time Inc. in 1989, then what unambiguous public law interest did Chancellor Allen's ruling possibly serve? "*Time-Warner's* language about a valuable corporate 'culture' does invoke public interest concerns, but neither the Court nor the approving commentators have offered any serious analysis of what public interest there might be in Time's corporate culture—as an occasional reader of the magazine over the past thirty years, I am skeptical—and why it would have been threatened by Paramount."[23]

Here, then, is the point of extending judicial protection to a form of organization rather than to any putative substantive quality of a corporation. Constituents and informed observers can recognize in common whether a form of organization is present in corporate governance structures. They cannot recognize in common whether corporate rituals are in place and being honored or whether a corporate culture is otherwise "distinctive and important." They also cannot recognize in common why these substantive qualities merit judicial protection in a market for corporate control. The presence of corporate collegial formations means that corporate officers are acting more disinterestedly than one-sidedly when making major corporate decisions at these sites. Because these formations institutionalize an ongoing procedural normative mediation of positional power in a structured situation in civil society, courts can credibly claim they are advancing an unambiguous public law interest when they protect these formations. This is what courts in equity do, not what courts in common law typically do.

III. Mediating Corporate Power in Civil Society

1. Collegial Formations and Institutional Design

Even if judges (and legal scholars) see merit in taking the procedural turn we proposed in Chapter 11, they would nonetheless correctly point to practical problems of implementation. For instance, how can corporate officers demonstrate to a court's satisfaction that a governance structure, not their own entrenchment or unilateral managing, merits judicial protection on a public law ground? Given our previous discussion, they can demonstrate this in three steps:

1. They can demonstrate that they organized this structure long ago in the collegial form and that over the years they have maintained its integrity in normal business operations as well as in hostile situations.
2. They can demonstrate that this formation's integrity is indeed jeopardized by a proposed change in corporate control brought to the court's attention by a derivative suit.[24]
3. Third, and equally important, they can demonstrate that this formation's presence has not jeopardized the corporation's domestic profitability and international competitiveness in the past, and its continued presence is not likely to do so now and in coming years.

By taking these three steps, corporate officers are *not* establishing that their company contains a "distinctive culture" that somehow merits judicial protection in substance. Rather, they are establishing that a structure of corporate governance merits judicial protection in form. Moreover, rather than jeopardizing the domestic profitability and global competitiveness of corporate America, the agency costs involved in maintaining corporate collegial formations do not necessarily exceed those of maintaining bureaucratic formations, patron-client networks, or formally democratic bodies. For that matter, because many uncertainties in today's business environments can be traced to qualitative factors whose value for any management team eludes pricing, corporate collegial formations do not necessarily carry greater agency costs than unmediated drift toward unilateral managing, shareholder contracting, or stakeholder balancing.

Our three steps, however, keep the burden of proof where it belongs. Management teams seeking judicial protection on this qualitative ground, this procedural normative ground, in the face of credible allegations of breach of fiduciary duty bear the burden of demonstrating to a court's satisfaction that the three steps indeed apply *in their case*:

- Is the collegial form already present within the boardroom or else-where in the governance structure?
- Does the contested transaction really threaten this formation, or does it simply threaten the careers of individual managers and the "stakes" of other constituents?
- Is the continued presence of the collegial form vital to the corpora-tion's major product lines,[25] and thereby consistent with its domestic profitability and global competitiveness?

Placing the burden of proof here brings into view the greatest weakness in Chancellor Allen's *Time-Warner* decision and also the greatest strength in Vice Chancellor Jacobs' *QVC* decision and in the *Macmillan* and *Technicolor* decisions preceding it. The weakness in *Time-Warner* is that Chancellor Allen did not ask Time Inc. attorneys to answer even the first question above, let alone the other two. In the absence of explicit answers to these questions, any references to "Time culture" were strictly self-aggrandizing, ideological in the most classic sense. Time Inc. attorneys were manipulating Chancery rather than elaborating with reasons Time managers' decision to merge with Warner Communications rather than entertain Paramount's hostile bid.

The strength in *QVC*, in turn, is that Vice Chancellor Jacobs required the Paramount board to deliberate over a hostile bid even though there was no evidence that this corporation's board had ever acted in this way in the past, had ever been organized in the collegial form. Thus, this decision did not mark a partial return to *Revlon*, as many legal scholars believe.[26] To the con-trary, it radicalized the procedural turn we proposed in Chapter 11. Jacobs essentially encouraged all target management teams to adopt a form of or-ganization with which many of them may not be familiar. And he and other Delaware judges likely appreciate this will be an uphill battle in corporate America. Corporate boards have often been toadies of the CEO and corpo-rate officers (as *Van Gorkom* illustrates), not independent, deliberative, col-legial bodies. After interviewing 60 directors in the late 1970s and early 1980s and then synthesizing what they told him, T. L. Whistler came up with an only slightly tongue-in-cheek set of "norms of director conduct": no fighting, support your CEO, serve your apprenticeship, no crusades, we don't manage the company, we don't set strategy, and keep your distance from subordinate company executives.[27]

On the other hand, Vice Chancellor Jacobs' message about how to han-dle hostile situations is nonetheless also "in the air" in the United States because the presence of corporate collegial formations is consistent with the institutional design of a democratic society. Delaware court decisions in *Macmillan* and *Technicolor*, and earlier in *Van Gorkom* and *Weinberger*, elaborate this doctrinal rationale for either supporting or opposing defensive actions by target management teams.

2. Can Courts Overextend Protection of Collegial Formations?

Compare the specificity of the three steps we just presented, and their potential to orient the corporate judiciary as an institution, to the way legal scholars *sympathetic* to the *Time-Warner* decision characterize it. First, Jeffrey Gordon:

> The core of the socio-historical account is the rejection of markets as the ultimate (or at least exclusive) decision-maker over economic resources, in favor of human agency. This principle fits with a proxy contest, which ultimately entails an appeal to shareholders about the wisdom of replacing a management team and changing a course of business conduct. The decision mechanism for a proxy battle, unlike a hostile tender offer, is not a marketplace exchange. To be sure, a tender offer also entails a certain kind of shareholder persuasion—that the bid price is higher than any price they are likely to be offered for their shares in the foreseeable future. Nevertheless there is an important distinction between persuading shareholders to exercise voice versus exit. This distinction maps onto the difference between decisions made by continuing participants in the enterprise, acting in response to multiple variables, as opposed to decisions by impersonal markets reacting to a single, economic variable.[28]

Ultimately, Gordon is offering yet another rationale for stakeholder balancing, for dividing corporate agency. He substitutes a metaphor of corporation-as-representative-body for that of corporation-as-indivisible-entity.[29] With this, he inadvertently subordinates the courts' public law interest in seeing to it that corporate governance structures broadly support institutional design to the courts' private law interest in seeing to it that immediate externalities are minimized for corporate constituents.

Second, David Millon's proposed rationale for *Time-Warner*:

> [M]anagement of any substantial company that has become an established feature of the business landscape and on which the public has come to rely may be entitled to protect the corporation from the disruptive and potentially ruinous impact of a hostile takeover—even though self-preservation

comes at the expense of a robust market for corporate control and its attendant benefits to shareholders.[30]

Ultimately, Millon's rationale recapitulates the weakest parts of Chancellor Allen's reasoning. It, too, attempts to interrelate directly a substantive normative standard of corporate culture with a substantive normative standard of the latter's putative institutional benefits for the larger society. The problem, as Gordon acknowledges more generally, is that these standards are "vague, fuzzy, and indeterminate."[31] They bring controversy and inconsistency to judicial rulings, not legitimacy and consistency. Were state courts to enforce the doctrinal principle implicit in *Time-Warner* as it stands, and thereby attempt to enforce a substantive normative approach to corporate purpose, they would likely bring corporate law to full-blown crisis. This is why Millon concedes he cannot refute the proposition that Dunkin' Donuts' corporate culture, too, contributes a "significant public interest dimension" to American society.[32] This means he cannot refute the argument that Dunkin' Donuts also merits judicial protection from hostile bids even when the latter guarantee a Pareto optimal outcome for shareholders.

Unlike Gordon's and Millon's characterization of *Time-Warner*, our three steps escape vagueness and controversy in two ways. First, they revolve around corporate officers' fidelity to norms that only one form of organization institutionalizes in civil society. Judges can identify interpersonally when corporate officers exhibit fidelity to procedural norms and the collegial form even when they otherwise interpret differently the substance of corporate officers' behavior and the substance of transactions' outcomes. Second, a threshold standard and the collegial form come into play only when corporate officers' fidelity to both is economically practicable, when their presence in governance structures is at all appropriate to corporation's domestic profitability and global competitiveness. This ensures that courts will not overextend judicial protection of corporate collegial formations.

But why does this follow from our general argument about the relationship between corporate governance and institutional design? Why is there little likelihood that state courts will misapply our three steps, and particularly given the fact that the *QVC* decision and then the *Macmillan* and *Technicolor* decisions have already radicalized the procedural turn we are proposing?

In the first place, managers of routine production facilities face such severe systemic pressures of rationalization that they have little reason to feign

deliberation, let alone to feign institutionalizing it with collegial formations. In the second place, consider what would happen if judges extended
judicial protection to corporations in which deliberation over qualities is
inconsistent with their product lines and thus their domestic profitability
and global competitiveness. Such judicial activism would so increase agency
costs, and so jeopardize shareholder wealth, that courts would not for long
maintain their own legitimacy and authority as an institution. Their rulings
would run counter to existing social norms and both elite and general public opinion.

Stating this point in more general terms, judges overextend judicial protection when they take any one of the following actions: first, when they enforce anachronistic (that is, substantive normative) mandatory rules directly; second, when they declare that a particular corporate culture merits
judicial protection as an end-in-itself; third, when they enforce fiduciary
law's relational norms—norms designed to mediate how power is exercised
between positions of trust and positions of dependence—to compel corporate officers to maximize shareholder dividends, as contractarians propose;
and fourth, when they enforce these relational norms to protect the careers
of particular managers, the strategic plans of particular management teams,
or the fixed assets of particular stakeholders. None of these judicial decisions serves any self-evident public law interest.

3. Societal Constituents, Corporate Constituents

Consider, on the other hand, what judges are doing when they extend
judicial protection to corporate collegial formations or, as the *QVC, Technicolor,* and *Macmillan* decisions illustrate, when they go further by requiring boards and management teams to deliberate over proposed
changes in corporate control. They are applying fiduciary law's relational
norms to a form of organization. This converts these norms into a procedural standard that mediates unilateral managing, shareholder contracting, and stakeholder balancing, *and updates the fiduciary law tradition at
a conceptual level.* Judges are delimiting fiduciary law's scope of application in today's global economy to an identifiable set of structured situations in corporate America.

Distinguishing between the form and substance of mandatory rules is
critical to the corporate judiciary retaining any linkage to its fiduciary law
tradition. When judges employ fiduciary rhetoric when protecting corporate collegial formations rather than corporate entities as long-term enter-

prises, they are normatively mediating *how* corporate officers *and anyone else in their position* maximize share price or growth, protect stakeholders, or formulate and implement strategic plans. With this, they are normatively mediating possible institutional externalities of corporate governance, *including how corporate officers otherwise exhibit loyalty to an entity consistent with fiduciary law tradition.*

By monitoring whether corporate officers make major decisions within collegial formations, judges can also draw another distinction in consistent ways: They can identify one set of stakeholders who indeed merit representation (and possibly standing), but only in one narrowly defined respect. These are the stakeholders whose positional interest in a company's future is to maintain the integrity of collegial formations in its governance structure. These stakeholders merit representation in corporate decision making (and possible standing in court) because when they advance this narrow, analytically distinguishable positional interest, they simultaneously advance the public law interest of normatively mediating exercises of positional power in structured situations short of one-sidedness. These stakeholders might include:

- outside directors, who have a positional interest in maintaining the collegial form within boardrooms;
- proponents of minority views in sitting management teams, who have a positional interest in maintaining the collegial form elsewhere in the governance structures;
- professional chemists or biologists, who have a positional (and professional) interest in maintaining the collegial form in research divisions;
- house counsel, who has a positional (and professional) interest in maintaining the collegial form in legal divisions;
- editors and journalists (for instance at Time Inc.), producers and directors (for instance at Paramount Communications Inc.), who have a positional interest in maintaining the collegial form, respectively, in news and entertainment divisions.

Again, these stakeholders comprise a distinct, identifiable subset of corporate constituents. And the positional interest at issue is narrow, indeed one-dimensional. It is not coterminous with their entire stake in a company's future. Only when they act on this positional interest do they simultaneously advance an unambiguous public law interest. Thus, *we may think of these stakeholders as societal constituents.*[33] Edward Rock makes this point, but more narrowly.[34] He proposes that derivative litigation helps to clarify corporate norms, a public law interest, and this justifies awarding attorney fees to plaintiff shareholders. We would say that plaintiff shareholders *may* be societal constituents, namely when their claims draw attention to the presence or absence of collegial formations in corporate governance structures. But we also go further than this. We identify societal constituents in terms of the positions of trust and responsibility they occupy within corporate governance structures—an identifiable set of structured situations in civil society. We do not try to identify them more directly, by pointing to the substance or "intrinsic value" of their investments or stakes. Because societal constituents advance a public law interest from which everyone benefits, namely supporting institutional design, we cannot reasonably expect them to bear all of the costs involved. Rather, their efforts to advance this narrowly defined positional interest merit judicial support *as a mandatory rule.*

This doctrinal option, extending judicial protection to corporate collegial formations and then to societal constituents who have a stake in maintaining their integrity, is neither a heuristic device nor an ideal aspiration. Rather, it is consistent in three respects with existing corporate law and current judicial practice. It permits opting out of mandatory rules that place substantive limitations on management business judgment, shareholder contracting, or stakeholder balancing. It identifies an unambiguous public law interest within the issue of corporate purpose. And it retains greater continuity with the business judgment rule than does shareholder contracting or stakeholder balancing. We elaborate each of these in turn.

First, our doctrinal option—updating fiduciary law with a procedural turn—permits management, with shareholder approval, otherwise to opt out of mandatory rules that limit contractual freedom in substance. It permits broadening stakeholder representation, if this is what management wishes to do, with shareholder approval. But our doctrinal option normatively mediates inadvertent *drift* toward unilateral managing, shareholder contracting, or stakeholder balancing—that is, when any of these decision making options reduces the presence of collegial formations in corporate governance structures.

Second, our doctrinal option identifies the public law interest at issue in corporate purpose at least within democratic societies. Thus, it retains continuity with mandatory rules, including courts' long-standing enforcement of management loyalty to the corporate entity. However, this loyalty is no longer defined as one to a corporation in substance. Rather, fiduciary loyalty is now defined as one to a form of organization found in selected corporate governance structures. Courts lend judicial support to the form, not to the particular corporate officers acting through it at any particular time. Thus, courts will permit changes in corporate control as long as friendly or hostile bidders make plans to maintain existing corporate collegial formations. Correlatively, courts will support defenses against changes in corporate control when the latter place these formations in jeopardy.

Third, by distinguishing societal constituents from other corporate constituents, our doctrinal option even retains greater continuity with the business judgment rule than does drift toward contracting or balancing. As long as judges extend judicial protection to corporate collegial formations (or insist that directors learn to deliberate), they may then otherwise defer to management's business judgment, if they wish. Or, if they wish, they may defer instead to the business judgment of hostile bidders. It does not really matter. Judges now safely treat all substantive claims and interpretations as strictly private law matters. They now safely leave these disputes and conflicts to corporate constituents to resolve among themselves within governance structures by negotiating and renegotiating suppletory rules and enabling rules. Similarly, since extending representation to other corporate constituents does not serve any identifiable public law interest, courts need not concern themselves with *encouraging* stakeholder representation.[35]

13

Explaining and Predicting Judicial Behavior in a Global Economy

The corporate judiciary is grappling today with two major issues of corporate governance:

- Whether to keep corporate agency unified or to divide it along with
  legal responsibility for corporate power. *This is the issue of corporate
  agency.*
- Whether to impose mandatory rules on corporate officers or to drift,
  toward unilateral managing, shareholder contracting, or stakeholder
  balancing. *This is the issue of corporate purpose.*

These issues trouble the corporate judiciary today, but it is not possible to
resolve them satisfactorily within today's orthodoxy.[1]

The procedural turn we propose orients judges differently and, actually, more consistently with existing corporate law and ongoing judicial
practice. Yet it is more consistent with republican vigilance than liberal
complacency. Our alternative orients judges to subordinate issues of corporate agency and corporate purpose to a single issue: Either permit corporate governance structures to be organized in any form for which management gains shareholder (and stakeholder) approval; or protect corporate collegial formations more explicitly, and then permit managing,
contracting, or balancing only to that point at which corporate officers
encroach against these formations.

The primary importance of our procedural turn is that it recasts the issue
of corporate purpose in particular into manageable, empirically researchable terms. It identifies the relationship between corporate governance and
institutional design, and it draws courts' attention to collegial formations

and to societal constituents who have a positional interest in broadening their presence and maintaining their integrity.

We saw in the previous chapter that the corporate judiciary as an institution can, in principle, identify the presence and integrity of corporate collegial formations with relative consistency across cases irrespective of how differently particular judges otherwise rule on the two issues of corporate governance. As long as the corporate judiciary extends legal protection to corporate collegial formations and the narrow positional interest of societal constituents as a mandatory rule, particular judges may otherwise either unify corporate agency or divide it; either broaden corporate governance with stakeholder representation or narrow it by supporting unilateral managing or shareholder contracting; and either enforce other mandatory rules or permit opting out.

Similarly, as long as the corporate judiciary takes our procedural turn, it does not matter how particular management teams otherwise react to uncertainties in their business environments, and it also does not matter: whether corporations located in the United States are American owned or foreign owned;[2] whether corporations are privately owned or publicly traded; whether corporate governance is dominated by management teams, controlling shareholders, or stakeholder coalitions; whether state legislatures place corporate constituency statutes or other public law norms in their General Corporation laws; and whether particular judges are imposers, contractarians, or balancers.

We believe this procedural turn also better accounts for what Delaware courts have been doing for over two decades, albeit unevenly and implicitly. By contrast, contractarians, imposers, and balancers fail to account for more of this judicial behavior.[3] We believe this is a result of their failing to convert the issue of corporate purpose into any explicitly stated connection between corporate governance and institutional design even as this implicitly informs them at least in some part as they analyze and resolve major governance disputes. A handful of legal scholars comes closest to explaining what Delaware courts are endeavoring to accomplish: Alan Palmiter, Edward Rock, Lawrence Cunningham and Charles Yablon, and Margaret Blair and Lynn Stout. In each case, these legal scholars fail in places to carry their analyses through. By bringing our procedural turn and focus on the institutional externalities of corporate governance into their analyses, we (a) identify these places, (b) reveal ways to get around them, and therefore (c) propose more parsimonious ways of explaining Delaware court behavior.

I. Judicial Behavior in Legal Scholarship

1. Palmiter's "Duty of Independence"

Alan Palmiter at Wake Forest Law School proposes that Delaware courts and other state courts at times implicitly impose on corporate directors a new fiduciary duty, one he calls "independence." By his account, this is "a duty . . . to avoid being influenced by [management] colleagues whose [positional] interests diverge from those of the corporation and its shareholders." Palmiter sees courts imposing on directors in particular an extracontractual, normative obligation to remain generally informed about and disinterested when evaluating management decisions and actions. He perceives this duty as operating in practice much like judicial efforts to maximize disclosure.[4] Directors bear their "new" fiduciary duty when they monitor how management advances its own positional interests and how it interprets the corporate entity's collective interests.[5] Palmiter does not see independence requiring directors to concern themselves with the details of management actions, thus challenging management's business judgment. Rather, he acknowledges that courts cannot realistically expect outside directors in particular to dedicate this much time to detailed oversight.

A. INDEPENDENCE IN PRACTICE: *VAN GORKOM*

Palmiter's most important illustration of the independence standard in action is, ironically, the Delaware Supreme Court's *Van Gorkom* decision in 1985, the same year as its *Unocal* decision. He sees, of course, that the aftermath of this case hardly supports his general thesis. In *Van Gorkom*, to recall, the Court imposed a personal liability on Trans Union directors for failing to take due care in selling the company on their CEO's request. A year and a half later, the Delaware General Assembly changed its General Corporation law specifically to protect directors from such liability in the future, and 30 other states followed suit.[6] With this, the Delaware General Assembly explicitly subordinated Palmiter's proposed duty of independence, *along with the two more traditional duties of care and loyalty,* to Lockean principles of contracting and Madisonian principles of balancing. It did this in two ways. On the one hand, it accepted that the priced outcome of the Trans Union board's actions was indeed Pareto optimal and wealth maximizing. On the other hand, it also accepted that a CEO has every right, as do other corporate constituents, to try to influence a board of directors. Easterbrook and Fischel capture these points well:

It is not hard to see why the case produced such a swift and sweeping reaction. Judicial inquiry into the amount of information managers should acquire before deciding creates the precise difficulties that the business judgment rule is designed to avoid. Information is necessary for corporate managers to maximize the value of the firm. But there is a limit to how much managers should know before making a decision. . . . Information is costly, and investors want managers to spend on knowledge only to the point where an additional dollar generates that much in better decisions. Exactly how much information to gather depends on such factors as how much the managers already know, the costs of obtaining additional information, the likely benefit of such information, and the variance of possible outcomes. Perhaps the Supreme Court of Delaware has changed course again, for in 1985 it remarked that "informed decision to delegate a task is as much an exercise of business judgment as any other." Managers can delegate this task to the market as easily as to investment bankers—and markets are cheaper. The ultimate issue is who should decide how much information to acquire in advance of a business decision. Allowing shareholders to challenge business decisions that they say were not "informed" has the effect of substituting the business judgment of some shareholders, their attorneys, and a court for that of managers. Because the managers have the best incentives (particularly when, in a case like *Van Gorkom*, they hold large blocs of the firm's stock), the legal process is distinctly inferior.[7]

In short, Delaware's legislature and many others considered the Delaware Supreme Court's concern with norms of equity and disinterested behavior to be too controversial to support with personal liability.

In one respect, the General Assembly's reaction was not particularly surprising. After all, it is consistent with a "race to the bottom" explanation for Delaware's success in competing for charters. Yet others see something of a tug-of-war in Delaware, between often presuming business judgment rule protection for unilateral management but at times favoring shareholders in hostile situations.[8] The Supreme Court decision in *Van Gorkom*, however, supports the fourth explanation for Delaware's success. It illustrates that Delaware courts are deliberative bodies that bring qualitative standards of analysis to governance disputes, as opposed to reducing everything to priced outcomes. This likely accounts for why Palmiter sees a duty of independence implicit in this decision.

What is also intriguing about *Van Gorkom*, however, is how traditionalists other than Palmiter portray what is at stake in this decision. For instance, Robert Clark calls the decision "surprisingly strict," and he approves of the Assembly's reaction even as he appreciates it allows management to lobby directors and shareholder majorities relentlessly to "opt out" of *otherwise applicable fiduciary duties*.[9] Indeed, it was in the context of the Assembly's reaction to *Van Gorkom* that contractarian Frank Easterbrook called on state courts (and state legislatures) to go further, to permit opting out of corporate officers' loyalty to a corporate entity, the most basic fiduciary duty of all.[10]

To his credit, Palmiter sees this episode differently. Unlike Clark and other traditionalists, he sees the controversy surrounding *Van Gorkom* giving traditionalists an opening to challenge the nexus of contracts approach at a basic, doctrinal level. And, actually, Delaware courts would soon develop this opening by sanctioning breaches of due care similarly to the way they sanction breaches of loyalty rather than reducing (or eliminating) these sanctions, as Easterbrook advised. They took this course of action despite the fact that the General Assembly eliminated personal liability from breaches of due care (but not from breaches of loyalty). The problem in Palmiter's account is he ultimately failed to take fuller advantage of this opening himself as he elaborated his concept of independence. We seek the source of this failure in his otherwise promising review of how American state courts have endeavored over the years to enforce fiduciary law.

B. THREE FIDUCIARY "REGIMES"

When Palmiter discusses fiduciary law's two traditional duties, as well as the new independence duty, he refers to each as a legal "regime." Thus, he explores how courts operate under a care regime, under a loyalty regime, and (implicitly) under an independence regime. Each orients courts in terms of a different rationale for analyzing and resolving governance disputes. The problem, as Palmiter sees it, is that over the last two or three decades the first two rationales have resulted in courts steadily narrowing their enforcement of fiduciary law's relational norms, the norms mediating how power is exercised between positions of trust and positions of dependence in structured situations.

When Palmiter was writing, in the late 1980s, courts typically enforced a care regime, except in *Van Gorkom*, only when management engaged in egregious misconduct, say in making investments that were literally irrational. Short of this, courts typically presumed business judgment rule protection for management, *effectively vitiating this traditional duty*. Courts enforced a loyalty regime similarly. They imposed sanctions on management only when its behavior either unambiguously jeopardized shareholder dividends or unambiguously jeopardized the corporate entity itself *as a long-term enterprise.* This tended to be the case, however, only when management's self-dealing or dishonesty was so egregious that a court could not reconcile its behavior with any credible interpretation of an entity's collective interests, *thereby effectively vitiating this traditional duty.*[11] In *Unocal,* Delaware courts simply added that management may take stakeholders' positional interests into account when exercising its business judgment. However, as we have seen, all of this changed in later decisions, in *Technicolor* and *QVC* (and Cunningham and Yablon, whom we discuss next, focus on how it changed).

For now we follow Palmiter's argument by asking: Why did this narrowing occur through the late 1980s? Or, put differently, why was it not possible for courts to reverse themselves and once again enforce management's duty of loyalty more strictly, as at least a few traditionalists, such as Eisenberg and Brudney, were advising? A return to stricter enforcement of loyalty was no longer a viable option because the market for corporate control revealed starkly that management at times used this putative duty to the corporate entity to its own one-sided advantage. More strict enforcement of loyalty, therefore, would put the courts directly at odds with the two norms underlying today's orthodoxy—Lockean contracts and Pareto optimal outcomes. Thus, if judges tried to enforce loyalty more strictly, they would in at least two respects harm the corporate judiciary as an institution. First, they would bring even greater attention to fissures riddling corporate law doctrine. In particular, they would expose the gulf between (a) judicial drift toward contracting and balancing over recent decades and (b) the rigidity of corporate law's most central mandatory rule. Second, they would also diminish the courts' legitimacy as an institution: By enforcing loyalty more strictly, courts could very well jeopardize the domestic profitability and global competitiveness of corporate America.[12]

As courts narrowed their enforcement of both traditional fiduciary duties and began drifting toward contracting beginning in the late 1970s, they left themselves with another problem, however: "[M]any of the most significant corporate decisions [coming before the courts] . . . fall into neither of [the] two narrow categories" of care and loyalty.[13] Here Palmiter saw the situation as clearly as anyone. His point is that courts heard many cases in which positional conflicts between management and shareholders are indeed irreconcilable, particularly in hostile situations, and yet management's intentions are unclear. In addition, the implications of management's actions for the larger society either escape view or are ambiguous. This means

that two important facts about these cases were subject to competing interpretations. The first is whether management fulfills its contractual obligations to shareholders and stakeholders. The second is whether management
exhibits sufficient loyalty to the corporate entity as a long-term enterprise.

Palmiter's point in proposing that judicial behavior during this period
implies courts were enforcing a new duty of independence is that even as
many governance disputes fell outside fiduciary law's two traditional
"regimes," courts nonetheless hesitated to embrace contracting (or balancing) outright. Thus, he sees some courts implicitly attributing a "duty of independence" to directors (and then to other corporate officers). To be sure,
Palmiter also found precedents for this judicial behavior as early as the
1930s. His central argument, however, is that only by the mid-1980s did
some state courts really act as if there is "a conceptually separate [fiduciary]
duty of independence." With this, he summarizes the state of fiduciary law
in the late 1980s by formulating the question he believes each "regime" orients judges to ask.[14]

- Under a care regime: What might the result have been had the board
  acted rationally (in market-mimicking ways) to achieve some corporate purpose?
- Under a loyalty regime: What would the result have been in an "arm's-
  length" or disinterested transaction, in which directors were not influenced by "extraneous" conflicting interests?
- Under an independence regime: What would the result have been if
  directors had been truly independent, free even of management's
  influence?

We can see how narrowly corporate purpose is defined under the care
regime of the late 1980s, consistent with today's orthodoxy. We can also see
why this effectively vitiated enforcement of this duty, short of egregious
breakdowns in management's business judgment.

C. LIMITATIONS OF THE INDEPENDENCE CONCEPT

There is a major problem with the concept of director "independence,"
one that Palmiter acknowledges. He ends his promising discussion by saying he cannot identify specifically what "independence" actually means in
practice.[15] Finding the effort "futile," he acknowledges he cannot really instruct judges about how they might recognize director "independence" with
consistency across cases.[16] This is hardly a minor concession. Palmiter is
saying he cannot identify the scope of application of his proposed fiduciary

duty even as he finds clear empirical evidence that some courts bring a qualitative standard of analysis implicitly to governance disputes other than traditional care and loyalty. In addition, director or board independence (from management and powerful stakeholders) does not guarantee that corporate officers will in fact act disinterestedly. Rather, "independent" directors and boards may act one-sidedly in their own *positional* interests (rather than their own personal interests).[17]

We can identify independence more specifically by standing back from Palmiter's discussion and asking a basic question: What must independence involve, in practice, when this orients courts to enforce norms of behavior as mandatory rules? In order for this "regime" to stem drift, and challenge today's orthodoxy, it must at the very least orient courts to support *qualities* of corporate governance that judges can identify with consistency. Thus, independence cannot be reducible to encouraging market-mimicking behavior by corporate officers, their efforts to maximize priced outcomes for shareholders (or stakeholders).[18] After all, if "independence" boils down to this, then Palmiter's entire inquiry becomes superfluous. Courts can leave the enforcement of "independence" to a robust market for corporate control. Moreover, in order for qualities of any kind to merit judicial protection on a public law ground, they must also carry some institutional benefit for the larger social order. They cannot simply carry "meaning" or "intrinsic value" for particular directors, corporate officers, or other constituents.

Thus, if Palmiter's discovery of an implicit duty of independence is to retain its promise, if it is eventually to orient the corporate judiciary explicitly as an institution, then it needs to have at least two characteristics. First, it needs to revolve around qualities of corporate governance that judges are capable of identifying and supporting in consistent ways. Second, the public law interest it serves must be so unambiguous that even judges otherwise sympathetic to managing, contracting, or balancing will nonetheless acknowledge the importance of enforcing independence as a mandatory rule.

2. Cunningham and Yablon's "New Unified Standard"

Where others see confusion, inconsistency, even schizophrenia in major Delaware court decisions of the 1980s and early 1990s, Lawrence Cunningham and Charles Yablon of Cardozo Law School see "a unified standard."[19] They acknowledge that many legal scholars see *Unocal* (in 1985), *Revlon* (in 1986), and *Macmillan* (in 1988) demonstrating that Delaware courts analyze takeover cases in terms of different standards of fiduciary duty. They also acknowledge that Delaware judges and legal scholars alike have insisted for decades that directors' duty of care is distinct from their duty of loyalty. Yet they propose "a fundamental doctrinal shift in Delaware fiduciary law" is unifying these cases, and these duties, within a single, more abstract, qualitative standard of analysis. Delaware courts are "imposing on all corporate directors a single, highly general obligation of good faith and fair dealing based on reasonably informed judgment."

The "unified standard" they see is actually a two-step standard of review in takeover situations. Legal scholars have long seen the second step: Any breach of fiduciary obligation, whether termed care or loyalty, "yields the same strict 'intrinsic fairness' standard of review." What is new, in the view of Cunningham and Yablon, is *a similarly unified* first step of "intermediate review": In deciding *whether* a breach of fiduciary duty occurred in a particular takeover situation, the "intermediate standard" is "an 'enhanced scrutiny' review." Under its terms, directors successfully rebut *credible* allegations of breach by establishing to a court's satisfaction that they acted on adequate information in a disinterested way. With this, the disputed transaction retains the presumption of business judgment rule protection; in its absence, Delaware courts may rescind the transaction or else determine damages using an intrinsic fairness review.[20]

Cunningham and Yablon's thesis is that "this single [intermediate] standard is potentially applicable to a broad range of managerial decisions regarding control and other extraordinary corporate events." Courts can apply this standard generally because it never demands any particular course of action from corporate officers in takeover situations, whether holding a *Revlon* auction for their companies or erecting *Unocal* or *Time-Warner* defenses. Instead, the unified standard requires corporate officers to exercise informed judgment as they endeavor to obtain, in the wording of the *QVC* decision, "the best value reasonably available to the stockholders."

Cunningham and Yablon accept that others can credibly read what the Delaware courts have been doing differently. Some can say these courts are simply condemning "sleazy" or egregious misbehavior by management. Others can say Delaware courts are repudiating their own earlier lenience in approving defensive tactics, in *Unocal* and *Time-Warner*. Still others, including Yablon himself in 1989 and Chancellor Allen in 1992, can say Delaware courts move back and forth on a pendulum, from shareholder-friendly decisions (in *Revlon*), to more pro-management decisions (in *Time-Warner*), to more shareholder-friendly decisions (in *QVC*). But Cunningham and Yablon make their case for a unified, two-tier standard by focusing on the 1993 written decisions in *Technicolor* and *QVC* because these "mark the first concrete articulations of a broader unification of Delaware fiduciary law."

Technicolor in particular was "novel" in holding that violations of care imply substantially the same consequences as violations of loyalty, thus reaffirming what the Delaware Supreme Court had said in *Van Gorkom*—but this time without holding directors to any personal liability.[21] Before the *Van Gorkom* decision in 1985, *all* commentators agreed that only loyalty really mattered; due care was more formality than mandatory rule.[22] Palmiter believed this in 1989; Brudney continues to believe this.[23] Thus, all actions by directors and other corporate officers fell into only two categories, those in which they had a material conflict of interest, thereby a breach of loyalty, and those in which they did not. The problem, as we noted in Chapter 5, is that hostile takeover situations place corporate officers in positions that do not fall easily into either traditional category.[24] Courts needed an "intermediate" category and standard of analysis in order to decide whether to presume business judgment rule protection or to initiate an intrinsic fairness review. To this end, courts also needed either to reduce their entire fiduciary law tradition to loyalty, to corporate officers' conflicts of material interest, or else identify other duties corporate officers bear as mandatory rules.

It was in this context that the *Van Gorkom* decision suddenly challenged the received wisdom about due care being mere formality, but then Delaware's General Assembly seemed to reassert this received wisdom.[25] Thus, like Palmiter, Cunningham and Yablon also see *Van Gorkom* and its aftermath as a critical event in the evolution of Delaware fiduciary law. But what they see that Palmiter could not in 1989 is the *Technicolor* case of 1993.

In *Technicolor*, two directors stood to derive personal material benefit from a merger, and each disclosed this to the board—thereby eliminating any breach of loyalty. Chancellor Allen expressed "grave doubts" that the board exercised due care but, since everyone agreed shareholders received more than fair value, he dismissed this allegation. He confirmed the received wisdom that when loyalty is not at issue, corporate officers' fiduciary duties end here.[26] But Delaware's Supreme Court responded on appeal that once a breach of due care is credibly alleged, the burden shifts. Defendant directors must establish to a court's satisfaction the intrinsic fairness of the disputed transaction (in this case a merger) under the standard established in *Weinberger* in 1983, two years before *Van Gorkom*. Here is where Cunningham and Yablon see a new unified standard of review first emerging.[27] And here is where the Delaware Supreme Court essentially moved Chancery around the General Assembly's *Van Gorkom* statute by reasserting fiduciary law's relational norms regarding how power is to be exercised between positions of trust and positions of dependence in structured situations.

Cunningham and Yablon read the Delaware Supreme Court as saying that a breach of care demands the same level of scrutiny as a conflict of interest, a breach of loyalty. Thus, they see the Court "broadening" fiduciary law to span three elements, not two: traditional loyalty, traditional care, and corporate officers' subjective intent, good faith. Still, the way Folk, Ward, and Welsh word the relationship between these elements seems more credible: "[C]onsiderations of good faith are irrelevant in determining the threshold issue of whether directors as a board exercised an informed business judgment."[28] A credible allegation of a breach in any one of these three areas—but, if Folk, Ward, and Welsh are right, particularly in either of the first two areas—deprives corporate officers of a presumption of business judgment rule protection. It exposes them to the *possibility* that a disputed transaction will be subjected to an intrinsic fairness review.[29] The point for Cunningham and Yablon is that this makes due care far more than a formality: Corporate officers now have as much of a legal obligation to be reasonably informed as they do to avoid conflicts of interest and to act in good faith.[30]

Cunningham and Yablon also see evidence of the new unified standard of review in Vice Chancellor Jacobs' *QVC* decision. He held that "*Revlon* and *Unocal* do not represent any departure from the bedrock fiduciary principles" because these decisions are simply particular applications *of the duty of care*, now hardly a formality. When Delaware Chief Justice Veasey affirmed this decision, within hours, he emphasized that board decisions are subject to "enhanced scrutiny"—intermediate review—whenever (a) there is a sale of control, (b) management erects defenses against hostile activity, or (c) management reduces or alters shareholder voting rights.[31] Cunningham and Yablon therefore see both Delaware courts rejecting the proposition that *Revlon* and *Unocal* mandate two distinct, that is contradictory, options in hostile takeover situations. They see Delaware courts holding that corporate officers will be held to one standard when dissatisfied shareholders credibly allege a breach of any fiduciary duty: enhanced scrutiny.

Indeed, Cunningham and Yablon see this unified standard applying not only to hostile takeover situations but "to all management decisions that substantially alter shareholder interests in the corporation."[32] We amend this wording slightly. The unified standard applies to all decisions of substantive importance to shareholders (and possibly others). When a corporate governance structure permits corporate officers to make such decisions by exercising their positional power in what appear to be one-sided ways, then their actions receive enhanced scrutiny to see if a full fairness review is warranted. Thus, we read the unified standard boiling down to Delaware courts requiring corporate officers to establish and maintain collegial formations as they make substantively important decisions. Corporate officers do not meet this standard simply by getting shareholder approval at the time, or simply by negotiating an outcome that is Pareto optimal for shareholders. They meet this standard only if they do these things in procedurally correct ways, for instance by being candid with shareholders rather than failing to inform them fully.

Cunningham and Yablon come closest to our amended wording in two places. The first instance is at the end of their article, when they quote from Chief Justice Veasey's written opinion in the *QVC* case. An enhanced scrutiny review "could be triggered by all decisions that involve any fundamental change in the 'nature of the corporate enterprise from a practical standpoint.'"[33] The second and more important instance is when Cunningham and Yablon insist that the primary reason Delaware courts seek a unified standard is internal to these courts, not *at all* a product of external interest group pressures on them. Delaware courts are certainly not driven to a unified standard of intermediate review under pressure from management, which much prefers that courts presume broader business judgment rule protection. They are also not driven to a unified standard by the practicing bar or academic legal commentators, which, after all, often prefer uncertainty in corporate law to predictability. Nor, finally, are they driven to a unified standard because Delaware judges wish either to encourage or discourage hostile activity in a market for corporate control. Delaware judges have less of a stake, less of a positional interest, in whether hostile activity increases or decreases than in whether their rulings in major governance disputes are widely perceived across the corporate judiciary and bar to be consistent, thereby legitimate.

It is true that Delaware courts have an enormous stake in avoiding any mass exodus of corporations from their state. Thus, they have a stake in not doing anything that manifestly annoys management *or shareholders*. But within the grand middle ground of maneuvering then left to them, they can uphold as many possible doctrines or standards of review as they wish.[34] The point, as Cunningham and Yablon see it, is Delaware courts are driven to a unified standard by norms of legal craft. Delaware judges want their

rulings to be widely perceived as consistent across cases, as reasoned or publicly justifiable, and, because they are courts in equity, as yielding substantively fair outcomes.[35]

We add to this interpretation a central point of our procedural turn in
explaining Delaware court behavior. Part of Delaware judges' sense of legal
craft—and of their sense of what is consistent, reasoned, and substantively
fair—is their responsibility, sitting in equity, to identify and reduce possible
institutional externalities of corporate governance.[36] Delaware judges are
responsible when exercises of power between positions of trust and positions of dependence in structured situations become one-sided. Our evidence for characterizing the notion of legal craft in this broader way is a
point Cunningham and Yablon miss as they think through the scope of application of their unified standard thesis. They end their article by proposing that Delaware courts bring executive compensation and corporate charitable contributions into the situations covered by enhanced scrutiny review.[37] They also wonder whether Delaware courts recognize shareholder
interests both long term and short term.[38]

Our explanation for why Delaware courts have not brought enhanced
scrutiny review to these situations and, we predict, are not likely to do so in
the future is that at most these situations involve immediate externalities of
corporate governance for shareholders (that is, agency costs). Irrespective of
how these governance disputes are settled, they do not bear in any way on
institutional design. We predict, therefore, that Delaware courts will leave it
to management and shareholders, including institutional investors, to settle
these disputes as best they can, in their own positional interests. We also
predict that should Delaware courts ever bring enhanced scrutiny review to
these situations, this will dramatically and immediately raise doubts about
their reputation as this country's premier corporate courts. Delaware judges
have no greater expertise in evaluating management compensation, corporate charitable contributions, or shareholders' long-term interests than the
parties directly involved and their advisors.

We propose, therefore, that our procedural turn better explains current
judicial behavior and more accurately predicts future judicial behavior. It
accounts for why Delaware courts resuscitated due care as a fiduciary duty,
placing it on a par with loyalty despite the General Assembly's move in the
opposite direction. It accounts for why Delaware courts chose to link both
traditional duties to a more abstract notion, that of good faith. Delaware
courts are telling corporate officers that if they wish to retain business judgment rule protection, decisions and transactions that substantially affect

shareholders (and possibly others) must be made within and through a collegial formation. And they are telling all observers, albeit more implicitly or indirectly, that there is indeed a relationship between corporate governance and institutional design and they are taking responsibility, as courts in equity, for monitoring it. After all, if Delaware courts are not concerned with the institutional externalities of corporate governance, why would they *ever* criticize, let alone rescind, a transaction that unambiguously benefits shareholders materially—no matter how it was made? They certainly would not do so because corporate officers who otherwise have no personal material stake in the action (and so do not breach loyalty) nonetheless fail to exhibit sufficient "care" along the way. Yet Delaware courts do indeed criticize and at times rescind such transactions because, we propose, they are concerned about institutional design.

Our interpretation also better explains why Delaware courts keep their applications of enhanced scrutiny review, a qualitative standard of analysis, relatively restricted in scope, despite calls by Brudney as well as Cunningham and Yablon to broaden its scope. They are quite willing to tolerate boards and management teams that do not hold an auction, do not take stakeholder interests into account, do not maximize share price, and do not maximize corporate growth *because none of these actions, none of these exercises of positional power, harm institutional design.* At most, these actions may harm discrete constituents—shareholders, stakeholders, or third parties—at particular times.

An enhanced scrutiny review allows "precisely the kind of flexible, fact-based, case-by-case inquiry so characteristic of Delaware corporate law opinions."[39] Yet why do Delaware courts bring any qualitative standard of analysis to governance disputes (other than to give them something interesting to do)? They do this, we propose, because applying qualitative standards of behavior to corporate officers makes it more difficult for them to feign deliberation and disinterestedness, as opposed actually to establishing and then maintaining collegial formations in governance structures. Regardless, Delaware courts do not like to see legal practitioners treating the distinctions they draw between cases as formalities that corporate officers can try to manipulate as they act one-sidedly in their own interests.[40]

3. Rock's "Moral Community"

Cunningham and Yablon's final piece of evidence for their thesis that Delaware courts have developed a new unified standard is that by the early

1990s these courts were characterizing their major decisions of the 1980s as expressions of the same legal standards.[41] The unified standard calls on corporate officers to change their behavior, but it allows them to act in countless ways other than maximizing shareholder wealth in the short run. Edward Rock, of University of Pennsylvania Law School, builds on this unified standard thesis and, in particular, on Cunningham and Yablon's point that Delaware courts prefer to analyze and decide governance disputes with detailed, contextual reviews of contested transactions than with formal rules, what legal scholars call "bright-line rules."[42]

Rock's thesis is that Delaware courts are best described as the "moral voice" of an elite community, namely that of directors, senior managers, and legal counsel of large, publicly traded companies.[43] With this, Rock holds that the rulings and written opinions of Delaware courts regarding breaches of fiduciary duty are "moral narratives," not fixed standards of conduct. These courts issue "corporate law sermons" designed to remind "members" of their "community's" substantive norms of proper behavior, norms that Rock asserts "members" have already internalized in common, as shared personal beliefs.[44] Here we see Rock recapitulating Useem's explanation for why directors and corporate officers at times act in disinterested ways: An "inner circle" of elites somehow shares internalized substantive beliefs.[45] What Rock adds to Useem's account is that Delaware courts literally shame corporate officers into acting disinterestedly.[46] They do so by adding substance to the abstract concept of "good faith" that is not easy for corporate officers to ignore. Delaware courts present "fact-intensive, normatively saturated descriptions of manager, director and lawyer conduct, and of process." The result is not unpredictable law but "reasonably precise standards" that, however, "are not reducible to rules or algorithms."[47]

Rock illustrates his thesis by focusing on Delaware court decisions in management buyout cases of the late 1980s and early 1990s, cases in which conflicts of interest are rife. MBO disputes did not come before Delaware courts "in appreciable numbers" until 1985, at the earliest, and Delaware courts did not work out the norms they would apply to these situations until 1988, at the earliest.[48]

In MBO transactions, Rock notes, "kindergarten" norms of "loyalty and cooperation" do not provide courts with much guidance because loyalty, for instance, is always in dispute.[49] Corporate directors in particular find themselves in a *position* in which they cannot avoid conflicts of interest, and thereby the possibility of being charged with breaching loyalty. On the one hand, directors often have personal ties with senior managers.

On the other, they owe contractual duties to shareholders, to maximize their wealth, and fiduciary duties of care and loyalty to the very corporate entity some senior managers are trying to buy.[50] Making matters worse, directors and other corporate officers also have inside information and often can control the timing of any buyout or other change of control (by taking either more or less time to become "informed" as they bear their duty of care). What behavior is appropriate or proper in these situations, therefore, is hardly clear.[51]

The closest precedent or analogy Delaware courts had to MBO transactions was to cases in which (a) a parent *corporation* acquires additional shares of a partially owned subsidiary and (b) *management* buys a division from the corporation it manages.[52] Delaware courts were more familiar with parent-subsidiary transactions. "The most common situation in which the Delaware courts apply the entire fairness test in the merger context is when a parent corporation acquires the minority-held stock of its subsidiary."[53] In the 1970s, Delaware courts gave serious consideration to prohibiting all parent-subsidiary mergers because of the conflicts of interest inherent in these transactions.[54] In the 1980s, they did the same with MBOs.

We can interject here one of our central points: If these transactions pose no possible harm to institutional design, why would Delaware courts even consider prohibiting them? Why would they even consider assuming that these transactions cannot maximize shareholder wealth and thereby increase social wealth—irrespective of the conflicts of interest inherent in them?

What Delaware courts eventually decided is that a legitimate business purpose of a parent company *might* justify a parent-subsidiary merger, subject to review by a court.[55] Moreover, Delaware courts confirmed our account of their behavior by emphasizing the importance of these and other unusual transactions being carried out within and through a collegial formation. In *Weinberger v. UOP, Inc.* (in 1983), to recall, Delaware's Supreme Court held that UOP could not cash out minority shareholders of a subsidiary it partially owned unless it established an independent committee to represent these shareholders' interests.[56] Management buyouts of divisions of the corporations they managed were more exotic than parent-subsidiary mergers. The first case came to Delaware in 1982 (in *Field v. Allyn*).[57]

Delaware courts initially approached MBO cases with the same two concepts they used in other changes of corporate control during the early 1980s, namely, the business judgment presumption and the entire fairness standard. As applied to directors in particular, a presumption of business judgment rule protection has three core elements. It protects them from liability and their decisions from rescission if they are independent (of management and any interested party), act in good faith, and exhibit due care.[58] Moreover, consistent with a presumption in directors' favor, the burden of proof was on plaintiff shareholders to allege credibly that directors failed to act consistently with any of these standards. Once they did this, directors' behavior was then subjected to an entire fairness review and, with this, the burden of proof shifts to them. Defendant directors must now demonstrate to a court's satisfaction that the transaction at issue was entirely fair to the corporation, both in its outcome and in the process through which it was undertaken.[59]

Rock's point is that these are normative, qualitative standards of analysis, not bright-line rules. What these standards mean hinges on the narratives Delaware courts tell when they rule in each case, not just the decision itself.[60] As Delaware courts decided and discussed MBO cases, therefore, directors adjusted their behavior accordingly, as they heard the new "moral sermons."[61] By Rock's account, three Delaware cases in particular, "the defining trilogy," brought substance to the norms governing MBO transactions: *Macmillan* I and II (1988–1989), *Fort Howard* (1988), and *RJR Nabisco* (1989).[62]

The norms Rock sees emerging from these cases are captured only in part by the summary he provided of Delaware court sermons.[63] Given that any summary is deficient, Rock turns to how these norms are conveyed to corporate officers and, given his thesis about "community" and shared substantive beliefs, he spends considerable time describing how judicial shaming keeps corporate legal counsel, and then corporate officers, in line.[64] Thus, Rock notes, "Delaware norms disfavor": "strong-willed CEOs who dominate directors," personal antipathy that interferes with board consideration, boards that tilt toward management's preferred bidder.[65] But he has problems establishing that corporate officers are really personally shamed by any of this, in fact that they care less what Delaware courts are sermonizing about one way or the other. He establishes only that they care whether or not they win in court. More important for our purposes, what Rock interprets as efforts by Delaware courts to shame particular people, by playing on their putatively internalized substantive beliefs, we can explain more parsimoniously, and less metaphysically.

We propose that many actions taken by Delaware courts are efforts to uphold the integrity of collegial formations in boardrooms (including how the special committees responsible for MBO transactions conduct themselves) and corporate governance structures more generally (including how management or controlling shareholders conduct themselves in these transactions). This judicial behavior, we hold, has nothing to do with shaming the individuals within these formations, except for those who act in particularly egregious ways. Rather, this judicial behavior has everything to do with seeing to it that directors and corporate officers recognize *cognitively* two procedural norms of behavior. First, a collegial formation is to be put in place in these situations and given exclusive authority over these transactions. Second, directors and corporate officers participating in this formation, and in this transaction, are not to feign independence and disinterest while acting as a pawn of the management buyout group.

At a minimum, we believe, Delaware courts are endeavoring to maintain the integrity of collegial formations currently present in boardrooms and corporate governance structures. At a maximum, they are endeavoring to establish collegial formations and support their authority by instructing all corporate officers that in hostile or unusual situations the presence of these formations allows them to attain two of their most important goals simultaneously. First, the presence of collegial formations not only normatively mediates excesses (one-sidedness) by corporate officers *but also protects them from excesses (problematic tender offers) by hostile bidders and mobilized shareholders.* Second, the presence of collegial formations also keeps courts at bay, allowing corporate officers relatively easily to pass Delaware's intermediate standard of enhanced scrutiny and then, if necessary, its ultimate standard of intrinsic fairness. On the other hand, of course, a collegial formation in boardrooms, or in special committees, means management buyout groups may lose to a hostile bidder or their plans may otherwise be vetoed after deliberation has occurred.

4. Blair and Stout's "Mediating Hierarchy Model"

Margaret Blair and Lynn Stout, of the American Enterprise Institute and Georgetown Law School, seek a way of reconciling not only shareholder contracting and stakeholder balancing but also the nexus metaphor and the entity metaphor. Rather than treating management as agent and shareholders as principal and focusing narrowly on agency costs for shareholders, they take a "team production" approach to the corporation. It is not possible, they point out, for management to anticipate by contract all of the rewards and responsibilities attending team production. This explains why complex teams develop "an institutional substitute for explicit contracts," namely the law of publicly traded corporations.[66] All team members, managers, stakeholders, and shareholders alike, give up important rights to a legal entity, its governance structure and, ultimately, its board of directors. Blair and Stout's point is that what distinguishes a publicly traded corporation from a close corporation is not the relationship between ownership and agency. Rather, it is the presence of an independent board of directors coupled with a self-regulating stock market where dispersed investors buy and sell shares in the company.[67]

Shareholders are not really owners of publicly traded corporations. Their legal rights and powers over a board of directors are "remarkably limited."[68] A board, therefore, is the ultimate authority in any publicly traded corporation, but it, too, does not own the company. Consistent with corporate law tradition and long-standing judicial practice, Blair and Stout propose that a board is the trustee of the team as a whole, of the entity.[69] Its central function, therefore, is not exclusively to reduce agency costs and maximize shareholder wealth. Rather, a board's central function is directly or indirectly to encourage all constituents to make the firm-specific investments necessary to keep team production going, to keep the entity going.[70]

Rather than seeing their team production approach supporting "communitarian" or "progressive" criticisms of a nexus of contracts approach, however, Blair and Stout see it supporting shareholder contracting in one important respect. Communitarians and progressives advocate changing corporate law in order to make directors more accountable to stakeholders, often including local communities. But Blair and Stout's point about a board being "independent" of management, shareholders, and stakeholders alike is that it stands atop a "mediating hierarchy." Corporate law, in turn, does not need to be changed. It already instructs courts to see to it that senior managers, controlling shareholders, or any other constituents do not directly control the boards of directors of public traded corporations. This is very similar to Palmiter's point about directors implicitly bearing a fiduciary duty of independence.

What is most important, and also consistent with Palmiter, Blair and Stout propose that their team production, mediating hierarchy approach better explains how corporations and law actually work.[71] The corporation is not so much a nexus of arm's length contracts as a nexus of firm-specific investments. Their point is that it is difficult to entice stakeholders to dedicate their intermediate products or human capital to a corporation when they see shirking and opportunism going uncontrolled or when they are worried that a governance structure might permit this to happen. Stakeholders will only make these investments if they see a decision making procedure in place that they believe is fair and reliable. Thus, a corporation is a mediating hierarchy, with a board of directors at its peak.[72] The board is the internal "court of appeals" for all investors who have disputes with management.

In turn, rather than directors controlling corporations directly, a top management team makes most day-to-day decisions, along with other constituents (such as middle managers) at lower levels in the hierarchy. Blair and Stout's point is that all constituents—high and low in the hierarchy—share an interest in resolving their disputes and conflicts before they reach the board, the internal court of appeals.[73] However, once disputes reach the board, its decisions are final; they cannot be overturned by appealing *directly* to any outside authority, whether a court or a shareholder majority.

Courts do enforce explicit contracts among management and between management and constituents. They also enforce criminal and civil laws more generally, such as minimum wage laws. But courts do not intervene into the internal governance of a corporation unless directors or other corporate officers act in ways that threaten the corporate entity's existence, by violating their fiduciary duties *to the entity*.[74] Derivative suits by shareholders, to recall, are proxies for proper behavior by directors, made on behalf of the corporate entity. Moreover, derivative suits only reach court after dissatisfied shareholders first make a "demand" on a board to do its job. Courts typically do not permit dissatisfied shareholders to go around a board, and thereby to bring suit directly on the entity's behalf.

Here, however, is where Blair and Stout's reading of judicial behavior is too narrow and where a procedural turn can help out.[75] Courts also intervene into the internal governance of corporations when the existence of corporations as entities is not an issue, when their ownership is simply changing hands. Consider again transactions between parents and partially owned subsidiaries, and management buyouts of divisions or corporations. Courts intervene when directors and corporate officers fail to show due care, even when maximizing shareholder wealth or protecting stakeholder interests and outcomes redound unambiguously to the benefit of a corporate entity. Courts intervene, that is, when the hierarchy, the governance structure, fails to operate within and through a collegial formation and thereby threatens institutional design, not a corporate entity's existence.

We see the same judicial behavior in derivative suits as an institution, as an established practice. Blair and Stout acknowledge that shareholders have two sets of rights that other constituents lack—a right to bring a derivative suit on behalf of the corporate entity against directors accused of breaching their duties, and a right to vote for directors (and their removal) and on "fundamental" corporate changes. But their point is that corporate law nonetheless insulates directors from all constituents, including shareholders. It awards shareholders the rights above only because they, not other constituents, are at times in the best position to represent the interests of the entity, namely when directors act at the entity's expense. After all, successful derivative action results in the entity receiving benefits, not the shareholders bringing suit.[76] Moreover, boards may take control of these suits, and then terminate them, by establishing investigating committees comprised of truly independent directors whose behavior is not credibly challenged.[77]

Here again we see clearly that courts are prepared at any time to defer to a collegial formation in a corporate governance structure. But, unlike Blair and Stout, we do not reduce the point of this judicial deference to whether actions taken by directors or board committees necessarily have anything to do with a corporate entity's continued existence. Our point is that judicial deference to corporate collegial formations benefits institutional design, and then may or may not bear on a particular corporate entity's existence.

The significance of our institutional approach to corporations and law comes into fullest view where Blair and Stout try to explain how corporate law keeps directors relatively "faithful" to the corporate entity rather than allowing them to act one-sidedly, to become "despotic." They point to three "aspects of corporate law and culture" that likely encourage directors to serve the entity's collective interests.[78] First, directors have a positional and "reputational" interest in meeting at least minimum demands of major constituents because otherwise firm-specific investments will lag and efficiency will decline. Second, corporate law limits directors' opportunities to act one-sidedly. Third, corporate law treats directors not only as agents but also as trustees, and contract theory assumes implicitly the presence of a fair, trusted mediator of disputes.

The first aspect is so minimalist that, aside from bankruptcy situations, it is irrelevant. We add to the other two aspects that constituents as well as observing judges can only identify when directors are acting "faithfully" or disinterestedly in terms of a procedural normative standard of behavior. They can identify directly when directors exhibit fidelity to the threshold standard of consistent rule enforcement and, therefore, maintain the integrity of a boardroom's collegial form of organization. They cannot do so more directly in terms of any substantive normative standard (as traditional fiduciary law suggests) or in terms of any quantitative standard (as contractarians propose). Using these standards directly, constituents and judges typically cannot agree that directors have been acting in disinterested ways, a qualitative end-in-view. Agreement typically breaks down among constituents because they have different, often competing stakes in what directors are doing in substance, which color how they interpret any qualitative end-in-view. Judges are similar. They often have different subjective interpretations regarding what directors are doing in substance, and why they are doing it, which have the same effect.

Indeed, Blair and Stout acknowledge that observing economists have difficulty identifying when directors act in "trustworthy" ways in substance. Actually, economists have the same difficulty "modeling the behavior of judges," whether directors (acting as a corporation's internal court of appeal) or corporate law judges.[79] Blair and Stout conclude from this that heterogeneous constituents will only trust directors (and judges) when the latter (a) establish reputations for integrity, independence, and service, and then also (b) maintain a personal desire to protect and enhance their reputations.[80] This desire, in turn, "must be reinforced by powerful social norms," and here is where economists become most uncomfortable.[81] The key to seeing that these combinations of qualities actually come together, by Blair and Stout's account, is carefully to select trustworthy individuals as directors, those who will behave in good faith with an eye to appropriate social norms.[82]

But we have seen this solution before. It focuses attention too directly on the substantive normative beliefs that directors putatively share as individuals (Rock's "community") and then, even worse, on the social psychology of these individuals (their capacity to be shamed personally by "corporate law sermons"). Our account of director (and judicial) behavior is quite different. We focus attention on the form in which boardrooms and corporate governance structures are organized, and then on individuals' behavior within this form, on how they exercise positional power within it. We focus on whether they *cognitively* recognize that a collegial formation is present in a boardroom or governance structure, and we propose that whether they do or not is reflected in their *behavioral* fidelity to a threshold standard of procedural norms, not in their internalized beliefs (whatever they are). We have no way of divining the substantive beliefs or social psychology of these individuals, and certainly not in advance of actually seeing how they perform their duties. We do not propose *a priori* that they comprise any "inner circle" or "moral community," and certainly not one any more "inner" or "moral" than what we might find in any neighborhood or local community. We assume they think and act like any individuals who exercise positional power in structured situations in civil society and whose behavior is monitored by courts. The key for us is that the courts now at issue sit in equity and thus keep an eye on the relationship between corporate governance and institutional design.

II. An Opening in Palmiter's Implicit Duty

Palmiter concedes that he cannot identify "independence" at a conceptual level, but we wish to convert his analysis of judicial precedents into practicable instructions for judges. We read his approach as an investigation into how different state courts, at different points in time, have endeavored to encourage corporate officers to establish and maintain collegial formations within corporate governance structures.[83] In turn, we also read this ongoing endeavor in the *Weinberger, Van Gorkom, Macmillan, Technicolor,* and *QVC* decisions, and we reinterpret the *Time-Warner* decision in this light. After all, with the exception of *Time-Warner,* Delaware courts did not attempt in these cases to impose on corporate officers any particular, substantive normative standard of behavior. A sermon lacking substantive norms is a curious one, even if it does draw attention to egregious misbehavior by particular individuals.

The problem with Palmiter's own references to "independence" is he explicitly assumes or asserts that the opposite is the case. His wording conveys that when state courts call on boards and individual directors to exhibit "independence" from the influence of management and "extraneous" interests, they are placing substantive limitations on unilateral managing and shareholder contracting alike. He says explicitly, for instance, that independence is "a higher substantive standard" than the traditional fiduciary duty of care.[84]

1. Re-reading Palmiter

There is a more defensible way of understanding board and director independence in light of the procedural turn we are proposing. Palmiter documents that the corporate judiciary retains a positional interest as an institution in restraining one-sidedness. We see this in its uneven but discernible efforts in recent years to support the presence of deliberative bodies in structured situations.[85] But we need to add three points to Palmiter's discovery of an implicit duty of independence, if it is to orient judges explicitly and in consistent ways.

First, judges must begin to state explicitly that they are extending judicial protection to existing corporate collegial formations, as deliberative bodies. As Vice Chancellor Jacobs demonstrated, they are already prepared at times to go further, to compel recalcitrant directors and corporate officers to adopt this form irrespective of what their corporation's "culture" happens to be. Second, judges must also begin to appreciate that the presence of collegial formations is reflected in director and corporate officer behavior, not in their beliefs, intent, social psychology, or sensitivity to shame, sermons, or substantive social norms. Collegial formations are only present when, at the very least, corporate officers exhibit fidelity to procedural norms they cognitively apprehend, not emotionally sense. Third, judges must appreciate too that the threshold standard of procedural norms we discussed in Chapter 11 is uniquely institutionalized only in democratic social orders, *and always only contingently.* This is why extending judicial protection to corporate collegial formations advances an unambiguous public law interest. Such judicial behavior is an essential ingredient in maintaining the institutional design of any democratic society.

This way of explaining how Delaware judges are (increasingly) analyzing governance disputes also allows us to solve problems that Mark Roe and Michael Useem have raised independently about possible "collegial monitoring" of management by boards of directors. Roe holds that such monitoring depends on boards recruiting expert individuals who also have sufficient financial incentives to be involved and well informed. Thus, he expects representatives of institutional investors to have both expertise and incentives, whereas he is skeptical that individuals holding large blocks (and, thus, incentives) will have sufficient expertise.[86] But then Roe adds two complications and Useem another. First, Roe says we have no reason to expect financial intermediaries to run corporations any better than management, and, regardless, "professional pride makes managers and directors try hard even if the organizational constraints acting on them are weak." Markets and financial analysts monitor corporate officers' behavior, and media reporting embarrasses them when they perform poorly.[87] This gets us back to Useem and Rock on substantive norms and shaming. Second, Useem notes more recently that corporate officers find portfolio managers' personal and professional qualifications more appealing than their ownership stakes. Thus, when portfolio managers are elected to boards (which Useem recommends against), management does not treat them as representing any special constituency at all.[88] Finally, Roe notes that there is no prominent theory—efficient markets, indexing strategies, portfolio theory—which extols coupling large block investing with presence in boardroom.

Our procedural turn addresses all three problems. First, it provides a theory that can accommodate, if not extol, the presence in boardrooms of institutional investor representatives. As long as boardrooms are organized in the collegial form, and directors exhibit fidelity to procedural norms, directors do not exercise positional power one-sidedly and will not tolerate those among them who try. Second, our procedural turn converts Useem's problem into a virtue: Boardrooms that value director expertise and knowledge, not whether they putatively represent any constituency in substance, is precisely what Delaware courts are trying to encourage and what Palmiter's notion of independence captures well. Third, the point of a corporate board is not to run companies better than management, irrespective of who the directors are. The point is for the board to see to it that positional power is not exercised in one-sided ways anywhere in a corporation where governance disputes, and derivative suits, might emerge.

2. Can a New Fiduciary Duty Orient Courts Explicitly?

Contractarians' reluctance to acknowledge that court-enforced norms ever properly mediate Pareto optimal outcomes is understandable. What is mysterious is judicial imposers' failure to see what Palmiter has accomplished with his discovery. He has given them the opening they need to challenge today's orthodoxy by reestablishing a direct linkage to the fiduciary law tradition. He points the way to identifying a specific relationship between corporate governance and institutional design. Equally mysterious are the intentions of the judges whose decisions Palmiter reviews. What exactly do they think they are doing when they hold corporate officers to norms of behavior that mediate Pareto optimal outcomes?

What eludes these judges and imposers are four important points about this judicial behavior. First, the duty of independence implied by this behavior differs significantly from fiduciary law's two traditional duties. Unlike the latter, it cannot be read historically as delimiting management's discretion and business judgment in substance. Put differently, a duty of independence need not place substantive limitations on the corporation's legitimate place and purpose in American society.

Second, judges whose behavior implies they are enforcing a duty of independence have yet to consider what is actually involved in enforcing this duty consistently across cases as a mandatory rule.[89] At a minimum, it would involve them stating explicitly that this mandatory rule instructs them to impose a *procedural* normative mediation on certain exercises of positional power in certain structured situations. By contrast, Palmiter tried to identify this duty by drawing a more direct analogy to fiduciary law's traditional *substantive* normative duties of care and loyalty. Thinking directly about what "independence" means in substance, he quickly declared the effort "futile." He fails to appreciate that independence is served by the presence of a particular form of organization, not by any behavior required in substance outside the form. Given this failure, Palmiter never really appreciates either the doctrinal implications *or institutional significance* of the judicial behavior he otherwise describes so accurately.[90]

Third, the duty of independence can replace both traditional duties. Precisely because it can be tied to the presence of a particular form of organization, it eliminates the difficulties judges face whenever they otherwise attempt to enforce social norms of behavior more directly. When judges overextended fiduciary law in the past, they undermined courts' capacity as an institution to recognize and then normatively mediate one-sided exercises of positional power, let alone corporate behavior that does not carry institutional externalities.[91] By contrast, the duty of independence successfully updates this legal tradition. It permits judges once again to recognize in common when exercises of positional power in structured situations fall unambiguously within the core scope of application of the entire fiduciary law tradition. It permits them to recognize this behavior independently of management's positional interests, independently of individual directors' or individual managers' interpretations of their corporations' collective interests, and, certainly, independently of any state legislature's references to corporate "citizenship," "social responsibility," or any other morality of aspiration.

Fourth, judges whose behavior implies they have been enforcing a duty of independence have yet to appreciate that this duty can normatively mediate managing, contracting, and balancing in ways that are practicable in today's global economy. Coupled with our procedural turn, it instructs judges to enforce mandatory rules with two ends in view, one quantitative and instrumental and the other qualitative and institutional. It instructs them *simultaneously* (a) to facilitate corporations' domestic profitability and global competitiveness and yet (b) to extend judicial protection to collegial formations in structured situations. Because this second end is institutional and advances a public law interest, it assumes higher legal status than the first. Fiduciary obligations always trump contractual obligations. Yet, giving enforcement priority to this qualitative standard of analysis does not in any way jeopardize American corporations' domestic profitability and global competitiveness. The qualitative standard is a procedural normative mediation of management business judgment, shareholder contracting, and stakeholder balancing, not a substantive normative limitation. As such, judges can enforce the standard consistently while otherwise facilitating corporate officers' market-mimicking behavior and while otherwise tolerating a broad range of "corporate cultures." The only "corporate cultures" that they cannot tolerate or accommodate are those that encourage corporate officers to encroach against corporate collegial formations and procedural norms.

III. In the Absence of a Procedural Turn

What is likely to happen if Delaware courts fail to take the procedural turn we propose (or some equivalent)? They are likely to drift, usually incrementally but at times more dramatically. This is the way in which legal scholars and the business press interpreted Vice Chancellor Jacobs' 1993 *QVC* decision before Cunningham and Yablon published their article proposing that it is part of a unified standard of intermediate review. Legal scholars originally read Jacobs' decision as a return to *Revlon* and a repudiation of *Time-Warner*.[92] They read it as a return to the doctrinal principle that directors are obliged to seek the highest price for a company once it enters a market for corporate control. They did not read it as a more sophisticated wording of *Time-Warner*, a decision consistent with Palmiter's implicit duty of independence. They did not read it as supporting the doctrinal principle that directors are expected to deliberate disinterestedly over a company's collective interests, including any qualities that they believe elude pricing (such as the presence of sites of disinterested governance itself).

What difference would it make if the *QVC* decision was interpreted in this narrow way and state courts continued to drift? The aftermath of the *Van Gorkom* decision aptly illustrates three developments that would likely unfold. First, it illustrates that state courts can accede to midstream opting out of all mandatory rules, all qualitative standards of analysis in corporate governance disputes. State courts not only can try to operate exclusively with the quantitative standard of Pareto optimality for shareholders (and then possibly stakeholders) but can also come to regard it, by default, as the highest *moral* or substantive normative standard of corporate governance. They can accord higher legal status to Pareto optimal *outcomes* than to traditional fiduciary duties of fair *dealing* in structured situations. This means they can accord to Pareto optimal outcomes higher legal status than corporate officers' behavioral fidelity to procedural norms that only collegial formations institutionalize. With this, the corporate judiciary effectively narrows corporate purpose, and its social vision, to immediate externalities of corporate decision making, at best. It removes from its concerns any broader view of corporate purpose, and the possible institutional externalities of corporate governance. It thereby brings liberal complacency into the very center of corporate law doctrine for the first time in American history.

Second, and related, the aftermath of *Van Gorkom* illustrates that state courts can fail to treat each component part of today's orthodoxy of liberal complacency as an independent variable. They can hypostatize the first part, thereby focusing exclusively as an institution on whether shareholder wealth is maximized. With this, they increasingly neglect considering whether maximizing private wealth may fail at times to advance social wealth, and they lose the legal terminology needed even to raise concerns about possible harms to institutional design. With this, state courts become "available" as an institution first to tolerate, then to accommodate, one-sided exercises of positional power within and around corporations and other major intermediary associations—as long as priced outcomes are Pareto optimal. At first, they tolerate inadvertent instances of one-sidedness. Over time they become "available" to tolerate more purposeful encroachments against the integrity of the collegial form and procedural norms. Meanwhile, their tolerance of encroachments within and around corporations can inadvertently encourage one-sidedness by administrators of hospitals, universities, and other sites of professional practice.[93]

Third, *Van Gorkom*'s aftermath also illustrates why dividing corporate agency and drifting toward stakeholder balancing can neither orient nor legitimate the corporate judiciary as an institution. Balancing is not consistent with this institution's long-standing practice of extending judicial protection on a public law ground to individuals who occupy positions of dependence in structured situations. Thus, the courts' drift toward stakeholder balancing is not self-evidently consistent with maintaining their own integrity as an institution.

In addition, legal commentary in support of contracting or balancing in the absence of any explicitly taken procedural turn can only encourage Delaware courts to contribute to three developments in corporate law and corporate governance that they have been resisting as an institution for over a century. One development is an ongoing narrowing of all normative restraints on corporate officers. Given that even the traditional fiduciary duty of loyalty was losing "interdicting power" during the 1980s, the only restraints that corporate officers might eventually face will be strictly strategic.[94] Management, for instance, will face mobilized institutional shareholders and stakeholder coalitions. It will no longer face *norm-based* restraints that courts enforce independently of all constituent interests, as mandatory rules. Rather, state courts and state legislatures will treat either management or shareholder majorities as the corporate agent, or, alternatively, formally divide corporate agency. This last decision will bring the metaphor of the corporation as representative-body into the very center of corporate law doctrine. As these actions permit or encourage one-sidedness within structured situations in American civil society, this can only culminate in a legitimation crisis for these courts as an institution.

The second development in corporate law and judicial practice to which judicial drift will contribute comes into play, ironically, when courts attempt in this context to address the public law issue of corporate purpose. They will find that today's orthodoxy fails to offer them practicable doctrinal options. Judicial drift in the 1980s nearly delegitimated the duty of loyalty. Yet this was the duty that ultimately kept the fiduciary law tradition alive within the corporate judiciary and bar. In the absence of an explicitly taken procedural turn, any resumption of judicial drift can culminate in eliminating all considerations of equity, all qualitative standards of analysis, from judges' concerns.

The third development to which judicial drift will contribute is further to politicize corporate law and corporate governance. In the absence of an explicitly taken procedural turn, judicial interventions into corporate governance disputes will exacerbate, not ameliorate, existing positional conflicts. Cunningham and Yablon's advice that Delaware courts broaden their applications of their intermediate standard of review to management compensation and related matters would instantly have this effect. Such judicial behavior will exacerbate, not ameliorate, power struggles within other major intermediary associations, including the professions. In short, a new round of judicial drift will increase the uncertainties with which corporate managers and association administrators live every day. In such a state of uncertainty and flux, judges will have no way of identifying when certain exercises of private power carry institutional externalities for the larger social order.

If state courts fail explicitly to extend judicial protection to corporate collegial formations as a mandatory rule, then the only doctrinal options available to them other than management sovereignty, shareholder contracting, or stakeholder balancing will be to revert to some type of doctrinal fundamentalism. This would be marked by judges' (inherently unsuccessful) efforts to impose substantive standards of behavior on corporate officers directly as mandatory rules.[95] It would be marked by (inherently unsuccessful) efforts to require corporate entities to exhibit qualities of "citizenship" or "social responsibility."[96] This is the thrust, after all, of what Rock calls Delaware courts' "moral sermons." Because this is impracticable in a global economy, and impossible to enforce with consistency regardless, doctrinal fundamentalism can only decrease courts' legitimacy and authority as an institution (as Chancellor Allen acknowledges).[97]

Thus, the most likely turn for state courts to take in the absence of a procedural turn during times of renewed hostile activity will be to divide corporate agency. They will institutionalize stakeholder balancing as a qualitative standard of analysis in corporate governance disputes. With this, they will at times challenge the legal status of shareholders' private property and the "moral" standing of Pareto optimal outcomes. They will convert corporate governance structures, as well as state courts, into representative bodies. All three institutions will be dedicated to balancing competing group interests literally as an end-in-itself. Max Weber could have predicted this institutional convergence. Unlike contractarians, however, he would also have coldly drawn attention to its institutional externalities for the larger social order.

Notes

1. We find this example being used by both social democrats (Dugger 1989) and communitarians (Etzioni 1993, 1996; Selznick 1992).

1. Kaysen (1996a:5).

2. Useem (1993, 1996), Davis and Thompson (1994); for Europe, see Baums, Buxbaum, and Hopt (1994).

3. Compared to 8.2 percent from 1991 to 1993 and, more important, to 6.5 percent from 1985 to 1987 (Stevenson 1996). "A Chicago-based employment consulting firm, Challenger, Gray & Christmas, Inc., reported last week that major corporations announced 108,000 layoffs in January [1994], the highest monthly level since it began tracking the figures in 1989" (Lohr 1994).

4. Applebome (1998), citing Harvard economist James Medoff. See Gordon (1996) for the argument that U.S. corporations remain bloated bureaucracies, and real wages keep falling.

5. See Harrison (1994) for a general analysis that anticipated greater competitiveness by large corporations; also Smith and Dyer (1996:55–56) and Calomiris and Ramirez (1996:164–65) for more specific statements.

6. Uchitelle (1999).

7. Kilborn (1999).

8. In reviewing chapters written by social scientists and legal scholars for his collection, Kaysen (1996a:16) notes that if "the quadrivium" of socioeconomic virtue is efficiency, progress, stability, and equity, "the contributors give the corporation high marks for the first two and often regard the last two as not appropriate measures."

9. The legal scholars who come closest to explaining what the Delaware courts are doing and why are Alan Palmiter (1989), Lawrence Cunningham and Charles Yablon (1994), Edward Rock (1997), and Margaret Blair and Lynn Stout (1999). We discuss their accounts at length in Chapter 13.

10. British management scholars Kay and Silberston note that the term

"corporate governance" is relatively recent, emerging 20 or 25 years ago; yet the fact that corporations perform a governance function has been known for generations (1997:49). Anne Carver, a legal scholar at University of Hong Kong, finds the term "governance" being applied first to corporations in 1984, by Robert Tricker (1997:71). Economists Shleifer and Vishny (1997:737) define corporate governance narrowly, as the ways in which suppliers of finance to corporations assure themselves of getting a return on their investment. Why this definition is narrow will become more and more apparent as this book unfolds.

11. This is the central issue that Blair and Stout (1999) and Bratton (1995) see in corporate governance disputes.

12. Kay and Silberston put the matter even better, saying a company is a set of systems and routines and a structure of organization (1997:54–55). "The essence of the company is a structure of internal relationships among the staff, and a collection of external relationships with suppliers." Blair and Stout (1999) explore a "team production approach" to corporate governance.

13. Coffee (1990), Pound (1993), Davis and Thompson (1994), Useem (1993, 1996), Fligstein (1996), Smith and Dyer (1996).

14. Bruyn traces the term to Mintzberg's 1983 textbook (1991:79–80, 381 note 37). Legal scholars often use the term "stakeholder" when exploring the points at which the interests of creditors and employees conflict with those of shareholders and management (e.g., Coffee 1990:1499). Japanese managers act on behalf of a stakeholder coalition rather than on behalf of shareholders more exclusively (Kester 1991:75–81).

15. See Morrill (1995) for an ethnographic account of top managers' interactions at thirteen corporations.

16. Williamson (1985, 1988a, 1988b). This terminology— governance function, production function—is common in both law and economics journals.

17. Compare this approach to that by Nohria and Gulati (1994).

18. See Gregory Mark (1995:74) for the view that "law school historians rarely ... take the political culture into account in their work on the corporation"; but exceptions he cites are Mark Roe, Herbert Hovenkamp, and James Hurst. For a general statement about the economy and culture, see DiMaggio (1994).

19. See in particular Roy (1997), Butler and Ribstein (1995), Roe (1994), Romano (1993a).

20. See Roy (1997:144–75) on the relative autonomy of corporate law from both social forces and political interests.

21. This is why Patfield (1995) and Freedman (1995) say that unless "society" is clear about what "it" expects corporate law to accomplish, this law will not somehow independently, or automatically, guard society.

22. In Chapter 11 we distinguish limited government from formal democracy.

23. On the fiduciary law tradition, see Sciulli (1999:chap. 5) and the literature cited there.

24. Melvin Eisenberg's "first principle" of corporate law is that agents whose interest may materially diverge from the interests of their principal "should not have the power to unilaterally determine or materially vary the rules that govern those divergencies of interest" (1989:1474).

25. The Williams Act of 1968, for instance, regulates the timing of tender offers, not how target management teams may or may not react to them within the statutory time frame (e.g., Loewenstein 1989). John Kozyris (1989) calls on the federal government to protect "interstate stock," and Henry Butler and Larry Ribstein want the federal government to reduce restrictions of state corporate law by enforcing the interstate commerce clause more vigorously. They do not, however, want corporate law federalized (1995:148 note 16).

26. Parsons (1968).

27. See Rock (1997:1014) for the two legal questions, and then also for a different wording of the second sociological question that follows.

28. The phrase is from Etzioni (1988).

29. This paragraph and the next generally follow Sciulli (1999:43–44).

30. See Banfield (1958) for a now classic statement about "familism," and Putnam (1993) for a similar position. Tribalism is not the correct term for ethnic conflict in subsaharan Africa and therefore, Young (1976) and other area specialists do not use it in this context. Yet the term conveys well the point we are making about how corporate constituents react when subjected to arbitrary private governance. See Morrill (1995).

31. See Orts (1998b:283) who notes that this aspect of corporations moves us beyond the methodological individualism of economic theory and brings us to legal theory; and, I would add, social theory. Legal scholars who endeavor to identify corporations' collective interests and how corporations exercise collective power in society call this an "enterprise" approach.

32. See Parkinson (1993:1–50) for a standard general statement of this additional burden corporate officers bear.

33. Commentators trace the origin of legal contractarianism to a 1972 article by Alchian and Demsetz in *American Economic Review* and then "the watershed," the 1976 article by Jensen and Meckling in *Journal of Financial Economics*.

34. Legal scholars typically characterize these "harms" in exceedingly vague terms. Parkinson, for instance, refers to the "social disfigurement" that corporations might cause (1993:35).

35. See Acs and Steuerle (1996) for a well-reasoned, representative example, and Parkinson (1993) for an impressive theoretical justification for holding corporate officers accountable for these externalities. See Dragun (1983), Cornes and Sandler (1986), and Dahlman (1988) for general statements. See Macey (1989) for an example of how narrowly contractarians define externalities of corporate governance.

36. Blair and Stout (1999), Folk, Ward, and Welch (1998:141:15), Brudney (1997:599 note 9), Parkinson (1993:73–96).

37. Parsons (1964).

38. For a recent general theoretical approach to management-constituent relations, see Rindova and Fombrun (1999).

39. Hylton (1992).

40. Orts (1993:1577–78).

41. Blair and Stout (1999:258–65).

42. For a more comprehensive discussion, see Sciulli (1999).

43. For discussion, see Millon (1990) and Blumberg (1993).

44. Delaney (1992).

45. All state legislatures placed limitations on the amount of capital a corporation could accumulate, and even a state as sophisticated as New York held to a limit of $2 million in 1881, and then one of $5 million in 1890 (Friedman 1973/1985:523, Millon 1990:206–10).

46. Millon (1990:206).

47. Millon (1990:209–13).

48. Millon (1990:215).

49. Bratton (1989a:1474, 1485–89), Millon (1990), Blumberg (1993:27).

50. Butler (1989:101).

51. Hovenkamp (1991:247–48, 266).

52. Chancellor Allen (1992a).

53. For example, see Chancellor Allen (1992b:263–64, 272–81), Millon (1993: 1373).

NOTES TO CHAPTER 2

1. A hostile bid is under way "when one corporation [or raider] directly purchases another firm's stock from its shareholders without first approaching the firm's management with a proposal to combine" (Palmer et al. 1995:470).

2. See Useem (1993, 1996) and Morrill (1995) for managers' subjective impressions of their situation.

3. Chandler (1990:621–28); also see note 14 below. See Smith and Dyer (1996:32–33) for the point that Chandler's work in the late 1950s and early 1960s was "as much indebted to Weber and Parsons as to accumulating historical research on business."

4. The United States had undergone four previous waves of build-up takeovers, but why the fourth wave began in the mid-1960s, rather than earlier or later, remains a mystery to economists. For example, see Williamson (1988a) and Auerbach (1988). See Sobel (1984) for a general history.

Regardless, the fourth wave crested in 1969, with 6,107 takeovers (Kester 1991:10). See Palmer et al. (1995) for an empirical study of this period. In comparison, Japan underwent its first wave of mergers and acquisitions in the mid-1980s, with only small privately traded companies involved (Kester 1991:8–17). From 1971 to 1989, there had been only two major tender offers in Japan, both friendly and one by an American firm: Bendix International Finance Corp. (Kester 1991:99). Ames and Young found that there were only 32 foreign acquisitions of Japanese firms from 1955 through 1984, 19 by American corporations (Kester 1991:137). From 1984 to 1989, there were 24 others. See Kester (1991:138–39) for a complete list of American acquisitions of Japanese firms during this period. Japanese regulations clearly favor target management teams (Kester 1991:101).

    5. Chandler (1990:623). Today, about 2,000 U.S. firms have subsidiaries in foreign countries, with the typical firm in this group reporting eight (Vernon 1996: 75–76).

    6. The quotation is from Anders (1992:198), but see Roe (1996:113) for the general point that conglomerates made it possible to make money by severing top management because the latter was already treating divisions and subsidiaries like capital assets.

    7. Calomiris and Ramirez (1996:157).

    8. Calomiris and Ramirez (1996:157–58).

    9. Kaysen (1996a:10–11), Calomiris and Ramirez (1996:159).

    10. Useem (1996:24).

    11. Chandler (1990:625).

    12. Hurst (1970:87).

    13. Palmer et al. (1995) discuss both friendly and "predatory" corporate acquisitions in the 1960s, but they acknowledge difficulties in identifying the predatory type. At first (1995:470), they define it as "when one corporation directly purchases another firm's stock . . . without first approaching the firm's management with a proposal to combine." However, later they acknowledge (1995:477 note 8) that some acquiring bids were followed by silence on the part of target management and, therefore, were likely "friendly combinations in which the target firm's managers . . . for legal reasons disguised their role in the acquisition." Finally they add, "only three of the firms in our sample experienced a significant predatory bid in the 1960s and avoided either hostile takeover or acquisition by a 'white knight'" (1995:487). They never indicate how many firms experienced a significant predatory bid. Pound (1993:1015–16) is being similarly vague in defining hostile activity when he says there were fewer than ten cash tender offers each year without management consent or notification in the United States from 1956 to 1960. Then in 1963, there were 29 for firms listed on the New York Stock Exchange.

    14. Chandler's fifth and sixth developments elaborate the fourth: The fifth refers to portfolio managers' activities in capital markets, and the sixth to how these markets evolved into a market for control over the corporation itself.

    15. Yago (1991:26) contends it was the takeover of Electric Storage Battery by International Nickel in the mid-1970s. This calls into question Palmer et al.'s contention that there were truly "predatory" acquisitions in the 1960s. Pound (1993:1015–16) dates the first "cash tender offer for shares . . . without the consent

or notification of management" in 1956, without identifying the firm or firms involved, and without indicating whether it was really hostile or not.

16. Johnson (1990:903 note 150). Of the largest 478 publicly traded industrial corporations in the United States in 1962, only 71 were acquired from 1963 through 1968 (and another 13 disappeared through merger) (Palmer et al. 1995:476). At most, using the loosest definition, only 37 of the 71 acquisitions could possibly qualify as hostile or predatory (Palmer et al. 1995:477, plus note 8).

17. Palmer et al. (1995:476 note 6) found no evidence that either free cash flow or indebtedness affected the likelihood of acquisition during the 1960s. This continued to be the case even as the pace of corporate takeovers escalated in 1981, beginning with duPont's purchase of Conoco, the ninth largest U.S. oil company, for $7.68 billion. Conoco stock rose from under $50 a share to $98, for a total increase in premium of $3.2 billion; DuPont's premium fell $800 million. Ivan Boesky earned $40 million on this single deal in arbitrage (Stewart 1991:83–84; Easterbrook and Fischel 1991:196).

18. Coffee (1986:4 note 5), Jensen (1988:37).

19. Whether investment grade or junk, bonds yielded interest twice a year, they "matured in anywhere from three to 20 years, and they generally were sold in lots of $1 million or larger to big institutional investors" (Anders 1992:82). By the late 1980s, small investors were pooling their life savings into junk bond *funds*. "A medical-supply salesman in Maine put $7,000 into a junk-bond fund to finance his children's college education. An 89-year-old widow in Florida switched most of her $250,000 savings into junk-bond funds" (Anders 1992:103). Over $18 billion was accumulated in these funds from 1986 through 1988 (Anders 1992:103).

20. Lipton (1987:11–12), Stewart (1991:90ff).

21. Jensen (1988:39).

22. Stewart (1991:102, 114).

23. Yago (1991:108). See Anders (1992:8, 20–43) on the history of LBOs. "Senior debt" refers to investment bank loans or investment grade bonds, whereas "subordinate debt" refers to junk bonds and less secured loans.

24. Anders (1992:8), Burrough and Helyar (1990:140), Rock (1997:1026). *Field v. Allyn* involved an MBO of a division, not an entire corporation.

25. Others were Clayton & Dubilier, Forstmann Little & Co., Adler & Shaytkin, and Gibbons Green van Amerongen (Anders 1992:36–37).

26. The company was Houdaille Industries, Inc. of Fort Lauderdale FL, a Fortune 500 manufacturer of machine tools, pumps, and automobile bumpers (Burrough and Helyar 1990:139). According to Anders, KKR successfully completed three leveraged buyouts in 1977, but had none in 1978.

27. Anders (1992:14), Burrough and Helyar (1990:138).

28. Across the rest of the decade: 41 at $10.38 billion in 1985, 43 at $24.91 billion in 1986, 32 at $22.43 billion at 1987, 74 at $26.54 billion at 1988, 59 at $50.03 billion in 1989—and finally falling off in 1990 to 25 at $8.14 for billion (for rea-

sons we explore in time) (Rock 1997:1091, citing LBO Signposts and Leveraged Buyout Trends).

29. Anders (1992:156).

30. Anders (1992:272).

31. See Yago (1991:28–29) for the first four.

32. Consider Samuelson's general discussion of bonds (1948:122):

[Bonds] are nothing but special kinds of promissory notes printed on fancy paper and issued in $100 or other denominations so as to be readily marketable for resale. A bond is a security promising to pay a certain number of dollars every six months for a number of years until it matures. At that time the borrowing company promises to pay off the principal of the bond at its face value. . . . Ordinarily, the [biannual] coupons and principal must be paid on time regardless of whether the company has been making earnings or not. Otherwise the company is in default of its obligations and can be taken to court like any debtor. (Occasionally the bonds are also covered by a mortgage on the corporation's factories or equipment so as to give the lenders extra security). Of course, there is no particular reason why a partnership could not borrow by the use of bonds; but ordinarily it would not be well enough known to succeed in interesting any lenders. For that matter a small corporation is rarely in a position to raise capital by issuing bonds.

33. Easterbrook and Fischel (1991:175–76).

34. An investment grade corporate bond fund market is literally nonexistent in Japan, to say nothing of a junk bond market. Japanese taxes and regulations subtly encourage companies to take banks loans instead of issuing bonds. Moreover, there are no trustworthy corporate bond rating agencies in Japan and, as a result, no standard corporate bond market. Japanese underwriters traditionally sell their rare issues of corporate bonds at discounts to preferred customers. As a result, announced bond pricing in Japan is at times unrealistic. See Litt et al. (1990). On December 9, 1991, the Nippon Telegraph and Telephone Corp., which is 75 percent owned by the Japanese government, startled Japan's major securities firms by breaking two precedents. It would issue an estimated $390 million in bonds at the same price to all investors, with a maturity from 6 to 10 years and a rate of interest 1.25 percent over the rate for 10-year Japanese government bonds. And it would use the American securities house Morgan Stanley & Company as underwriter—the first time that an outside securities house would lead a domestic Japanese securities underwriting (Sterngold 1991).

35. Yago (1991:30–31).

36. See Calomiris and Ramirez (1996) for a fascinating description of how financial intermediaries identify where to invest capital and how corporations identify where to seek capital.

37. Yago (1991:4–5).

38. Anders (1992:49).

39. Useem (1996:25–26).
40. Anders (1992:42–43).
41. Anders (1992:50).
42. Barenberg (1994), Reich (1991), Weiler (1990), Friedman (1988); compare to Sabel (1982).
43. Anders (1992:19).
44. Stewart (1991:41).
45. See Roe (1994) for a methodical discussion of the restrictions placed on banks as well as on mutual funds, insurers, and pension funds.
46. Of course, commercial banks can nonetheless lend capital to finance leveraged buyouts and other corporate takeovers. What they cannot do is to underwrite or arrange the sale of corporate bond issues.
47. Herman (1981:117). The roles performed by American financial intermediaries can be contrasted to that of a "universal bank." The latter has three characteristics: it operates large networks over a wide geographic range; it provides customers with access to a broad range of activities (lending, underwriting bonds, portfolio management, deposit taking); and it is allowed to hold a variety of types of claims (debt and equity) on corporate customers (Calomiris and Ramirez 1996:137).
48. Herman (1981:118), Calomiris and Ramirez (1996:148).
49. See Easterbrook and Fischel (1991:282) on this factor.
50. Stewart (1991:46–48).
51. As such, this period in Drexel's history is an exemplar of contractarians' nexus of contracts approach.
52. Stewart (1991:46–48), Yago (1991:23).
53. See Easterbrook and Fischel (1991:125, 145, 150, 161, 186) on the importance of a "reservation price."
54. Stewart (1991:46).
55. For example, see Anders (1992:94) on Drexel's fees and (1992:73, 95) on KKR's.
56. Yago (1991:24), Anders (1992:84).
57. See Jensen (1988:37), Lipton (1987:15–19) for various strategies employed by raiders.
58. See Yago (1991:19–20) and Anders (1992:84) on senior and junior forms of debt. Also see Anders (1992:61, 75) on how KKR approached banks for loans and on why banks could not resist financing leveraged buyouts.
59. Lipton (1987:14).
60. Coffee (1986:3, plus note 4).
61. Lipton (1987:11, 62 note 288).
62. Loewenstein (1989:85 note 71).
63. Anders (1992:69–75, 95–97, 113–14) offers a journalistic account of the Beatrice deal, including the fees involved (1992:73, 95). On the fees in the RJR Nabisco buyout, "a bizarre and unseemly action," see (1992:127, 131).

64. Yago (1991:20).
65. Yago (1991:25). Ironically, Standard & Poor's, Moody's, and Duff & Phelps were then expanding from rating bonds to rating life insurance companies. By the late 1980s, the reputation of this field's leading rater, A. M. Best, was faltering because of the seizure of Executive Life Insurance Company and other problems in the industry. In 1989, Martin Weiss entered this rating field with Weiss Research, and startled the industry by giving even some large insurance companies low ratings (Berg 1992).
66. Yago (1991:207–10).
67. Jensen (1988:25).
68. Yago (1991:36).
69. Lipton (1987:12).
70. The savings and loan debacle stems in large part from this. For instance, by mid-1986, Columbia Savings & Loan owned $2.33 billion in junk bonds, comprising 28 percent of its portfolio (Lipton 1987:63).
71. Stewart (1991:114).
72. Jensen (1988:37).
73. Yago (1991:199).
74. Yago (1991:199).
75. Cary and Eisenberg (1988:195–96).
76. Lipton (1987:7).
77. This largely explains why the average volume of shares traded daily on the New York Stock Exchange in the 1980s exceeded that of the 1960s, after a lull in the 1970s (Burk 1988:96–97). Burk notes that during the 1960s the daily volume had nearly quadrupled, and the dollar value of stock rose from $43.5 billion in 1960 to over $186.3 billion in 1969.
78. Lipton (1987:8–9).
79. See Morrill (1995) for an ethnographic account.
80. See Useem (1996). Ironically, this change in ethos was initially facilitated, not restrained, by statutes covering tender offers (both the Williams Act and statutes found in states' General Corporation laws). For instance, the Williams Act typically compelled management teams faced with hostile bids to respond within 20 business days—hardly enough time to erect defenses, or to find alternative bidders. Lipton (1987:62) called for this to be extended to 120 calendar days, and other legal scholars wanted it extended at least 60 calendar days (e.g., Loewenstein 1989:69).
81. Coffee (1981:150).
82. See Easterbrook and Fischel (1991:193–205) for a survey of the literature.
83. Coffee (1986:4–5 note 6).
84. Anders (1992:131). Into the 1990s, shareholders could still benefit considerably from the market for corporate control. Viacom stock rose from $37 on April 22, 1993, when Martin Davis and Sumner Redstone began exploring the possibility

of a merger, to $67.50 on September 13, 1993, the day after they publicly announced their plans (Norris 1994).

85. Legal scholar Rinaldi (1990:760 note 1) defines a corporate restructuring vaguely as "any transaction that could have an effect on equity ownership, including a merger, a management buyout or a recapitalization." Sociologist Useem defines it as "a multifaceted revamping of the corporation" (1996:143).

86. Coffee (1986:4–5).

87. Easterbrook and Fischel (1991:178).

88. Coffee (1990:1505–6).

89. Compare these figures to the paltry number of corporate acquisitions across the 1960s in Palmer et al. (1995).

90. Coffee (1986:5–6), citing the *Wall Street Journal.*

91. Jensen (1988:22). If we look at all foreign takeovers of American corporations across the decade, beginning in 1979, British investors ranked first (692), and then Canadians (423), Germans (152), and French (132). Japanese investors ranked fifth (120) (Kester 1991:11). Why did a market for corporate control emerge in the United States but not in Japan, Germany, or Great Britain? One factor was that in 1980–1981, many American states granted public employee pension funds greater investment freedom. The managers of these funds opted to finance leveraged buyouts (Anders 1992:49). Another factor was that Europe and Japan simply have far fewer corporations participating in their stock exchanges. Yet a third factor was that capital markets in Europe and Japan differ significantly from those in the United States. European and Japanese corporations continue their historical practice of maintaining long-term relationships with banks and other financial institutions. They rarely raise investment capital independently by entering the corporate bond market.

92. Anders (1992:280–81).

93. Useem treats a restructuring as "a multifaceted revamping of the corporation" that spans six areas: greater shareholder voice, changes in workforce size, redesign of decision making, changes in company strategies, changes in executive leadership and succession, and changes in corporate governance (1996:143–64).

94. Coffee (1986:54).

95. Coffee (1986:54).

96. Jensen (1988:23), citing Grimm.

97. Coffee (1986:6 note 11).

98. Jensen (1988:22–23), Easterbrook and Fischel (1991:194–98).

99. See Roe (1994: 83–87) on insurers' conservatism.

100. Burrough and Helyar (1990:140–41).

101. Easterbrook and Fischel (1991:171–74), also Roe (1994:153–54).

102. Jensen (1988:32).

103. Anders (1992:37), Burrough and Helyar (1990:139).

104. Burrough and Helyar (1990:142).
105. Burrough and Helyar (1990:140).
106. Burrough and Helyar (1990:150).
107. Anders (1992:55).
108. See Anders' appendix (1992:285–93) for a list of KKR's acquisitions, and when they were resold.
109. Anders (1992:158).
110. Anders (1992:162–63).
111. Jim Johnston and John Greeniaus at RJR Nabisco, and Robert Kidder and Charles Perrin at Duracell followed (Anders 1992:172–75). See Burrough and Helyar (1990) on the RJR Nabisco saga.
112. Coffee (1986:6–7).
113. Coffee (1986:42).
114. Coffee (1986:41–42).
115. Delaney (1992:23, 26).
116. Cowan (1994).
117. Davis et al. (1991:1).
118. Cowan (1994).
119. Gordon (1996:34–60).
120. Coffee (1986:70–71).
121. Yago (1991:168).
122. Lohr (1992), citing Graef Crystal.
123. Kroll (1997).
124. Lohr (1992), citing Graef Crystal.
125. Kroll (1998).
126. Cowan (1994).
127. Wayne (1993:21).
128. Wayne (1993:23). See Useem (1996), Roe (1994), and Baums, Buxbaum, and Hopt (1994) more generally on institutions' monitoring of management performance.
129. Wayne (1993), quoting John Pound. But see Useem (1996:70–106) on how managers characterize investors' oversight of their business judgment.
130. Jensen (1988:35), Easterbrook and Fischel (1991:102).
131. Anders (1992:165). See Burrough and Helyar (1990:92–96) on fat at RJR Nabisco.
132. Easterbrook and Fischel (1991:182).
133. Reich (1991:214).
134. Yago (1991:168–69).
[A]cquired firms do not reduce wages or close plants at a rate any different from that of similar, but independent, firms. New owners undoubtedly make many changes in acquired firms, and some of these affect labor. . . . Yet there

is no visible difference between the results of voluntary acquisitions in mergers and those accomplished by hostile tender offer. Changing wages are an outcome of deregulation (Easterbrook and Fischel 1991:201).

135. Anders (1992:228).

136. Roe (1994:152), citing Romano.

137. Yago (1991:27, 181). We discuss this takeover attempt at length in Chapter 5.

138. Anders (1992:221).

139. Anders (1992:234).

140. Anders (1992:220).

141. Anders (1992:236).

142. Yago (1991:212–13).

143. Anders (1992:272).

144. Anders (1992:234–35). Of course, this does not compare with Black Monday, the crash of October 19, 1987.

145. Anders (1992:237).

146. Anders (1992:247, 250–51).

147. Stewart (1991:16, 54, 437), Anders (1992:247–49). It must be kept in mind that Milken personally earned $45 million in salary and bonuses as early as 1982, and he earned $550 million in 1986 alone.

148. Anders (1992:279–80).

149. Anders (1992:233).

150. Orts (1992:35 note 112).

151. Gordon (1991:1931).

152. Orts (1992:35 note 12).

153. Gordon (1991).

154. See Easterbrook and Fischel (1991:253–75) for a partial defense of these practices.

155. Orts (1992:39).

156. Holson (1998).

157. For examples, see Bartley (1992) and Reich (1991).

158. For example, see Yago (1991:200–204).

159. Yago was confident this would soon lower the cost of investment capital in the United States to Japanese and German levels, and he seems to have been correct. "In fact, by the 1990s the cost of capital was coming to be about the same in all advanced nations" (Reich 1991:264).

160. For example, see Anders (1992:165) on Union Texas and Owens-Illinois.

161. See Anders (1992:xvi) for the opposite view, and yet (1992:157–61) for confirmation of Yago's position.

162. See Useem (1996) and Morrill (1995).

163. Anders (1992:222).

164. Henriques (1991).

165. Norris (1993, my emphasis).
166. Goldman (1998).
167. Teitelbaum (1999).
168. See Davis and Greve (1997) on the "diffusion" of poison pills and golden parachutes across corporate America during the 1980s.
169. Useem (1993:2), Davis and Thompson (1994:143).
170. Useem (1996:296).
171. Useem (1996:311–12).
172. For example, see Coffee (1986:56 note 164).
173. See Romano (1992), Orts (1992:124–26), Easterbrook and Fischel (1991: 194–98), and Jensen (1988) for reviews of the early empirical literature. Then see the following studies and reviews and the literatures cited therein: Healey, Palepu, and Ruback (1992), Blair (1993), Finkelstein and Hambrick (1996), Stearns and Allan (1996), Shleifer and Vishny (1997), Avery, Chevalier, and Schaefer (1998), Core, Holthausen, and Larcker (1999), Vafeas (1999).
174. Holson (1999a), citing a research firm, KDP Investment Advisors, of Montpelier VT.
175. Calomiris and Ramirez (1996:164–65); also see Uzzi (1999).
176. Calomiris and Ramirez (1996:167–68).
177. Eaton (1994a).
178. Holson (1998).
179. Holson (1999b).
180. Holson (1999b). One exception today is Pfizer's pending suit in Delaware's Chancery to get Warner-Lambert to rescind anti-takeover provisions in its merger agreement with American Home products, including a $1.8 billion breakup fee. On the breakup fee, see Norris (1999).
181. Hansell (1998).
182. Fisher and Holson (1998), citing Securities Data Company.
183. Gilpin (1998), citing data from Salomon Smith Barney.
184. See Roe (1994:161) for the view that "few anti-takeover laws are showstoppers."

NOTES TO CHAPTER 3

1. Influential early statements include: Winter (1977), Posner (1977), Fischel (1978, 1982, 1984), Hessen (1979), Fama (1980), Posner and Scott (1980), Easterbrook and Fischel (1981, 1982, 1983), Gilson (1981), Fama and Jensen (1983), Carlton and Fischel (1983), Kraakman (1984).
2. Representative statements include Easterbrook and Fischel (1991:12–13), Butler and Ribstein (1995:vii, 145 note 1, 7–12), Shleifer and Vishny (1997:737).
3. Judge Richard Posner is an important link between the broader movement and contractarianism in corporate law (see Posner 1977; Posner and Scott 1980).

The economic bases for legal contractarianism can be traced to Alchian and Demsetz (1972) and Jensen and Meckling (1976), and then more indirectly to Coase (1937).

4. See Coase (1960) for an early statement.

5. Bratton notes (1995:152) that contractarians associate the moral component of fiduciary law with the threat of statism.

6. Butler and Ribstein (1995:vii–viii) are representative of this rhetoric, holding that judges and legal scholars who resist the nexus of contracts approach "apply an outmoded understanding of the corporation."

7. Butler and Ribstein (1995:viii).

8. Roe ends his long discussion of the political and legal restrictions placed on American financial intermediaries by calling not for law to encourage activism by institutional investors but rather for law to permit "more variation" (1994:263).

9. Easterbrook and Fischel (1991:12), Butler and Ribstein (1995:145 note 2). Roe prefers corporate monitors to be institutional investors with larger holdings rather than dispersed investors because now "American managers owe fiduciary duties to an abstraction, a faceless stock market" (1994:237). He does not want managers to owe fiduciary duties to the corporate entity, as interpreted by courts.

10. The two seminal statements are by Klein (1982) and student editors of *Yale Law Journal* (Note 1982). See the next chapter and Chapter 8 for discussion.

11. Patfield is representative in Great Britain (1995:15–20), and Orts (1992) explores where balancing might lead future judicial decisions in American governance disputes.

12. See Blair and Stout (1999) for a particularly impressive presentation of this position.

13. Easterbrook and Fischel (1991:37).

14. See Knight (1921/1948:303) and Keynes (1936:152–53) for representative statements.

15. Easterbrook and Fischel (1991:126, 145) see maximizing shareholder wealth or corporate growth resulting automatically in Pareto optimal outcomes and, with this, institutional externalities are not a possibility.

16. See Brudney (1997:595) for a representative statement about mandatory rules.

17. The notion of a normative capsule is from Etzioni (1988).

18. Actually, Delaware law views the corporation both as a "distinct entity" and as "a creature made up of its membership." See Folk, Ward, and Welch (1998:122:4), quoting a 1928 Chancery decision.

19. Roe (1994:chaps. 17–21) sees this only in part. On the one hand, he acknowledges that "good overall corporate performance" cannot be traced to governance. On the other, he fails to appreciate that corporate performance is not the point of governance at all, but rather the mediation of one-sided exercises of positional power. Thus, when Roe says blithely "governance can be seen as competition's

assistant" (1994:233), he obscures the entire point of why American courts have intervened, and continue to intervene, into corporate governance disputes. They are not endeavoring to assist economic competition; they are endeavoring to mediate private power in structured situations.

20. Folk, Ward, and Welch (1998:109:2–3).

21. Eisenberg (1989:1461; 1990a:1321); also Orts (1993:1578–87).

22. This factor affects everything that Morrill (1995) and other ethnographers report about management's disputes, and whether and how they escalate into conflicts that third parties help to resolve.

23. Folk, Ward, and Welch (1998:109:2, 6).

24. Folk, Ward, and Welch (1998:109:9–14).

25. "[A]s the charter is an instrument in which the broad and general aspects of the corporate entity's existence and nature are defined, so the by-laws are generally regarded as the proper place for the self-imposed rules and regulations deemed expedient for its convenient functioning to be laid down." See Folk, Ward, and Welch (1998:109:3), quoting *Gow v. Consolidated Coppermines Corp.*, a 1933 Chancery decision.

26. Folk, Ward, and Welch (1998:121:3).

27. Clark (1989:1706).

28. See Easterbrook and Fischel (1991:63–89) on shareholder voting.

29. Black (1990:587–88).

30. Easterbrook and Fischel also call them "mandatory terms" and "directive rules" (1991:15).

31. See Easterbrook and Fischel (1991:63–89, 162–211, 276–314).

32. Gregory Mark notes that "we lack even bad histories of many of the most important doctrines in basic corporate law," including the duty of loyalty (1995:75).

33. Bebchuk (1989a:1395–97).

34. Brudney (1997:627).

35. Butler and Ribstein hold that the "supposed" mandatory rules of corporate law "are so easily avoided" that "they are, in substance, optional" (1995:20–21). See the 1989 symposium on opting out in *Columbia Law Review.*

36. Easterbrook and Fischel (1991:1–39), Butler and Ribstein (1995:1–28), Shleifer and Vishny (1997). Coffee (1989:1632) describes their view well. Easterbrook and Fischel go further at times, asserting that corporate law *is* enabling: "The corporate code in almost every state is an "enabling" statute. An enabling statute allows managers and investors to write their own tickets, to establish systems of governance without substantive scrutiny from a regulator" (1991:2). At other times, however, they hedge: "The normative thesis of [their] book is that corporate law should contain the terms people would have negotiated, were the costs of negotiating at arm's length for every contingency sufficiently low. The positive thesis is that corporate law almost always conforms to this model. It is enabling rather than directive" (1991:15). Unfortunately, social scientists at times treat Easterbrook and

Fischel's prescription for corporate law as if it is a neutral description (e.g., Davis and Greve 1997:5).

37. Folk, Ward, and Welch (1998:109:4).

38. Easterbrook and Fischel (1991:124–290), plus their discussion of the "appraisal remedy" (1991:145–61).

39. Easterbrook and Fischel (1991:15), Butler and Ribstein (1995:14).

40. Brudney (1997:629).

41. Branson notes (1995:97) that the Delaware Supreme Court reaffirmed in the 1990s that some "immutable rules and principles" continue to govern corporations, and he adds that this court's "polar stars" are "fairness and good conscience."

42. Easterbrook and Fischel (1991:21). One of fiduciary law's central concepts, structured situations, is very close to economists' concept of externalities: both "impede voluntary exchange."

43. For example, see Easterbrook and Fischel (1991:93, 113, 136, 180, 206–9, 317).

44. Butler and Ribstein, like other contractarians, accept that the interests of shareholders and stakeholders differ (e.g., 1995:3–4). What they refuse to accept is that stakeholders enter a structured situation, or one that eludes contract protection (1995:24).

45. Morrill (1995) leaves the impression that top managers see themselves as constantly under assault and therefore at war—particularly with their fellow top managers. If we add positional conflicts to Morrill's account of managers' interpersonal conflicts, then the "war" metaphor seems even more apt.

46. The question, again, is when, if ever, is judicial oversight of corporate governance on qualitative grounds necessary, and why exactly is it necessary, as opposed to leaving any oversight to investment bankers and capital markets? See Millon (1995:2, 9–10) on the "problem of nonshareholder vulnerability" and then (1995:30–31) for his tentative "communitarian" remedy.

47. We must keep in mind that shareholder minorities and hostile bidders have legal standing to bring suit in state court whereas stakeholders do not. See Chapter 4 on standing.

48. See Easterbrook and Fischel (1991:12–13) for an example. By contrast, see Thompson (1967), Mintzberg (1983), Bratton (1989a:1505–16), and Parkinson (1993).

49. Economist Oliver Williamson typically begins his discussion of corporations by saying explicitly that he focuses on the issue of efficiency, and neglects the issue of collective power (e.g., Williamson and Bercovitz 1996:327).

50. See Brudney (1997:599) for this criticism of contractarianism.

51. Easterbrook and Fischel (1991:12).

52. Roe tries to do the same thing with the Delaware courts, and claims that he

succeeds. Yet he calls attention along the way to actions taken by these courts that cannot be attributed to group pressures (1994:160–67).

53. Easterbrook and Fischel (1991:10).

54. Also Butler and Ribstein (1995:1, 145 note 1).

55. Social theorist Niklas Luhmann is remarkably similar when thinking about the possibility of "arbitrariness" in "autopoietic systems." See an interview in Sciulli (1994).

56. When Butler and Ribstein discuss "the court's deficiencies in formulating governance rules," they do so in terms of whether judicial rulings can ever be sufficiently market mimicking and they conclude, of course, that they cannot be (1995:25). They have no way of considering even the possibility that Delaware courts formulate governance rules with an eye to institutional design. Romano (1993b:449) points out that Easterbrook and Fischel fail to account for "one datum that any theory of fiduciary duty must explain [namely] why certain relations [that is, structured situations] are subject to statutory regulation [that is, mandatory rules], which mandates obligations, rather than left to the common law, which permits contractual flexibility." As a contractarian herself, however, Romano also lacks the concepts with which to account adequately for this datum.

57. This is Roe's thesis (1994) even though he acknowledges at times that he cannot explain all manifestations of "state paternalism," and particularly the behavior of Delaware courts, using this public choice account.

58. Roe (1994) sees "populists" often doing this.

59. Roe (1994) focuses on the origin of public law statutes that place restrictions on financial intermediaries. Yet he says that legislative actions may at times have served the public interest—a major, and curious, concession for a contractarian to make. Consider the following: "I spend little time on the public interest explanations [for legislative interventions into institutional investing] not because they are unimportant, but because they are obvious" (1994:77). Roe continues this in passing (1996:106) when he accounts for why law at times constricts corporate actions and at other times relaxes restraints and even protects corporations. He never considers that the corporate judiciary might act legitimately with an eye to institutional design *in either situation*.

60. My point is not that liberal complacency is a subjective or ideological preference of individual contractarians and neoclassicists. My point is that this implicit political economic position is inextricably embedded in their concepts, their analytical distinctions. This is the case irrespective of what their subjective preferences or ideological positions happen to be as individuals. See Sciulli (1992b) for an application of this point to rational choice theory, and Sciulli (1995) for an application to Donald Black's structural approach to the "behavior" of law and social control.

61. Easterbrook and Fischel (1991:1–39), Roe (1994), Butler and Ribstein

(1995:7–11). See, more generally, Chandler (1962, 1990), Herman (1981), Fligstein (1990, 1996), Coffee (1990), Streeck (1992), Useem (1993: chap. 4), Davis and Thompson (1994), Roy (1997), Orts (1998b), Rindova and Fombrun (1999), Blair and Stout (1999).

62. Powell (1990), Romanelli (1991).

63. See Stinchcombe (1990).

64. The literature on corporate crime attests to this (e.g., Braithwaite 1984, 1985).

65. This is a central thesis in Sciulli (1992a, 1999). See also Chapters 10–13 in this volume.

66. For a sample, see what Easterbrook and Fischel have to say about loony decisions (1991:100), looting (1991:125, 129–30), shareholder squeezeouts (1991:134–39), manager exploitation (1991:140–42), winners' curse and bidders' hubris (1991:184–85), state and corporate survival of the fittest (1991:227), and fraud (1991:280–86).

67. Easterbrook and Fischel (1991:7).

68. Roe (1994:chaps. 17–21).

69. For examples, see Easterbrook and Fischel (1991:17, 23, 90, 124–25, 130, 205–9, 272).

70. Easterbrook and Fischel (1991:17).

71. Easterbrook and Fischel (1991:38).

72. The first question runs prominently through all contractarian accounts. The second question is equally central to contractarian accounts, but often not displayed as prominently in their works. See Easterbrook and Fischel (1991:126, 145) for clear, explicit statements that they are "simply applying Pareto principles of welfare economics" to corporate transactions and governance disputes.

73. Easterbrook and Fischel (1991:35).

74. Plus Williamson and Bercovitz run into another empirical problem (1996:350–51). They find that four types of boards of directors are possible—directors, trustees, workers (a German two-tier board), and overseers—and the overseer board is the most efficient way to handle stakeholder representation. Director and trustee boards review management decisions and appoint and compensate top managers whereas an overseer board simply discloses contract-relevant information and then allows all constituents to contract for their own advantages and protections. Williamson and Bercovitz's empirical problem is that the overseer board is yet to be adopted, and they have no explanation for this fact. Our answer is that Delaware courts monitor corporate governance, including boards, with an eye to institutional externalities, an eye to institutional design. An overseer board allows one-sided exercises of positional power in structured situations in American civil society. The fact that these exercises are accepted by participants by contract does not reduce the harm they can do to institutional design.

75. Easterbrook and Fischel (1991:207, also 136). Roe is even more uncertain,

and therefore unwilling to attribute this judicial behavior to superstition or knee-jerk "state paternalism." He acknowledges that there may be a "public-regarding dimension" to Delaware court behavior, and acknowledges, too, that he is unable to identify what it is (1994:154–67).

76. As Roe's concluding chapters illustrate (1994:chaps. 17–21).

77. For example, see Easterbrook and Fischel (1991:36, 94).

78. Easterbrook and Fischel (1991:94 note 3).

79. Easterbrook and Fischel (1991:171, my emphasis).

80. Anders (1992:164, also 175).

NOTES TO CHAPTER 4

1. Coffee (1990:1497). Also see Millon (1995), Dallas (1995), Blair and Stout (1999).

2. Johnson (1992:2220 note 26). See Easterbrook and Fischel (1982:705 note 15) for an example.

3. Whereas Easterbrook and Fischel (1991:4) do assume this about the relationship between managers and investors.

4. See Zald (1969) for a discussion of how boards of directors operated in the absence of today's more extensive judicial monitoring precipitated by derivative suits.

5. This is why contractarians endeavor to redefine management's fiduciary duties, as being owed to shareholders, not to the corporate entity. See Easterbrook and Fischel (1993).

6. Loewenstein (1989:66–67). See the next chapter for specific Delaware court rulings.

7. Bratton notes (1995:141) that Berle and Means were the first to articulate a new theory of fiduciary duties tied to the notion of maintaining shareholders' expectations, as opposed to maintaining the integrity of the entity's governance structure.

8. We will see in Chapter 8 that once state legislatures either encouraged or required management to consider stakeholder interests by statute, balancers could conclude that the fiduciary duty of loyalty is no longer necessary.

9. See Wolfe and Pittenger (1998:516–612). More generally, consider this statement by Bumiller:

Standing is a device used in constitutional language to limit jurisdiction of official and public action, in fact, to remove private interests from judicial view. The issue of standing means in practice that the person making a legal claim has suffered recognized legal harms and that the court is capable of providing remedies for those harms. The issue is raised when public and private boundaries become problematic (in some domains, the public nature of the contested issue is accepted, e.g., questions of fundamental constitutional rights; in other domains, the division between state and private interests is in dispute, e.g., environmental litigation). The interests of individuals are only considered in constitutional and administrative law proceedings when they fit into legal categories of "who" is harmed (class, group, etc.), and when their harm can be cast in terms of public values. By these means, private interests are selectively redefined as legal cases. Legal identities shift the boundaries of the law; they are concepts that create tunnel vision in the law. (Bumiller 1988:60–61; the last sentence starts a new paragraph)

10. The Delaware courts hear disputes in which *contract* provisions between a corporation and CEO in some way infringe on the board's authority. See Folk, Ward, and Welsh (1998:141:12–13).

11. There are exceptions, of course, but they do not bear on the point being made in the text. See Wolfe and Pittenger (1998:515–25). The American judiciary recognized shareholder derivative action as a means to redress breaches of fiduciary duty by corporate officers in the first two decades of the nineteenth century (Loewenstein 1999:1).

12. Blair and Stout (1999:293).

13. Wolfe and Pittenger (1998:515); also see Easterbrook and Fischel (1991:104).

14. Blair and Stout (1999:287–89, 294–95). Courts award successful share-holder-plaintiffs lawyers' fees, but only after scrutinizing them and often agreeing to a lesser amount than requested (Loewenstein 1999:3 note 7).

15. Easterbrook and Fischel (1991:101). They think this results at times in shareholders "with tiny holdings" bringing claims without considering how they might affect other shareholders.

16. Loewenstein (1999:4–5).

17. Loewenstein (1999:9).

18. Most notably Klein (1982) and *Yale Law Journal* student editors (Note 1982).

19. Orts (1992:27). Also see Wallman (1991).

20. Gordon (1991:1932 note 2).

21. See Easterbrook and Fischel (1991:218–27), Romano (1993a:xi, 52–84), Roe (1994:160–63), Butler and Ribstein (1995:52–53).

22. Sociologist Alan Wolfe (1993:1689–92) also embraces balancing.

23. The single most impressive statement came later in Eisenberg (1989).

24. For example, see Stone (1982). See Orts (1992:22) for the connection between the earlier corporate social responsibility movement and legal traditionalism. Sociologist Wolfe defends the notion of corporate social responsibility even as he acknowledges there is "no developed theory" here that can compete with the nexus of contracts approach (1993:1688).

25. See the 1988 symposium in *Yale Law Journal* on republicanism.

26. For examples, see Frug (1980, 1984) and, more recently, David Gordon

(1996). See Orts (1993:1570 note 15) for the view that "Frug's analysis of corporate legal theory deserves to be taken more seriously than it has been."

27. Eisenberg was chief reporter for the America Law Institute's Corporate Governance Project, whose mandate was to establish principles of governance and regulation of American corporations. Corporate law was so contentious during the 1980s that ALI did not issue its report for 15 years.

28. Lawrence Mitchell and Margaret Blair may also be included here, but at times they endeavor to defend mandatory rules more directly.

29. See Mitchell's (1995) collection, and especially the opening chapter by Millon and then the second chapter by Dallas.

30. Patfield is representative when she says that her rationale for company law "is that of facilitating business activity and legitimatising [*sic*] the power which results from that activity by the recognition of a whole range of stakeholder interests, including the public interest" (1995:15).

31. This is Parkinson's (1993) project.

32. See Dallas' "power coalition theory" for an example (1995:51–59), Orts's (1992) defense of stakeholder balancing for another, and then also Klein (1982), Coffee (1990), and Bratton (1993). See Wolfe (1993:1689–95) and Fligstein (1996) for similar views by sociologists. Other legal scholars express reservations but fail adequately to identify the harms that concern them, e.g., Gordon (1989, 1991), Mitchell (1992), Parkinson (1993), and Millon (1995).

33. Orts (1992) is clear about this.

34. Traditionalist Brudney is adamant that fiduciary obligations not be extended directly to stakeholders (1997:611 note 41), as are Blair and Stout (1999). Orts (1992) has no such reservations, nor do other legal scholars who favor European corporatism or Germany's two-tier boards. See Charkham (1994) and Roe (1994) for discussions, and Parkinson (1993) for advocacy.

35. Coffee (1990), Pound (1993), Davis and Thompson (1994), Blair and Stout (1999).

36. See Lowi (1969).

37. Chancellor Allen (1993:1399).

38. We noted earlier that courts have yet to adopt the nexus metaphor outright, and one of our major goals is to explain this resistance. Our point is that the burden of proof has shifted to judges who enforce mandatory rules, not to those who permit opting out. Chancellor Allen acknowledges this, and in no uncertain terms (1993:1399–1407). Consider the following passage:

> In the United States the [contractarian] account of and prescription for corporate law is the dominant legal academic model and will remain so for some time. The coherence and power of the economic model, as it is applied to corporations, have for many an all but irresistible appeal. Moreover, in our pluralistic society, it may be especially difficult to formulate an alternative comprehensive theory of corporations that takes its animating power from a

conception of human connectedness and responsibility. Finally, in an age of global competition and fading expectations, the plausible claims of greater efficiency (wealth maximization) that the nexus of contracts theory makes also renders this way of thinking powerfully attractive (1993:1406).

39. For representative examples, see Phillips (1997), Blair and Stout (1999) and, more generally, Leventhal (1980).

40. See note 32.

41. For examples, see Millon (1993:1380), Orts (1992), Parkinson (1993).

42. Gordon (1989:1550–51).

43. Butler and Ribstein (1995:19).

44. A notable but only partial exception is Douglas Branson. The title of his chapter in the Mitchell collection is in part "the death of contractarianism." Yet in the body of the chapter he says "their movement is regressing" only in that it is returning to its proper place as useful analysis for some purposes (1995:94). This hardly sounds like the nexus approach is dead, been soundly defeated, or even that the burden of proof has shifted against them. More credible is Bratton's view that legal scholarship today is marked by a "compromise" (1995:139). The nexus of contracts approach retains its "primacy" but more judges and legal scholars have become "cautious about process, the integrity of internal decision-making mechanisms."

45. Blair and Stout (1999:287).

NOTES TO CHAPTER 5

1. Kaouris (1995:966 note 6, 1004).

2. Rock (1997:1023 note 32).

3. Quoted by Kaouris (1995:982).

4. Rock (1997:1024). See Easterbrook and Fischel (1991:154–57) on problems in assessing fair price or fair value.

5. Rock (1997:1022–23).

6. Brudney and Chirelstein (1978).

7. Cunningham and Yablon (1994:1601–2).

8. And Easterbrook and Fischel say bluntly that none of these grounds "holds water" (1991:206).

9. See Easterbrook and Fischel generally on "Delaware's intermediate standard" (1991:205–8), but then especially Cunningham and Yablon (1994).

10. Heyman (1998).

11. The title of Simon's 1993 article says it all: "What Difference Does It Make Whether Corporate Managers Have Public Responsibilities?"

12. Easterbrook and Fischel point explicitly to "procedural but not substantive review of conflict-of-interest transactions" but the procedures they discuss are those that privilege shareholders when managers' interests conflict with sharehold-

ers' interests (1991:104–5). The procedures we have in mind are those that identify the relationship between corporate governance and institutional design (see Chapters 10–13).

13. This is why Easterbrook and Fischel end up declaring that Delaware courts remain instructed by "superstition" and employ "earth is flat reasoning" (1991:109–44, 205–11). This is also why Parkinson refers vaguely to corporations causing "social disfigurement" rather than stating explicitly what he means (1993:35). As a result, he also never establishes why either "profit sacrificing social responsibility" or "employee participation" matters (1993:304–46, 397–434).

14. The duty of care originated in the law governing the conduct of banks (Mark 1995:77), and to this day it is usually directors of financial institutions who are brought before courts on charges of violating care (Brudney 1997: 599–600 note 12).

15. Folk, Ward, and Welch (1998:141:34); the quotation is from Bayless Manning. See Cunningham and Yablon (1994:1597 note 29).

16. Palmiter (1989:1384–94).

17. Folk, Ward, and Welsh (1998:14–15).

18. Folk, Ward, and Welch (1998:141:34–35).

19. Folk, Ward, and Welch (1998:141:34).

20. Palmiter (1989:1394). Easterbrook, Fischel and other contractarians, of course, think the Court went over the deep end.

21. See Eisenberg (1989), Gordon (1989), Coffee (1989), Romano (1989), Black (1990), Mitchell (1990b), Easterbrook and Fischel (1991:103), Block, Maimone, and Ross (1993), Cunningham and Yablon (1994), Rock (1997).

22. See Easterbrook and Fischel (1991:107–8).

23. Here Easterbrook and Fischel are representative (1991:107–8).

24. Cunningham and Yablon (1994:1597), Olson (1992:1020–23).

25. Romano (1993a:49).

26. Romano (1993a:49).

27. Loewenstein (1989:72 note 22).

28. In 1996, the Delaware General Assembly went further, exculpating monetary damages of any kind for violations of care (Brudney 1997:599–600 note 12).

29. Folk, Ward, and Welch (1998:102:20–23).

30. Cunningham and Yablon (1994:1597–98).

31. Thus, contractarian Mark Loewenstein (1989:69) called for the time period to be extended to 60 calendar days in order to facilitate an auction, and traditionalist Martin Lipton (1987:62) called for 120 calendar days in order to given target management teams sufficient time to defend themselves.

32. Loewenstein (1989:65–68).

33. See Johnson (1990:911), Gordon (1991:1933–36).

34. Folk, Ward, and Welch (1998:141:54).

35. Folk, Ward, and Welch (1998:141:58, note 171).

36. Folk, Ward, and Welch (1998:141:58).
37. Folk, Ward, and Welch (1998:141:58–59).
38. Folk, Ward, and Welch (1998:141:60).
39. Folk, Ward, and Welch (1998:141:55–56), quoting the Court.
40. Folk, Ward, and Welch (1998:141:56–57). Chancery has since held that, unlike a two-tiered tender offer, an all shares, all cash offer does not threaten to coerce shareholders into tendering their shares. But Chancery has recognized other threats to corporate policy that might attend such noncoercive offers (1998:141:62.2–3).
41. Folk, Ward, and Welch (1998:141:61–62), quoting the *Unitrin* decision.
42. Folk, Ward, and Welch (1998:141:62).
43. Folk, Ward, and Welch (1998:141:62–63, plus note 198).
44. Loewenstein (1989:95), Easterbrook and Fischel (1991:206).
45. By contrast, Delaware's Chancery Court still tended to measure any threat at hand more narrowly in terms of whether or not shareholders received an adequate or fair price (Gordon 1991:1939). See Easterbrook and Fischel (1991: 150–57) on the "fair value" standard, and (1991:136–37) for criticisms of "fairness" for all shareholders.
46. Folk, Ward, and Welch (1998:141:57–58).
47. Orts (1992:20–22).
48. See Gordon (1991:1939) for a different view of the Delaware courts' actions.
49. We will see in Chapters 10–13 that judicial intervention on behalf of a corporation as a long-term economic enterprise is ultimately not consistent with the fiduciary law tradition. What is consistent is judicial intervention into intracorporate structured situations, into exercises of power between positions of trust and positions of dependence.
50. Aichele (1990:97).
51. Easterbrook and Fischel (1991:200).
52. Folk, Ward, and Welch (1998:141:87).
53. Millon (1990:234). Easterbrook and Fischel (1981) and Gilson (1981) anticipated this move.
54. Folk, Ward, and Welch (1998:141:87–88). We will see that in *Macmillan*, the Court will add that directors' responsibility in these situations is to get the highest value reasonably attainable for the stockholders.
55. Loewenstein (1989), Rinaldi (1990). Easterbrook and Fischel do not see loyalty as a distinct duty (1991:103), and they see it obligating management to serve shareholders, not the corporate entity (1991:93).
56. Folk, Ward, and Welch (1998:141:88).
57. Folk, Ward, and Welch (1998:141:88–89), citing *Mills Acquisition Co. v. MacMillan, Inc.* 1989.
58. Folk, Ward, and Welch (1998:141:89).
59. Folk, Ward, and Welch (1998:122:6–7).
60. Folk, Ward, and Welch (1998:141:117–18).

61. Folk, Ward, and Welch (1998:141:118–19).
62. Folk, Ward, and Welch (1998:141:95–96).
63. Folk, Ward, and Welch (1998:141:97–98).
64. Folk, Ward, and Welch (1998:141:99–102).
65. Folk, Ward, and Welch (1998:141:107).
66. Ronald Rinaldi argues (1990:760, 778), for instance, that this properly refers only to situations in which a proposed transaction would cause shareholders to give up their equity ownership or would otherwise change the share-ownership relationship as such. It does not properly refer to changes in corporate governance short of this. Alan Palmiter argues that in *Revlon* the Delaware Supreme Court recognized that a corporate board's independence from the undue power or influence of a target management team is the most basic foundation today of any application of fiduciary law to corporate governance. But he concedes that this and other courts "have referred to a duty of independence . . . without defining it" (1989:1444–45). We explore Palmiter's intriguing position in Chapter 13.
67. See Loewenstein (1989:78) and Easterbrook and Fischel (1991:104–5), plus Parkinson on "social responsibility as a process concept" (1993:344–46).
68. Gordon (1991:1932–33).
69. Cunningham and Yablon (1994:1609) call *Macmillan* "the high water mark of fragmentation" in Delaware court rulings.
70. Cunningham and Yablon (1994:1610–12).
71. Rock (1997:1040). The other two MBO cases are *In re Fort Howard Corp. Shareholders Litigation* (1988) and *In re RJR Nabisco, Inc. Shareholders Litigation* (1989), the latter the largest LBO of all time. Rock shows that the Delaware courts heard only 15 MBO cases from 1985 through 1990, compared to a total of 274 LBOs during the same period, and compared to 130 LBOs earlier, from 1981 through 1984 (1997:1091–93).
72. My account of both *Macmillan* cases relies on Rock (1997:1040–49).
73. Rock (1997:1062).
74. Rock (1997:1082).
75. Rock (1997:1102).
76. *Paramount Communications v. Time, Inc.* (Delaware Chancery Court 1989). See Gordon (1991), Millon (1990, 1993), Johnson and Millon (1990), Johnson (1993), and Simon (1993) for legal scholars' commentary on the significance of this decision, and both Clurman (1992) and Anders (1992:219ff) for journalists' accounts.
77. Millon (1990:251–55).
78. Easterbrook and Fischel (1991:206). See the beginning of Chapter 6 for their muddling-through explanation for the Delaware courts' behavior.
79. Gordon (1991:1932).
80. Johnson (1990:929–30).
81. Rinaldi (1990).

82. See Clurman (1992:188–200) on the original deal.

83. This is also consistent with the Delaware courts' "intrinsic value" notion.

84. The European view of intermediary associations may be traced to Gierke's notion of a corporate personality (Kay and Silberston 1997:56–57). See Ringer (1969) on German organic metaphors of social order and individual cultivation. See Clurman (1992:201–2) on "Time culture" in particular, and Gordon (1991:1962–82) on the Delaware courts' "sociohistorical" approach more generally. Bratton (1992) and Orts (1992) are optimistic about the benefits of such a turn.

85. It is worthwhile to note in passing that Chancellor Allen is married to a Chicago-trained sociologist, Ruth Horowitz, whose specialty is American race and ethnic relations.

86. Gordon (1991:1940–41) praises Allen's decision as a "doctrinal retreat" from Chancery's earlier drift toward contracting.

87. Actually, there were also enormous personality conflicts between Martin Davis, Paramount's CEO, and both Time's top management team of J. Richard Munro, Gerald Levine, and Nicholas J. Nicholas Jr., and Warner's CEO Steven J. Ross. More than anything else, this soured Time Inc. management on the Paramount deal at the outset, and it drove Time Inc. management to reassess their initially negative impression of Ross.

88. Quoted by Millon (1990:257, my emphasis). See Clurman (1992:241–52, 287–88), then Allen (1992b, 1993) for his reflections.

89. Folk, Ward, and Welch (1998:141:73–74).

90. By contrast, the view of all corporations at Kohlberg Kravis Roberts and Company, even those regarded "as never-to-be-sold treasures," was strictly pecuniary. For KKR's George Roberts, the reasoning was simple: "I don't think you should fall in love with anything except your wife and kids. To do otherwise is looking for trouble" (Anders 1992: 197). Roberts was referring to Golden West Broadcasting.

91. Millon (1990:257).

92. Clurman (1992:203). Clurman, a former *Time* chief of correspondents, and John Gregory Dunne (1992), a former *Time* correspondent, both document the earlier collapse of the editorial staff's independence from business divisions.

93. Ariel Sharon's successful liable suit in 1985 came in response to a story published February 21, 1983. Using the rationale of protecting the company from future suits, the business and publishing divisions of Time Inc. then asserted greater control over editorial decisions.

94. Clurman (1992:198).

95. Clurman (1992:199).

96. Gordon (1991:1982).

97. Folk, Ward, and Welch (1998:141:74–77).

98. Cunningham and Yablon (1994).

99. Cunningham and Yablon (1994:1598).

100. Cunningham and Yablon (1994:1597–98).

101. Cunningham and Yablon (1994:1596).

102. My account of the facts of the case relies on Kaouris (1995:987–993).

103. This paragraph and the next follow Cunningham and Yablon (1994: 1598–1600).

104. Cunningham and Yablon (1994:1600).

105. In *Weinberger,* The Delaware Supreme Court held that Signal Companies, which owned 50.5 percent of UOP and nominated 6 of 13 UOP directors, breached its fiduciary duties in cashing out minority shareholders of UOP because of an absence of an independent committee to represent public shareholders. This "led to a near universal use of 'special committees' of independent directors in MBOs" (Rock 1997:1025–26).

106. I rely on Block, Maimone, and Ross (1993:92–95) for the details of this case.

107. Cunningham and Yablon (1994:1600 note 45).

108. Folk, Ward, and Welch (1998:141–46).

109. Cunningham and Yablon (1994:1600–1601).

110. Cunningham and Yablon (1994:1601, note 52).

111. Fabrikant (1994), Kaouris (1995:994), Taylor (1996:839–40, plus note 9).

112. Taylor (1996:840 note 14).

113. Taylor (1996:841).

114. Taylor (1996:840).

115. For example, see Antilla (1993).

116. Taylor (1996:842).

117. Taylor (1996:842).

118. Taylor (1996:843).

119. In *QVC Network, Inc. v. Paramount Communications, Inc* (Delaware Chancery Court 1993).

120. In *Paramount Communications, Inc. v. QVC Network, Inc.* (Delaware Supreme Court 1993). See Fabrikant (1993a, 1993b).

121. Cunningham and Yablon (1994:1593).

122. Cunningham and Yablon (1994:1604–5).

123. See Millon (1993:1376) and Bratton (1993:1457) for comments.

124. Fabrikant (1993a), quoting Jacobs.

125. Cunningham and Yablon (1994:1603–4).

126. Fabrikant (1993b).

127. Cunningham and Yablon (1994:1604).

128. Fabrikant (1993a).

129. Fabrikant (1993b).

130. John Coffee, paraphrased by Cowan (1993).

131. Fabrikant (1993a).

132. Jacobs (1993).

133. Harvey Goldschmid, quoted by Cowan (1993).
134. Cunningham and Yablon (1994:1605–6).
135. Cunningham and Yablon (1994:1607).
136. Green (1993).
137. Jacobs (1993).
138. Jacobs (1993).
139. Cunningham and Yablon (1994:1594).
140. Cunningham and Yablon (1994:1594–96).

NOTES TO CHAPTER 6

1. Loewenstein (1989:95).
2. Easterbrook and Fischel (1991:206). All of the insertions in brackets are mine.
3. For example, see Easterbrook and Fischel (1993:436–38; 1991:93, 104).
4. Macey (1989) is representative. I have not seen a single work by a contractarian economist or legal scholar in which this possibility is raised, let alone addressed.
5. But see Easterbrook and Fischel generally (1991:162–211).
6. Easterbrook and Fischel concede this (1991:176) but then hedge (1991:184).
7. Also see Reich (1991:75, 281).
8. Anders (1992:158).
9. This waned when interest rates began to fall in the mid-1990s. Much like homeowners, corporations refinanced their loans.
10. Easterbrook and Fischel (1991:176). More generally, see Delaney (1992) and Sullivan, Warren, and Westbrook (1989).
11. Bourdieu (1979:309–10).
12. Useem (1993, 1996).
13. Consider Galbraith's *New Industrial State* (1967) for a sense of how dramatically the world of American top managers has changed in the last three decades.
14. Useem (1996).
15. "While many states move to further insulate directors from personal liability for business decisions, th[e] insolvency exception can result in director liability for conduct that a troubled company's directors may not perceive as erroneous" (Davis et al. 1991:3). More generally, see Hopt and Teubner (1985).
16. Anders (1992:176–93).
17. Useem (1996).
18. Calomiris and Ramirez (1996:169–70). Roe (1994) is similar, and yet less sanguine about the benefits this will bring to corporate governance.
19. See Clarke and Short (1993) for a review of sociological approaches to risk, plus Douglas (1985), Heimer (1988), Stinchcombe (1990), and Luhmann (1993).
20. Recall the statement about the Rockefellers in Chapter 1.
21. The first two types of risk either may be reflected in priced outcomes or may elude pricing, but the third type is strictly qualitative.

22. Coffee (1986:61–63).

23. Morrill (1991:609).

24. See the debate in *Journal of Marriage and the Family* over David Popenoe's (1993) "conservative" defense of the family as an institution. In addition, there is a robust literature in law journals about "marrying up."

25. James Coleman's efforts (1990:579–609) to interrelate the study of corporations with the study of child-rearing is a promising start, even as this seems to fall outside the scope of application of Coleman's own rational choice concepts. See also Menaghan (1991) for a review of the literature.

26. Morrill (1991:608), citing Paul Hirsch.

27. Noble (1992), Freudenheim (1992).

28. See also Anders (1992:28).

29. Coffee (1986).

30. Kahneman and Tversky (1979). Coffee (1986:65) draws centrally on this study.

31. Coffee (1986:65–66).

32. See Piore and Sabel (1984:248) for an early example. This conjecture can be supported empirically by comparing top managers' rates of suicide, alcoholism, drug abuse, theft and corporate crime over time. See Carol Aneshensel's review of the literature that "differentiates the stressful consequences of social organization from the stressful antecedents of psychological disorders" (1992:15).

33. Williamson (1988a, 1988b). Also see Lipton (1987), Coffee (1990), Mitchell (1990a), and Davis et al. (1991) for accounts of this.

34. Millon (1990:232), Cornett, Million, and Tehranian (1992), Craypo and Nissen (1993), Shleifer and Vishney (1997), Avery, Chevalier, and Schaefer (1998), Core, Holthausen, and Larcker (1999). It also may reverberate across society more indirectly, as institutional externalities; but it will take several more chapters for me to demonstrate this.

35. Coffee (1986:13–15, 53–56).

36. Here we offer a conjecture. Sociologists have difficulty relating the literature of work and occupations to shifts in the direction of cultural and social change. See Abbott (1993) for a review of this literature and, more generally, Higley et al. (1991), Higley and Burton (1989), and Etzioni-Halevy (1989).

37. Norris (1992).

38. See Ludwig (1993) for a history and analysis of the swap market.

39. Losses in the swap market led to the bankruptcy of Orange County CA, as well as to bankruptcies in several municipalities, including Lakewood OH.

40. Berton (1994).

41. Eaton (1994b).

42. Anders (1992:212, also 281–83).

43. Hart (1989:1758).

44. Meyer (1994:556). Meyer proposes that we gauge performance measures by

three standards: their informativeness (which he acknowledges changes over time), their differentiation (which he acknowledges often originates in management's own actions), and change (which means we cannot expect continuity in performance measures) (1994:569–74). Parkinson (1993:97) defines corporate "efficiency" as "expenditure of appropriate levels of effort and skill on the part of directors and top managers," a decidedly qualitative standard. Parkinson acknowledges that courts cannot enforce any such standard (1993:108–10).

45. Fischel (1982:1272).

46. Also Butler and Ribstein (1995:25). Traditionalist Eisenberg agrees (1990a). See Etzioni (1968) for an earlier rejection of both central planning and muddling through in favor of "mixed scanning," a tacking between strategic policy making and tactical operations.

47. For example, see the collection edited by Campbell, Hollingsworth, and Lindberg (1991). For a more general acknowledgment that "today's sociologists have a lot of work to do on macroeconomic issues," see Swedberg and Granovetter (1992:19).

48. Johnson (1990, 1992) and Gordon (1991) are explicit about this.

NOTES TO CHAPTER 7

1. Brudney (1997) is a recent, representative example of both failures.

2. Kanter (1977), Mintzberg (1983), Knowlton and Millstein (1988), John Scott (1991), Finkelstein and Hambrick (1996), Davis and Greve (1997).

3. See Mizruchi (1996) for an excellent review of this literature.

4. "With a handful of notable exceptions, there is little useful information available today on what American corporate directors actually do. Few case writers or investigative reporters have penetrated the mysterious recesses of that holy of bodies, the boardroom" (Knowlton and Millstein 1988:169). The literature has long abounded with popular accounts (e.g., Mueller 1974, 1984), information and advice for practitioners (e.g., Houle 1960, 1989; Mills 1981; Vance 1983; Worthy and Neushel 1983; Waldo 1985; Anderson and Anthony 1986), and critical accounts of directors' failures to serve shareholder interests (e.g., Mace 1971).

5. Another exception is Zald (1969). He explores the norms and responsibilities of directors during a period when Delaware courts intervened into the internal governance of corporations less frequently, when interested and disinterested transactions were easier to distinguish.

6. Useem (1984:53); also see Lorsch (1989:91–95).

7. Lorsch (1989:1–2). The key factor that he finds in boards that successfully challenge CEO-chairmen, however, is social psychological, not institutional (or legal), namely the "serendipitous emergence of a leader from among the outside directors" (1989:15, also 102–39, 164–67). One of Lorsch's central concerns is finding

ways to enhance the authority of corporate boards by increasing openness and candor in their deliberations. To this end, he advocates "systemic" changes in the law (1989:91–95, 172–93). Yet his proposed reforms are neither dramatic (that is, "systemic") nor likely to have the effect he seeks (that is, to increase board independence from management teams). Lorsch proposes that chairmen be appointed independently of boards, that constituents other than shareholders be represented, that directors devote more time to board affairs, and that directors be given formal authority to name their own successors.

8. Contractarians usually make this substitution in the context of downplaying the significance of corporate law history, and instead emphasize the importance of today's economic analysis of corporations and law (e.g., Butler and Ribstein 1995:19–25). As Butler and Ribstein put it, "the fight is over the value of economic analysis," not over history (1995:23); they are tired of corporate law's traditional origins "continu[ing] to rule from the grave" (1995:20).

9. Contractarian Fischel (1982:1268–69) posed this challenge early in the 1980s, traditionalist Clark (1989:1708) acknowledges its credibility, and contractarian Black (1990) adds rhetorical flourishes. The same challenge began surfacing in Japan at the end of the decade (Kester 1991:244–54).

10. Weinrib (1975:18).

11. Legal traditionalist Mark notes that the general assumption today is that corporate law is significant to shareholders but not "to the corporation's place and influence in society." Thus, he finds it "problematic" that changes in the internal rules governing corporations can alter this institution's place in society (1995:84).

12. Kaysen (1996a:18). Again, recall Parkinson's concern that corporations may cause "social disfigurement" (1993:35).

13. Branson calls this symposium "the high water mark of contractarianism" (1995:95). See Bebchuk (1989a) for the introduction to this symposium, and then Eisenberg (1989) and McChesney (1989). The debate then extended to another issue of *Columbia Law Review* (Eisenberg 1990a; McChesney 1990) and elsewhere (Eisenberg 1990b).

14. What follows are major points raised across this debate as a whole, not a recapitulation of points in the actual order in which they were presented. Each debater had ample opportunity to address the other's points and either decided to do so or not.

15. Eisenberg (1990a:1330–31).

16. McChesney (1990:1336–39).

17. For Butler and Ribstein, as for other contractarians, the only credible approach in corporate law today is "to presume in favor of private ordering" until a "market failure" occurs *and* it is also demonstrated that only corporate law can correct the problem (1995:27).

18. See Millon (1993:1386) for another representative example of this.

19. For example, see Chancellor Allen (1993:1399).

20. For instance, see what Easterbrook and Fischel do with the Delaware court view that corporations have "intrinsic value" (1991:136, 154–57, 205–9).

21. He failed to establish this two years earlier as well, in his excellent, largely sociological discussion of the common law tradition (Eisenberg 1988).

22. For examples, see Coffee (1981, 1989), Block, Maimone, and Ross (1993), and Brudney (1997). Parkinson (1993:369–72) and Cunningham and Yablon (1994) call for further extension today. See Chapter 13 for discussion.

23. See Sciulli (1999:122–25).

24. Eisenberg (1989:1488–89).

25. Eisenberg (1989:1523–24).

26. See Sciulli (1999:141–44). Economists approach corporations with five assumptions that can be traced to Alfred Marshall's general theory of rational behavior in self-regulating markets: The internal governance of corporations is more consensual than conflictual. No matter who manages a corporation, and no matter how they govern it and resolve disputes, corporate managers will endeavor to balance marginal rates of productivity with marginal costs of factors of production. Rational shareholders are passive investors, not active owners. Intracorporate contracts are complete, unambiguous, and delimited economic arrangements. And qualities of the larger social order do not and cannot affect these characteristics of corporate performance in self-regulating markets.

27. Eisenberg is silent about their effect on shareholder majorities (1989: 1488–89). Brudney addresses this in 1997 in the context of discussing how fiduciary law frames the contracts and agreements into which investors enter with management.

28. Brudney (1985:1411–12); Easterbrook and Fischel (1991).

29. On the difficulties institutional investors have even in Great Britain in forming coalitions to challenge corporate management, see Black and Coffee (1994), Buxbaum (1994), Charkham (1994), Roe (1994), Rock (1996), and Patfield (1995, 1997).

30. Easterbrook and Fischel insist that "governance structures are open and notorious" regardless (1991:7). The allegory of shareholder self-help is remarkably similar to that of the constituent force that informed the Glorious Revolution and the American Revolution. All of the same limitations come to the fore when either allegory is brought without amendment to modern conditions (see Sciulli 1992a:233–39). A New York Times guest opinion devoted to institutional shareholders' recent stirrings (as well as those by outside directors) carries the headline "The Glorious Oversight Revolution" (Pound 1992). John Pound is a political scientist at Harvard's Kennedy School, and he elaborated his view a year later in the New York University Law Review (1993).

31. See note 26 and economists' third assumption about corporations.

32. The closest the "real world" gets to this game of chicken today is likely the

situation of publicly traded companies in Russia. Contractarians Bernard Black and Reiner Kraakman (1996) explore what "corporate law" means in a country the lacks authoritative courts, credible legal precedents, and legislative expertise. And they find, not unsurprisingly, that suitable social norms are needed in this situation, not just quantitative standards of analysis oriented to maximizing shareholder wealth. This is akin to calls by rational choice theorists Brennan and Buchanan (1985) for a civil religion to take greater hold in the United States in order to support constitutionalism and the rule of law. There is nothing wrong with both conclusions as such, but both run counter to their writers' central concepts and assumptions.

33. More recently, Brudney calls on courts to tighten limits on one-sidedness in corporate governance if they wish "to be faithful to their proclaimed origins in fiduciary premises"—hardly a rousing counterargument to contractarians' criticisms of mandatory rules (1997:631). His only other rationale is similar, namely that the need to prevent and discourage a trustee's appropriation of a beneficiary's assets requires that the aspiration of maximizing shareholder wealth be removed from the center of corporate law doctrine (1997:638–39). Patfield (1995:7) says simply that "we" need to figure out which burdens on corporations are justified, but she never addresses what the burdens are supposed to accomplish except to refer vaguely to "justice" (1995:14). Parkinson calls for "profit sacrificing social responsibility" (1993:304–46), extending the scope of fiduciary duties (1993:369–72), and greater employee participation in corporate governance (1993:397–434). However, he never identifies the dire consequences that will result if these steps are not taken or, therefore, how these steps will reduce these harms.

34. Blumberg is just as blunt (1993:147): "Market efficiency is not an appropriate standard in cases involving the construction of statutory law and determination of the outer boundaries of a statutory regulatory regime." The irony is that this sentence concludes one of his chapters, and he never states specifically what an appropriate legal standard is.

35. White (1985:1418).

36. See Easterbrook and Fischel (1991:35–36) for an explicit rejection of any such approach.

37. For similar statements, see Bratton (1993), Mitchell (1993), Orts (1993), and Parkinson (1993).

38. And, even here, Nietzsche (1887) reminds us how long it took for human beings actually to internalize these restrictions, and Freud (1930) reminds us why this was the case. Clearly, norms of proper and improper corporate conduct have not been with us as long.

39. It does not matter whether they accept these beliefs or rebel against them: An individual must first have internalized or otherwise been exposed to substantive beliefs in order to rebel against them later in life. Thus, these beliefs frame later

rebellion no less than later conformity. The same is true of the beliefs inculcated into individuals during their secondary socialization in school and then later in career training.

40. For general statements about elites (including top management), see Finkelstein and Hambrick (1996), Campbell, Hollingsworth, and Lindberg (1991), Bourdieu (1989, 1996), Lamont (1992), and Lamont and Fournier (1992).

41. See Cookson and Persell (1985) for this estimate of board members' educational backgrounds. But see Rock (1997) for an argument that corporate officers, and their lawyers, operate within a small community of norms, an argument that he asserts rather than establishes with evidence. See Chapter 13 for discussion.

42. This is the case even in Japan, Korea, and Poland, which are often cited as relatively homogeneous societies—and, thus, putatively rare exceptions to the modern rule of heterogeneity.

43. See Sciulli (1992a:chap. 7). Compare this to Hechter (1987).

44. See Halle (1992) on the difference between purchasing abstract art and having a cultivated understanding of it, or at least an understanding that distinguishes an "elite" owner from a "working-class" observer. The working class tends to prefer landscapes. What surprised Halle is that most of the upper middle class people he interviewed who expressed a preference for abstract act, and in some cases had such art on display in their homes, nonetheless reported that they saw landscapes in them.

45. See the collection by Lamont and Fournier (1992), in which the Halle chapter can be found, for a series of discussions of how "taste" differs across class-based status groups, and then, too, how dramatically constructions of the meaning of art objects differ within each such group.

46. Bourdieu (1979, 1989, 1996), Bellah et al. (1985), Lamont (1992).

47. Cookson and Persell (1985). Also see Zweigenhaft and Domhoff (1991).

48. Bourdieu (1979:1).

49. Bourdieu explores this at length in *The State Nobility* (1989) and *The Rules of Art* (1996).

50. Bourdieu (1979:562).

51. Schrecker (1986:12–13).

52. Strauss (1978).

53. Turner and Killian (1957). French social theorist Michel Maffesoli (1985) describes fleeting interactions in urban settings as an "orgy." Individuals can get caught up in the moment, spending an entire week's wages, or tarnishing their reputations, or running afoul of the law, all on a whim. American sociologist Jack Katz (1988) traces the genesis of most crimes, including the most violent crimes, to such situations.

54. Easterbrook and Fischel (1991:136).

55. Easterbrook and Fischel (1991:209, my emphasis, and I remove their emphases).

56. Parkinson assumes the same thing when he considers the merit of "profit-sacrificing social responsibility" (1993:304–46).

57. See Lon Fuller (1964/1969:5–19) for this distinction. Unfortunately, Fuller's own term for such a social duty is a "morality of duty"; equally unfortunate is the title he selected for his major work, *The Morality of Law*. I explain why in Chapter 11.

NOTES TO CHAPTER 8

1. See the symposium in *Washington and Lee Law Review* (1993) and also the collections edited by Mitchell (1995) and Patfield (1995, 1997).

2. Corporate law doctrine may have been in flux in the 1980s, and may well have changed considerably over time. But there are certain core ways of operating that courts would be loathe to abandon under any conditions. These are the institutional practices to which any proposed alternative to existing corporate law and judicial behavior must conform.

3. See Easterbrook and Fischel (1991:12–22).

4. Easterbrook and Fischel insist, with other contractarians, that "the 'personhood' of a corporation is a matter of convenience rather than reality" (1991:12). Mitchell and other traditionalists see corporate personhood as "critical" to everything else (1993:1481). Blumberg (1993) wants courts to treat the corporate enterprise as an agent, at least for some legal purposes, rather than treating each corporate unit or subsidiary as an "entity" unto itself. He calls this alternative enterprise law, as opposed to entity law. See Orts (1998a) for a review of books by Henry Hansmann and G. P. Stapledon that also explore enterprise law. Orts traces the origins of this approach to Alfred Conard at University of Wisconsin Law School.

5. A judge cannot be said in this instance to be "piercing the corporate veil" because this occurs only in close corporations or within corporate groups (that is, parent-subsidiary transactions), not in publicly traded corporations (Thompson 1991:1038). Legal scholar I. Maurice Wormser coined this phrase in 1912, applying it to situations in which judges look for particular corporate officers who engaged in fraud or otherwise committed crimes (Blumberg 1993:66–67). Over time others have applied it to situations in which judges endeavor to identify who bears legal responsibility in any disputed corporate behavior. Gabaldon (1995:113) notes that the notion of piercing the corporate veil has a high profile and yet is not well understood (and Thompson 1991:1036 is similar). Gabaldon sees the rise of limited liability companies in the early 1990s as efforts to stave off these sorts of interventions by courts so that investors and managers are not held liable for what close corporations do. Easterbrook and Fischel discuss the "doctrine of piercing the corporate veil" while considering why courts ever relax shareholders' limited liability protection in order to "allow creditors to reach the assets of shareholders" (1991:54–55). They accept that this makes economic sense

in close corporations, where "limited liability provides minimal gains from improved liquidity and diversification, while creating a high probability that a firm will engage in a socially excessive level of risk taking." It is unclear, however, how Easterbrook and Fischel's concepts allow them to recognize when risk taking ever reaches this level. More important for present purposes, they question courts' test in applying this doctrine, namely "whether a corporation has a 'separate mind of its own,' [or] whether it is a 'mere instrumentality.'"

6. Giddens (1984:9); also see Fine (1993:69–70).

7. Jensen and Meckling (1976:308).

8. See Prechel (1997) on divisions and subsidiaries.

9. See Easterbrook and Fischel (1991:66) on why shareholders do not have "appropriate incentive to study the firm's affairs and vote intelligently."

10. Again, corporate constituents' interests in enhancing their positional power are analytically distinct from individuals' self-interests in, say, shirking or goldbricking at others' expense.

11. See Blair and Stout (1999:297). Germany's two-tier boards of directors essentially institutionalize, and thereby tame, this activity. See Streeck (1992) and Charkham (1994:6–58).

12. See Millon (1995:13–16) for the notion of a "multifiduciary model" of corporate governance and why it troubles many legal scholars, including those who are critical of contractarianism. See Orts (1992) for greater enthusiasm.

13. Bourgin (1945/1989), Buchanan (1958).

14. See Bratton (1993:1474) for a rare call for American corporate law to take a European turn toward corporatism, and Parkinson (1993:397–434) for a rare call in Great Britain. See Gabaldon (1995:110–37) for an intriguing comparison of the divergent evolution of investor liability and product liability.

15. There is consensus about this, but for specific statements, see Shleifer and Vishny (1997:769–73), Williamson and Bercovitz (1996:334–35), Roe (1994:233), and Charkham (1994:349–66).

16. Easterbrook and Fischel (1991:14). Shleifer and Vishny (1997:737) do the same thing, by asking which corporate governance structure best assures "suppliers of finance" of receiving "a return on their investment."

17. Dent (1989:920, quoted by Orts 1992:128 note 769). In addition, see the works cited in note 14 along with Smitka (1994), Litt et al. (1990), Kester (1991:244–53), Hamilton and Biggart (1988) for different views of corporate behavior in Japan.

18. See Simon (1990) for an apt statement of corporate law's doctrinal crisis in the 1980s.

19. See Easterbrook and Fischel (1991:132–34) on whether managers should be permitted to sell their positions. Their answer:

Managers may agree, as part of the sale of a controlling block of shares, to turn over their offices. In such cases part of the premium reflects the value of the office. Managers may also accept payment for recommending that the shareholders approve a merger, when the payment is disclosed and the managers simultaneously sell their own shares. The sale of office violates the fiduciary principle [which they define as a duty to maximize shareholder wealth] only when the office is sold by itself.

20. Simon (1990:399–400).

21. As Morrill (1995) documents ethnographically.

22. Useem (1996), Shleifer and Vishney (1997).

23. Easterbrook and Fischel (1991:171–72).

24. Useem (1993, 1996), Black and Coffee (1994).

25. See Sciulli (1999:chap. 6).

26. "Given a bid [to buy a corporation] . . . an attempt [by management] to engross the profits by defense or auctioneering—privately rational for the target [corporation] or its managers—leads to too little future monitoring. Conclusion: Managers should leave to shareholders and rival bidders the task of 'responding' to offers" (Easterbrook and Fischel 1991:174).

27. Useem (1993, 1996).

28. Smith and Dyer (1996:52–53).

29. Berle and Means raised the earliest concerns about dividing corporate agency, in 1932. See a 1983 symposium in *Journal of Law and Economics* on the fiftieth anniversary of their publication.

30. Note (1982:1653 note 50). The federal statutes that *Yale Law Journal* student editors cite are the Securities Act of 1933, the Trust Indenture Act of 1939, and the Investment Advisors Act of 1940. See Burk (1988:23–44) on the historical context of federal securities legislation, which includes not only the Securities Act of 1933 but also the Glass-Steagall Act of 1933 and the Securities Exchange Act of 1934 (also Sobel 1984:76–121; Roe 1994).

31. Aleinikoff (1987), McDowell (1982, 1988), Stewart (1976).

32. Aleinikoff (1987:945), Lowi (1969).

33. See Sciulli (1999:130–33). The courts' turn toward balancing is the "sociological jurisprudence" that Hans Kelsen roundly criticized and Roscoe Pound espoused, following Rudolph von Jhering (Aleinikoff 1987:958).

34. See Ravitch (1983:114–81) on how administrative and judicial strategies of race balancing in education trumped the doctrine of color-blind admissions and treatment, and how this complicated rather than facilitated their implementation of the Supreme Court's Brown decisions. See Belz (1991) for a history of affirmative action. See Stewart (1990) on splintering in administrative law, which he calls "Madison's nightmare."

35. Ringer (1969) remains an important statement of what happens when all legal institutions and intermediary associations are politicized rather than any retaining relative independence from interest group competition as truly deliberative bodies. Arendt (1951) offers a grander historical sweep and richer conceptual

framework in support of the same point. I read Donald Black's propositions regarding the "behavior" of law and social control as documenting the decline of deliberative bodies in some U.S. criminal and civil courts and organizations (Black 1976, 1989, 1993; see Sciulli 1995).

36. Klein (1982:1542–43). As did student editors of *Yale Law Journal* (Note 1982) as they surveyed judicial rulings. Subsequent calls for dividing corporate agency came from the MIT Commission of Industrial Productivity (see Lindberg and Campbell 1991:392–95 for comments), Columbia legal scholar John Coffee (1990:1549), and economist Charles Craypo and labor scholar Bruce Nissen (1993:244). The same thing was happening in Great Britain (Patfield, 1995, 1997) and balancing had long been institutionalized in Japan, Germany and, to a lesser degree, France (Charkham 1994; Roe 1994:169–221). Kester sees Japanese corporate governance as

> a coalition of stakeholders—suppliers, lenders, customers, shareholders—holding a complex blend of senior and junior, short-term and long-term, conditional and unconditional, implicit and explicit claims against the company. . . . Under these conditions, corporate growth tends to emerge as the common denominator among the stakeholder groups. . . . Within [this context], good management is measured not so much by its ability to maximize the welfare of any one isolated stakeholder as by its ability to maximize the aggregate size of the revenue pie and maintain the stability of the coalitions. (1991:76–78)

Craypo and Nissen overstate the novelty of balancing.

37. Coffee (1990) believes courts should tolerate, not endeavor to regulate, coalitions of interests within and across corporate governance structures. By contrast, Mark (1987:1443) and many other legal scholars insist that the metaphor of *the* corporate person is "vital" to corporate law doctrine.

38. Blair and Stout (1999) elaborate this insight even more effectively.

39. Klein's concern about whether corporate governance advances social wealth appears also in *Yale Law Journal* student's Note of the same year. This reflects how broadly the notion of stakeholder balancing appealed at the time even to new observers of the corporate judiciary and bar. Also see the management text by Freeman (1984) for an earlier appreciation of stakeholder balancing.

40. "By a faction, I understand a number of citizens, whether amounting to a majority or a minority of the whole, who are united and actuated by some common impulse of passion, or of interest, adverse to the rights of other citizens, or to the permanent and aggregate interest of the community" (Madison, Hamilton, and Jay 1788:123). Still, this passage also convey's Madison's republican vigilance. He expresses a concern about the majority by proposing that there is a more "permanent" community interest, one that transcends majority will as well as balancing.

41.

Extend the sphere, and you take in a greater variety of parties and interests; you make it less probable that a majority of the whole will have a common motive to invade the rights of other citizens; or if such a common motive exists, it will be more difficult for all who feel it to discover their own strength, and to act in unison with each other. (Madison, Hamilton, and Jay 1788:127)

42. Compare this wording to Fligstein's approach to the rise of finance managers in corporate governance (1985, 1990) and to his more recent "political model" (1996).

43. Coffee (1990:1496). Pound (1993) carries this view to its logical conclusion, as do Davis and Thompson (1994), Parkinson (1993) and Orts (1992). See Donaldson and Preston (1995) for a review of empirical studies.

44. Actually, sociologists have long approached the individual in the way that proponents of balancing approach the corporation. Sociologists study the roles individuals perform in their everyday lives, and the status positions into which they enter—not individuals as wholes, as indivisible persons. Roles and status positions can be isolated analytically. Thus, sociologists essentially concede that individuals are too complicated to study more directly. See Demo (1992).

45. See Kozyris (1989:1110). "[I]t must be remembered that state anti-takeover statutes are a recent phenomenon. When the Williams Act was enacted in 1968, just one state (Virginia) had such a statute, and even there only for one year" (Easterbrook and Fischel 1991:223).

46. Roe (1994:157–60).

47. Kozyris (1989:1110). Kozyris calls Edgar the "apogee" of invalidations of stake anti-takeover statutes (1989:1127).

48. Judge Richard Posner, a prominent proponent of the law and economics movement, decided this case (Orts 1992:88).

49. Kozyris (1989:1112–13).

50. Kozyris (1989:1111–12).

51. Roe (1994:159–60).

52. Kozyris (1989:1110–11).

53. Romano (1993a:81), Kozyris (1989:1111).

54. Kozyris (1989:1113–25).

55. Pennsylvania took the lead in 1983 and then kept it by passing the toughest anti-takeover legislation at the time in 1989, 1990, and 1992 (Orts 1992:27; plus Yago 1991:192). Orts notes (1992:49–56) that whether today's corporate constituency statutes violate the Commerce Clause remains "an unresolved issue," even as he is confident that they do not.

56. See Romano (1993a), Butler and Ribstein (1995).

57. Yago (1991:189), Orts (1992:37–39).

58. Orts (1992:16).

59. See Wallman (1991) and also Gordon (1991:1932 note 2), Hansen (1991: 1355, 1372–74), Millon (1990:234), Kozyris (1989:1112–24), Lipton (1987:41).

60. The others are:. Kentucky (in 1984), then Illinois, Missouri, and Ohio (1985–1986), followed by Arizona, Connecticut, Florida, Georgia, Hawaii, Indiana, Idaho, Iowa, Louisiana, Maine, Massachusetts, Minnesota, Mississippi, Nebraska, New Jersey, New Mexico, New York, Oregon, Rhode Island, South Dakota, Tennessee, Virginia, Wisconsin, and Wyoming (Orts 1992:27). Connecticut requires management to consider stakeholders' interests, and Idaho requires corporate directors to consider the long-term as well as short-term interests of the corporation and its shareholders (Orts 1992:29, plus note 68). Arizona and Virginia are ambiguous. They permit management to consider stakeholder interests, but fail to specify any of the interests that may be considered (Orts 1992:27). Orts believes that only Connecticut requires management to consider stakeholder interests (1992:29, plus note 68). This says something about these statutes' clarity even to those trained in the law.

61. Millon (1990:233).

62. See Romano (1992) for a review of empirical studies of these statutes' effects on corporate performance. Not surprisingly, she finds that they strengthened management's positions.

63. Orts (1992:128).

64. Bratton (1993:1474), Orts (1992:132).

65. Kozyris (1989:1125 note 59). He proposes that Congress reassert the importance of interstate commerce by establishing "interstate stock" governed by federal law.

66. "The 'nexus of contracts' approach to corporations has many problems, but an inability to accommodate the interests of nonshareholder constituencies is not among them" (Simon 1993:1699). See Easterbrook and Fischel (1982:703 note 15) for their position, namely that they "do not necessarily rule out arguments that directors owe fiduciary duties to employees and other groups."

67. Orts (1992:123–35), Bratton (1993:1468). The same process is under way in Japan. However, the Japanese emphasis on trust—preserving existing claims by stakeholders and long-term ties with major banks and other corporations in the keiretsu system—is not likely to lead to a convergence with American corporate governance (Kester 1991:4–7, 54–55). "Companies belonging to keiretsu account for only one-tenth of one percent of all incorporated businesses in Japan, but group members are generally much larger than the median Japanese firm" (1991:55).

68. Alchian and Allen (1964/1972:283).

69. Easterbrook and Fischel argue that the price of a corporation's stock reflects not only investors' assessment of its current value but also their anticipation of its future value (1991:183):

Stock is valued for the returns through the years. If a given investor puts too much value on the present and too little on the future, someone else can make a lot of money by taking the stock off his hands at a bargain price. The process should continue (because there continues to be profit in it) until the price of stock fully reflects its long-term value. They already are assuming the presence of a market for corporate control.

70. Alfred Chandler Jr. believes, for instance, that the critical mark of corporate efficiency and effectiveness is the recruitment and training of managers at middle and lower levels, not just at top levels (e.g., 1990:594). But this is strictly his preference, not a standard that is self-evidently superior to all others. Indeed, even the measurement of "profit" is controversial. Alchian and Allen (1964/1972:288–90) offer four alternatives, and acknowledge that "of these gauges of wealth or income changes, only the capital-value (wealth) measure is directly measurable in the market." Beyond the problem of measurement, they also discuss alternative definitions of the term "profit" itself (1964/1972:297–98).

71. Samuelson (1948:510).

72. Klein (1982:1542); also Coffee (1990:1496).

73. Klein (1982:1544).

74. For example, see Lindberg, Campbell, and Hollingsworth (1991:8, 33).

75. Recall Roe's proposal that legislatures and courts permit greater variation (1994:233–87).

76. Stinchcombe (1990).

77. Samuelson (1948:510).

78. Lindberg, Campbell, and Hollingsworth (1991:5, 7–8), Shleifer and Vishny (1997).

79. Klein (1982:1542).

80. See Blair and Stout (1999) for a recent, impressive argument in favor of this general position.

81. Bratton (1993:1468). This is a central theme running through Orts (1992) and then also in evidence in Mitchell's 1995 collection and Kaysen's 1996 collection (1996b).

82. Millon (1995:12–16).

83. Smith and Dyer (1996:57).

84. Roe (1996:114–16).

85. Freeman and Evan (1990), cited and discussed by Williamson and Bercovitz (1996:338–39).

86. Klein (1982:1527–33).

87. Mitchell (1990a:1224–25, 1229).

88. Richard Stewart sees this occurring already in American administrative and regulatory law. Japanese corporations face stakeholder pressure, but they resist it by centralizing power in the hands of professional managers who share information and prohibit "hidden action" by any stakeholders. Stakeholders who violate managerial policies are literally reported to the press (Kester 1991:32–33). Japanese organized crime syndicates, or yakuza, use this to their advantage. They "acquire

shares in a target company and then threaten to disrupt shareholder meetings with public disclosures of scandalous management behavior unless they are paid off" (Kester 1991:245). Kester sees systemic pressures expanding management's discretion, at shareholders' expense (1991:167–68, 219ff).

89. Williamson (1985:311–12), Lipton (1987:43–45), Williamson and Bercovitz (1996:338–49).

90. Williamson and Bercovitz (1996:355 note 9); Blair and Stout (1999) agree.

91. Aleinikoff (1987:977). Williamson and Bercovitz (1996:340–49) seek criteria by which to predict which stakeholders can succeed in establishing "contractual regularities" to protect their stakes.

92. See Aleinikoff (1987:992) on the Supreme Court and Sciulli (1999:chap. 5) on the corporate judiciary.

93. Eisenberg (1989:1461, my emphasis).

94. Meyer and Rowan (1977) would object. Efficient performance cannot be distinguished this sharply, they would insist, from nonrational "myths" institutionalized in corporations' environments. Yet, how Meyer and Rowan can identify "myths" without presupposing that efficient performance can be distinguished from them in one way or another is a mystery.

95. Eisenberg (1989:1461, my emphasis).

NOTES TO CHAPTER 9

1. By 1991, Chancellor Allen went further, in *Credit Lyonnais v. Pathe Communications Corp.* He not only allowed directors "to consider the concerns of all stakeholders," but also "requires the board to consider certain stakeholders' concerns under certain circumstances" (see Hartman 1993:1764).

2. Easterbrook and Fischel (1991:223).

3. As long as management business judgment is not tied to stakeholder balancing by law, contractarians are otherwise content: "It is better to insulate all honest decisions from review than to expose managers and directors to review by judges and juries who do not face market pressures. The business judgment rule does this" (Easterbrook and Fischel 1991:100, also 182–83, 208).

4. Orts (1992:111).

5. Johnson (1990:909). Worse, these statutes apply only to domestic corporations, not to multinationals incorporated overseas (Kozyris 1989:1110). Thus, in principle, takeovers of multinationals are facilitated by potentially pricing American corporations "artificially" out of the market for corporate control. Yet, in practice, Japan and Western Europe still lack the junk bond market that helped fuel hostile activity in the United States, and their regulations (unlike those in Great Britain) still favor sitting management teams.

6. See Greenfield (1997) for a rare, enthusiastic advocacy of the notion of cor-

porate social responsibility today, and Parkinson (1993) for a more typical, muted advocacy.

7. Fischel (1982:1260–61). And Fischel was right about the notion of social responsibility being out of touch. Today's liberal and radical critics of contractarianism, the "progressives" or "communitarians," no longer try "to superimpose social obligations on the corporation." Rather, they look for ways to improve the public goals of the corporation from within, that is, by improving its governance function. See Mitchell (1995:xiv–xv) in the preface to his collection. The sole exception in the collection is Orts (1995:261), who considers a multinational's "corporate social responsibility" to be that of "a citizen of the world."

8. Millon (1993:1380).

9. Contractarians advocate bringing greater economic competition into corporate governance structures, but they oppose bringing greater constituent competition into these structures. Yet this would seem to be consistent at a conceptual level with a nexus of contracts approach. This may be what Bebchuk has in mind when he notes (1989a:1399, 1408–9) that advocacy of deregulation does not necessarily follow as a corollary of the contractarian position.

10. For example, see Mitchell's discussion of contractarians' behavior (1993: 1477).

11. Recall from Chapter 7 Eisenberg's characterization of three normative beliefs that legitimate the American economy: Shareholders own corporations, appointed agents should govern corporations, and these agents are sufficiently restrained by markets.

12. Recall our discussion of constitutional law and balancing in Chapter 8.

13. I explore this issue at length in the context of discussing Etzioni's communitarianism (Sciulli 1997c).

14. Bratton's call for a turn to European corporatism, for instance, is not tied to any constitutional or doctrinal foundation (1993:1474).

15. See Sciulli (1999:chap. 5). It might be possible to interpret the Constitution in such a way as to demonstrate that these norms come into play as part of the Framers' background assumptions. Haar and Fessler (1986) read these norms into the American common law tradition, but this ignores over 400 years of British history in which fiduciary law and common law developed along different tracks. The problem is that exegesis directed to the Framers' "original intent" is hardly in favor today. See Dworkin (1986) for criticisms.

16. Haddock, Macey, and McChesney (1987).

17. For examples, see Easterbrook and Fischel (1982, 1983:401), Coffee (1989: 1678), Bebchuk (1989b:1824).

18. Easterbrook and Fischel (1993). Butler and Ribstein (1995:6, 11–12) see fiduciary duties serving contracts, by being "gap-filling"; they do not see fiduciary duties legitimately mediating contracting. Thus, they insist that parties to any

contract have the choice of opting out of all "fiduciary duties." For a lengthy discussion of how contractarians deal with fiduciary law, see Sciulli (1997a). Bratton says contractarians endeavor to "supress the moral conception of fiduciary duty," but their strenuous efforts here testify to its "enduring power" (1995:152).

19. See Frankel (1983).

20. See the next four chapters. DeMott (1988) is representative in failing to distinguish structured situations from agency relationship in general.

21. Easterbrook and Fischel (1993).

22. See the 1989 symposium in *Columbia Law Review*, plus Butler and Ribstein (1995:15–18).

23. Bebchuk (1989a:1399).

24. For example, see Easterbrook and Fischel (1991:4–5, 12–17).

25. See Bernard Black (1990:564–68).

26. Clark (1989:1725).

27. Our distinction between immediate externalities and voluntary exchange turns upside down Easterbrook and Fischel's rationale for management's fiduciary duties to shareholders (1993:437). As one example, managers often fail fully to recompense suppliers whose intermediate products have been depreciated more than expected (Williamson 1988a, 1988b). Similarly, managers also often fail fully to recompense middle managers whose expertise became dedicated to the company rather than being marketable elsewhere.

28. See Bratton (1995:150) on "process defects" in midstream opting out.

29. For example, see Easterbrook and Fischel (1991:6–7,17–18,90).

30. For example, see Easterbrook and Fischel (1991:222–23) on Delaware's "innocuous" anti-takeover rules.

31. Legal traditionalist Clark (1989:1722) argues persuasively that contractarians also accept that elites may decree the meta-rules, the constitutional principles, that then frame all subsequent contracts. Clark's point is that this raises enormous problems of political theory (we would say, of institutional design) which contractarians are understandably reluctant to address (see Easterbrook and Fischel 1991:15–16 for an example). Brennan and Buchanan (1985) are rare in at least offering a solution, even as it is one that clearly moves beyond the scope of application of their own neoclassical concepts. They call for a renewed civil religion.

32. Easterbrook and Fischel (1991:104–5). See Bebchuk (1989b:1852–57) for criticisms of their earlier views.

33. Bratton (1995:175 note 64).

34. Bebchuk (1989a:1406).

35. Carlton and Fischel (1983). And here contractarians have a point: Insider trading does not fall unambiguously within fiduciary law's scope of application. Traditionalist Weinrib acknowledges, for instance, that "the insider trading cases mark the beginning of a substantially new conceptual direction for the fiduciary re-

lation" (1975:15). Japan, Germany, Great Britain, and many other industrialized countries either lack or fail to enforce insider-trading laws. In Germany, insider trading is not illegal; it is purportedly barred by a voluntary code. In Japan and Great Britain, insider trading is illegal, but enforcement is rare. See Strudler and Orts (1999) for an effort to treat insider trading as fraud, a breach of contract not of fiduciary duty.

36. Also Klein (1982:1525–26). See Bebchuk (1989b:1822) and Clark (1989: 1704–5 note 6) for critical comments. Bratton says that few contractarians supported unqualified opting out, but Butler and Ribstein (1990) came closest (1995:150).

37. Roe (1994:23, 263).

38. Easterbrook and Fischel (1991:124–44). Millon (1990:239 note 152) criticizes this when commenting on Macey (1989).

39. Sunstein (1990:7–8).

40. This was when neoclassical economics and legal pragmatism successfully supplanted classical political economy and moral philosophy. See Sciulli (1999: chap. 6) and the literature cited there.

41. See Sciulli (1999:chap. 4) and the literature cited there.

42. I showed earlier in this chapter that it is futile today for judges to rely on the business judgment rule alone to orient them toward consistent rulings.

43. See Blair and Stout (1999) for an example, and Chapter 13 for discussion.

44. With some hedging, Bratton essentially concedes this (1993:1468):

The constituency statutes do bear expansive interpretations as a linguistic and structural proposition. But the statutes do not compel that interpretation. A look at the context makes it safe to predict that we are unlikely to see an expansive interpretation in the law. The fragmented process that led to the statutes' adoption does not provide judges with a solid basis to assume that a material expansion of the definition of the corporation was the statutes' intended or inevitable role. The management-driven process of enactment did not force the implications of constituency empowerment forward as a matter for legislative consideration. These facts invite an ordinarily cautious interpreting judge to fit the statutes into corporate law's inherited framework of management empowerment: Since constituency rights disempower managers, the statutes do not imply them. In any event, the statutes have not yet prompted a leading case, even as we now enter the fifth year following the collapse of the 1980s takeover market.

45. Chancellor Allen holds correctly to the more traditional wording of a duty of loyalty to the corporate entity:

In fact, in every corporation law case in which the gist of the complaint is a breach of loyalty—in every case involving self-dealing by a controlling shareholder or involving any manipulation of the voting process, for example—compliance with the more or less clear technical rules of corporation law is not the determinative issue. A contestable judgment about fairness—the historic mission of chancery—is. (1993:1404)

NOTES TO CHAPTER 10

1. Johnson (1990:896–97), Gordon (1991:1982).
2. Johnson (1990:871).
3. In this regard the American corporate judiciary and bar is very much a "system" in Niklas Luhmann's sense (see an interview in Sciulli 1994). It addresses problems and issues generated within itself, and it is largely self-referential, what Luhmann calls "autopoietic." Whether the same is true of any other part of the judiciary and bar is an open question.
4. Compare the discussion in this chapter to that in Sullivan and Conlon (1997).
5. Kaouris (1995:966, note 3).
6. Romano (1993a:xii). Delaware receives another benefit from its corporate chartering. The U.S. Supreme Court held in 1993 that unclaimed dividends and interests, that is, assets held in bank and brokerage accounts whose owners cannot be located, are the property of the state of incorporation of the holder of the asset (Romano 1993a:38).
7. Kaouris (1995:966 note 6, 1004).
8. Kaouris (1995:1000–1001).
9. Romano (1993a:34).
10. See Kaouris (1995:1012–43) for the figures, and also for a listing of each reincorporation.
11. Kaouris (1995:977 note 78).
12. Kaouris (1995:970), Wolfe and Pittenger (1998:14 note 5)
13. Kaouris (1995:971 note 40, 1016 fig. 1).
14. I cannot explore here the jurisdictional problems that state chartering creates, as opposed to federal chartering. Goldsmith (1989) discusses how dividing corporate agency renders state governments incapable of protecting the corporations in which they have vested interests from being sued or otherwise brought into court by outsiders. Consider the case of an automobile manufacturing company that (a) is incorporated in Delaware, (b) has most of its manufacturing facilities in the Midwest, and yet (c) sells most of a particular line of trucks or vans in still another region of the country, say the Southwest. Which state is to be granted jurisdiction in a suit or class action claiming negligence or defective assembly in this product line? Clearly, the vested interests that states have in the outcome of such a suit differ substantially. Uncertainty about which state will in fact be granted jurisdiction affects both the corporation and any prospective litigant. The same uncertainty emerges in bankruptcy proceedings because "a court may impose [a fiduciary duty to creditors] under the laws of a state that is not the state of incorporation" (Davis et al. 1991:3).

15. Cunningham and Yablon (1994:1615).

16. Kaouris (1995:1004).

17. Kaouris (1995:1009).

18. Kaouris (1995:973).

19. Kaouris (1995:972–75).

20. Romano (1993a:42).

21. Skeel (1997:133 plus note 17).

22. Folk, Ward, and Welch (1998).

23. Kaouris (1995:975–76), Wolfe and Pittenger (1998:12), Skeel (1997:134–35).

24. Romano (1993a:39–40).

25. Wolfe and Pittenger (1998:12).

26. Skeel (1997:134).

27. Skeel (1997:133).

28. Skeel (1997:133–34 note 19).

29. Skeel (1997:134).

30. Rock (1997:1014).

31. Rock (1997:1102).

32. Wolfe and Pittenger (1998:5).

33. Easterbrook and Fischel (1991:164 note 1).

34. Wolfe and Pittenger (1998:6).

35. Wolfe and Pittenger (1998:33).

36. Kaouris (1995:977).

37. Skeel (1997:134, plus note 21).

38. Kaouris (1995:975–76). Contractarians concede this, along with everyone else, e.g., Butler and Ribstein (1995:25).

39. Wolfe and Pittenger (1998:1).

40. As one example of the combination, appellate courts usually do not conduct jury trials, but may in certain circumstances. As another example, appellate courts usually operate with judges questioning attorneys, rather than with attorneys engaging in criminal law's adversarial process of cross-examining witnesses. See Sciulli (1999:chap. 5).

41. Wolfe and Pittenger (1998:193).

42. Wolfe and Pittenger (1998:5 note 16).

43. Wolfe and Pittenger (1998:5 note 16).

44. Wolfe and Pittenger (1998:14).

45. Wolfe and Pittenger (1998:35), quoting from *IBM Corp. v. Comdisco* (1991).

46. Wolfe and Pittenger (1998:36–39). An inadequate remedy at law occurs when: multiple suits at common law would be required fully to remedy an injury; an award of compensatory damages would be inadequate, cannot be calculated, or would never be collected; litigants seek some declaratory judgment; or class actions (typically, in this case, by shareholders) would otherwise lead to multiple suits (Wolfe and Pittenger 1998:58–75, 613).

47. Wolfe and Pittenger (1998:13).

48. This practice began in 1951. Prior to that, Delaware had no permanent supreme court justices. It called on lower court judges not involved in the case to hear the appeal, thereby constituting the "supreme court" (Skeel 1997:135, plus note 23).

49. Skeel (1997:136, plus note 29)

50. Skeel (1997:129).

51. Indiana divided 58 times in 1995, and New Jersey 29 times. Looking only at states with smaller populations, the numbers in 1995 were: North Dakota (60), South Dakota (54), Connecticut (44), Vermont (26), and then New Hampshire (5) and Rhode Island (4) (Skeel 1997:132–33 note 16).

52. Skeel (1997:137).

53. Skeel (1997:136, plus note 31).

54. Kaouris (1995:977–78).

55. Kaouris (1995:1004–5).

56. Kaouris (1995:1008).

57. Romano (1993a:42).

58. Romano (1993a:44).

59. Romano (1993a:49).

60. See Bernard Black (1990:549–51) for the four explanations. We are keeping in mind that California incorporates more businesses overall than Delaware, but Delaware's corporations tend to be larger and more prominent. Easterbrook and Fischel (1991:215) are being cute when they ask: "Why do so few firms incorporate in Delaware?" Compared to California, and then, of course, to all other states combined, Delaware's slice of the entire pie of corporate charters is "thin." Yet this state incorporates nearly half of this country's largest corporations.

61. Cary (1974). Also see Easterbrook and Fischel (1991:213).

62. Traditionalist Eisenberg sees it this way (1989:1513–14), as does political economist (and former Labor Secretary) Reich (1991:297–99). In 1948, economist Paul Samuelson accepted the race to the bottom argument matter of factly: "[I]f the corporation is of any size, you may prefer to establish token headquarters in some state like Delaware or New Jersey, where the regulations governing corporations are made much lighter than in other states in order to attract corporations" (1948:118). It is still accepted matter-of-factly by many legal scholars:

> Missing from your discussion of the contest between Viacom and QVC over acquisition of Paramount . . . is whether a decision of such importance to the nation's communications systems, its economy and Paramount's employees and shareholders should be made under Delaware law. . . . Delaware courts and Delaware law are generally considered to be biased in favor of management and against the interests of shareholders and other corporate constituents. This is not surprising since it is managers who decide where to incorporate or reincorporate. In the competition for incorporation and license

fees, Delaware has led the race to the bottom of corporate managers' responsibility. (Peck 1993)

63. Wolfe and Pittenger (1998:7–8).

64. Branson (1995:103–4).

65. Wolfe and Pittenger (1998:8–9). This is very similar to the way Branson reads Delaware court decisions in the early 1990s (1995:103–5). Legal communitarian Greenfield asserts that Delaware "firmly supports shareholders" rather than stakeholders (1997:4).

66. Baysinger and Butler (1985), Easterbrook and Fischel (1991:213–14).

67. Romano (1993a:14–15).

68. Easterbrook and Fischel (1991:227).

69. Romano (1993a:32).

70. Delaware retains the notion, which Easterbrook and Fischel consider equivalent to believing that witches' brooms cause tornadoes, that a corporation may have an "intrinsic value" not reflected in the stock market (Easterbrook and Fischel 1991:136, 206–7). We show in the next chapter that if "intrinsic value" refers to substantive qualities that corporations putatively contribute to the larger society, then Easterbrook and Fischel are correct. But if "intrinsic value" refers to procedural qualities of corporate governance, then it reveals a vital relationship to institutional design.

71. Janofsky (1993).

72. Easterbrook and Fischel (1991:213).

73. Romano (1993a:32).

74. Romano (1993a:32–33).

75. Romano (1993a:37–38, 32).

76. See Gordon (1989:1553–54 note 16) for a partial list of Delaware's mandatory rules, and Romano (1989) for criticisms of them.

77. Norris (1993). This may be why Bernard Black believes that Delaware's advantage is smaller than the fourth set of legal scholars believes. He nonetheless concludes that other states are not likely to challenge Delaware, but only because the pace of state competition for charters has slowed considerably over the past few decades. The transaction costs of reincorporating certainly fail to pose any obstacle to such a challenge. Reincorporation runs between $40,000 and $80,000—far less than any top manager's annual salary (Black 1990:587–88).

78. Eisenberg (1989:1508–14). Here is where Romano continues to disagree. She acknowledges Delaware's other advantages but nonetheless attributes Delaware's reputation to its "hostagelike dependence on franchise tax revenues" (1993a:38–39).

79. For example, see Gordon (1991).

80. Kaouris (1995:977).

81. Skeel (1997:155).

82. Skeel (1997:171).

83. Skeel (1997:153, 157–59).

84. Skeel (1997:161–62).
85. Romano (1993a:31).
86. Romano (1993a:9,30).
87. Skeel (1997:163).
88. Skeel (1997:170, plus note 132).
89. Cunningham and Yablon (1994:1615).
90. Cunningham and Yablon (1994:1618).
91. Cunningham and Yablon (1994:1619–20).
92. Rock (1997:1013–14).
93. Rock (1997:1015).
94. Rock (1997:1015–17).
95. Rock (1997:1102).
96. Rock (1997:1101, plus note 255).
97. Roe (1994:152, citing Romano).
98. Romano (1993a:59–60).
99. Romano (1993a:59, 67–68). The same goes for California, but for a slightly different reason. California's corporate clientele is physically present within its borders, but also exceedingly heterogeneous, including both targets and hostile bidders. The same cannot be said, as examples, of Midwestern states once dominated by the automobile industry or steel industry, or Oklahoma, Texas, and Louisiana, once dominated by the oil industry, or Northwestern states once dominated by the logging industry.
100. Johnson (1990:907–8).
101. This is what Chancellor Allen did in *Credit Lyonnais v. Pathe Communications Corp.* (1991).
102. Reich (1991:265).
103. Which Chancellor Allen acknowledges (e.g., 1992a:34–35 note 49).
104. For example, see Easterbrook and Fischel (1991:136, 206–7).
105. Easterbrook and Fischel (1991:205–6). Ultimately, sociologist Alan Wolfe shares this view (1993:1689–92).
106. See the 1993 symposium in *Washington and Lee Law Review* to which Chancellor Allen contributed.
107. For example, see Easterbrook and Fischel (1991:207–9).
108. Johnson (1990:877–78).
109. Quoted by Orts (1993:1606 note 212). Also see Chancellor Allen (1993:1405).
110. Johnson (1990:897), citing Eisenberg (1988:15, 29).
111. Johnson (1990:897).
112. Johnson (1990:934). This makes Bratton less than sanguine about the prospects for an alternative to today's orthodoxy (1993:1471):

We cannot look to Delaware to redefine the firm and break the context. The possibility of an outbreak of regulatory competition keeps it faithful to man-

agement interests. Nor is there much point in looking to any other state. Management makes its influence felt nationwide. Furthermore, lawmakers can be expected to be disinclined to undertake reform schemes that carry any risk of wealth depressive effects and feel well justified in doing so.
113. Johnson (1990:891).
114. Gordon (1991:1983).

NOTES TO CHAPTER 11

1. See Sciulli (1999:chap. 5) and the literature cited there.
2. White (1985), Dugger (1989), Gordon (1996), Parkinson (1993).
3. Harvard legal theorist Lon Fuller first identified these procedural normative qualities of consistent law enforcement in 1964 (1964/1969:46–84).
4. See Summers (1984) for an intellectual biography of Fuller that places him among the four most important legal theorists of the twentieth century, the other three being Holmes, Pound, and Llewellyn.
5. A structured situation, to recall, is one in which someone in a position of trust exercises power over someone in a position of dependence who, for whatever reason, cannot easily or readily leave this position.
6. See O'Donnell, Schmitter, and Whitehead (1986) and the literature cited there.
7. Eisenstadt (1996:367–76), Nakane (1970), Schmitter (1981, 1983), Streeck (1992), Banfield (1958), Putnam (1993). See more generally Etzioni-Halevy (1989) and Friedrich (1941, 1974).
8. See Sciulli (1992a) and the literature cited there, along with Frankford (1994). On the social psychology of democratic societies, see Perez-Diaz (1993) and, earlier, Etzioni (1968). For discussion, see Sciulli (1999, 1997c).
9. Again, see Sciulli (1999:chap. 5) and the literature cited there, and also Brown, Maimone, and Schoell (1998) for an assessment of mandatory requirements of disinterestedness "under Delaware law."
10. See Parkes (1828) for a classic statement. Parkes never questioned, however, the importance of Chancery's mission, and so he called for its reform rather than its abolition. Where common law courts decided disputes over land ownership on private law grounds, Chancery decided disputes over property use on public law grounds.
11. See Hawkins (1984) for several examples of this in British environmental law enforcement, and Stewart (1990) for a general statement about the same flaws in American administrative law.
12. Palmiter (1989). Also see Brown, Maimone, and Schoell (1998).
13. For examples, see Easterbrook and Fischel (1991:35–39, 86–87, 91–93, 98–100, 104–5, 124–25, 129–31, 166).
14. This is precisely Brudney's (1997) ultimate defense for mandatory rules

today. Delaware courts must continue to enforce mandatory rules because the fiduciary law tradition demands it, not because this serves any public law interest that Brudney identifies or even suggests.

15. We show in the next chapter that formally democratic formations are rarely present in corporate governance structures.

16. Compare this to legal scholar Edward Rock's (1997:1072–1107) quite different account of how corporate officers, and their legal counsel, learn what Delaware courts expect (see Chapter 13 for discussion).

17. I can only assert here that the same thing happened with the fiduciary duties that English Chancellors imposed on barons, and then on trustees and certain other agents. See Sciulli (1999: chap. 5) for discussion.

18. It is not surprising that a two-party system for mass elections emerged fully, for the first time in history, at the same time. See Duverger (1963), Sorauf (1964).

19. See Easterbrook and Fischel (1991:142–43) for this point about the law, and see Finkelstein and Hambrick (1996) on "strategic leadership" within corporations.

20. See Easterbrook and Fischel (1991:145–61) on the "appraisal remedy."

21. White comes closest to seeing the need to distinguish procedural norms from substantive norms when he notes (1985:1420) that economics as a discipline lacks the concepts with which to account for the rules of the game that frame everyday economic activity. Brennan and Buchanan (1985) also acknowledge this. Frank Knight appreciated this in 1933: "[T]he more vital problems are not problems of economy, but of maintaining social unity in the face of economic interests. . . . The social problem is preserve respect for the rules, and to make such rules as result in the best game for all, players and spectators" (1921/1948: xxx–xxxi). White sees that contractarians and traditionalists alike overlook this conceptual gap in economics, and we propose that this reflects their shared liberal complacency. They share the faith that American society, the "noneconomic background" against which corporations perform their governance and production functions, is inherently benign.

22. Chancellor Allen (1992b).

23. Easterbrook and Fischel (1991:86–87, 101).

24. See Mitchell (1995:189) on the (narrower and vaguer) "model of procedural fairness" in corporate law. Social scientists also study "procedural justice" in organizations (e.g., Newman 1993; Sheppard et al. 1992; Tyler 1988; Leventhal 1980). However, they often add substantive norms to their very definitions of procedural justice (rather than linking the latter more exclusively to a form of organization). For example, Leventhal's sixth standard of procedural justice is "conformity to prevailing ethical standards" (see Watts 1993:1526 for discussion). I have not seen other social scientific studies that link norms of procedural justice to the presence of any particular form of organization, and then to the latter's effect on institutional design. This interrelationship marks the core of what I call societal constitutionalism (Sciulli 1992a). See Frankford (1994) for comments and criticisms. Indeed, social scientists typically do what Useem and Lorsch did, namely link norms of procedural

justice immediately to individuals' personal behavior and social psychology within organizations (e.g., Victor and Cullen 1988; Etzioni 1988). For instance, Newman draws attention to the "moral climate of an organization." Yet she acknowledges that "no consistent agreement exists in the literature about the method of classifying the moral climates of organizations" (1993:1495–99; also Watts 1993 for comments).

NOTES TO CHAPTER 12

1. For commentary, see Gordon (1991:1943–47), Johnson (1990, 1992), Palmiter (1989), and Bratton (1989b).

2. See Gordon (1991:1936–91) on doctrine prior to *Time-Warner*.

3. This question is consistent not only with population ecology but also with a resource dependence approach in the sociology of organizations. See Pfeffer (1972), Pfeffer and Salancik (1978), Hannan and Freeman (1989), Hannan and Carroll (1992).

4. See Finkelstein and Hambrick (1996) more generally.

5. The paragraph that follows, including the definition of collegial formations, is drawn from Sciulli (1999:59–60). This definition, in turn, slightly modifies the wording in Sciulli (1992a:80) in order to fit our discussion of corporations and intermediary associations.

6. Sociologist Wolfe captures more generally the problem posed by self-interested or economizing behavior that is unmediated by norms: "The market leaves us with no way to appreciate disinterest" (1989:102).

7. Curiously, Morrill reports *elements* of collegiality in what he calls "atomistic organizations" (1995:52–58, 141–76). On the one hand, Morrill finds evidence of disinterested behavior: Decisions are made on the merits, not on the basis of whether they are supported by superiors. On the other hand, Morrill finds little evidence of deliberation, of robust discussion.

8. See Chapter 7, page 146.

9. If we read Useem's work in this way, then it is certainly also a description of how outside directors' shared substantive beliefs are indeed delimiting their strictly instrumental and strategic efforts to improve their own corporations' performances. This is what misleads sociologists into assuming that elites' similar primary and secondary socialization predisposes them to act in similar ways—to act not only on similar material interests but also on similar beliefs. If sociologists said the same thing about any other demographic group, or any other segment of the stratification system, they would be accused of being inordinately naive or simplistic—or, worse, of being classist, sexist, racist, etc. Cookson and Persell (1985) as well as Zweigenhaft and Domhoff (1991) convey quite vividly how difficult it is today for elite American and British families to pass along their substantive beliefs even to their own children. And recall, too, our discussion of university presidents (Chapter 7, pages 159–60).

10. I assume throughout this discussion that Robert Michels' (1911) iron law of oligarchy is indeed an iron law, just as I assume that Max Weber's (1914–1920) concerns about rationalization cannot be ignored or dismissed. See Sciulli (1997b) for how institutionalists in the sociology of organizations deal with Weber's concept of rationalization. Thus, in order to account for the presence of any democratic *society* today, over eighty years after Weber's death, one must methodically address his concerns at a conceptual level. To adopt a political economic position of liberal complacency as a matter of faith is simply to ignore these concerns. Moreover, one must also accommodate Michels' iron law at a conceptual level. One cannot simply substitute some idealized alternative of participatory democracy or substantive consensus. This does not mean that I am closing off the possibility of a more robust democracy *a priori*, at a conceptual level. It does mean, though, that I appreciate that this possibility is rarely, if ever, realized in practice. Indeed, because no empirical example has falsified Michels' iron law since he first published it, in 1911, it is fair to say that the burden of proof is on those who wish to substitute an ideal.

11. Morrill discusses the "mechanistic bureaucracy" at length (1995:45–52, 92–140). Of course, scores of intrigues may be found within and around a chain of command. What cannot be found in the bureaucratic form, however, is a pattern of behavior that challenges the chain itself. Such a pattern would mean individuals are organized in another formation, most likely the patron-client.

12. See Morrill's discussion of "matrix systems" (1995:59–67, 177–216).

13. See Smitka (1994) on how Japanese managers establish relationships with suppliers, and see Useem (1996) on how American managers establish relationships with investment bankers and institutional investors.

14. Morrill (1995) does not report any examples of this.

15. For example, see Easterbrook and Fischel (1991:63–89).

16. Lorey (1992), Cleaves (1987).

17. I cannot explore the point here, but the relative size of Mexico's middle class is a separate, substantive issue. Japan and Italy in the 1920s, Germany in the 1930s, and France in the 1940s had sizable middle classes. What they lacked were collegial formations across their major intermediary associations, and then judicial or administrative support for them institutionalized in the larger society.

18. It can be traced to researchers' tendency to follow Max Weber in overextending the ideal type of bureaucracy to any large enterprise irrespective of how it is actually organized. See Sciulli (1999:chaps. 1–3; 1997b) on this tendency in the new institutionalism in the sociology of organizations. Dugger (1989:14) is typical for economists, and Frug (1984) and Orts (1993:1570 note 15) are typical for legal scholars. Researchers then attribute normative mediations of instrumental behavior within bureaucracies to shared substantive beliefs that leaders putatively internalize in common and then act on in common at particular sites, as corporate cultures or subcultures (e.g., Perez-Diaz 1993). They do not attribute these mediations to distinctive qualities of intermediary associations

themselves, supported in turn by distinctive institutional arrangements in their "environment," the larger social order.

19. Moreover, it is a safe bet that it is easier for Useem or other social scientists to gain access to corporate boards that adopt the collegial form than to those organized in hierarchies or patron-client networks. Again, it is difficult to imagine a corporate board really being formally democratic for any sustained period of time. See Lorsch (1989:169–93).

20. Again, it is a separate issue whether corporate constituents who recognize and understand this in common then either accept or reject the importance of keeping these qualities in view, and of acting voluntaristically to this end.

21. Reich (1991). For discussions of the qualitative ends over which professionals deliberate, see Abbott (1988: chap. 2). For a more general discussion, see Sciulli (1992a:chap. 7).

22. In the social sciences, value-neutral observation and description refer ultimately to social scientists' interpersonal recognition and understanding of the same descriptions and explanations of states of affairs in the world. It does not refer to their measuring "facts" more immediately (Popper 1934; Parsons 1937; Habermas 1967, 1968).

23. Simon (1993:1703).

24. It is not sufficient to show that the change jeopardizes the career security of particular directors or managers, editors, or reporters. Nor is it sufficient to show that the change jeopardizes the continued presence of a particular board, a particular team, or a particular division. In other words, if a raider wishes to spin off a corporation's research & development division, this is legally acceptable. But if a raider wishes to keep this division, then courts can examine whether the new management team is taking steps to maintain its integrity as a collegial formation. Similarly, if a raider wishes to dismiss most members of a corporation's board, this too is legally acceptable. But if the board had a history of operating in a collegial way, rather than bureaucratically, then courts can examine what the new owners say and do about this. We saw in Chapter 5 that Vice Chancellor Jacobs went further in his *QVC* decision: He demanded that Paramount's board deliberate even though it had no history of being organized in the collegial form.

25. After all, if a corporation is engaged in "routine production," then its claim to possess deliberative bodies or collegial formations is more likely feigned than genuine. On the other hand, if corporate divisions are engaged in "symbolic analysis," then its case for maintaining existing corporate collegial formations may be credible. It is at least worthy of "enhanced scrutiny" by a court. See Reich (1991) on the distinction between routine production and symbolic analysis.

26. See Millon (1993), Bratton (1993). Nor did *QVC* hinge on a principle of "maximizing disclosure," which Coffee proposes (1989) and Easterbrook and Fischel criticize (1991:276–314).

27. T. L. Whistler (1984), quoted by Finkelstein and Hambrick (1996:229).

28. Gordon (1991:1984).
29. Also Chancellor Allen (1992b).
30. Millon (1990:258).
31. Gordon (1991:1984).
32. Millon (1990:257–58).
33. This is intended to call to mind the Founders' concern about maintaining a vigilant citizenry, which others call a "constituent force" (Sciulli 1992a:68–69, 202–22). It is also intended to call to mind what I call a theory of societal constitutionalism. Also see Frankford (1994).
34. Rock (1997:1089–90, 1097–98, 1102).
35. Compare this to Chancellor Allen (1993).

NOTES TO CHAPTER 13

1. For example, see Wolfe (1993:1692–95).
2. If a corporation is foreign owned but operated on American soil, and thereby employs American citizens, courts serve a public law interest by protecting its collegial formations and the narrow positional interest of its societal constituents. How this might be done is something I leave to legal scholars. Here courts impose procedural norms on "outsiders," not substantive norms or "national culture"; thus, the behavior expected is within foreign managers' ability to perform, consistent with Fuller's threshold.
3. Bratton, for instance, sets out to assess "the wreckage of corporate fiduciary law" (1995:140).
4. Which Coffee advocates (1989).
5. Also Coffee (1989:1653–64).
6. Loewenstein (1989:72 note 22).
7. Easterbrook and Fischel (1991:107–8).
8. For example, see Norris (1993).
9. Clark (1989:1704).
10. Clark (1989:1704–5, plus notes 1 and 6).
11. This is why Easterbrook and Fischel collapse loyalty and duty (1991:103).
12. Coffee may well be correct that traditional fiduciary law, which is a set of substantive limitations rather than a set of procedural mediations, is ultimately hostile to the (longer-term) interests of management and other employees (1989:1626 note 18).
13. Palmiter (1989:1453).
14. Palmiter (1989:1450–52).
15. Palmiter (1989:1452–54).
16. Compare Palmiter's reticence to the following effort by Lorsch (1989:13): "Previous discussions of corporate governance have avoided references to the con-

cept of power, preferring to stress the need for outside directors to be *independent*. However, independence means freedom from unresolvable conflicts of interests with other companies (the duty of loyalty), and autonomy vis-à-vis management. In our view, being a truly independent director means having sufficient power to govern." But then, a paragraph later, Lorsch hedges: "In truth, other than their legal mandate, the directors' only power advantage is their capacity to act as a group by reaching a consensus, but doing this requires group cohesion and time for discussion, often scarce commodities in the typical boardroom."

17. Folk, Ward, and Welsh quote the Delaware Supreme Court's definition of "independence" in *Aronson v. Lewis* (1984) (1998:141:23):

Independence means that a director's decision is based on the corporate merits of the subject before the board rather than extraneous considerations or influences. While directors may confer, debate, and resolve their differences through compromise, or by reasonable reliance upon the expertise of their colleagues and other qualified persons, the end result, nonetheless, must be that each director has brought his or her own informed business judgment to bear with specificity upon the corporate merits of the issues without regard for or succumbing to influences which convert an otherwise valid business decision into a faithless act.

The Court goes on to say that any credible allegation that independence has been breached must show that a director had an "actual financial interest" in the disputed transaction, not a "personal affinity alone." This makes independence synonymous with loyalty.

18. Yet this seems to be the way the Delaware Supreme Court defined independence in 1984 (see note 17).

19. All quotations in this paragraph and the next two are from Cunningham and Yablon (1994:1594–96), unless otherwise footnoted.

20. Cunningham and Yablon (1994:1620).

21. Folk, Ward, and Welsh agree with this analysis; see (1998:141:14–15).

22. Cunningham and Yablon (1994:1597).

23. Brudney (1997:599).

24. Cunningham and Yablon (1994:1601).

25. Folk, Ward, and Welch (1998:102:23).

26. Cunningham and Yablon (1994:1598–99).

27. Cunningham and Yablon (1994:1599–1600).

28. Folk, Ward, and Welsh (1998:141:15). In 1989, Chancellor Allen placed loyalty first, good faith second, and due care third when describing a "threshold review" to see if business judgment rule protection would hold for management in *In re RJR Nabisco Shareholders Litigation*. As Folk, Ward, and Welsh put it (1998: 141:31–32): A threshold review of the objective financial interests of the board (i.e., independence), a review of the board's subjective motivation (i.e., good faith), and

an objective review of the process by which it reached the decision (i.e., due care). But they also point out that only a breach of care or loyalty rebuts the presumption of the business judgment rule, not a breach of good faith.

29. To recall, a judicial inquiry into director and management action under intrinsic fairness requires both fair dealing and fair price. "Fair dealing" encompasses the timing of a merger, how it was initiated, structured, negotiated, disclosed to directors, and how the approvals of directors and stockholders were obtained. "Fair price" encompasses the economic and financial aspects of a merger, including the corporation's market value, future prospects, and any other considerations an investment banker might make. Cunningham and Yablon (1994:1600 note 45).

30. Cunningham and Yablon (1994:1600).

31. Cunningham and Yablon (1994:1603–5), in which they quote Jacobs, then Veasey.

32. Cunningham and Yablon (1994:1606). They note that the unified standard also accounts for the disclosure obligations that Delaware courts impose on directors and officers (1994:1614 note 138).

33. Cunningham and Yablon (1994:1621).

34. Cunningham and Yablon (1994:1615–16, 1618).

35. Cunningham and Yablon (1994:1615, 1618).

36. This may be what Branson is getting at when he says that focus on "fair dealing" focuses attention only on harm to the corporation and thereby robs fiduciary law of a part of its "aspirational content" (1995:100). Mitchell sees only immediate externalities in corporate officers' breaches of the fiduciary duty of care (breakdowns of "trust"), not institutional externalities (1995:193). He sees everything in interpersonal terms, e.g., "You cannot trust another unless you are, yourself, trustworthy" (1995:194), or else in terms of "shared values" (1995:195). He ends by discussing "trust as a virtue" and the importance of having a "trust-based society" (1995:199–202). O'Connor is interested in extending fiduciary law protection to displaced workers, saying that this law's "moral mandate" is to act in parties' joint interests (1995:219); she never alludes to any connection to institutional design (see 1995:232–34).

37. Brudney does the same (1997:634–35).

38. Cunningham and Yablon (1994: 1621, 1625–26).

39. Cunningham and Yablon (1994:1607).

40. Cunningham and Yablon (1994:1619).

41. Cunningham and Yablon (1994:1620). Their thesis is important because it moves legal commentary beyond reacting to Delaware court decisions by advocating the positional interests of one constituent or another, whether management (Taylor 1996), shareholders (Romano 1993a; Butler and Ribstein 1995; Siegel 1999), hostile bidders (Loewenstein 1989), or employees and other stakeholders (Johnson and Millon 1990; O'Connor 1995; Blair and Stout 1999). See Cunningham and Yablon (1994:1615–16).

42. See Black and Kraakman (1996) for numerous uses of this phrase in the context of discussing how to reform corporate law in Russia.

43. The phrase is Etzioni's (1993, 1996).

44. Rock's use of religious metaphors when describing the behavior of courts in equity is apt for many reasons. One, of course, is that the first English chancellors were all clerics—for two centuries (Sciulli 1999:chap. 5). Another is that to this day an appeal for equitable relief from a court of equity is called a "prayer." See, for example, Wolfe and Pittenger (1998:55).

45. Also see Bratton (1995:141, 144, 152) on the "core mandate" of corporate law being "a norm of honorable conduct" and "scruples about appropriate behavior among business actors." See Mitchell (1995) on the importance of trust and the "reasonable" expectations of parties in corporate law.

46. See Braithwaite (1989) on the importance of shaming in criminal law enforcement.

47. Rock (1997:1013–17).

48. Rock (1997:1024–25).

49. Rock (1997:1017).

50. Rock (1997:1017–18).

51. Rock (1997:1022–23).

52. Rock (1997:1025).

53. Folk, Ward, and Welch (1998:251:41).

54. Orts notes that Germany regulates parents and subsidiaries more heavily than does the United States, but he does not elaborate (1995:275 note 75).

55. Rock (1997:1025).

56. Rock (1997:1026).

57. Rock (1997:1026).

58. Rock (1997:1023, plus note 32).

59. Rock (1997:1023–24).

60. Rock (1997:1024).

61. Rock (1997:1028).

62. Rock (1997:1040–56).

63. Rock (1997:1061–62). See Chapter 5, page 115.

64. Rock (1997:1065–1107).

65. Rock (1997:1080–81).

66. Blair and Stout (1999:250).

67. Blair and Stout (1999:251–2, plus note 9).

68. See Kay and Silberston (1997:53–54) for Honore's 11 characteristics of ownership and why shareholders fail to qualify as owners; they are investors, as are stakeholders.

69.

A fundamental precept of Delaware corporation law is that it is the board of directors, and neither shareholders nor managers, that has ultimate responsibility for the management of the enterprise. . . . The board may not either formally or effectively abdicate its statutory power and its fiduciary duty to manage or direct the management of the business and affairs of the corporation. (Folk, Ward, and Welsh (1998:141:11–12)

70. Blair and Stout (1999:253). Patfield proposes that this is how managers in fact typically act; they endeavor to run an efficient enterprise (1995:12–13), and Orts explores this more general "enterprise" notion (1998a).

71. Blair and Stout (1999:253–55).

72. Blair and Stout (1999:274–76).

73. Blair and Stout (1999:282).

74. Blair and Stout (1999:290–91).

75. And they continue this narrow reading later when discussing directors' fiduciary duty of care; see Blair and Stout (1999:299–301).

76. Blair and Stout (1999:287–89, 294–95).

77. Blair and Stout (1999:294–95, plus note 109).

78. Blair and Stout (1999:315–16).

79. Donald Black's structural approach to law and social control (1976, 1989, 1993) also leaves no room for disinterest and deliberation in collegial formations. See Sciulli (1995).

80. Bratton emphasizes the importance of "reputational incentives" in game theory (1995:155).

81. Blair and Stout (1999:317–18). In elaborating the implications of findings from game theory for legal theory, Bratton also sees the importance of bringing social norms into play (1995:165–66). Recall that rational choice theorists Brennan and Buchanan (1985) do the same thing.

82. Blair and Stout (1999:318–19).

83. Palmiter (1989:1376–94).

84. Palmiter (1989:1394).

85. See Branson (1995:95) for the view that corporation law across advanced societies is moving toward "mandatory structure," not mandatory rules, for corporations. But he is vague in identifying this structure, pointing only to "a governance model that is comprised of a majority of independent directors, with a well thought out committee structure and whose mission is one of monitoring the chief executive."

86. Roe (1994:11–12).

87. Roe (1994:13, 16).

88. Useem (1996:224–25).

89. For example, see Palmiter (1989:1436–60).

90. This is a good example of how epistemology trumps methodology, how an empirically defensible description of a state of affairs in the world can nonetheless distort its meaning and significance. That is, even empirically sound descriptions only escape distortion when they are embedded within a framework of concepts

that allows researchers to see their implications for individuals' everyday lives and for institutional arrangements.

91. Easterbrook and Fischel's most recent criticism of the fiduciary law tradition points directly to this breakdown of meaning. "The many agency relations that fall under the 'fiduciary' banner are so diverse that a single rule could not cover all without wreaking havoc" (1993:425). Their criticism is overstated: It is not necessary for traditionalists to defend any and all extensions of fiduciary law's relational norms. It is only necessary for them to isolate a core "jurisdiction" or scope of application, and then to explain why dire institutional consequences would result if contracting were allowed to encroach into it.

92. See Millon (1993), Bratton (1993).

93. Thus, *Van Gorkom* elaborates the examples we discussed in Chapter 4 illustrating why the maximization of private wealth can not be assumed invariably to contribute to the other two corporate purposes. It shows that not all "anomalies" of buyouts and takeovers are immediate externalities; some involve institutional externalities.

94. This is what Brudney foresaw with his thought experiment of a game of chicken (see Chapter 7).

95. Including, for example, Millon's (1993:1388) and Green's (1993:1419) notions of "multifiduciary duties."

96. For example, see Wolfe (1993:1688).

97. Chancellor Allen (1993:1404–7).

References

Abbott, Andrew. 1988. *The System of Professions: An Essay on the Division of Expert Labor.* Chicago: University of Chicago Press.

———. 1993. "The Sociology of Work and Occupations." *Annual Review of Sociology* 19:187–209.

Acs, Gregory, and Eugene Steuerle. 1996. "The Corporation as a Dispenser of Welfare and Security." Pp. 360–81 in Carl Kaysen (Ed.). *The American Corporation Today.* New York: Oxford.

Aichele, Gary J. 1990. *Legal Realism and Twentieth-Century American Jurisprudence.* New York: Garland Publishing.

Alchian, Armen A., and William R. Allen. 1964/1972. *University Economics: Elements of Inquiry.* 3d ed. Belmont, CA: Wadsworth.

Alchian, Armen A., and Harold M. Demsetz. 1972. "Production, Information Costs, and Economic Organizations." *American Economic Review* 62:777–95.

Aleinikoff, T. Alexander. 1987. "Constitutional Law in the Age of Balancing." *Yale Law Journal* 96:943–1005.

Alexander, Jeffrey C. 1989. *Twenty Lectures.* New York: Columbia University Press.

Allen, (Chancellor) William T. 1992a. "Our Schizophrenic Conception of the Business Corporation." Paper presented at Cardozo Law School.

———. 1992b. "Our Schizophrenic Conception of the Business Corporation." *Cardozo Law Review* 14:261–81.

———. 1992c. "Corporate Directors in the Dawning Age of Post-Managerialism." Paper presented at Stanford University, Center for Economic Policy Research, May 1.

———. 1993. "Contracts and Communities in Corporation Law." *Washington and Lee Law Review* 50:1395–1408.

Anders, George. 1992. *Merchants of Debt: KKR and the Mortgaging of American Business.* New York: Basic.

Anderson, Charles A., and Robert N. Anthony. 1986. *The New Corporate Directors.* New York: John Wiley.

Aneshensel, Carol S. 1992. "Social Stress: Theory and Research." *Annual Review of Sociology* 18:15–38.

Antilla, Susan. 1993. "Hard Lessons of Paramount's Saga." *New York Times* (December 26, Section 3).

Antilla, Susan, and Geraldine Fabrikant. 1993. "Bankers for Paramount under Fire for Advice on Bid." *New York Times* (December 6).

Applebome, Peter. 1998. "Second Acts, and Beyond: Check Out the 'Me, Reborn' Generation." *New York Times* (November 22).

Arendt, Hannah. (1951) 1958. *Origins of Totalitarianism*. Cleveland: Meridian.

Auerbach, Alan J. (Ed.). 1988. *Corporate Takeovers: Causes and Consequences*. Chicago: University of Chicago Press.

Avery, Christopher, Judith A. Chevalier, and Scott Schaefer. 1998. "Why Do Managers Undertake Acquisitions? An Analysis of Internal and External Rewards for Acquisitiveness." *Journal of Law, Economics, and Organizations* 14:24–43.

Banfield, Edward C. 1958. *The Moral Basis of a Backward Society*. New York: Free Press.

Barenberg, Mark. 1994. "Democracy and Domination in the Law of Workplace Co-operation: From Bureaucratic to Flexible Production." *Columbia Law Review* 94: 753–983.

Bartley, Robert L. 1992. *Seven Fat Years—and How to Do It Again*. New York: Free Press.

Baums, Theodor, Richard M. Buxbaum, and Klaus J. Hopt (Eds.). 1994. *Institutional Investors and Corporate Governance*. Berlin: Walter de Gruyter.

Baysinger, Barry, and Henry N. Butler. 1985. "Race for the Bottom v. Climb to the Top: The ALI Project and Uniformity in Corporate Law." *Journal of Corporate Law* 10:431–62.

Bebchuk, Lucian Arye. 1989a. "The Debate on Contractual Freedom in Corporate Law." *Columbia Law Review* 89:1395–1415.

———. 1989b. "Limiting Contractual Freedom in Corporate Law: The Desirable Constraints on Charter Amendments." *Harvard Law Review* 102:1820–60.

Bellah, Robert N., et al. (1985) 1986. *Habits of the Heart: Individualism and Commitment in American Life*. New York: Harper and Row.

Belz, Herman. 1991. *Equality Transformed: A Quarter Century of Affirmative Action*. New Brunswick, NJ: Transaction Books.

Berg, Eric N. 1992. "The Bad Boy of Insurance Ratings." *New York Times* (January 5, Section 3).

Berle, Adolf Jr., and Gardiner C. Means. (1932) 1967. *The Modern Corporation and Private Property*. Reprint. New York: Harcourt Brace and World.

Berton, Lee. 1994. "Some Smaller Losses from Derivatives Can Go Undetected." *Wall Street Journal* (April 15).

Black, Bernard S. 1990. "Is Corporate Law Trivial? A Political and Economic Analysis." *Northwestern University Law Review* 84:542–97.

Black, Bernard S. and John C. Coffee Jr. 1994. "Hail Britannia? Institutional Investor Behavior under Limited Regulation." *Michigan Law Review* 92:1997–2087.

Black, Bernard, and Reinier Kraakman. 1996. "A Self-Enforcing Model of Corporate Law." *Harvard Law Review* 109:1911–82.

Black, Donald. 1976. *The Behavior of Law*. New York: Academic Press.

———. 1989. *Sociological Justice*. New York: Oxford University Press.

———. 1993. *The Social Structure of Right and Wrong*. San Diego: Academic Press.

Blair, Margaret M. (Ed.). 1993. *The Deal Decade: What Takeovers and Leveraged Buyouts Mean for Corporate Governance*. Washington, DC: Brookings Institution.

———. 1995. *Ownership and Control: Rethinking Corporate Governance for the Twenty-First Century*. Washington, DC: Brookings Institution.

Blair, Margaret M., and Lynn A. Stout. 1999. "A Team Production Theory of Corporate Law." *Virginia Law Review* 85:247–328.

Block, Dennis J., Michael J. Maimone, and Steven B. Ross. 1993. "The Duty of Loyalty and the Evolution of the Scope of Judicial Review." *Brooklyn Law Review* 59:65–105.

Blumberg, Phillip I. 1993. *The Multinational Challenge to Corporation Law: The Search for a New Corporate Personality*. New York: Oxford University Press.

Bourdieu, Pierre. (1979) 1984. *Distinction: A Social Critique of the Judgment of Taste*. Cambridge: Harvard University Press.

———. (1989) 1996. *The State Nobility: Elite Schools in the Field of Power*. Stanford: Stanford University Press.

———. 1996. *The Rules of Art: Genesis and Structure of the Literary Field*. Stanford: Stanford University Press.

Bourgin, Frank. 1945/1989. *The Great Challenge: The Myth of Laissez-Faire in the Early Republic*. New York: George Brazilier.

Braithwaite, John. 1984. *Corporate Crime in the Pharmaceutical Industry*. London: Routledge & Kegan Paul.

———. 1985. "White Collar Crime." *Annual Review of Sociology* 11:1–25.

———. 1989. *Crime, Shame and Reintegration*. Cambridge: Cambridge University Press.

Branson, Douglas M. 1995. "The Death of Contractarianism and the Vindication of Structure and Authority in Corporate Governance and Corporate Law." Pp. 93–110 in Lawrence E. Mitchell (Ed.). *Progressive Corporate Law*. Boulder, CO: Westview.

Bratton, William W. Jr. 1989a. "The New Economic Theory of the Firm: Critical Perspectives from History. *Stanford Law Review* 41:1471–1527.

———. 1989b. "The 'Nexus of Contracts' Corporation: A Critical Appraisal." *Cornell Law Review* 74:407–65.

———. 1992. "Public Values and Corporate Fiduciary Law." *Rutgers Law Review* 44:675–98.

———. 1993. "Confronting the Ethical Case against the Ethical Case for Constituency Rights." *Washington and Lee Law Review* 50:1449–75.

———. 1995. "Game Theory and the Restoration of Honor to Corporate Law's Duty of Loyalty." Pp. 139–83 in Lawrence E. Mitchell (Ed.). *Progressive Corporate Law*. Boulder, CO: Westview.

Brennan, Geoffrey, and James M. Buchanan. 1985. *The Reason of Rules: Constitutional Political Economy*. Cambridge: Cambridge University Press.

Brown, Grover C., Michael J. Maimone, and Joseph C. Schoell. 1998. "Director and Advisor Disinterestedness and Independence Under Delaware Law." *Delaware Journal of Corporate Law* 23:1157–1201.

Brudney, Victor. 1985. "Corporate Governance, Agency Costs, and the Rhetoric of Contract." *Columbia Law Review* 85:1403–1444.

———. 1997. "Contract and Fiduciary Duty in Corporate Law." *Boston College Law Review* 38:595–665.

Brudney, Victor, and Marvin A. Chirelstein. 1978. "A Restatement of Corporate Freeze-Outs." *Yale Law Journal* 87:1354–75.

Bruyn, Severyn T. 1991. *A Future for the American Economy: The Social Market*. Stanford, CA: Stanford University Press.

Buchanan, Scott. 1958. *The Corporation and the Republic*. New York: Fund for the Republic [28-page pamphlet].

Bumiller, Krisin. 1988. *The Civil Rights Society: The Social Construction of Victims*. Baltimore: Johns Hopkins University Press.

Burk, James. 1988. *Values in the Marketplace: The American Stock Market under Federal Securities Law*. Berlin: Walter de Gruyter.

Burrough, Bryan, and John Helyar. 1990. *Barbarians at the Gate: The Fall of RJR Nabisco*. New York: Harper and Row.

Butler, Henry N. 1989. "The Contractual Theory of the Corporation." *George Mason University Law Review* 11:99–123.

Butler, Henry N., and Larry E. Ribstein. 1990. "Opting Out of Fiduciary Duties: A Response to the Anticontractarians." *Washington Law Review* 65:1–72.

———. 1995. *The Corporation and the Constitution*. Washington, DC: American Enterprise Institute Press.

Buxbaum, Richard M. 1994. "Comparative Aspects of Institutional Investment and Corporate Governance." Pp. 3–21 in Theodore Baums, Richard Buxbaum, and Klaus J. Hopt (Eds.). 1994. *Institutional Investors and Corporate Governance*. Berlin: Walter de Gruyter.

Calomiris, Charles W., and Carlos D. Ramirez. 1996. "Financing the American Corporation: The Changing Menu of Financial Relationship." Pp. 128–86 in Carl Kaysen (Ed.). *The American Corporation Today*. New York: Oxford University Press.

Campbell, John L., J. Rogers Hollingsworth, and Leon N. Lindberg (Eds). 1991. *Governance of the American Economy*. Cambridge: Cambridge University Press.

Carlton, Dennis W., and Daniel R. Fischel. 1983. "The Regulation of Insider Trading." *Stanford Law Review* 35:857–95.

Carver, Anne. 1997. "Corporate Governance—Capitalism's Fellow Traveller." Pp. 69–88 in Fiona Macmillan Patfield (Ed.). *Perspectives on Company Law*. Vol. 2. London: Kluwer Law International.

Cary, William L. 1974. "Federalism and Corporate Law: Reflections upon Delaware." *Yale Law Journal* 83:663–705.

Cary, William L., and Melvin Aron Eisenberg. 1988. *Corporations: Cases and Materials.* 6th ed. Mineola, NY: Foundation Press.

Chandler, Alfred D. Jr. 1962. *Strategy and Structure: Chapters in the History of the American Industrial Enterprise.* Cambridge, MA: MIT Press.

———. 1977. *The Visible Hand: The Managerial Revolution in American Business.* Cambridge: Harvard University Press.

———. 1990. *Scale and Scope: The Dynamics of Industrial Capitalism.* Cambridge: Harvard University Press.

Charkham, Jonathan P. 1994. *Keeping Good Company: A Study of Corporate Governance in Five Countries.* Oxford, UK: Clarendon Press.

Clark, Robert C. 1989. "Contracts, Elites, and Traditions in the Making of Corporate Law." *Columbia Law Review* 89:1703–47.

Clarke, Lee, and James F. Short Jr. 1993. "Social Organization and Risk: Some Current Controversies." *Annual Review of Sociology* 19:375–99.

Cleaves, Peter S. 1987. *Professions and the State: The Mexican Case.* Tucson: University of Arizona Press.

Clurman, Richard M. 1992. *To the End of Time: The Seduction and Conquest of a Media Empire.* New York: Simon and Schuster.

Coase, R. H. (1937) 1988. "The Nature of the Firm." Pp. 33–55 in *The Firm, the Market, and the Law.* Chicago: University of Chicago Press.

———. (1960) 1988. "The Problem of Social Cost." Pp. 95–156 in *The Firm, the Market, and the Law.* Chicago: University of Chicago Press.

Coffee, John C. Jr. 1981. "From Tort to Crime: Some Reflections on the Criminalization of Fiduciary Breaches and the Problematic Line between Law and Ethics." *American Criminal Law Review* 19:117–72.

———. 1986. "Shareholders versus Managers: The Strain in the Corporate Web." *Michigan Law Review* 85:1–109.

———. 1989. "The Mandatory/Enabling Balance in Corporate Law: An Essay on the Judicial Role." *Columbia Law Review* 89:1618–91.

———. 1990. "Unstable Coalitions: Corporate Governance as a Multi-Player Game." *Georgetown Law Journal* 78:1495–1549.

Coleman, James S. 1990. *Foundations of Social Theory.* Cambridge: Harvard University Press.

Cookson, Peter W. Jr., and Caroline Hodges Persell. 1985. *Preparing for Power: America's Elite Boarding Schools.* New York: Basic.

Core, John E., Robert W. Holthausen, and David F. Larcker. 1999. "Corporate Governance, CEO Compensation, and Firm Performance." *Journal of Financial Economics* 51:317–406.

Cornes, Richard, and Todd Sandler. 1986. *The Theory of Externalities, Public Goods, and Club Goods.* Cambridge: Cambridge University Press.

Cornett, Marcia Million, and Hassan Tehranian. 1992. "Changes in Corporate Performance Associated with Bank Acquisitions." *Journal of Financial Economics* 31:211–34.

Cowan, Alison Leigh. 1993. "Caution Signal for Corporate Boards." *New York Times* (November 25).

———. 1994. "The Business of Bankruptcy Hits Hard Times of Its Own." *New York Times* (January 12).

Cowen, Tyler. 1988. "Public Goods and Externalities: Old and New Perspectives." Pp. 1–26 in Tyler Cowen (Ed). *The Theory of Market Failure: A Critical Examination*. Fairfax, VA: George Mason University Press.

Craypo, Charles, and Bruce Nissen (Eds.). 1993. *Grand Designs: The Impact of Corporate Strategies on Workers, Unions, and Communities*. Ithaca, NY: ILR Press [School of Industrial and Labor Relations, Cornell University].

Cunningham, Lawrence A., and Charles M. Yablon. 1994. "Delaware Fiduciary Duty Law after QVC and Technicolor: A Unified Standard (and the End of Revlon Duties?)." *Business Lawyer* 49:1593–1628.

Dahlman, Carl L. 1988. "The Problem of Externality." Pp. 209–34 in Tyler Cowen (Ed.). *The Theory of Market Failure: A Critical Examination*. Fairfax, VA: George Mason University Press.

Dallas, Lynne L. 1995. "Working toward a New Paradigm." Pp. 35–65 in Lawrence E. Mitchell (Ed.). *Progressive Corporate Law*. Boulder, CO: Westview.

———. 1997. "The Global Corporate Board of Directors: A Proposal for Reform." Pp. 109–19 in Fiona Macmillan Patfield (Ed.). *Perspectives on Company Law*. Vol. 2. London: Kluwer Law International.

Davis, Gerald F., Kristina A. Diekmann, and Catherine H. Tinsley. 1994. "The Decline and Fall of the Conglomerate Firm in the 1980s: The Deinstitutionalization of an Organizational Form." *American Sociological Review* 59:547–70.

Davis, Gerald F., and Henrich R. Greve. 1997. "Corporate Elite Networks and Governance Changes in the 1980s." *American Journal of Sociology* 103:1–37.

Davis, Gerald F., and Tracy A. Thompson. 1994. "A Social Movement Perspective on Corporate Control." *Administrative Science Quarterly* 39:141–73.

Davis, Lewis U., et. al. 1991. "Corporate Reorganization in the 1990s: Guiding Directors of Troubled Corporations through Uncertain Territory." *Business Lawyer* 47:1–32.

DeBow, Michael E., and Dwight R. Lee. 1993. "Shareholders, Nonshareholders, and Corporate Law: Communitarianism and Resource Allocation." *Delaware Journal of Corporate Law* 18:393–424.

Delaney, Kevin J. 1992. *Strategic Bankruptcy: How Corporations and Creditors Use Chapter 11 to Their Advantage*. Berkeley: University of California Press.

Demo, David H. 1992. "The Self-Concept over Time: Research Issues and Directions." *Annual Review of Sociology* 18:303–26.

DeMott, Deborah A. 1988. "Beyond Metaphor: An Analysis of Fiduciary Obligation." *Duke Law Journal* 1988:879–924.

Demsetz, Harold. 1988. *Ownership, Control, and the Firm.* Vol. 1, *The Organization of Economic Activity.* Oxford, UK: Basil Blackwell.

Demsetz, Harold, and Kenneth Lehn. 1985. "The Structure of Corporate Onwership: Causes and Consequences." *Journal of Political Economy* 93:1155–77.

Dent, George W. Jr. 1989. "Toward Unifying Ownership and Control in the Public Corporation." *Wisconsin Law Review* 1989:881–924.

DiMaggio, Paul J. 1994. "Culture and Economy." Pp. 27–57 in Richard J. Smelser and Richard Swedberg (Eds.). *The Handbook of Economic Sociology.* Princeton, NJ: Princeton University Press.

DiMaggio, Paul J., and Walter W. Powell. 1983. "The Iron Cage Revisited: Institutional Isomorphism and Collective Rationality in Organizational Fields." *American Sociological Review* 48:147–60.

Donaldson, Thomas, and L. E. Preston. 1995. "The Stakeholder Theory of the Corporation: Concepts, Evidence, and Implications." *Academy of Management Review* 20:65–91.

Douglas, Mary. 1985. *Risk Acceptability According to the Social Sciences.* New York: Russell Sage.

Dragun, Andrew K. 1983. "Externalities, Property Rights, and Power." *Journal of Economic Issues* 17:667–80, reprinted in Warren J. Samuels (Ed.). 1988. *Institutional Economics.* Vol. 3. Hants, UK: Edward Elgar (pp. 324–37).

Dugger, William M. 1989. *Corporate Hegemony.* New York: Greenwood.

Dunne, John Gregory. 1992. "Your Time Is My Time" [review of Clurman. 1992. *To the End of Time*]. *New York Review of Books* 39 (8): 49–55.

Duverger, Maurice. 1963. *Political Parties.* New York: John Wiley.

Dworkin, Ronald. 1986. *Law's Empire.* Cambridge: Harvard University Press.

Easterbrook, Frank H., and Daniel R. Fischel. 1981. "The Proper Role of a Target's Management in Responding to a Tender Offer." *Harvard Law Review* 94: 1161–1204.

———. 1982. "Corporate Control Transactions." *Yale Law Journal* 91:698–737.

———. 1983. "Voting in Corporate Law." *Journal of Law and Economics* 26: 395–428.

———. 1991. *The Economic Structure of Corporate Law.* Cambridge: Harvard University Press.

———. 1993. "Contract and Fiduciary Duty." *Journal of Law and Economics* 34:425–46.

Eaton, Leslie. 1994a. "1980s Redux? Deals Making a Comeback." *New York Times* (July 17, Section 3).

———. 1994b. "Paine Webber to Bail Out Fund Battered by Complex Securities." *New York Times* (July 23).

Eisenberg, Melvin Aron. 1988. *The Nature of the Common Law*. Cambridge: Harvard University Press.

———. 1989. "The Structure of Corporation Law." *Columbia Law Review* 89: 1461–1525.

———. 1990a. "Contractarianism without Contracts: A Response to Professor Mc-Chesney." *Columbia Law Review* 90:1321–31.

———. 1990b. "Bad Arguments in Corporate Law." *Georgetown Law Journal* 78: 1551–58.

Eisenstadt, S. N. 1996. *Japanese Civilization: A Comparative View*. Chicago: University of Chicago Press.

Etzioni, Amitai. 1968. *The Active Society: A Theory of Societal and Political Processes*. New York: Free Press.

———. 1988. *The Moral Dimension: Toward a New Economics*. New York: Free Press.

———. 1993. *The Spirit of Community: The Reinvention of American Society*. New York: Touchstone.

———. 1996. *The New Golden Rule: Community and Morality in Democratic Society*. New York: Basic.

Etzioni-Halevy, Eva. 1989. *Fragile Democracy: The Use and Abuse of Power in Western Societies*. New Brunswick, NJ: Transaction.

Fabrikant, Geraldine. 1993a. "QVC Network Wins Court Round In Its Bid to Take Over Paramount." *New York Times* (November 25).

———. 1993b. "Delaware Court Ruling Aids QVC in Struggle to Acquire Paramount." *New York Times* (December 10).

———. 1994. "Who'll Survive in Media Deal?" *New York Times* (January 10).

Fama, Eugene F. 1980. "Agency Problems and the Theory of the Firm." *Journal of Political Economy* 88:288–307

Fama, Eugene F., and Michael C. Jensen. 1983. "Separation of Ownership and Control." *Journal of Law and Economics* 26:301–25.

Fine, Gary Alan. 1993. "The Sad Demise, Mysterious Disappearance, and Glorious Triumph of Symbolic Interactionism." *Annual Review of Sociology* 19:61–87.

Finkelstein, Syndey, and Donald C. Hambrick. 1996. *Strategic Leadership: Top Executives and Their Effects on Organizations*. Minneapolis/St. Paul, MN: West.

Fischel, Daniel R. 1978. "Efficient Capital Market Theory, the Market for Corporate Control, and the Regulation of Cash Tender Offers." *Texas Law Review* 57:1–46.

———. 1982. "The Corporate Governance Movement." *Vanderbilt Law Review* 35:1259–92.

———. 1984. "Labor Markets and Labor Law as Compared with Capital Markets and Corporate Law." *University of Chicago Law Review* 51:1061–77.

Fisher, Lawrence M., and Laura M. Holson. 1998. "Mentor Makes a Hostile Bid for Quickturn." *New York Times* (August 13).

Fligstein, Neil. 1985. "The Spread of the Multidivisional Form among Large Firms, 1919–1979." *American Sociological Review* 50:377–91.

———. 1990. *The Transformation of Corporate Control.* Cambridge: Harvard University Press.

———. 1996. "Markets as Politics: A Political-Cultural Approach to Market Institutions." *American Sociological Review* 61:656–73.

Folk, Ernest L. III, Rodman Ward Jr., and Edward P. Welch. 1998. *Folk on The Delaware General Corporation Law: A Commentary and Analysis.* 3d ed. 3 vols. New York: Aspen Law and Business, Aspen Publishers.

Frankel, Tamar. 1983. "Fiduciary Law." *California Law Review* 71:795–836.

Frankford, David M. 1994. "The Critical Potential of the Common Law Tradition" [Review Essay on *Theory of Societal Constitutionalism*]. *Columbia Law Review* 94:1076–1123.

Freedman, Judith. 1995. "Reforming Company Law." Pp. 197–221 in Fiona Macmillan Patfield (Ed.). *Perspectives on Company Law.* Vol. 1. London: Kluwer Law International.

Freeman, R. Edward. 1984. *Strategic Management: A Stakeholder Approach.* Boston: Pittman.

Freeman, R. E., and W. M. Evan. 1990. "Corporate Governance: A Stakeholder Interpretation." *Journal of Behavioral Economics* 19:337–59.

Freud, Sigmund. (1930) 1961. *Civilization and Its Discontents.* New York: W. W. Norton.

Freudenheim, Milt. 1992. "Medical Insurance Is Being Cut Back for Many Retirees: Most Appeals Court Decisions Uphold Employers' Rights to Change Benefit Plans." *New York Times* (June 28).

Friedman, Benjamin M. 1988. *Day of Reckoning: The Consequences of American Economic Policy under Reagan and After.* New York: Random House.

Friedman, Lawrence M. 1973/1985. *A History of American Law.* New York: Simon and Schuster.

Friedrich, Carl J. 1941. *Constitutional Government and Democracy: Theory and Practice in Europe and America.* Boston: Little Brown.

———. 1974. *Limited Government: A Comparison.* Englewood Cliffs, NJ: Prentice-Hall.

Frug, Gerald E. 1980. "The City as a Legal Concept." *Harvard Law Review* 93: 1059–1154.

———. 1984. "The Ideology of Bureaucracy in American Law." *Harvard Law Review* 97:1276–1388.

Fuller, Lon L. (1964/1969) 1975. *The Morality of Law.* Rev. ed. New Haven: Yale University Press.

Gabaldon, Theresa. 1995. "Experiencing Limited Liability: On Insularity and Inbreeding in Corporate Law." Pp. 110–37 in Lawrence E. Mitchell (Ed.). *Progressive Corporate Law.* Boulder, CO: Westview.

Galbraith, John Kenneth. (1967) 1971. *The New Industrial State*. Boston: Houghton Mifflin.

Giddens, Anthony. 1984. *The Constitution of Society: Outline of the Theory of Structuration*. Cambridge, UK: Polity.

Gilpin, Kenneth N. 1998. "Finding Flaws in an Old Barometer." *New York Times* (July 19).

Gilson, Ronald J. 1981. "A Structural Approach to Corporations: The Case against Defensive Tactics in Tender Offers." *Stanford Law Review* 33:819–91.

Goldman, David P. 1998. "Make Way for Junk." *Forbes Magazine* (April 20).

Goldsmith, Jack L. III. 1989. "Interest Analysis Applied to Corporations: The Unprincipled Use of a Choice of Law Method." *Yale Law Journal* 98:592–616.

Gordon, David M. 1996. *Fat and Mean: The Corporate Squeeze of Working Americans and the Myth of Managerial "Downsizing."* New York: Free Press.

Gordon, Jeffrey N. 1989. "The Mandatory Structure of Corporate Law." *Columbia Law Review* 89:1549–98.

———. 1991. "Corporations, Markets, and Courts." *Columbia Law Review* 91: 1931–88.

Green, Ronald M. 1993. "Shareholders as Stakeholders: Changing Metaphors of Corporate Governance." *Washington and Lee Law* Review 50:1409–21.

Greenfield, Kent. 1997. "From Rights to Regulation in Corporate Law." Pp. 1–25 in Fiona Macmillan Patfield (Ed.). *Perspectives on Company Law*. Vol. 2. London: Kluwer Law International.

Haar, Charles M., and Daniel W. Fessler. 1986. *The Wrong Side of the Tracks: A Revolutionary Rediscovery of the Common Law Tradition of Fairness in the Struggle against Inequality*. New York: Simon and Schuster.

Habermas, Jurgen. (1967) 1988. *On the Logic of the Social Sciences*. Cambridge, MA: MIT Press.

———.(1968) 1972. *Knowledge and Human Interests*. Boston: Beacon Press.

Haddock, David C., Jonathan R. Macey, and Fred S. McChesney. 1987. "Property Rights in Assets and Resistance to Tender Offers." *Virginia Law Review* 73: 701–46.

Halle, David. 1992. "The Audience for Abstract Art: Class, Culture, and Power." Pp. 131–51 in Michele Lamont and Marcel Fournier (Eds.). *Cultivating Differences: Symbolic Boundaries and the Making of Inequality*. Chicago: University of Chicago Press.

Hamilton, Gary G., and Nicole Woolsey Biggart. (1988) 1992. "Market, Culture, and Authority: A Comparative Analysis of Management and Organization in the Far East." Pp. 181–221 in Mark Granovetter and Richard Swedberg (Eds.). *The Sociology of Economic Life*. Boulder, CO: Westview.

Hannan, Michael T., and Glenn R. Carroll. 1992. *Dynamics of Organizational Populations: Density, Legitimation, and Competition*. New York: Oxford University Press.

Hannan, Michael, and John Freeman. 1989. *Organizational Ecology.* Cambridge: Harvard University Press.

Hansen, Charles. 1991. "Other Constituency Statutes: A Search for Perspective." *Business Lawyer* 46: 1355–75.

Hansell, Saul. 1994. "G.A.O. Study Seeks Regulation of Derivatives." *New York Times* (May 19).

———. 1998. "Computer Associates Drops Hostile Bid for Computer Sciences Corp." *New York Times* (March 6).

Harrison, Bennett. 1994. *Lean and Mean: Why Large Corporations Will Continue to Dominate the Global Economy.* New York: Guilford.

Hart, Oliver. 1989. "An Economist's Perspective on the Theory of the Firm." *Columbia Law Review* 89:1757–74.

Hartman, Rima Fawal. 1993. "Situation-Specific Fiduciary Duties for Corporate Directors: Enforceable Obligations or Toothless Ideals?" *Washington and Lee Law Review* 50:1761–90.

Hawkins, Keith. 1984. *Environment and Enforcement.* Oxford, UK: Clarendon.

Healey, Paul M., Krishna G. Palepu, and Richard S. Ruback. 1992. "Does Corporate Performance Improve after Mergers?" *Journal of Financial Economics* 31:135–75.

Hechter, Michael. 1987. *Principles of Group Solidarity.* Berkeley: University of California Press.

Heimer, Carol A. 1988. "Social Structure, Psychology, and the Estimation of Risk." *Annual Review of Sociology* 14:491–519.

Henriques, Diana B. 1991. "A Revival Is Seen for 'Junk Bonds' as Market Gains." *New York Times* (June 26).

Herman, Edward S. (1981) 1982. *Corporate Control, Corporate Power: A Twentieth Century Fund Study.* Cambridge: Cambridge University Press.

Hessen, Robert. 1979. "A New Concept of Corporations: A Contractual and Private Property Model." *Hastings Law Journal* 30:1327–50.

Heyman, Kurt M. 1998. "Expedited Proceedings in the Delaware Court of Chancery: Things of the Past?" *Delaware Journal of Corporate Law* 23:145–70.

Higley, John, and Michael G. Burton. 1989. "The Elite Variable in Democratic Transitions and Breakdowns." *American Sociological Review* 54:17–32.

Higley, John, et al. 1991. "Elite Integration in Stable Democracies: A Reconsideration." *European Sociological Review* 7:35–53.

Holson, Laura M. 1998. "The Incredible Shrinking Banker." *New York Times* (August 2).

———. 1999a. "In Nabisco's Return to Its Older Self, Memories of a Buyout Strategy's Flaws." *New York Times* (March 14).

———. 1999b. "Global Consolidation Redefines the Hostile Takeover." *New York Times* (November 12).

Hopt, Klaus J., and Gunther Teubner (Eds.). 1985. *Corporate Governance and*

Director's Liabilities: Legal, Economic, and Sociological Analyses of Corporate Social Responsibility. New York: Aldine de Gruyter.

Houle, Cyril O. 1960. *The Effective Board*. New York: Association Press.

———. 1989. *Governing Boards*. San Francisco: Jossey-Bass.

Hovenkamp, Herbert. 1991. *Enterprise and American Law, 1836–1937*. Cambridge: Harvard University Press.

Hurst, James Willard. 1970. *The Legitimacy of the Business Corporation in the Law of the United States, 1780–1970*. Charlottesville: University of Virginia Press.

Hylton, Richard D. 1992. "Rockefellers Trying to Keep a Fortune From Dissipating." *New York Times* (February 16).

Jacobs, (Vice Chancellor) Jack B. 1993. "Excerpts from Ruling in Paramount Case." *New York Times* (November 25).

Janofsky, Michael. 1993. "Ruling on QVC Bid Faces an Expert Review." *New York Times* (November 26).

Jensen, Michael C. 1988. "Takeovers: Their Causes and Consequences." *Journal of Economic Perspectives* 2:21–48.

Jensen, Michael C., and William H. Meckling. 1976. "Theory of the Firm: Managerial Behavior, Agency Costs, and Ownership Structure." *Journal of Financial Economics* 3:305–60.

Johnson, Lyman. 1990. "The Delaware Judiciary and the Meaning of Corporate Life and Corporate Law." *Texas Law Review* 68:865–936.

———. 1992. "Individual and Collective Sovereignty in the Corporate Enterprise" [review of Frank H. Easterbrook and Daniel R. Fischel. 1991. *The Economic Structure of Corporate Law* (Cambridge: Harvard University Press) and Robert N. Bellah et al. 1991. *The Good Society* (New York: Knopf)]. *Columbia Law Review* 92:2215–49.

———. 1993. "Conclusion: New Approaches to Corporate Law." *Washington and Lee Law Review* 50:1713–23.

Johnson, Lyman and David Millon. 1990. "The Case beyond Time." *Business Lawyer* 45:2105–25.

Kahneman, Daniel, and Amos Tversky. 1979. "Prospect Theory: An Analysis of Decision under Risk." *Econometrica* 47:263–91.

Kanter, Rosabeth M. 1977. *Men and Women of the Corporation*. New York: Basic.

Kaouris, Demetrios G. 1995. "Is Delaware Still a Haven for Incorporation?" *Delaware Journal of Corporate Law* 20:965–1043.

Katz, Jack. 1988. *Seductions of Crime: Moral and Sensual Attractions in Doing Evil*. New York: Basic.

Kay, John, and Aubrey Silberston. 1997. "Corporate Governance." Pp. 49–67 in Fiona Macmillan Patfield (Ed.). *Perspectives on Company Law*. Vol. 2. London: Kluwer Law International.

Kaysen, Carl. 1996a. "Introduction and Overview." Pp. 3–27 in Kaysen (Ed.). *The American Corporation Today*. New York: Oxford University Press.

————— (Ed.). 1996b. *The American Corporation Today.* New York: Oxford University Press.

Kester, W. Carl. 1991. *Japanese Takeovers: The Global Contest for Corporate Control.* Boston: Harvard Business School Press.

Keynes, John Maynard. 1936. *The General Theory of Employment Interest and Money.* New York: Harcourt, Brace.

Kilborn, Peter T. 1999. "Help Desperately Wanted, So the Help Can Be Fussy." *New York Times* (November 6).

Klein, William A. 1982. "The Modern Business Organization: Bargaining under Constraints." *Yale Law Journal* 91:1521–64.

Knight, Frank. 1921/1948. *Risk, Uncertainty, and Profit.* Boston: Houghton Mifflin

Knowlton, Winthrop, and Ira M. Millstein. 1988. "Can the Board of Directors Help the American Corporation Earn the Immortality It Holds So Dear?" Pp. 169–191 in John R. Meyer and James M. Gustafson (Eds.). *The U.S. Business Corporation: An Institution in Transition.* Cambridge, MA: Ballinger.

Kozyris, P. John. 1989. "Corporate Takeovers at the Jurisdictional Crossroads: Preserving State Authority over Internal Affairs While Protecting the Transferability of Interstate Stock through Federal Law." *UCLA Law Review* 36:1109–66.

Kraakman, Reiner H. 1984. "Corporate Liability Strategies and the Costs of Legal Controls." *Yale Law Journal* 93:857–98.

Kroll, Luisa. 1997. "Catching Up." *Forbes Magazine* (May 19).

—————. 1998. "Warning: Capitalism Is Contagious." *Forbes Magazine* (May 18).

Lamont, Michele. 1992. *Money, Morals, and Manners: The Culture of the French and American Upper-Middle Class.* Chicago: University of Chicago Press.

Lamont, Michele, and Marcel Fournier (Eds.). 1992. *Cultivating Differences: Symbolic Boundaries and the Making of Inequality.* Chicago: University of Chicago Press.

Leventhal, Gerald S. 1980. "What Should Be Done with Equity Theory? New Approaches to the Study of Fairness in Social Relationships." Pp. 27–55 in Kenneth J. Gergen et al. (Eds.). *Social Exchange: Advances in Theory and Research.* New York: Plenum Press.

Lindberg, Leon N., and John L. Campbell. 1991. "The State and the Organization of Economic Activity." Pp. 356–95 in John L. Campbell, J. Rogers Hollingsworth, and Leon N. Lindberg (Eds.). *Governance of the American Economy.* Cambridge: Cambridge University Press.

Lindberg, Leon N., John L. Campbell, and J. Rogers Hollingsworth. 1991. "Economic Governance and the Analysis of Structural Change in the American Economy." Pp. 3–34 in John L. Campbell, J. Rogers Hollingsworth, and Leon N. Lindberg (Eds.). *Governance of the American Economy.* Cambridge: Cambridge University Press.

Lipton, Martin. 1987. "Corporate Governance in the Age of Finance Corporatism." *University of Pennsylvania Law Review* 136:1–72.

Litt, David G., et. al. 1990. "Politics, Bureaucracies, and Financial Markets: Bank Entry into Commercial Paper Underwriting in the United States and Japan." *University of Pennsylvania Law Review* 139:369–453.

Loewenstein, Mark J. 1989. "Toward an Auction Market for Corporate Control and the Demise of the Business Judgment Rule." *Southern California Law Review* 63:65–105.

———. 1999. "Shareholder Derivative Litigation and Corporate Governance." *Delaware Journal of Corporate Law* 24:1–26.

Lohr, Steve. 1992. "Amid Layoffs and the Recession, Executives' Pay Is under Scrutiny." *New York Times* (January 20).

———. 1994. "Economic Recovery: Manhandle with Care." *New York Times* (February 13, Section 4).

Lorey, David E. 1992. *The Rise of the Professions in Twentieth Century Mexico*. Los Angeles: UCLA Latin American Center Publications.

Lorsch, Jay W. (with Elizabeth MacIver). 1989. *Pawns or Potentates: The Reality of America's Corporate Boards*. Boston: Harvard Business School Press.

Lowi, Theodore. 1969. *The End of Liberalism: Ideology, Policy, and the Crisis of Public Authority*. New York: W. W. Norton.

Ludwig, Mary S. 1993. *Understanding Interest Rate Swaps*. New York: McGraw-Hill.

Luhmann, Niklas. 1993. *Risk: A Sociological Theory*. New York: Aldine de Gruyter.

Mace, Myles L. (1971) 1986. *Directors: Myth and Reality*. Boston: Harvard Business School Press.

Macey, Jonathan R. 1989. "Externalities, Firm-Specific Capital Investments, and the Legal Treatment of Fundamental Corporate Changes." *Duke Law Journal* 1989:173–201.

Madison, James, Alexander Hamilton, and John Jay. (1788) 1987. *Federalist Papers*. London: Penguin Books.

Maffesoli, Michel. (1985) 1993. *The Shadow of Dionysus: A Contribution to the Sociology of the Orgy*. Albany: State University of New York Press.

Manne, Henry G. 1965. "Mergers and the Market for Corporate Control." *Journal of Political Economy* 73:110–20.

Mark, Gregory A. 1987. "The Personification of the Business Corporation in American Law." *University of Chicago Law Review* 54:1441–83.

———. 1995. "Some Observations on Writing the Legal History of the Corporation in the Age of Theory." Pp. 67–92 in Lawrence E. Mitchell (Ed.). *Progressive Corporate Law*. Boulder, CO: Westview.

McChesney, Fred S. 1989. "Economics, Law, and Science in the Corporate Field: A Critique of Eisenberg." *Columbia Law Review* 89:1530–48.

———. 1990. "Contractarianism without Contracts? Yet Another Critique of Eisenberg." *Columbia Law Review* 90:1332–39.

McDowell, Gary L. 1982. *Equity and the Constitution: The Supreme Court, Equitable Relief, and Public Policy*. Chicago: University of Chicago Press.

————. 1988. *Curbing the Courts: The Constitution and the Limits of Judicial Power.* Baton Rouge: Louisiana State University Press.

Menaghan, Elizabeth G. 1991. "Work Experiences and Family Interaction Processes: The Long Reach of the Job?" *Annual Review of Sociology* 17: 419–44.

Meyer, John, and Brian Rowan. 1977. "Institutionalized Organizations: Formal Structure as Myth and Ceremony." *American Journal of Sociology* 82:431–50.

Meyer, Marshall W. 1994. "Measuring Performance in Economic Organizations." Pp. 556–87 in Neil J. Smelser and Richard Swedberg (Eds.). *The Handbook of Economic Sociology.* Princeton, NJ: Princeton University Press.

Michels, Robert. (1911) 1949. *Political Parties.* Glencoe, IL: Free Press.

Millerson, Geoffrey. 1964. *The Qualifying Associations.* New York: Humanities Press.

Millon, David. 1990. "Theories of the Corporation." *Duke Law Journal* 1990: 201–62.

————. 1993. "Communitarians, Contractarians, and the Crisis in Corporate Law." *Washington and Lee Law Review* 50:1373–93.

————. 1995. "Communitarianism in Corporate Law: Foundations and Law Reform Strategies." Pp. 1–33 in Lawrence E. Mitchell (Ed.). *Progressive Corporate Law.* Boulder, CO: Westview.

Mills, Geoffrey. (1981) 1985. *On the Board.* London: George Adler & Unwin.

Mintzberg, Henry. 1983. *Power in and around Organizations.* Englewood Cliffs, NJ: Prentice-Hall.

Mitchell, Lawrence E. 1990a. "The Fairness Rights of Corporate Bondholders." *New York University Law Review* 65:1165–1229.

————. 1990b. "The Death of Fiduciary Duty in Close Corporations." *University of Pennsylvania Law Review* 138:1675–1731.

————. 1992. "A Theoretical and Practical Framework for Enforcing Corporate Constituency Statutes." *Texas Law Review* 70:579–643.

————. 1993. "Groundwork of the Metaphysics of Corporate Law." *Washington and Lee Law Review* 50:1477–88.

Mitchell, Lawrence E. (Ed.). 1995. *Progressive Corporate Law.* Boulder, CO: Westview.

Mizruchi, Mark. 1996. "What Do Interlocks Do? An Analysis, Critique, and Assessment of Research on Interlocking Directorates." *Annual Review of Sociology* 22:271–98.

Morrill, Calvin. 1991. "Conflict Management, Honor, and Organizational Change." *American Journal of Sociology* 97:585–621.

————. 1995. *The Executive Way.* Chicago: University of Chicago Press.

Mueller, Robert Kirk. 1974. *Board Life.* New York: Amacom.

————. 1984. *Behind the Boardroom Door.* New York: Crown.

Nakane, Chie. 1970. *Japanese Society.* London: Weidenfeld and Nicolson.

Newman, Karen L. 1993. "The Just Organization: Creating and Maintaining Justice in Work Environments." *Washington and Lee Law Review* 50:1489–1513.

Nietzsche, Friedrich. (1887) 1969. *On the Genealogy of Morals*. New York: Vintage.

Noble, Barbara Presley. 1992. "Endangered: Retiree Health Benefits." *New York Times* (February 9, Section 3).

Nohria, Nitin, and Ranjay Gulati. 1994. "Firms and Their Environments." Pp. 529–55 in Neil J. Smelser and Richard Swedberg (Eds.). *The Handbook of Economic Sociology*. Princeton, NJ: Princeton University Press.

Norris, Floyd. 1992. "Swapping Woes: A Fed Official Sees Problems." *New York Times* (February 9, Section 3).

———. 1993. "Delaware Law: From a Muddle, Owners Win." *New York Times* (November 28, Section 3).

———. 1994. "Can't Tell Viacom From QVC?" *New York Times* (January 30, Section 4).

———. 1999. "Is $2 Billion Fair Payment for a Fiancee Left at the Altar?" *New York Times* (November 5).

Note. 1982. "Constitutional Rights of the Corporate Person." *Yale Law Journal* 91:1641–1658.

O'Connor, Marleen A. 1995. "Promoting Economic Justice in Plant Closings: Exploring the Fiduciary/Contract Law Distinction to Enforce Implicit Employment Agreements." Pp. 219–45 in Lawrence E. Mitchell (Ed.). 1995. *Progressive Corporate Law*. Boulder, CO: Westview.

O'Donnell, Guillermo, Philippe C. Schmitter, and Laurence Whitehead (Eds.). 1986. *Transitions from Authoritarian Rule*. 5 vols. Baltimore: Johns Hopkins University Press.

Olson, John M. 1992. "The Fiduciary Duty of Insurgent Boards." *Business Lawyer* 47:1011–29.

Orts, Eric W. 1992. "Beyond Shareholders: Interpreting Corporate Constituency Statutes." *George Washington Law Review* 61:14–135.

———. 1993. "The Complexity and Legitimacy of Corporate Law." *Washington and Lee Law Review* 50:1565–1623.

———. 1995. "The Legitimacy of Multinational Corporations." Pp. 247–79 in Lawrence E. Mitchell (Ed.). *Progressive Corporate Law*. Boulder, CO: Westview.

———. 1998a. "The Future of Enterprise Organization." *Michigan Law Review* 96:1947–74.

———. 1998b. "Shirking and Sharking: A Legal Theory of the Firm." *Yale Law & Policy Review* 16:265–329.

Ouchi, William G., and Alan L. Wilkins. 1985. "Organizational Culture." *Annual Review of Sociology* 11:457–83.

Palmer, Donald, et al. 1995. "The Friendly and Predatory Acquisition of Large U.S. Corporations in the 1960s: The Other Contested Terrain." *American Sociological Review* 60:469–99.

Palmiter, Alan R. 1989. "Reshaping the Corporate Fiduciary Model: A Director's Duty of Independence." *Texas Law Review* 67:1351–1464.

Parkes, Joseph. 1828. *A History of the Court of Chancery*. London: Longman, Rees, Orme, Brown and Green.

Parkinson, J. E. 1993. *Corporate Power and Responsibility: Issues in the Theory of Company Law*. Oxford, UK: Clarendon Press.

Parsons, Talcott. (1937) 1968. *The Structure of Social Action*. 2 vols. New York: Free Press.

———.(1964) 1967. "Evolutionary Universals in Sociology." Pp. 500–14 in *Sociological Theory and Modern Society*. New York: Free Press.

———. (1968) 1969. "On the Concept of Value Commitments." Pp. 439–72 in *Politics and Social Structure*. New York: Free Press.

Patfield, Fiona Macmillan (Ed.). 1995. *Perspectives on Company Law*. Vol. I. London: Kluwer Law International.

———. 1997. *Perspectives on Company Law*. Vol. 2. London: Kluwer Law International.

Peck, Cornelius J. 1993. "U.S. Should Regulate Corporate Maneuvers." Letter to the *New York Times* (December 4).

Perez-Diaz, Victor M. 1993. *The Return of Civil Society: The Emergence of Democratic Spain*. Cambridge: Harvard University Press.

Pfeffer, Jeffrey. 1972. "Size and Composition of Corporate Boards of Directors: The Organization and Its Environment." *Administrative Science Quarterly* 17:218–28.

Pfeffer, Jeffrey, and Gerald R. Salancik. 1978. *The External Control of Organizations: A Resource Dependence Perspective*. New York: Harper and Row.

Phillips, Robert A. 1997. "Stakeholder Theory and a Principle of Fairness." *Business Ethics* Quarterly 7:51–66.

Piore, Michael, and Charles Sabel. 1984. *The Second Industrial Divide: Possibilities for Prosperity*. New York: Basic.

Popenoe, David. 1993. "American Family Decline, 1960–1990: A Review and Appraisal." *Journal of Marriage and the Family* 55:525–42.

Popper, Karl R. (1934) 1968. *The Logic of Scientific Discovery*. New York: Harper and Row.

Posner, Richard A. 1977. *Economic Analysis of Law*, 2d ed. Boston: Little, Brown.

———. 1990. *The Problems of Jurisprudence*. Cambridge: Harvard University Press.

Posner, Richard A., and Kenneth E. Scott. 1980. *Economics of Corporate Law and Securities Regulation*. Boston: Little, Brown.

Pound, John. 1992. "The Glorious Oversight Revolution." *New York Times* (March 15, Section 3).

———. 1993. "The Rise of the Political Model of Corporate Governance and Corporate Control." *New York University Law Review* 68:1003–71.

Powell, Walter W. 1990. "The Transformation of Organizational Forms: How Useful Is Organization Theory in Accounting for Social Change?" Pp. 301–29 in Roger Friedland and A. F. Robertson (Eds.). *Beyond the Marketplace: Rethinking Economy and Society*. New York: Aldine de Gruyter.

Powell, Walter W., and Paul J. DiMaggio (Eds.). 1991. *The New Institutionalism in Organizational Analysis.* Chicago: University of Chicago Press.

Powell, Walter W., Kenneth W. Koput, and Laurel Smith-Doerr. 1996. "Interorganizational Collaboration and the Locus of Innovation: Networks of Learning in Biotechnology." *Administrative Science Quarterly* 41:116–45.

Prechel, Harland. 1997. "Corporate Form and the State: Business Policy and Change from the Multdivisional to the Multilayered Subsidiary Form." *Sociological Inquiry* 67:151–74.

Putnam, Robert D. 1993. *Making Democracy Work: Civic Traditions in Modern Italy.* Princeton, NJ: Princeton University Press.

Ravitch, Diane. 1983. *The Troubled Crusade: American Education, 1945–1980.* New York: Basic.

Reich, Robert B. (1991) 1992. *The Work of Nations: Preparing Ourselves for 21st-Century Capitalism.* New York: Vintage.

Rinaldi, Ronald J. 1990. "Radically Altered States: Entering the 'Revlon Zone.'" *Columbia Law Review* 90:760–82.

Rindova, Violina P., and Charles J. Fombrun. 1999. "Constructing Competitive Advantage: The Role of Firm-Constituent Interactions." *Strategic Management Journal* 20:691–710.

Ringer, Fritz K. (1969) 1990. *The Decline of the German Mandarins: The German Academic Community, 1890–1933.* Hanover, NH: University Press of New England, Wesleyan University Press.

Rock, Edward B. 1996. "America's Shifting Fascination with Comparative Corporate Governance." *Washington University Law Quarterly* 74:367–91.

———. 1997. "Saints and Sinners: How Does Delaware Corporate Law Work?" *UCLA Law Review* 44:1009–1107.

Roe, Mark J. 1994. *Strong Managers, Weak Owners: The Political Roots of American Corporate Finance.* Princeton, NJ: Princeton University Press.

———. 1996. "From Antitrust to Corporate Governance? The Corporation and the Law: 1959–1994." Pp. 102–27 in Carl Kaysen (Ed.). *The American Corporation Today.* New York: Oxford University Press.

Romanelli, Elaine. 1991. "The Evolution of New Organizational Forms." *Annual Review of Sociology* 17:79–103.

Romano, Roberta. 1989. "Answering the Wrong Question: The Tenuous Case for Mandatory Corporate Laws." *Columbia Law Review* 89:1599–1617.

———. 1992. "A Guide to Takeovers: Theory, Evidence, and Regulation." *Yale Journal of Regulation* 9:119–80.

———. 1993a. *The Genius of American Corporate Law.* Washington, DC: AEI Press.

———. 1993b. "Comment on Easterbrook and Fischel, 'Contract and Fiduciary Duty.'" *Journal of Law and Economics* 34:447–51.

Roy, William G. 1997. *Socializing Capital: The Rise of the Large Industrial Corporation in America.* Princeton, NJ: Princeton University Press.

Sabel, Charles F. 1982. *Work and Politics: The Division of Labor in Industry*. Cambridge: Cambridge University Press.

Samuelson, Paul A. 1948. *Economics: An Introductory Analysis*. New York: McGraw-Hill.

Schmitter, Philippe C. 1981. "Interest Intermediation and Regime Governability in Contemporary Western Europe and North America." Pp. 285–327 in Suzanne Berger (Ed.). *Organizing Interests in Western Europe*. Cambridge: Cambridge University Press.

———. 1983. "Democratic Theory and Neocorporatist Practice." *Social Research* 50:885–928.

Schrecker, Ellen W. 1986. *No Ivory Tower: McCarthyism and the Universities*. New York: Oxford University Press.

Sciulli, David. 1992a. *Theory of Societal Constitutionalism: Foundations of a Non-Marxist Critical Theory*. New York: Cambridge University Press (ASA Rose Monograph Series).

———. 1992b. "Weaknesses in Rational Choice Theory's Contribution to Comparative Research." Pp. 161–80 in James S. Coleman and Thomas J. Fararo (Eds.). *Rational Choice Theory*: Advocacy and Critique. Newbury Park, CA: Sage.

———. 1994. "An Interview with Niklas Luhmann." *Theory, Culture and Society* 11:37–68.

———. 1995. "Donald Black's Positivism in Law and Social Control." *Law and Social Inquiry* 20:805–28.

———. 1997a. "Fiduciary Law in the Balance: Narrowing the Corporate Judiciary's Social Vision" (120-page manuscript).

———. 1997b. "Rationalization" and "Institutionalization" in the New Institutionalism" (100-page manuscript).

———. 1997c. "Critical Functionalism: Etzioni's Social Theory" (13-chapter manuscript).

———. 1999. *Corporations vs. the Court: Private Power, Public Interests*. Boulder, CO: Lynne Rienner.

Scott, John. 1991. "Networks of Corporate Power: A Comparative Assessment." *Annual Review of Sociology* 17:181–203.

Selznick, Philip. 1992. *The Moral Commonwealth: Social Theory and the Promise of Community*. Berkeley: University of California Press.

Sheppard, Blair H., et al. 1992. *Organizational Justice: The Search for Fairness in the Workplace*. New York: Lexington Books.

Shleifer, Andrei, and Robert W. Vishney. 1997. "A Survey of Corporate Governance." *Journal of Finance* 52:737–83.

Siegel, Mary. 1999. "The Erosion of the Law of Controlling Shareholders." *Delaware Journal of Corporate Law* 24:27–81.

Simon, William H. 1990. "Contract versus Politics in Corporation Doctrine." Pp.

387–409 in David Kairys (Eds.). *The Politics of Law: A Progressive Critique*. Rev. ed. New York: Pantheon.

———. 1993. "What Difference Does It Make Whether Corporate Managers Have Public Responsibilities?" *Washington and Lee Law Review* 50:1697–1703.

Skeel, David A. Jr. 1997. "The Unanimity Norm in Delaware Corporate Law." *Virginia Law Review* 83:127–75.

Smith, George David, and Davis Dyer. 1996. "The Rise and Transformation of the American Corporation." Pp. 28–73 in Carl Kaysen (Ed.). 1996. *The American Corporation Today*. New York: Oxford University Press.

Smitka, Michael J. 1994. "Contracting without Contracts: How the Japanese Manage Organizational Transactions." Pp. 91–108 in Sim B. Sitkin and Robert J. Bies (Eds.). *The Legalistic Organization*. Thousand Oaks, CA: Sage.

Sobel, Robert. 1984. *The Age of Giant Corporations: A Microeconomic History of American Business, 1914–1984*. 2d ed. Westport, CT: Greenwood Press.

Sorauf, Frank. 1964. *Political Parties in the American System*. Boston: Little, Brown.

Stearns, Linda Brewster and Kenneth D. Allan. 1996. "Economic Behavior in Institutional Environments: The Corporate Merger Wave of the 1980s." *American Sociological Review* 61:669–718.

Sterngold, James. 1991. "Japanese Bond Offering Breaks with the Past." *New York Times* (December 10).

Stevenson, Richard W. 1996. "Revised Data Show Layoff Rate Constant in 1990's." *New York Times* (October 24).

Stewart, James B. 1991. *Den of Thieves*. New York: Simon and Schuster.

Stewart, Richard B. 1976. "The Reformation of American Administrative Law." *Harvard Law Review* 88:1669–1813.

———. 1990. "Madison's Nightmare." *University of Chicago Law Review* 57:335–56.

Stinchcombe, Arthur L. 1990. *Information and Organizations*. Berkeley: University of California Press.

Stone, Christopher D. 1982. "Corporate Vices and Corporate Virtues: Do Public/Private Distinctions Matter?" *University of Pennsylvania Law Review* 130:1441–1508.

Strauss, Anselm. 1978. *Negotiations*. San Francisco: Jossey-Bass.

Streeck, Wolfgang. 1992. *Social Institutions and Economic Performance: Studies of Industrial Relations in Advanced Capitalist Economies*. London: Sage.

Strudler, Alan, and Eric W. Orts. 1999. "Moral Principle in the Law of Insider Trading." *Texas Law Review* 78:375–438.

Sullivan, Daniel P., and Donald E. Conlon. 1997. "Crisis and Transition in Corporate Governance Paradigms: The Role of the Chancery Court of Delaware." *Law & Society Review* 31:713–62.

Sullivan, Teresa A., Elizabeth Warren, and Jay Lawrence Westbrook. 1989. *As We Forgive Our Debtors: Bankruptcy and Consumer Credit in America*. New York: Oxford University Press.

Summers, Robert S. 1984. *Lon L. Fuller*. Stanford: Stanford University Press.

Sunstein, Cass R. 1990. *After the Rights Revolution: Reconceiving the Regulatory State.* Cambridge: Harvard University Press.

Swedberg, Richard, and Mark Granovetter. 1992. "Introduction." Pp. 1–26 in Mark Granovetter and Richard Swedberg (Eds.). *The Sociology of Economic Life.* Boulder, CO: Westview.

Symposium. 1983. Corporations and Private Property. *Journal of Law and Economics* 26:235–496.

Symposium. 1988. The Republican Civic Tradition. *Yale Law Journal* 97:1493–1723.

Symposium. 1989. Contractual Freedom in Corporate Law. *Columbia Law Review* 89:1395–1774.

Symposium. 1993. New Directions in Corporate Law. *Washington and Lee Law Review* 50:1373–1723.

Taylor, Ellen. 1996. "New and Unjustified Restrictions on Delaware Directors' Authority." *Delaware Journal of Corporate Law* 21:837–94.

Teitelbaum, Richard. 1999. "Leveraged Buyouts for the Middling Wealthy." *New York Times* (April 25).

Thompson, James D. 1967. *Organizations in Action.* New York: McGraw-Hill.

Thompson, Robert T. 1991. "Piercing the Corporate Veil: An Empirical Study." *Cornell Law Review* 76:1036–74.

Turner, Ralph, and Lewis M. Killian. (1957) 1987. *Collective Behavior.* 3d. ed. Englewood Cliffs, NJ: Prentice-Hall.

Tyler, Tom R. 1988. "What Is Procedural Justice? Criteria Used by Citizens to Assess the Fairness of Legal Procedures." *Law and Society Review* 22:103–35.

Uchitelle, Louis. 1999. "Unemployment Rate at Lowest Level since 1970." *New York Times* (November 6).

Useem, Michael. 1984. *The Inner Circle.* New York: Oxford University Press.

———. 1993. *Executive Defense: Shareholder Power and Corporate Reorganization.* Cambridge: Harvard University Press.

———. 1996. *Investor Capitalism: How Money Managers Are Changing the Face of Corporate America.* New York: Basic Books.

Uzzi, Brian. 1999. "Embeddedness in the Making of Financial Capital: How Social Relations and Networks Benefit Firms Seeking Financing." *American Sociological Review* 64:481–505.

Vafeas, Nikos. 1999. "Board Meeting Frequency and Firm Performance." *Journal of Financial Economics* 53:113–42.

Vance, Stanley C. 1983. *Corporate Leadership, Boards, Directors, and Strategy.* New York: McGraw-Hill.

Vernon, Raymond. 1996. "How American Is the American Corporation?" Pp. 74–101 in Carl Kaysen (Ed.). *The American Corporation Today.* New York: Oxford University Press.

Victor, Bart, and John B. Cullen. 1988. "The Organizational Bases of Ethical Climates." *Administrative Science Quarterly* 33:101–25.

Waldo, Charles N. 1985. *Boards of Directors: Their Changing Roles, Structure, and Information Needs*. Westport, CT: Quorum Books.

Wallman, Steven M. H. 1991. "The Proper Interpretation of Corporate Constituency Statutes and Formulation of Director Duties." *Stetson Law Review* 21: 163–96.

Watts, Charles D. Jr. 1993. "In Critique of a Reductivist Conception and Examination of 'The Just Organization.'" *Washington and Lee Law Review* 50: 1515–28.

Wayne, Leslie. 1993. "New Proxy Rules Embolden Shareholders." *New York Times* (May 31).

Weber, Max. (1914–1920) 1968. *Economy and Society*. New York: Bedminster.

Weiler, Paul C. 1990. *Governing the Workplace: The Future of Labor and Employment Law*. Cambridge: Harvard University Press.

Weinrib, Ernest J. 1975. "The Fiduciary Obligation." *University of Toronto Law Journal* 25:1–22.

Whistler, T. L. 1984. *Rules of the Game: Inside the Corporate Boardroom*. Homewood, IL: Dow Jones-Irwin.

White, James Boyd. 1985. "How Should We Talk about Corporations? The Language of Economics and of Citizenship." *Yale Law Journal* 94:1416–25.

Williamson, Oliver. 1985. *The Economic Institutions of Capitalism: Firms, Markets, Relational Contracting*. New York: Free Press.

———. 1988a. "The Logic of Economic Organization." *Journal of Law, Economics, and Organization* 4:65–93.

———. 1988b. "Corporate Finance and Corporate Governance." *Journal of Finance* 43:567–91.

Williamson, Oliver, and Janet Bercovitz. 1996. "The Modern Corporation as an Efficiency Instrument: The Comparative Contracting Perspective." Pp. 327–59 in Carl Kaysen (Ed.). *The American Corporation Today*. New York: Oxford University Press.

Winter, Ralph K. Jr. 1977. "State Law, Shareholder Protection, and the Theory of the Corporation." *Journal of Legal Studies* 6:251–92.

Wolfe, Alan. 1989. *Whose Keeper? Social Science and Moral Obligation*. Berkeley: University of California Press.

———. 1993. "The Modern Corporation: Private Agent or Public Actor?" *Washington and Lee Law Review* 50:1673–96.

Wolfe, Donald J. Jr., and Michael C. Pittenger. 1998. *Corporate and Commercial Practice in the Delaware Court of Chancery: Procedures in Equity*. Charlottesville, VA: Lexis Law Publishing.

Worthy, James C., and Robert D. Neushel. 1983. *Emerging Issues in Corporate Governance*. Evanston, IL: Northwestern University Press.

Yago, Glenn. 1991. *Junk Bonds: How High Yield Securities Restructured Corporate America*. New York: Oxford University Press.

Young, Crawford. (1976) 1979. *The Politics of Cultural Pluralism*. Madison: University of Wisconsin Press.

Zald, Mayer N. 1969. "The Power and Functions of Boards of Directors: A Theoretical Synthesis." *American Journal of Sociology* 75:97–111.

Zweigenhaft, Richard L., and G. William Domhoff. 1991. *Blacks in the White Establishment? A Study of Race and Class in America*. New Haven: Yale University Press.

Index

Alchian, Armen A., 181–82
Allen, William R., 181–82
Allen, William T., 94, 117–20, 121–22. See also
Time Inc., Paramount Communications v.
(Time-Warner)
Anders, George, 143
Anti-takeover legislation, 50, 52, 174–80,
189–90, 354n. 5. See also Poison pill defense
Auctions of companies, 111–12, 113–15, 126,
127–28
Authoritarian regimes, 236–37
Authority issues, 11, 239–40. See also Directors

Balancers. See Stakeholder balancing
Banking, 36, 37–39, 40, 55, 137, 320n. 47
Bankruptcies, 27–28, 46, 50, 135
Bellah, Robert, 158
Bercovitz, Janet, 185, 330n. 74
Blair, Margaret, 95, 299–304
Board of directors. See Directors
Bondholders, 73–74, 86
Bond market, corporate, 36–37, 319n. 32
Bourdieu, Pierre, 158
Branson, Douglas, 216
Bratton, William, 180
Bright-line rules, 296–99
Brudney, Victor, 148–52, 345n. 33
Bureaucratic form of organization, 265, 271,
366–67n. 18
Business judgment: broadening scope of, 109;
contractarians' trust in, 79; in hostile
takeover environment, 100; judges with-
drawal of support for, 172; judicial defer-
ment to, 84, 113, 168; option to protect, 202;
and power of management, 29; and stake-
holder balancing, 175

Calomiris, Charles, 137
Capital investment, 34–37, 52

Care, fiduciary duty of: erosion of, 286–88;
historical use of, 335n. 14; vs. independence,
307; and mandatory rules, 21–22; and pro-
cedural norms, 245; QVC case, 125–26, 128;
Technicolor case, 122–23; and unified stan-
dard, 290–91; Van Gorkum case, 102–5,
284–85. See also Loyalty, fiduciary duty of
Cary, William, 215–16
Case law precedent, Delaware's, 221–22
Cede & Co. v. Technicolor, 120–23
Chancery Court. See Delaware courts
Chandler, Alfred Jr., 31
Charters, corporate, 68–70, 208–9, 215–21,
240, 358n. 14
Chief executive officer (CEO), 47, 146. See also
Corporate officers
Clark, Robert, 285, 356n. 31
Clurman, Richard, 119
Coffee, John Jr., 83
Collective interest, 10–11, 17, 21–22, 75–76,
269, 273. See also Entity, corporation as
collective
Collegial form of organization: constituency
issues, 278–81; and corporate officers,
243–49; and Delaware courts, 210, 219–20,
297, 298–99; and disinterested behavior,
262–68; importance of, 349–50n. 35; and in-
dependence duty, 304–8; and institutional
design, 274–76; overextending protection of,
276–78; range of value, 268–73
Compensation, top management, 47–48
Competition, corporate, 35, 355n. 9
Conflicts of interest, 10, 12, 99, 296–98. See
also Loyalty, fiduciary duty of
Consistently enforced laws, 235, 236–37, 249
Consistent rule enforcement, 240–42, 251, 255,
264
Constituency statutes, 178–79, 357n. 44
Constituents, societal vs. corporate, 279–81

About the Author

David Sciulli is a member of the Governing Bureau of the International Institute of Sociology and Professor of Sociology at Texas A&M University. He is the author of *Theory of Societal Constitutionalism* (1992), *Corporations v. the Court* (1999), and three collections. Sciulli is currently completing lengthy studies of Talcott Parsons and Amitai Etzioni and is bringing his approach to corporate power and law to professions and other voluntary associations in civil society.